FROM CHAOS TO COVENANT

Robert P. Carroll

FROM CHAOS
TO COVENANT

*Prophecy in
the Book of Jeremiah*

CROSSROAD · NEW YORK

For John Mauchline
a token of respect, affection
and gratitude

1981
The Crossroad Publishing Company
575 Lexington Avenue, New York, N.Y. 10022

Printed in the United States of America

Library of Congress Cataloging in Publication Data

Carroll, Robert P.
From chaos to covenant.

Bibliography: p.
Includes index.
1. Bible. O.T. Jeremiah—Criticism, interpretation,
etc.   I. Title.   II. Title: Prophecy in the Book of
Jeremiah.
BS1525.2.C37   224'.206   81-9801
ISBN 0-8245-0106-3   AACR2

CONTENTS

PREFACE

This book is the firstfruits of a decade of studying and teaching the book of Jeremiah. It is also a preparatory volume for a commentary on Jeremiah which will appear later.

As the product of research and teaching, countless lectures, seminars and discussions with students have contributed to it in an anonymous way rather like the building of medieval cathedrals. In being nameless they remain blameless. Others are not so fortunate, but I owe too much to too many not to name a few individuals by way of expressing my gratitude for help received. To Professor Peter Ackroyd of the University of London I continue to owe much for encouragement and advice and especially for commenting on a couple of chapters of this book, to Professor William McKane of the University of St Andrews I am deeply grateful for entering into correspondence so freely with me over points of interpretation in Jeremiah, to Professor Robert Davidson of the University of Glasgow for allowing me access to a number of books on Jeremiah, to Dr Graeme Auld of the University of Edinburgh for discussions and correspondence, and to my colleague Alastair Hunter for putting up with talk about Jeremiah interrupting our lunchtime sessions in 'The Western' and, especially, for the tedious task of proofreading.

I have dedicated this book to Professor John Mauchline, formerly Professor of Old Testament Language and Literature in the University of Glasgow. For my first five years as a lecturer in Glasgow University I worked closely with Professor Mauchline and came to admire and respect his old-fashioned integrity, competence and wit. After his retirement in 1972 we kept in touch until he left the Glasgow district for real retirement in the wilds of Argyll. His parting gift to me of some two hundred volumes in the field of Semitic and biblical studies from his library greatly enhanced my personal library, and as a gesture of gratitude and affection I dedicate this one volume to him in return.

Having written this book I am beginning now to see how wise were the Buddha, Socrates and Jesus in teaching without writing books.

ROBERT P. CARROLL

INTRODUCTION

Paris 1526 must seem like an *annus mirabilis* to the highly imaginative dramatist, poet or novelist. For in that year the city would appear to have housed three figures who were to leave their mark on the subsequent development of European culture – François Rabelais, John Calvin and Ignatius Loyola. History does not record a meeting of the three men, but the deficiencies of history may be made good by the imagination. An encounter between the apostles of austerity and the bawdy monk is a might-have-been of history to savour. Of one it has been said, 'Rabelais did not want to burn anybody – that's why so many wanted to burn him';[1] the other two have become bywords for intellectual systems, intolerance and narrowness. What might they have said to each other if chance (or providence as one of them would have called it) had thrown them together one evening in a Paris tavern? Unfortunately this is not the way history works so this reverie must be left to the poets and dramatists to develop. The biblical writers, closer to being poets and dramatists than being historians, could imagine fruitful and dramatic encounters of this kind and on occasion did construct imaginative stories like this one. Such an imaginative construction is the book of Jeremiah. That, at least, is the thesis of this book.

The book of Jeremiah is ill served by books in English, so my book is intended to meet a need of the market and to offer a distinctive treatment of the prophet whose contribution to the English language is a word meaning 'a long mournful lamentation or complaint'. I do not intend, however, to demonstrate that the historical figure of Jeremiah was, contrary to the dictionaries, a happy, serendipitous character. I am not at all sure that we can discover what the historical Jeremiah was like because the presentation of the prophet we have in the book bearing his name is so much the work of the traditionists who produced that book. This also is the thesis of my book.

The book of Jeremiah is not only the longest of the prophetic

books in the Bible; it is also one of the most difficult. Its mixture
of poetry and prose complicates interpretation because although
poetry is an end in itself, prose is significative. So we must analyse
the poems but interpret the prose. *Interpretation* (hermeneutic) is
the key to this enterprise. We live, to use Rilke's phrase, 'in an
interpreted world' (*in der gedeuteten Welt*),[2] so this book is full of
interpretations. The book of Jeremiah is the primary datum but it
is itself already a highly interpreted datum. So we are engaged in
interpreting interpretation! That takes us a couple of removes from
the real (?) Jeremiah. There are, of course, degrees of interpreted-
ness – the stones in the garden outside my office window are *less*
interpreted than the view that my bookshelves in the office contain
some of the *finest* works ever created by man; but both the stones
and the books are part of the interpreted world. Hermeneutic is
everywhere and rules over all. As an attempt at interpreting the
book of Jeremiah my interpretation is open to argument, but then
all interpretations are, and I would wish to avoid catching what
Socrates called 'the worst disease', namely 'to hate arguments'.[3] The
notes to this book contain sufficient argumentative positions to keep
Socrates and others in perfect health.

An overview of my approach would be that the book of Jeremiah
is a metaphor of the redactional and community activity which
produced it. The book is a series of strategies for survival in the
period after the collapse of the Judaean state. Responses to the
disasters of the fall of Jerusalem and deportation, power struggles
within the communities of the sixth century BCE and later, and
attempts at the legitimation of parties and policies in the reconstruction of the Jerusalem community have all contributed to the production of the Jeremiah tradition. It is as such that I use the word
metaphor to describe a central feature of the book. The metaphor
may be extended to cover society and consciousness of the period
but as my book is only a preliminary investigation of the tradition
it would be misleading to promise more than I have performed. A
commentary on Jeremiah is in preparation, so this book should be
treated as an introduction to some of the main issues involved in
the interpretation of Jeremiah. Its conclusions are therefore tentative
rather than final. Much thought, analysis and research remain to be
done, and further investigations will change my views on certain
matters and modify or extend the arguments of this book. New
ideas will have to be formulated and tested against the text. The
commentary therefore should be an improvement on this work. It
is as a work in progress that this book must be judged, though the

tentativeness of my judgments is as much determined by the difficulties of the subject as it is by the preliminary nature of the work. If I may rephrase Aristotle slightly in order to make his wise remarks about the study of politics apply to the study of any subject, I would say: 'In studying a subject we must be content if we attain as high a degree of certainty as the matter of it admits . . . It is a mark of the educated man and a proof of his culture that in every subject he looks for only so much precision as its nature permits.'[4] The study of Jeremiah is necessarily an imprecise one. That at least I hope this book will demonstrate.

I have taken the opportunity in a number of notes to continue, by other means, the discussion started in my previous book *When Prophecy Failed*. The subject matter of that book is not unconnected with aspects of the Jeremiah tradition, so it is appropriate that second thoughts should be made available as opportunity permits. To be critical of other people's work but not of one's own is academic folly of the worst order, and I have tried to avoid such folly by incorporating elements of the earlier discussion into the notes here. I have tried to limit the notes in size and number, but there is a great deal of work being done on the Jeremiah tradition so it is necessary to refer to and discuss such work. The comprehensive note has been eschewed. What is here is but the merest tip of a gigantic iceberg. In acknowledging the stimulation and insight gained from so many scholars whose work is mentioned in the notes, I must accept the sole responsibility for the ideas mooted in this book.

I have used the RSV with reluctance, but a public text is necessary for writer and reader to have a shared norm. The only liberty I have taken with the RSV is the modern convention of substituting 'Yahweh' for 'Lord'. The notes referring the reader to the Hebrew or Greek text are a necessary concomitant of using a shared translation. As another stage in the sufferings of Jeremiah (whose memory Heaven preserve), I hope my book will be a contribution to the investigation of the tradition.

1

The Quest of the Historical Jeremiah

Originally this book was intended to be a bringing up to date of John Skinner's classic *Prophecy and Religion: Studies in the Life of Jeremiah*.[1] The more immodest aim of replacing that book has been forestalled, or facilitated, by the fact that Skinner's book is now out of print. However the book that has been written is neither a replacement nor an updating of Skinner but an alternative account of the book of Jeremiah. This radical rethinking of the proper approach to Jeremiah has been necessitated by a close reading of the text and a careful consideration of recent scholarship on the book. Skinner's book forms the background for this introductory study of Jeremiah, but it is in opposition to his approach, which for convenience's sake I have called the Skinnerian approach, that the analysis has been made. In no sense is my analysis intended to denigrate the importance or influence of John Skinner's work nor to suggest that his book must now be discarded as obsolete. His influential work has been the starting point of my studies and, although the goal has changed radically, this book should be taken in some sense as a tribute to the influence of a book I have known and used for more than twenty years. It is time, however, that more recent thinking on the book of Jeremiah should be made available in the English language.

The Skinnerian approach. Jeremiah is the longest of the prophetic books in the Bible.[2] It is also the one which gives most promise of providing information on the life and thoughts of a prophet. This view is taken by so many scholars, commentators and writers on Jeremiah that there is little point in enumerating them all, but Sheldon Blank's view of the matter may stand as a fair sample of the position.

No prophet sits for his portrait so well as the Prophet Jeremiah. There is a full record of his life and thought . . . Jeremiah is a good subject for a portrait not only because of the length of the record, but also because of an unusual feature in the story: the prophet here sometimes speaks of himself. A biblical prophet rarely speaks of himself – autobiographically – but Jeremiah does so; and when he does he is more articulate than others. He is co-operative, and from the sources a plausible portrait looks out.[3]

In spite of the admission that it is rare for a biblical prophet to speak autobiographically, the presentation of the material in the book of Jeremiah is treated as evidence for reconstructing the life of the prophet. This approach is not only characteristic of the views of scholarship in the earlier part of this century, but also represents a good deal of current American and British writing on Jeremiah. Not all the writing on Jeremiah from a biographical standpoint is as lucid or judicious as Skinner's treatment, but it is a reasonably accurate categorization of the approach to call it Skinnerian. It indicates a position which is quite radically different from an approach to Jeremiah which sees the book as the product of many factors and processes, few of which permit the possibility of reconstructing the life of the prophet. Against interpretation or presentation the approach sees in Jeremiah a biographical and, at times, an autobiographical production. Hence it is possible to write a life of Jeremiah, which includes his thoughts and feelings, derived from the text as we have it now.

The Skinnerian approach is not an uncritical one, nor is it simply the conventional reading of the surface of the Bible. It accepts the existence of secondary material in the tradition and acknowledges the presence of a significant deuteronomistic influence on the shaping of the book. However, in spite of such factors it insists that either the ipsissima verba of Jeremiah or the gist of these are to be found in the book, and these may be used to gain insights into the mental processes of the prophet. The book is therefore extremely valuable as a document of personal religion, an anticipation of the New Testament and as a handbook of spirituality. At times in the books written in accordance with this approach Jeremiah emerges either as a Carlylean hero or a Protestant mystic. He battles alone against the forces of corrupt religiosity, fat priests and manipulative cult prophets, denounces a nation gone far from God, derides king and council and in the lonely retreats of his soul communicates his troubles to God. He stands against everybody, and everyone is ranged against him. Like a figure from a Herman Melville novel he rages against false institutions, corrupt officials and evil throughout the land – a veritable prophetic Ishmael![4] It is a very graphic approach to prophecy and it has a strong appeal for those who like to work with heroic figures. Being in agreement with a superficial reading of the text it also appeals to biblicists who prefer not to think about what they are reading. It therefore has a very wide range of support, from biblical scholars of the sophistication of Skinner and John Bright to ordinary Jewish and Christian believers. It has a functional capacity which few other approaches will ever have and that gives it great strength and appeal.

The essence of the approach sees in the various blocks of tradition in the book of Jeremiah a straightforward (with some exceptions) account of the life and thought of the prophet Jeremiah. His call in ch. 1 comes from the prophet, the poetry and much of the prose may be attributed to him, the confessions represent his inmost thoughts and feelings, and the lengthy narratives about his dealings with the kings also should be treated as authentic representations of the prophet's deeds and words. The precise role of Baruch may vary in different scholars' accounts, but he is essentially Jeremiah's amanuensis, writing down the words spoken by the prophet. Indeed, those scholars who favour the approach of rhetorical criticism sometimes go so far as to attribute the complex arrangements of the oracles to the prophet himself.[5] He thus becomes author and publisher as well as arranger and editor of his own work. Baruch does the actual work of writing everything down, but Jeremiah oversees the work and makes all the decisions. This is, no doubt, an extreme to which the Skinnerian approach seldom goes, but it is perfectly logical within the general approach. Given such a picture of the prophet's activities, why should the prophet not also be the publisher of his own work?

Books will continue to be written about Jeremiah following the Skinnerian approach, and even books which take a different view of the matter will acknowledge the stimulus and contribution of such an interpretation. The approach will constitute a limiting case for any alternative analysis, and, given the lack of prima facie evidence so characteristic of biblical material, will always be a possible interpretation of the data available. In this book, however, it is my intention to pursue a rather different approach to the book of Jeremiah from the Skinnerian position. This chapter will set out some of the reasons for such an approach and the rest of the book will analyse the text from that different perspective.

Problems of reconstructing a life of Jeremiah. The intelligent reader
of the Bible will be struck by a number of peculiar features in the
book of Jeremiah. Apart from its length (compared to the Book of
the Twelve), the amount of poetry is matched by a significant
quantity of prose. A great deal of this prose is in language already
encountered in the books dealing with the history of the kings of
Israel and Judah. The thought patterns of much of the prose are
similar to the theological dogmas of that history and also of the
book of Deuteronomy. A comparison of the poetry and the prose
produces a number of problems relating to the consistency of the
prophet's thought. For example, the poetic oracles indicate a corrupt
society incapable of changing its ways (cf. 6.10; 8.4–6; 13.23),
whereas the prose sermons regularly appeal to the community to
repent (cf. 7.3; 18.7–11; 26.3). The conflict between oracles of doom
and promises of salvation is not peculiar to Jeremiah, but the problem constituted by it is exacerbated by the strongly critical nature
of Jeremiah's oracles. A prophet who said so many harsh things
about the community can hardly have said such positive things
without serious problems of interpretation arising. This general
problem of the biblical prophetic traditions has its particular problematic aspects in Jeremiah. Schematic explanations which permit
a volte-face after the destruction of Jerusalem presuppose a very
superficial attachment between the prophet and his convictions.[6]

A further striking feature of the Jeremiah tradition is the way in
which double accounts appear for a number of events. The temple
sermon in 7.1–15 appears also in ch. 26; the attack on the cult of
the queen of heaven in 7.17–19 is given in a different version in
44.15–25; the prophet's interview with Zedekiah occurs in two
accounts in chs. 37 and 38; and conflict between Jeremiah and the
prophets is presented in 23.9–32 in poetic forms and in chs. 27–29
in narrative forms. These samples of double accounts are not to be
explained away by theories of a bifid construction of the book,
whereby essentially the same material is presented in both halves of
the book in order to facilitate the circulation of a lengthy work in
equal halves.[7] A careful reading of the text will show that these
double accounts have rather different treatments of the subject
matter, so that reading one account will not convey adequately the
thought of both accounts.

The presence of certain verses, phrases and motifs throughout
the book of Jeremiah indicates a redactional feature of the book
rather than a tendency on the prophet's part to repeat himself in
different contexts. Such redactional activity removes a saying from

whatever its original context (if any) may have been and uses it in a rhetorical way to construct the tradition. Examples of this technique include 6.12–15 = 8.10–12; 16.14–15 = 23.7f.; 23.19f. = 30.23f., where it is a moot point which context is better suited to the occurrence of the verses. The notion of the community's incurable wound (30.12f.) is also used of the prophet's response to the city's fate (8.18–22; 10.19), and in the so-called confessions (15.18). The motif of the divine destruction and building of nations (1.10) is used regularly throughout the tradition in a number of different ways (cf. 12.14–17; 18.7–10; 24.5–7; 31.27f., 40; 42.9f.; 45.4). The variations in context and meaning reveal a complex redactional employment of the elements in the motif but do not afford a simple account of that activity. These examples could be multiplied significantly for the tradition as a whole but the point is made effectively with this small selection. The similarity between the so-called confessions of Jeremiah (see ch. 5 below), the Psalms and the book of Job raises many questions about construction and influences and casts severe doubt on any account of them being the confessions *simpliciter* of the prophet. Each of these features suggests that the book of Jeremiah underwent a complicated series of editing techniques which, in fact, created the book and hint at the possibility that we may have better grounds for attempting to reconstruct the history of redaction than the life and work of the prophet Jeremiah.

Further pointers in this direction are to be found in the problematic relationship between the poetic oracles and the prose sermons in the tradition. Taking the core of the poetic oracles as the work of the poet/prophet Jeremiah (probably the only a priori judgment used in this book), there is a profound difference of language, thought and outlook between it and the prose sermons and narratives. This difference is less likely to be accounted for by arguments about the deuteronomistic prose style being the kind of prose everybody spoke in Judah of that period, than by explanations which recognize that two rather different kinds of material have been put together in the construction of the book of Jeremiah.[8] I am not denying that Jeremiah, like Monsieur Jourdain, spoke prose in everyday life. My point is rather that a major poet, and there is little doubt that Jeremiah was indeed such a poet, does not use banal prose for the majority of his most important statements. That the prose is also in the idiom of the deuteronomistic writers makes it even less likely that the prophet used it. If the poetic tradition as the basis of Jeremiah's work is to be maintained, then to saddle the prophet with the infelicities of the repetitive and banal pieties of the

prose sections is to call in question his poetic abilities and make him
more of an inferior scribe than a poet. Such a reduction of ability
cannot be ruled out but, if it is to be maintained, then the poetic
material must be attributed to some other poet. The judgment being
expressed here is that in order to understand the prophet as poet
(a similar judgment applies to the Isaiah tradition) it is necessary to
rid ourselves of the notion that he is also a speaker or writer of *other
people*'s prose. It is not simply a question of whether he only wrote
poetry or whether he wrote prose as well! It is a matter of whether
he spoke or wrote this kind of prose, i.e., deuteronomistic material.
If the prose elements were distinctive or unique in the biblical
traditions, then a case might be made out for accepting them as the
prophet's. That they are not and, furthermore, that they are traceable to specific sources (i.e., deuteronomistic) warrant their rejection
as part of the prophet's original work.

Another strong indication of redactional construction of the tradition is the significant difference between the Hebrew and Greek
traditions of Jeremiah. The Greek version is much shorter than the
Hebrew; about twelve and a half per cent shorter (roughly one-
eighth less). Often the shorter text provides a more coherent account
in the narrative sections.[9] There is also a different arrangement of
the sections in the two traditions: the Hebrew has oracles of judgment against Judah followed by oracles of salvation, and the oracles
against the nations (46–51) form a third section. The Greek has
oracles of judgment against Judah followed by the oracles against
the nations (25.13a following), and the oracles of salvation form the
third section. Different editorial policies are at work in the versions,
though some would argue that there is greater logic in the Greek
arrangement. What cannot be denied is the role of redactional activity in the construction of the different versions. Whichever may be
the original arrangement, the fact that they are different indicates
the freedom with which the versions developed and therefore emphasizes the significance of redaction in the Jeremiah tradition.

These then are some of the problems involved in reconstructing
the life of the prophet from the sources available for such a task. I
have discussed only a few of the problems, and very briefly at that,
but elements of the discussion will be expanded in the rest of this
book. The arguments cannot be a conclusive demonstration of the
truth of one position and the falseness of all other positions. Biblical
data do not provide the grounds for such proof or disproof. Strong
dissatisfactions with the conventional view of the authorship of
Jeremiah in relation to the text allied to views about poetry and

deuteronomism in the Bible as well as some recent research on the editing of Jeremiah underwrite the approach of this analysis. The matter is too complex for simple solutions, but the view towards which this book is working is that the Jeremiah tradition was constructed out of the poetry of Jeremiah, worked on by many redactional circles, including a major deuteronomistic redaction, and produced over a lengthy period of time. Some of these factors demand further discussion and will be treated briefly in this introductory chapter.

The poetic tradition. The primary datum about Isaiah, Jeremiah, Ezekiel, Amos or any of the biblical prophets is that they were poets. From that fact come their traditions. The heavily developed traditions (Isaiah, Jeremiah, Ezekiel) are the development of the poetic elements in a number of directions, in particular the addition of prose elements and the selection and arrangement of the material.[10] The difficulties encountered by biblical scholars in determining which elements are primary and which secondary may be modified by attending to the poetic sections as primary, with some poetic additions, and the rest as secondary. It is not a resolution of all the problems but it suggests a way of working with the primary material which highlights the definitive feature of prophecy. An initial poetic tradition is built up over a period of time by further poetic additions (perhaps even as accretions by attraction). Prose elements are added by way of explanation, often taking the form of biographical presentations of the prophet acting *as* a prophet (cf. Isa. 6.1–9.1 [Hebrew 8.23] for the prime example of such a construction). Such additions are determined by later generations attempting to give flesh to the bones of the poems – the redaction of many psalms to give them titles, identifying the poems with events and experiences in the life of David, illustrates the practice.[11] The book of Jeremiah develops the practice in a different direction and also in a more thoroughgoing way. Under the influence of deuteronomistic editors the poetic tradition associated with Jeremiah is built up into the largest of the prophetic traditions, though the development is much more in terms of prose and narrative elements than poetry (in contrast to the development of the Isaiah tradition – Isa. 36–39 apart). However, this way of treating the prophetic collections can only be suggested here, and the radical rethinking of prophecy that may be entailed by it will have to await much more concentrated analysis. Whether prophecy should be seen as being rooted in poetry or as a later accommodation to specific poetic

traditions is too large an issue to attempt a resolution here, but it
is an important aspect of the relation between prophecy and
poetry.[12]

If the development of the Isaiah tradition appears to be a supple-
mentation of poetry by further poetry, the Jeremiah tradition is
quite distinctive in that there is a sharp contrast between the poetic
sections and the lengthy prose elements. A rather different process
has given rise to the Jeremiah tradition – a process, no doubt,
strongly associated with the deuteronomistic character of the edition
and serving purposes other than just the maintenance of a poetic
tradition. The poetic elements predominate in Jer. 1–25 with prose
elements interwoven with poetry, but in chs. 26–45 the prose elements are dominant except for the book of consolation in chs. 30–
31. The oracles against the nations in chs. 46–51 are poetry, but the
collection is concluded by a lengthy prose extract from the history
of the kings of Judah (ch. 52). As is usual in the poetic oracles
throughout the prophetic traditions, the poems are not presented as
essays in biography or autobiography; it is the prose sections which
construct pictures of the prophets at work or reacting to events.
Such a division of the material raises important questions about the
precise relationship between prophecy and poetry, and nowhere in
the biblical traditions is the relationship more important or more
problematic than in the book of Jeremiah.

The approach to the problem taken in this book is to see in the
poetic oracles the basis of the tradition; its development via further
poetic pieces and lengthy prose sections is taken to be the work of
the redactors, deuteronomists and others, building up that tradition.
I have explained already some of the reasons why attributing the
prose material to Jeremiah is probably a mistaken notion. Some
commentators who would relate the prose sections to Jeremiah in
some sense prefer to argue that the prophet's amanuensis Baruch
wrote such pieces and gave the gist of what Jeremiah said rather
than his ipsissima verba. There may be such elements in the tradition which have been developed from words of the prophet, but,
as a general attempt to rescue the tradition from its redactors, it
tends to substitute one set of problems for another set. The reduction of poetry to a prose précis or gist does serious damage to the
work of a poet. Such a reductionistic approach to poetry fails to
grasp the essential feature of poetry which relates to the way in
which a thing is said. The switch from poetry to paraphrase includes
a semantic shift which introduces changes in meaning and removes
attention from the speaker's utterance to a third-hand report sum-

marizing what may have been said. It introduces more problems for interpretation than it resolves and is therefore not a solution to the problematic relation between prose and poetry in the Jeremiah tradition. The constant assumption of commentators that a piece of the tradition, though not coming from the prophet, expresses his sentiments often begs the question. It would be a better principle to work on the assumption that the redactors have put their own words into the prophet's mouth, a practice for which there is much evidence in the literature of other cultures as well as in the Bible, than to maintain a position which so reduces the poet to the level of mediocrity that grave doubts must arise about his poetic ability.

This account of the prophet as poet substantially reduces the amount of material in the tradition which can be attributed to Jeremiah with any certitude. It therefore follows those commentators (especially Bernhard Duhm and his followers) who see the basic tradition as a small collection of poems by the poet-prophet Jeremiah and the rest of the book as the development of the tradition by other sources. As such it is hardly to be wondered at that the argument of this chapter maintains the unlikelihood of being able to reconstruct the life and thought of Jeremiah from the book associated with his name. Too many other factors have contributed to the growth of the book for us to be able to assert with any confidence: 'Here is a record of the life and times of Jeremiah'. The reduction of the poetry to prose is too similar a process to turning wine into water to be appealing or persuasive as an argument. To see, in the transformation of the poetic tradition into a presentation of the prophet and an interpretation of his life, a process whereby many factors helped to create the prophetic tradition of Jeremiah is a far more realistic appraisal of the book than the conventional reconstruction of the prophet, which has to ignore so many of the problems inherent in such a reading of the text. Although it does not solve all the problems of interpreting Jeremiah, such an approach does provide a rational account of most of the factors involved in the growth of the tradition. To some of those factors I now turn.

Deuteronomism. One of the most powerful influences and creative writing forces in the Hebrew Bible is what modern scholarship calls 'deuteronomism'. It produced an edition of the history of Israel from the entry into Palestine to the release of the exiled king in the Babylonian captivity (Joshua – II Kings), known as 'the deuteronomistic history'.[13] It also produced an edition of ancient legal material incorporated into a framework of deuteronomistic sermons known as Deuteronomy, edited the book of Jeremiah and may have contributed towards an edition of the twelve prophets.[14] Such wide ranging activity should not be subsumed under a monolithic understanding of the term 'deuteronomistic', but allowance must be made for a broad connotation of the term. Distinctive strands or branches of the deuteronomistic school should be made responsible for these different works: the history, Deuteronomy, Jeremiah, the prophetic traditions and even Lamentations. They are given their common features, which therefore demonstrate their association with the deuteronomistic school, by their common theological and stylistic elements. They are the products of the great scribal school of the deuteronomists.[15] The deuteronomists worked on traditions, collected and edited them, and gave them a final form in which they represented the theologoumena of the school. The works so edited carried the deuteronomistic theology and illustrated it in a variety of ways.

The deuteronomistic edition of Jeremiah may not be the final stage in the construction of Jeremiah, but it is one of the most important stages in the creation of the book. We do not know precisely how the prophetic traditions came into existence or what the relation was between the collections of oracles and the prophets with which they were associated. Followers of a prophet might have recorded and preserved the sayings of their leader and these over a period of time may have been developed in various ways – we do not know.[16] The Jeremiah material presumably came into the deuteronomists' keeping at some stage and they built it up in such a way as to make the prophet a spokesman for their school. The tradition does provide an account of how the book was first created. In ch. 36 Jeremiah is represented as instructing Baruch ben Neriah to write in a scroll all his words spoken from the time of Josiah until the fourth year of Jehoiakim (probably c. 627–605; cf. 25.3). Barred from access to the temple, the prophet sends Baruch to read the scroll to all the people on a fast day, with the possibility in mind that the community may persuade Yahweh to turn from his evil way (36.7). Baruch does as he is told and is summoned before the princes for a further reading of the scroll. Thereupon he is warned to go into hiding with Jeremiah (36.19) and the scroll is read before the king. The king dramatically cuts the scroll into strips as it is read and tosses the strips into the brazier burning in the winter house (36.23). Jeremiah then takes another scroll and dictates the oracles again to Baruch, adding a special piece for the king's benefit (36.29–

31), and also adding many similar words to the original oracles (36.32; in spite of the first scroll having contained *all* his words).

It is a very dramatic narrative, redolent of ironic observation and unstated power struggles, which many commentators have taken to be an account of how the Jeremiah tradition was created. However that aspect of the matter is to be adjudged, the involvement of a scribe in the proceedings gives fair indication of the scribal origins of the story. It is a story created by the deuteronomists, which accounts for their part in the construction of the tradition. Whether it is an accurate historical account or a story created by the redactors to justify their place in the tradition is a matter much debated by scholars.[17] Those scholars who accept the account in ch. 36 as a historical record tend to speculate about which bits of Jeremiah were contained in Baruch's scroll. It must have been fairly short, in order to have been read three times in the one day, and it must also have contained curses and threats exclusively to have warranted the king's complete rejection of it. As such it may have consisted of the bulk of threat oracles in chs. 2–6 and possibly 8.4–9.1 (Hebrew 8.23), but, as Georg Fohrer wisely observes, 'It is probably hopeless to try to reconstruct an original scroll.'[18] A number of scholars also associate the material in Jer. 26ff. with the memoirs of Baruch and see these as probably having been combined with his two collections of oracles.[19] Thus Baruch is the real creator of the Jeremiah tradition.

There are some features of the role of Baruch in the tradition which probably point to the important part played by the deuteronomistic scribal school in the presentation, preservation and creation of the Jeremiah tradition. However, it is most unlikely that the account in Jer. 36 is a historical one. It has all the marks of a dramatized encounter between king and prophet or, as in this case, prophet's representative, and is a literary creation designed to incorporate the scribal influence into the Jeremiah tradition. That is why the prophet is barred from the temple (and then by extension of the prophet's authority his representative must flee the king's presence and hide) and the scribe becomes all important in the transmission of the prophetic word via the medium of writing. No doubt the story reflects the reality of the scribal involvement in the development of Jeremiah's work, but as it stands it is an ideal account of the matter. It is a story created to legitimate the role of the scribe in the creation and transmission of the Jeremiah tradition, just as the finding of the lawbook in the temple in Josiah's time (II Kings 22.8–13) is an attempt to legitimate Deuteronomy by the deuteronomistic historians. That the story in Jer. 36 is such a project should be clear from its dramatic presentation, its separation of the people, princes and king into different roles (cf. similar structuring in Jer. 26), the protective role of the deity in the story, and the fact that the account is essentially a variation on 25.1–14. Such double accounts in which the second account is a heavily dramatized story are a feature of the Jeremiah tradition. In the developed tradition the tendency is for the redactors to reconstruct elements of the tradition in such a way that a narrative form carries the reconstructed elements and transforms their significance. The best example of that technique may be the development of the temple sermon in 7.1–15 in the direction of a complex tribunal narrative in ch. 26, but the technique is well displayed in the way 25.1–14 reappears as an entirely different narrative in ch. 36.[20]

It is difficult to demonstrate why the deuteronomists took up the Jeremiah poetic tradition and developed it into such a lengthy carrier of their theological outlook. Circumstances beyond our knowledge probably account for this strange symbiosis of radical poet-prophet and the ideological framework of the deuteronomists. One possible connection which has much to recommend it may be the fall of Jerusalem, which in many ways vindicated the preaching of the prophet who attacked the community, its institutions and its false sense of security. Perhaps the tradition was developed in its narrative form to bear out this vindication. Throughout the biblical works edited by the deuteronomists there is a deep awareness of either impending doom or doom already experienced by the community. Such an awareness is also to be found throughout the book of Jeremiah. The prophet is presented as constantly warning the community or bemoaning its inability to respond to his warnings. The inevitability of destruction seems to stalk the community, and nowhere is that so much the case as in the narratives about the prophet's dealings with the king in chs. 27–29, 34, 37–38. To what extent this factor belongs to the stories or to the deuteronomistic presentation of them is more difficult to determine, because there are very distinctive differences between the motif of an inevitable judgment and the more characteristic sermons of the deuteronomists, which are intended to persuade the community to amend its ways. This difficulty might be eased if the sermons urging amendment of life represent the exilic preaching of deuteronomistic circles, greatly reinforced by the recent events which vindicated the prophet's warnings.[21] Even Deuteronomy has been supplemented to include the possibility of repentance, now that the disaster has befallen the community (cf. Deut. 4.30; 30.2).[22] But there are some family resemblances between elements in the poetic tradition of Jeremiah and the deuteronomistic theology which provide sufficient overlap between the traditions to account for the taking up and development of Jeremiah by the deuteronomists.[23]

A final point about deuteronomism as used in this book is the role of *ideology* in the deuteronomistic writings. Ideology can be a confusing term because there are so many meanings of the word, and in modern political usage it has become a term of abuse. The general meaning of ideology is a body of ideas or a coherent set of (political) beliefs. Karl Marx introduced the pejorative use of the word to mean the false consciousness of social and economic realities or the collective illusion shared by members of a social class.[24] In the Marxian sense ideology is a distorting factor because it mistakes contingent historical facts for permanent and immutable ones, fails to ask certain questions and affirms false answers. Being against all forms of mystification, Marx dismissed ideology as alienation and evil. Ironically in the late twentieth century the most pervasive and perfidious forms of ideological distortion would appear to be maintained by the followers of Marx; it being one of the features of such ideology that modern Marxians would deny that their system of ideas was ideological at all. The positive sense of ideology includes a system of ideas which is capable of motivating behaviour, can be used to criticize false ideas and practices within the community and is a method of analysing the social structures operating in any society. Ideology fluctuates between positive and negative features, so that all systems of ideas need to be constantly criticized and checked for such ideological distortion.

In using the term ideology to describe elements of deuteronomism I am aware of the ambiguous and less than satisfactory aspects of the term, but few other terms convey the possibility of the distortion inherent in all systems of thought used to impose political control on communities as well as it does. Biblical scholars might prefer to use the word theology to describe the deuteronomistic outlook, but that naively overlooks the political organization and control intended by the deuteronomists. The way the deuteronomistic history criticizes and analyses the history of the two communities is just as much part of the ideology as the theological elements in its outlook. The varied criticisms made by scholars of the inadequate account of history in the deuteronomistic writings, as well as its oversimplified moralism, are further indicators of the ideological nature of the writings. The way every king's reign is reduced to the same formula

and each period of history is dismissed (with the exceptions of
Hezekiah and Josiah) points to ideology in the negative sense. Such
defects in the deuteronomistic analysis also appear in the Jeremiah
tradition: e.g., the same criticisms are made of the communities in
Egypt (ch. 44) as are made of the Jerusalem community (7.17–19);
no differentiation is made between communities, no new analysis is
provided, just the same stereotyped statements are used. Where
everything is reduced to the same bland state and the responses to
changed circumstances and new situations are the same as previous
judgments, then ideology in the negative sense is at work and serious
distortions are introduced into the analysis. I stress these aspects of
deuteronomistic ideology in order to draw attention to features of
the redaction of the Jeremiah tradition and to warn against a facile
acceptance of such elements. The deuteronomists produced an edition of Jeremiah to serve their own purposes in the exilic and
post-exilic political struggles for power in the community. Not to
recognize such factors is to fail to understand important elements
at work in the period and operating to produce an edition of Jeremiah which would support the party line of the deuteronomists.

The composition of Jeremiah. The two aspects of the development
of the tradition discussed so far have been the poetic kernel and the
deuteronomistic edition. Unfortunately the book of Jeremiah is
much more complicated than just being a combination of poetry
edited by deuteronomists. Its redaction is so complex that there is
no consensus among scholars as to the stages through which it went
or the processes which produced it. There are, however, many
theories about its composition, and various positions have been set
out which command some following among scholars. Perhaps the
most influential account has been that put forward by Sigmund
Mowinckel.[25] The gist of his modified account is as follows. Mowinckel designates three types of material in Jeremiah: A, B, and
C. Type A is made up of the prophetic oracles of Jeremiah which
are poetic and mostly found in the early part of the book. Examples
of type A include 4.5f.; 6.6f.; and some scholars would include the
'confessions' in this type. Type B is biographical material and nar-
rates incidents from the life of Jeremiah (e.g. chs. 26–29; 34–44).
This material is usually attributed to the work of the scribe Baruch.
Type C consists of prose discourses of a highly rhetorical nature
closely resembling the language and style of the deuteronomists
(e.g. 7.1–15; 16.1–13; 18.1–12; 19.1–13; 33). This type is the most
controversial in discussions about the composition of the book of

Jeremiah and is to be found scattered throughout the whole book. The independent development of these three sources and the complex interrelationships between them in the editing and transmission processes are extremely difficult to determine given the complete lack of information available for the task. Further difficulties are entailed in deciding the extent to which types B and C reflect any genuine information about the prophet or his activities. Here so many extra-biblical factors are involved, such as evaluation of sources, commitments to beliefs about the Bible, frameworks of reference and hermeneutic systems, that a healthy agnosticism about the matter is probably the most reasonable view to take.[26]

There has been some recent work done on the prose sections of Jeremiah which has attempted to deny much of the prose to the deuteronomists and attribute it to the prophet himself.[27] This work proceeds from the Skinnerian approach to Jeremiah, which would see in the book the work and words of the prophet, with only the most minimal contribution coming from other sources. It is a view which denies or ignores the possibility that the text went through a long history of transmission or that other hands were involved in that process. Jeremiah, using Baruch, produced his own work, arranged it and developed its themes in accordance with the language of the sixth century. Community activity, redactional elements, development and application of thought in relation to changing circumstances, and double accounts are not to be taken as evidence of composition processes but reflect the ways Jeremiah and Baruch handled the work. The flatness of the view of the book produced by these approaches does not contribute very much to the understanding of the complexities of the subject or the period, and the attempt to make Jeremiah a Carlylean hero is rather backward-looking. However, it is a view that will appeal to biblicist positions and, though out of sympathy with it, I note it as an alternative approach to the analysis of this book.

A much more positive approach has been taken by other recent research done on the question of the prose elements in the Jeremiah tradition.[28] This approach involves an analysis of the sermons and prose sections in relation to the circles which may have produced them and attempts to read the text for indications of the redactors' intentions. Again there is not a great deal of agreement between researchers – the data are too ambiguous for any such agreement – but the approach advances the discussion by not working with a vacuum for the background of the text's development. Some of the difficulties involved arise out of the nature of the text, i.e., the double accounts and regular shifts of perspective, and accounting for these requires a very flexible framework, with much allowance for variations and additions. One view, that of Ernest Nicholson, understands the sermons in the book of Jeremiah to have been addressed 'to a listening audience, more specifically, to gatherings of those in exile for worship and instruction'.[29] Such an account provides a context for the production of the sermons and shows how the Jeremiah tradition was built up by relating the life and work of Jeremiah to the new situation in which the exiles found themselves. A different view (e.g. that of Pohlmann) would relate some of the narratives (esp. chs. 37–44) to sources other than Babylon. Both views provide examples of the range of possible interpretations of the material and focus on the practical issues facing various communities after the fall of Jerusalem. The sermons and narratives arise out of community needs and are the responses of various circles which saw in the life and work of Jeremiah grounds for addressing groups of people and extending his work to new situations.

Such approaches are more promising and suggest ways of handling the very complex material. It would, however, be misleading if these analyses were seen as the resolution of all the problems. Too many elements appear to have contributed to the composition of Jeremiah to permit a straightforward account of the development of the tradition. The multiple sources include the original poetic tradition along with developments of it, the deuteronomistic edition produced during the exile, sermons and narratives from different sources (e.g. Egypt, Palestine, possibly Babylon), the salvation oracles developed in the book of consolation, additions to the tradition (e.g. 17.19–27; 32.36–44; 33), the oracles against the nations (chs. 46–51), and various post-exilic expansions of the tradition (e.g. 23.33–40). The extent to which some of this material was attached to the Jeremiah tradition because it was considered to be a development of the tradition cannot be determined now. Some of it probably came to be associated with the tradition for contingent reasons. Clearly the book of Jeremiah was one of the major forms of activity for some circles during the exilic and post-exilic period, though the precise features of such activity can only be guessed at now. It is highly unlikely that such circles worked purely in terms of recording and preserving the words and deeds of the prophet Jeremiah; that is a modern approach to history. But the initial stages of the development of the tradition will have been the poetic oracles of the prophet and some of the next stages probably developed that material by producing a presentation of the prophet's life in terms of a highly *interpreted* work. Other stages will have been directed to dealing with problems and issues in the life of the community and probably incorporated a good deal of diverse material into the construction of the tradition. At some stage the deuteronomists interested in Jeremiah produced an edition of the tradition, but whether they were the main traditionists or simply the ones with the most dominant ideology is very difficult to determine. Narratives from different sources (chs. 42–44 from Egypt?) were added at some stage and for such a development a single location is required. There is no agreement among scholars as to where the tradition was developed; all the possibilities have been suggested – Babylon, Egypt, Palestine – and the substantial differences between the Hebrew and Greek versions of the book suggest perhaps different locations for distinctive versions of the tradition.[30] A post-exilic edition produced in Palestine, with minor additions added later, would suit the general thesis of this book, but such a suggestion belongs to the realm of the reasonable hypothesis rather than to solid historical evidence. The material on the Babylonian exiles (24.4–7; 29.10–14) may have stemmed from Babylonian sources, but is equally explicable in terms of being the propaganda of a party of returned exiles in the post-exilic period when there were fierce political struggles for power during the reconstruction of life in Jerusalem. As such, certain elements in the Jeremiah tradition may have been part of the political programme of pressure groups in Jerusalem supported by returning deportees (the new covenant perhaps?). There is much scope for speculative reconstruction of the tradition but lack of primary evidence means that the composition of Jeremiah will continue to be a hotly debated issue in Jeremiah studies. That is a fitting state for a book whose central figure is presented as an argumentative and contentious character.

The exilic age. The historical background to the book of Jeremiah is the period of the decline of Assyrian power and the rise of the Babylonian empire (c. 640–570). During that period Judah enjoyed its last few decades of relative independence, came under the suzerainty of Egypt and then Babylon, disintegrated and collapsed as a nation state. Two invasions by the Babylonians led to deportations and the destruction of Jerusalem. It was a period which began with great chauvinism and expansionistic policies maintained by King Josiah, but ended with the complete humiliation of territory, people and cities.[31] Whatever the precise period of Jeremiah's activity (most likely c. 626–587), the background of the book is one of disintegrated communities living in reduced circumstances in Palestine, Egypt and Babylon. This is the period known in the standard textbooks as 'the exilic age'.[32] The term may stand as a conventional indication of a period in biblical history, but a few observations about it are warranted if misconceptions are to be avoided. To talk about 'the exilic age' is to take the perspective of the exiles. For those communities living in Palestine it may have been a time of great hardship but it certainly was *not* a time of exile! Behind such a use of the term is the presupposition that the real centre of the community, if not the whole community itself, was in exile. That is an understandable misconception because it is one put forward by a number of biblical writers (cf. Jer. 44.2, 14, 27; II Chron. 36.20f.). Also influencing such a view is the notion that the great writings of the period (Jeremiah, Ezekiel, Second Isaiah, the deuteronomistic history, the priestly writing) were all produced in Babylon, hence the exilic perspective for viewing the period.

To define the perspective as exilic is to decide the question of where these written documents were produced in favour of a Babylonian or even an Egyptian context. As there are difficulties with such a view and as the matter is rather complex and open to various interpretations, to define these pieces of literature as exilic is probably question-begging. It is certainly open to question and the possibility that most of the writings came from a Palestinian background has, at least, as much in its favour as an exilic setting. The phrase 'exilic writings' may stand if it is taken to refer to the period between the fall and rebuilding of Jerusalem, but to presuppose that the writings necessarily came from exilic locations goes further than the meagre evidence warrants. Although a term of convenience, the use of 'exilic' to qualify period, writings or thought can be misleading and some other term might be less open to debate, such as 'sixth-century'. With these reservations in mind it may still be meaningful to talk about the age of exile, but from a Palestinian perspective.

The elements in the Jeremiah tradition which boost the identity and confidence of the exiles in Babylon (e.g. 24.4–7; 29.10–14; cf. Ezek. 11.14–21) may give the impression of a shift of focus from Palestine to Babylon, but the main elements in the tradition are focused on Jerusalem. In spite of propagandist views on behalf of the exiles in Babylon the social and political centre of Judaean life probably remained Palestinian. Martin Noth's observation is a fair statement of what may have been the case:

Although the old way of life and the old traditions were maintained to some extent both in Babylonia and Lower Egypt, nevertheless the tribes left behind in the old country continued to be the centre of Israelite history and Israelite life. For them the events of 587 BC did not in any way signify the end.[33]

The old cult centre was there (cf. Jer. 41.5) and the primary narrative traditions related to the land of Palestine rather than anywhere else. Yet the emergence of communities living outside the land in Babylonia and Egypt gave rise to later expectations of a great return from exile of these scattered communities. In that sense a new focus began to develop in certain circles during the period of Babylonian dominance. It was to play a significant part in the development and reconstruction of political life in Jerusalem during the Persian period.

The sixth century was a period of major intellectual activity and saw the development of various movements designed to conserve the ancient traditions and to maintain a number of forward-looking schemes.[34] Such movements were not confined to the sixth century, but continued in the fifth century, and by the time of Ezra and Nehemiah the roots of Judaism had begun to take hold. In many ways the age may be seen as the period (some would call it a watershed period) out of which the Bible began to emerge, because the loss of certain institutions and the movements of conserving the past gave rise to the need for a canonization concept. Loss of faith in prophecy (cf. Lam. 2.14; Zech. 13.2–6) certainly must have contributed over the two centuries to such a demand, and the sense of a past (cf. Zech. 1.4–6; 7.7) gave impetus to the collecting of prophetic traditions. However, these are rather large, significant issues which cannot be dealt with here, nor can they be delineated with any great confidence.

It was an age of activity, and the various streams of tradition, focusing on the past and working for the future, produced three major prophetic collections: Jeremiah, Ezekiel and Second Isaiah. The Second Isaiah material with additions was incorporated into the already well developed Isaiah tradition, but the other two traditions were constructed independently. Any treatment of the thought of the period really should focus on the three traditions rather than one, because they contain many shared elements.[35] This is especially true in relation to hopes about the future. The circles which produced these prophetic traditions either shared similar outlooks or, what is more likely, included groups which thought alike and maintained certain collections of oracles relating to restoration, leadership and the reunification of the nations. Similarities between the three traditions will be noted at various points in this book, but I would not overemphasize the common streams they share. There are many differences between the three collections, differences distinctive enough to indicate separate signatures for each collection. It would be unwise to generalize about tradition streams, especially in a few lines, but some observations may be warranted. The Jeremiah tradition is marked by a very strong deuteronomistic element, a uniquely developed presentation of the life and deeds of a prophet, and a heavily worked over and highly reflective treatment of similar accounts produced in multiple versions. Apart from a relatively small collection in chs. 30–31 (with chs. 32–33 appended), the tradition is not over-optimistic about the future. Its hopes are, generally, modest and it appears to be more concerned with justifying the catastrophe of Jerusalem's destruction (theodicy) than with grandiose schemes for the future. In that modesty may be seen the controlling influence of the deuteronomists. Its focus on the presentation of Jeremiah in relation to that disaster gives it a very distinctive signature. The Ezekiel tradition is much more concerned with cultic matters, taking a cultic view of the corruption of temple and nation which justifies the destruction of both. That cultic concern is taken up by the traditionists who attached the programme for the restoration of the temple (Ezek. 40–48) to the tradition. The future hopes of the Ezekiel tradition are similar to those in Jeremiah, though spelled out in different ways and at greater length, which suggest that similar circles of traditionists contributed to both traditions. There is also a common concern with the problem of other prophets (Jer. 23.9–32; Ezek. 13.1–14.11) which both traditions reject in similar ways. The Second Isaiah tradition differs from the other two in that it is entirely devoted to salvation oracles for the community, with the occasional outburst against Babylon (Isa. 47). Such differences may be explained by background and period of production, as well as the relation of Isa. 40–55 to the Isaiah tradition. Prophetic conflict is no longer between Yahwistic prophets but concerns the experiences of the speaker in the tradition (cf. Isa. 50.4–9; 52.13–53.12).[36] It would require another book to investigate the distinctive theological workings and developments of these three traditions and the different ways they came to terms with the problems created by the destruction of Jerusalem and the exile of various groups of Judaeans. There is great scope for such a book, especially for the sensitive theologian, but I am not the person to write it.[37]

The Quest of the Historical Jeremiah. The title of this chapter owes more to Albert Schweitzer than just the English title of his famous book on the lives of Jesus.[38] In that book Schweitzer provides a thorough analysis of work done in the late eighteenth century and throughout the nineteenth century on the historical reconstruction of the life of Jesus and shows how negative its results were.[39] His conclusion is that the historical Jesus cannot be known in our time. The guiding principle in this chapter, and throughout this book is that if there are great difficulties in establishing the figure of the historical Jesus, then there are a fortiori even greater problems in finding the historical Jeremiah. The synoptic gospels at least provide three accounts of Jesus which permit some cross-checking for criteria of dissimilarity, but there is only one book of Jeremiah (the substantive Greek differences do not constitute a parallel account). Whatever the difficulties of discerning a historical figure in the gospel writings, they are increased by a factor of nearly six hundred years in the case of Jeremiah. The work of form and redaction critics on the gospel has demonstrated the heavy influence of post-resurrection church theology in the different presentations of Jesus. The circles which produced the fourth gospel indicate the great variety of approaches taken to Jesus in the first Christian century (cf. the letter to the Hebrews for an equally discrete presentation). Yet we have nothing like as much evidence for working on Jeremiah, so the degree of agnosticism experienced when analysing that tradition is necessarily much greater even than when working on the gospels. The principle of just accepting what is read in the text may be a good rule for pietists (Jewish and Christian), but it is very unsatisfactory as a scholarly and critical approach. Given problems of a textual, translational and interpretative nature, it may not even be a very good rule for pietists – and Jeremiah has more than its fair share of all these problems. So the analogy with Schweitzer's *The Quest of the Historical Jesus* is quite justified, provided it is remembered that establishing the historical Jeremiah is *much more* difficult than finding the historical Jesus.[40]

Behind the scepticism about the quest of the historical Jeremiah is a framework of biblical hermeneutic which understands the text in a number of ways which make it much less likely that we have in the book of Jeremiah a historical account of the prophet. I do not deny for one moment that the book tells the story of Jeremiah: his life, actions, innermost thoughts, and relations with other people. What is being asserted is that this story represents the construction of the traditionists during, and possibly after, the exile (sixth century) and that this tells us more about the development of thought in that period than about the historical Jeremiah. Just as we cannot construct the historical Jesus from the church's theological views about him, so we cannot reconstruct Jeremiah from the highly developed theological presentations in the book of Jeremiah (only more so!). No doubt there may be an original figure somewhere behind all these developments, just as there was a Jesus of Nazareth, but the book, as we now possess it, has buried that figure beneath a massive amount of later presentation, interpretation and functional development. As biblical scholarship is used to taking this approach to the patriarchs, Moses, the exodus and settlement periods, and the early kingdoms of Saul, David and Solomon, it should not be very difficult to extend it to those prophetic traditions which contain so-called biographical elements (e.g. Isa. 6–8).

Part of the argument is this: at some period, most likely during the time after the fall of Jerusalem and up to, at least, the Ezra-Nehemiah era, the development and editing of the prophetic traditions included an element of tradition building which concretized aspects of some of the traditions in the form of 'lives and deeds of the prophets'. Isaiah, Jeremiah, Ezekiel, and, to a certain extent, Amos are the traditions with such an element in them (the story of Jonah illustrates the principle). The exilic era and the subsequent period of reconstruction are the most likely periods for such a development, because the fall of Jerusalem severely dislocated thought and belief in Judah. The development is a crisis response, a reaction to catastrophe and exile (this is clear from Isa. 6.9–13). It is also a response to problems of prophetic conflict, identity and control. The concentration of material on prophetic conflict in the Jeremiah and Ezekiel traditions is symptomatic of the period and indicates the breakdown of prophetic authority in society. So it is hardly surprising to find in these traditions a claim to divine authority being made on behalf of certain prophets and a rejection of all other prophets. The fall of Jerusalem became the criterion of the genuine prophet and the other prophets were held responsible for the community's collapse. The editing of these traditions with their presentations of genuine prophets may have been intended to make claims for particular interpretations of prophecy and to reject other prophetic movements.

A study of Jeremiah will show two distinctive views of prophecy running through the tradition. There is Jeremiah in conflict with the other prophets, whose false behaviour is held responsible for the disasters befalling the community (e.g. Jer. 23.9–32; 27–29), and there is the deuteronomistic ideology of prophecy as the sending of Yahweh's servants throughout history to the nation and their rejection by that stubborn nation (e.g. Jer. 7.25f.; 25.4; 26.5). The two views may be placed side by side and seen in terms of 'prophets who were sent by Yahweh' and 'prophets who were not sent by Yahweh'. Unfortunately the community listened to the wrong set and rejected the right set! Both traditions carry implicitly the view that Jeremiah is a proper prophet (the call narrative makes that very clear at the outset of the tradition). The community should have listened to him and *that* is precisely what the tradition is doing – it is constructing an account of the true prophet in action and calling upon the community (whether in exile or in Palestine or in both places) to take him as an authoritative prophet. An even more explicit account of the prophet as the only legitimate authority in the community is given in the Isaiah tradition for Isaiah (cf. Isa. 8.16–22).

The deuteronomists' presentation of Jeremiah, particularly in narrative and sermonic forms, is the most comprehensive picture of prophecy in the Bible. All the fragmentary and isolated stories of prophets in the deuteronomistic history (the Elijah-Elisha sagas are the most closely comparable to the Jeremiah material) do not constitute as powerful a statement about prophecy as the book of Jeremiah. In it the redactors, both deuteronomistic and others, tell the story of the closing decades of Judaean political life before the fall of Jerusalem in terms of the life of the prophet Jeremiah. They use that story to carry a great deal of information about their theological outlooks and to present an argued case for why the disaster happened. The key to the disaster is the community's attitude to Jeremiah, especially the failure of the kings to respond to his preaching. The whole book is marked by a concern to produce a theodicy, i.e., a reasoned statement which will justify the divine action of destroying city and community. The prophet becomes the linchpin of that argument and the other prophets become the target of many of the swingeing attacks on the community. It is difficult to imagine a more functional book in the whole Bible than Jeremiah, and because it is so functional and polemical it is very hard to treat it as a factual and historical reconstruction of the life of a prophet. It is too concerned with explaining the past, maintaining the present and creating hope for the future to be a work of sober history.

These analyses provide some of the grounds for scepticism about the quest of the historical Jeremiah, but there are equally good arguments for the thesis of this book in the text of Jeremiah itself.

These arguments will be unfolded in the following chapters, but may be anticipated here at one or two points. The poetic oracles from which the tradition developed contribute to the theodicy argument but that may only be a by-product of their incorporation into the tradition. The so-called confessions (to be found throughout chs. 11–20) are the most difficult part of the book from the point of view of interpretation. They are a favourite subject for pious exposition, and are usually treated as the inner thoughts of the prophet, expressing his self-doubts during dialogues with God. They can be so interpreted, but there are some problems with such an approach to them. In the first place, the language of these sections is very similar to that of the Psalms and Job. Now, I suppose, a great poet might use conventional language to express his inmost thoughts, but it is more likely that such expressions have been derived from other sources than that Jeremiah expressed himself in other men's language. It is a question of probability here, and other scholars may judge the matter differently (indeed many of them already have!). However, the subject matter and the linguistic turns of Job and the Psalms appearing in the confessions of Jeremiah raise important questions about sources and influences. It is my judgment that the poems come from the redactors who have created or used them to present the prophet in the familiar forms of the individual (or communal) lament. Again, it is a matter of response to the catastrophe of Jerusalem's destruction, and the prophet is represented as giving expression to that bitter experience. The confessions are open to many interpretations, so dogmatism is quite out of place here, but a very good case can be made for understanding them in this way as an example of the uses of prophecy in the tradition.

The very great degree of development in the different narratives about the prophet also underwrites the view that the book is not about the historical Jeremiah but represents a multi-layered presentation of a prophet from the perspective of later generations. The double accounts demonstrate this development by telling the same story in different ways, so as to produce a multiplex picture of the prophet in relation to all the social strata of the community. Yet each story is significantly different, and various blocks of tradition have very distinctive portrayals of the prophet. It is futile trying to reconcile these portraits, because they have arisen out of distinctive settings and are designed to represent different elements in the developing view of prophecy. The whole tradition answers the question 'How should a prophet behave in all manner of different situations?' and, more importantly, responds to the query 'What is the proper response to a prophet?' Such questions, and many more besides, must have been part of the communal response to the tragic events of the sixth century (cf. Lamentations for some of the responses). Each development of the tradition takes it further away from its poetic origins and makes the reconstruction of the historical Jeremiah more and more difficult. As the presentation of a factual account of the prophet would have had very little relevance to the exilic and depressed communities of the sixth century struggling to make sense of the disasters and to reconstruct the future, we must ask of the tradition 'What purposes did it serve?' 'What had the redactors in mind when they contributed to the creation of such a large tradition?' The answers to these questions will be community related. The tradition was developed by groups with specific communities in mind and as its audiences, so we must scrutinize the tradition for information (indirect) about such matters. Such an approach, i.e., the tradition as the answers to questions raised by the events and experiences of the period as well as by the communities seeking hope for the future, will take the researcher in a direction far removed from the quest of the historical Jeremiah.

Concluding introductory remarks. As a preliminary study of the book of Jeremiah this work cannot hope to deal with all the many questions raised by a particular approach to the interpretation of Jeremiah. The absence of a full-scale modern commentary in English on Jeremiah may be indicative of the almost insuperable problems awaiting the intrepid exegete. However there is a continuous stream of work being produced on Jeremiah in the journals, in monographs and festschrifts, and numerous commentaries in English are promised during the 1980s.[41] All this activity makes the task of interpreting Jeremiah easier in one sense and more difficult in another sense. The more views available on the subject the easier it is to develop one's own; but because there are more views appearing all the time, more time and energy are required to assimilate the new material. The constant production of monographs, commentaries and articles by German scholars on the subject of Jeremiah makes the researcher heavily indebted to such enterprise, and this book is no exception to that indebtedness. A number of German monographs have been used throughout the book, and I am deeply aware of just how much I have learned from the analyses of these books, though I have not always made as much use of them as I ought to have. The interpreter of the Jeremiah tradition faces a wide range of problems which seldom yield to anything but a very careful and diligent teasing out of their constituent elements, and in what follows I have attempted to begin that task of scrutinizing the text. I must stress the preliminary nature of the book which means that further research, thought, reflection and argument will inevitably modify or change views, opinions and interpretations offered at this stage of my investigations into the Jeremiah tradition.[42]

2

The Call of Jeremiah

After a brief commonplace editorial introduction to the book, giving details of family and period of work (cf. Isa. 1.1; Ezek. 1.1–3; Hos. 1.1; Amos 1.1; Micah 1.1; Zeph. 1.1; Hag. 1.1; Zech. 1.1), the book of Jeremiah opens with a partial account of Jeremiah's commission to be a prophet (1.4–10).[1] It is however, a strange truncated account providing no occasion for the call or circumstances under which the prophet became aware of being commissioned as a prophet. It has also been supplemented by two visions, one of which has been expanded considerably (1.11f., 13–19). Such factors in an opening section raise questions about the editor's aims and intentions and underline the remarkable fact that all the (so-called) call narratives in the prophetic traditions are problematic. To understand properly the forces at work in this presentation of Jeremiah as a prophet it is necessary to consider briefly the prophetic call narratives in order to see the patterns underlying and linking them and the disjunctive elements which make each account discrete.[2]

Patterns of prophetic call

The primary literary features of the call narratives have been analysed by Norman Habel and broken down into six divisions: (1) divine confrontation; (2) introductory word; (3) commission; (4) objection; (5) reassurance; (6) sign.[3] Habel pays particular attention to the calls of Gideon, Moses, Jeremiah, Isaiah, Ezekiel and Second Isaiah. He sees them as the products of later reflection and designed as proclamation rather than as providing autobiographical information. A critical consideration of his analysis suggests that his literary type (*Gattung*) of a prophetic call may only be derived loosely from the material available. The cases examined fit his analysis in a general way, sufficiently to indicate the presence of a pattern but not sufficiently enough to explain other prophetic call narratives such as those of Samuel, Hosea and Amos. Nor are his six divisions necessarily always present in a call narrative, not even in those analysed by Habel. For example, division 4, 'objection', applies to the stories of Moses, Gideon and Jeremiah but not to the others. Only by making Isaiah's question 'How long?' an exclamation of indignation and Second Isaiah's question 'What shall I cry?' a sharp cry of frustration can Habel fit their calls into his pattern. Each call narrative would appear to have certain elements present which suggest a pattern but also to have a number of distinctive features which tend to make each narrative uniquely particular.

In order to formulate the pattern of the call narrative more precisely it is necessary not only to look briefly at each story so as to be able to discern its *Gestalt* (i.e., its perceptual pattern or structure), but also to note the different ways in which collections of prophetic oracles are introduced and the kinds of legends told about anonymous men of God.[4] The variety of introductions to the prophetic traditions may be noted as follows: a series of oracles prefaced with the name of the prophet (e.g., Joel, Obadiah, Habakkuk, Malachi), a specific message directed to or against a particular place (Nineveh) associated with a named prophet (e.g., Jonah, Nahum), the identification of the prophet in relation to his family, house and times (e.g., Amos, Hosea, Micah, Zephaniah), a specific date for the reception of the divine word by a named prophet, further identified by family details (e.g., Haggai, Zechariah). Similar introductions are provided for Isaiah, Jeremiah and Ezekiel so that all the prophetic traditions have a formal introduction of one kind or another, though only a few of the traditions may be said to have a call narrative incorporated into it (e.g., Amos, Hosea, Isaiah, Jeremiah, Ezekiel). Further variations may be noted in the introductions (e.g., Malachi may not be a proper name but a phrase meaning 'my messenger', or the collections may be introduced by a variety of words 'word', 'oracle', 'vision') so that the formal pattern is capable of great diversity. The most important feature of this diversity for my analysis is the fact that a call narrative is not a necessary part of a prophetic tradition. Accounts are given of far more prophets for whom no call narrative exists (this is especially true of the relevant sections in the deuteronomistic history, i.e., Samuel – Kings) than of prophets whose traditions contain a call story. The view that such minor prophets were cult prophets (e.g., Joel, Nahum, Habakkuk, Obadiah)[5] may account for the lack of a call narrative but it is by no means a conclusive argument. The existence of call narratives for Moses, Samuel, Isaiah, Jeremiah and

Ezekiel (and in modified forms for Amos and Hosea) may reflect important developments in the traditions about these prophets rather than posit a necessary pattern for prophets in general.

Whatever the formal elements of a call narrative may be, in determining its *Gestalt* it is important to relate the story to its context. Where does it appear in the tradition? What precedes or follows it? Can the editor's intention be discerned by the answers to such questions? For the placing of the call narrative and its context are important elements in the building up of the tradition and are also further variations in the pattern of the call genre. Thus this analysis goes beyond the form-critical approach of dissecting the story and takes up the redactional development of the text. This is necessary because the form-critical method is too limited for dealing with the incorporation of the individual stories into the larger framework of the particular tradition, whereas the traditio-historical approach focuses on the redactional and transmissive elements of the completed text.[6] Form criticism, albeit a legitimate and important interpretative procedure, is too narrow a perspective for analysis of the biblical text and tends to reduce the material to common patterns, patterns which blur the distinctive elements in an individual story. This reductionism is an inappropriate and inadequate treatment of the hermeneutically rich prophetic traditions, and can be misleading when used to analyse the call narratives. So in the following analysis the individual call narratives are delineated in terms of their redactional features as well as their formal elements, in order to highlight the great variety of story-telling in the material.

Moses. The influence of the prophetic office on the telling of the story of Moses at the burning bush (Ex. 3.1–4.17) has long been recognized.[7] Leading his flock in the desert, Moses encounters God at Horeb when he turns aside to investigate a burning bush. Speaking to him from the bush, God identifies himself and commissions Moses to bring the people of Israel out of Egypt. Moses responds to this encounter by asserting his insignificance, his ignorance of the divine name, his inability to speak well (cf. also 6.12, 'a man of uncircumcised lips'), and the unlikelihood of the people believing him. These objections are countered by the deity with an assurance of divine presence (3.12), a revelation of the divine name (3.14f.), signs confirming the status of Moses (4.1–9), and finally the transfer of the role of speaker from Moses to Aaron (4.14–17). This amalgam of assertion and counter-assertion interrupts, and tends to conceal, the simplicity of Moses' response: 'Here am I . . . send, I pray,

some other person' (3.4; 4.13 contrast Isa. 6.8, 'Here am I! Send
me'). But in spite of the complexities of the redactional elements
governing and shaping the tradition,[8] the *Gestalt* of the story is fairly
clear: Moses encounters God in the desert, is commissioned to lead
the people out of Egypt, objects at length, but finally, accompanied
by Aaron (acting prophet to Moses as God 7.1), goes to Egypt and
engineers the exodus.

The commission of Moses is prefaced by accounts of the circumstances of the people in Egypt after the death of Joseph, the birth
of Moses, his reception into the Pharaoh's family and his later
experiences in Egypt which led to his fleeing from there to the land
of Midian. There he enters the employ of Reuel and marries into
the Midianite's family. These experiences set him in a context out
of which his commission comes. The commission complex is followed by equally lengthy complexes of material associated with the
exodus. Unlike the call narratives of the prophets, that of Moses is
set within a context of stories about his early life and the exodus,
so that the call of Moses includes circumstances as well as encounter.
Thus the element of encounter (Habel's division of confrontation)
in the formal pattern of the call narrative should be subdivided into
encounter simpliciter and encounter with circumstances. Both the
response and the sign elements of the Moses story are highly developed. The way the redaction has incorporated the different stories
and built them into the tradition makes the elements function in a
complex way. The sign element is very complex in that it includes
the burning bush, the Sinai event as confirmation of the call (3.12),
the use of signs to authenticate the office of Moses for the people
(4.1–9), and the development of the sign in the direction of the
plague narratives (4.9). The vision of the bush and the multiplex
use of signs associated with the call indicate that the formal element
of the sign can be developed in the call narratives into a substantive
block of tradition. The sign element therefore needs to be analysed
not only as an integral feature of the call but also for the way it may
be associated with the call narrative without being a part of it (e.g.,
Isa. 6; 7). To take account of this feature, the sign element category
should include sign as well as vision, and also an analysis of the
association of sign material with the call narrative. Clearly much
reflection and many elements have contributed to the construction
of the Moses tradition; analysis of the call narrative pattern must
therefore take cognizance of such complexity without imposing too
rigid a structure on the material.

Gideon. The story of Gideon (Judg. 6) is included in the analysis of call narratives because the account of his commission to be a deliverer of Israel has a number of features in common with the prophetic call narratives (esp. the section in Judg. 6.11–17). There are also various connections between the classical prophets and the judges which are brought out in the deuteronomistic presentation of the stories of the judges: e.g., Deborah is designated a 'prophetess' (Judg. 4.4), Ehud has a 'word' (*dābār*) from God for Eglon (Judg. 3.20), and Gideon asks for a sign that it is Yahweh who is speaking to him (Judg. 6.17).[9] The link between prophet and judge is best seen in the presentation of the prophet Samuel (cf. I Sam. 3.19–21; 7.15–17), where the redaction has produced a picture of Samuel as prophet *and* judge. So the inclusion of the story of Gideon in the analysis is justified as a contribution to the pattern of the call narrative. Like the story of Moses, the Gideon account is set in the context of the people's oppression, this time by the Midianites rather than the Egyptians (though throughout Judg. 6.7–18 the defeat of the Egyptians in the exodus period is an important motif in the story). Furthermore, Gideon's encounter with the divine is an encounter with circumstances included in the account. It was while he was beating out the wheat in the wine press that the angel of Yahweh appeared to him (6.11f.; cf. Ex. 3.2).[10] So the same pattern is used for the stories of Moses and Gideon. Variations in the pattern may be seen in the fact that Gideon's response comes before the commission to deliver Israel is defined (it is anticipated in the angel's reference to Gideon as a 'mighty man of valour', v. 12) and relates to the specific Midianite problem ('if Yahweh is with us, why then has all this befallen us?', v. 13). His commission consists of being sent to deliver Israel from the hand of Midian. This motif of the deity sending a person, particularly a prophet, is a dominant one in the call narratives pattern (cf. *šlḥ* in Ex. 3.10, 12, 13–15; Judg. 6.14; Isa. 6.10; Jer. 1.7; Ezek. 2.3f.; 3.5f.). As in the account of the call of Moses, the response of Gideon to his commission is an objection on the grounds of his insignificance and his incapacity. The variation occurs in the fact that Moses simply demurred because he was nobody, whereas Gideon objects that he is the least in the weakest clan in the tribe. It is essentially the same objection. The deity's response is the same in both cases: 'But I will be with you' (Ex. 3.12; Judg. 6.16; cf. Jer. 1.8). The sign element in the Gideon story is an extended one with a number of redactional complications.[11] In the first place it is used to confirm that it is Yahweh who has spoken to Gideon (Judg. 6.19–24) so it is an authenticating sign, though normally the authenticating element is used to legitimate the prophet in the eyes of others. This element does appear in the story but not in relation to the sign (cf. vv. 25–32). A second sign element is included in the story (vv. 36–38) in order to convince Gideon that he is the one to deliver Israel. This sign is repeated with a variation as further confirmation of his commission (vv. 39f.). However, the use of signs in the Gideon story illustrates the wide range of functions the sign element has in the call narratives. After the various confirmations of Gideon's call, the story of Gideon continues with a number of accounts of Gideon's military achievements (Judg. 7–8).

Samuel. The story of Samuel's call to be a prophet (I Sam. 3) is set in the context of stories about his birth and early life (I Sam. 1– 2). His encounter with the divine takes place in the sanctuary where he ministers before the ark, so the pattern of the encounter is similar to that of Moses and Gideon. He meets the divine while pursuing his normal work pattern. The redaction of the stories parallels that of Moses in that the pattern 'birth narrative – early life – sanctuary-related encounter (Horeb, Shiloh) during the pursuit of normal work' is used for both men.[12] Yet there are variations and differences in the story of Samuel. His becoming a prophet is not presented as a call to be a prophet but is an account of how the young Samuel is informed by Yahweh of the intended destruction of the house of Eli. Samuel passes this information on to Eli, and in doing so becomes a prophet (cf. I Sam. 3.19–4.1).[13] This passing on of information by a prophet to the community leader (usually the king) reflects the standard view of prophecy in the deuteronomistic history (esp. the books of Kings), so the Samuel story has been constructed along the lines of a prophetic paradigm. The account of Samuel's encounter with God is told in a way which uses the fact of his youthfulness to emphasize his ignorance of Yahweh (3.7). There may be here an element of a similar pattern found in the stories of Moses and Gideon: Samuel does not yet know Yahweh – did Moses or Gideon know Yahweh before their encounters with him? The question about the name and its identity (cf. Ex. 3.13; 6.2f.) may hint at ignorance of the name. Gideon's reply to the effect that if Yahweh had been with Israel the Midianite crisis would not have occurred (Judg. 6.13), as well as his demand for proof of the divine identity (Judg. 6.17), may point to a similar ignorance. The response element in Samuel's call is prolonged by having Samuel respond 'Here I am' three times, but on each occasion the response is made to the priest Eli. It is a good example of the paradigmatic (i.e., the proper response to God) use of the 'here am I' response (cf. Ex. 3.4; Isa. 6.8), but the variation here is due to the story in which it appears. When Samuel finally responds to Yahweh he does so in words provided by the priest (I Sam. 3.9f.). There is no element of objection or demurral in the story. Samuel listens to what is said and then remains in bed until morning. The element of vision is contained in the phrase 'and Yahweh came and stood forth (*wayyityaṣṣab*)' (v. 10) and the use of the term 'vision' (*marʾāh*, v. 15) to describe the event.[14] In keeping with the general approach of the Bible to visions of God, this aspect of the story is not developed. It is not clear from the text whether Samuel was supposed to convey the information received to Eli or was forced by Eli to divulge it, but Eli was certainly informed of the divine message. No sign element appears in the story, but a summary statement included at the end of the account (3.19–4.1) asserts the confirmation of Samuel as a prophet in Israel.

Nowhere in the story of Samuel is he called to be a prophet or commissioned to do or say anything. That he is a prophet is implicit in the story because that is the tradition the editors are working with and from which they draw their paradigms. The next stage of the redaction (I Sam. 4.1–7.2) uses extracts from the history of the ark to confirm by instantiation the authenticity of Samuel's word of doom to Eli. Thus the redactional treatment of the stories functions for the story of Samuel in the way signs function in the stories of Moses and Gideon, and affords further evidence for the variety of ways in which the elements of the call narratives may be used to construct the traditions.

The call narrative is a much more limited feature of the prophetic traditions (Isaiah – Malachi). It only appears in Isaiah, Jeremiah and Ezekiel and in modified or fragmented forms in Second Isaiah, Amos, Hosea and Jonah. The fact that so many of the prophetic traditions do not have a call narrative indicates that it is not a necessary element in being a prophet. The further fact that it is precisely in the three largest prophetic traditions (i.e., the three traditions most substantially built up over a long period) that the clearest form of a detailed call narrative appears says something significant about the Isaiah, Jeremiah and Ezekiel blocks of tradition. It may be the case that call narratives were part of the developing construction of these traditions which were related to problematic issues in the life of the community and also the growth towards canonic status of such traditions. The existence of a modified call narrative in Amos probably also points in this direction.

Isaiah. The call of Isaiah (Isa. 6) appears at the head of a section devoted to (auto)biographical accounts of the prophet and his followers (Isa. 6.1–9.7).[15] It does not appear at the beginning of the Isaiah tradition and so differs from the editing of the Jeremiah and Ezekiel traditions. Reasons of style and subject matter have been adduced for this placing of the call narrative other than at the beginning of the collected oracles, but the view taken in this analysis is that the section in 6.1–9.7, as it now stands, comes from the exilic or post-exilic period of editing and reflects the concerns of the later community with the problems of authority and authenticity among the prophets.[16]

The context of Isaiah's call is given as the year King Uzziah died, and Isaiah's encounter with the divine is located in the temple. Whether this represents Isaiah as a cult prophet going about his daily duties in the temple (thus making his encounter parallel that of Moses, Gideon and Samuel) or simply expresses the prophet's experience on the occasion of a visit to the temple cannot be determined from the text. The vision of God is the dominant element in the encounter, a vision of God the King sitting on his throne and attended upon by the seraphim.[17] Out of Isaiah's response to this vision comes a divine response which purifies the prophet and allows him to eavesdrop on the deliberations of the divine council. Isaiah is not called to be a prophet, but volunteers as a messenger, using the paradigmatic formula 'Here am I! Send me' (v. 8). Then follows the sending: 'Go, and say to this people' (v. 9) and a statement of the message to be delivered to the community. It is a word of terrible doom comparable with the word given to Samuel. There is no sign associated with the call narrative, but the occurrence of the Immanuel sign in 7.10–14 has been seen as a deliberate juxtaposition of material.[18] This redactional feature can only be seen as deliberate if the sign offered to Ahaz is one of judgment against his house (as developed in the additional sections of 7.18–25), in which case the encounter with Ahaz (Isa. 7) spells out in a different way the same message as the (so-called) inaugural vision – the land is to be devastated completely. The sign of Immanuel is a confirmatory one of the oracle given to Ahaz (7.7–9) but becomes with the redaction further confirmation of the judgment set out in 6.9–13. Although the ostensible reference is to the Assyrian period (cf. the glosses in 7.17, 20) it is the experience of the Babylonian exile which confirms the vision of Isaiah and the sign to Ahaz. Isaiah is thereby authenticated as a genuine prophet and the function of a call narrative may be seen as the legitimation of a prophet and also (probably) a proclamation of such status to the community at large.

The elements of encounter with circumstances, vision and response, sending and message with redactional juxtaposition of signs are all present in the account of Isaiah's call. There are, however, a number of distinctive features in the story. It is more vision than encounter. The first response to the vision is Isaiah's sense of being unclean (a sense equivalent to the objections of Moses, Gideon and Jeremiah?), to which the divine response (mediated by one of the seraphim) is not one of assurance 'I will be with you' (cf. Ex. 3.12; Judg. 6.16; Jer. 1.8) but one of purification (Isa. 6.6f.). No direct commission is given to Isaiah but he overhears the divine question and volunteers his services. That confident willingness is in striking contrast to the hesitations and objections of Moses, Gideon and Jeremiah but in keeping with the view expressed elsewhere in the prophetic traditions: 'The Lord Yahweh has spoken; who can but prophesy?' (Amos 3.8). He is sent with a message of destruction to 'this people' (Isa. 6.9f.), a contemptuous reference to Judah more characteristic of the book of Jeremiah than any other prophetic tradition.[19] The most distinctive feature of the commissioning of Isaiah story is its setting in relation to the divine council (indicated by the deity on the throne and the discussion about 'who will go for *us*'). Such a motif is absent from the accounts of the commissioning of Moses, Gideon and Jeremiah and suggests a different type of narrative for the Isaiah story. The appropriate comparative material for this type of story is the call of Ezekiel (Ezek. 2.1–3.11) and especially the story of Micaiah (I Kings 22.5–28).[20] There are very strong connections between the language of Isaiah's encounter with the divine council (Isa. 6.1–8) and the language of Micaiah's vision of the divine council (I Kings 22.19–21). In Micaiah's story an evil spirit deceives the prophets and entices King Ahab to his destruction; in Isaiah's story the prophet himself is sent to make sure the people do not turn from their ways and thereby avoid destruction. The differences between the two stories illustrate the variety of ways in which the stories of prophetic commissioning could be constructed.

Ezekiel. The account of Ezekiel being sent to speak the divine word to the people of Israel (Ezek. 2.1–3.11) is set in a complex context of visions of the divine and movements of the spirit.[21] The circumstances of Ezekiel's encounter with the divine are given thus: 'In the thirtieth year, in the fourth month, on the fifth day of the month, as I was among the exiles by the river Chebar, the heavens were opened, and I saw visions of God' (Ezek. 1.1).[22] As with Moses, Gideon, Samuel, Isaiah and also Amos, the life situation of Ezekiel is the setting for his encounter with the divine. The encounter is introduced and titled as 'visions of God' (*mar'ōt 'elōhīm*, cf. I Sam. 3.15) but in the commissioning section it is an auditory encounter. So vision, encounter, circumstances and commission are all elements of the Ezekiel story. The complex redactional problems of the material will be left unexplored here in order to focus solely on the pattern of Ezekiel's commissioning. After the lengthy vision of the appearance of the likeness of the glory of Yahweh, Ezekiel is commissioned to go to the rebellious house of Israel and, ignoring their reception of him and their hostility towards him ('though you sit upon scorpions', 2.6), to speak to them the word of Yahweh. This commission is given at great length with many repetitive phrases. It includes a brief section (2.8–3.3) which is similar to the call narrative of Jeremiah (cf. Jer. 1.4–10). Ezekiel is commissioned to be a prophet, commanded to be fearless and then given a scroll, with writing on both sides of it, to eat. Perhaps the stress on not being rebellious is the equivalent in Ezekiel to the element of objection in the narratives of Moses, Gideon and Jeremiah. The content of the scroll to be eaten is described as 'words of lamentation and mourning and woe' (2.10). So as with Samuel and Isaiah, Ezekiel's message is one of terrible import. The response element in Ezekiel's commission has no verbal feature; throughout the encounter Ezekiel says nothing. That is an unusual feature in the various narratives under consideration but must be accepted as a variation within a broad pattern of responses. Ezekiel's only response is to take the proffered scroll and to eat it. Throughout the account Ezekiel is passive: he watches the spectacle of the vision, is set upon his feet by the spirit (2.2), listens to the deity speaking, opens his mouth for the scroll, listens yet again to his commissioning and finally is lifted up and taken away by the spirit (3.12, 14). It is a remarkable study in passivity and makes an equally remarkable contrast with the other narratives where prophets respond, argue and demand signs. There are no signs in the Ezekiel account, but there is so much vision and movement of the spirit, and the symbolic action of eating the scroll, that signs would be superfluous. The fact of Ezekiel going to the house of Israel, whatever the reaction to him might be, will be confirmation that he is a prophet (2.5; cf. 3.11).

This is confirmation by obedient response to the commission. As in the commissionings of other prophets (e.g., Isa. 6.9; Amos 7.15), Ezekiel is sent to the people of Israel.

The redaction of Ezekiel has expanded the call narrative in 3.16b–21, and then in 3.22–5.17 has provided a series of symbolic actions of the prophet Ezekiel.[23] These symbolic actions convey Ezekiel's message and confirm his status as a prophet. They therefore function in the story of Ezekiel in a way analogous to the signs accounts of Moses and Gideon (cf. the symbolic actions of Jeremiah). However, the complexity of the redactional activity in the book of Ezekiel makes the call narrative of Ezekiel similar in many ways to the equally complex redactional material in the stories of Moses and Samuel. The simpler forms of the narrative in Isaiah and Jeremiah have had their influence on the Ezekiel narrative as well. So again we have evidence of the combination of pattern and variation in a call narrative with the redactional factor also making a contribution. The Ezekiel material also clearly demonstrates the focus of redactional activity on the call narrative.

To complete the analysis of the *patterns* of prophetic call, it is necessary to pay brief attention to the accounts of how Hosea and Amos became prophets. Other material such as the commissioning of Jonah, a story with its own distinctive problems for the interpretation of prophecy, and the anointing of Saul to be king (I Sam. 10.1–16), the story of which owes a good deal to the prophetic call pattern, must simply be recorded as potential contributors to the analysis. A more comprehensive treatment of the call pattern would take more account of them, but my concern with providing adequate background material for understanding the call of Jeremiah may safely pass over them in relative silence.

Hosea. The account of how Hosea came to be a prophet is a very distinctive one in the prophetic traditions (Hos. 1.2–9). Nothing is said about him being called to be a prophet nor of the circumstances under which he became one. After the formal introduction to his work, which is mainly concerned with the period when he was active (1.1), the matter is introduced thus: 'When Yahweh first spoke through Hosea, Yahweh said to Hosea, "Go, take to yourself a wife of harlotry and have children of harlotry, for the land commits great harlotry by forsaking Yahweh" ' (1.2).[24] No circumstance or occasion is provided for whenever Yahweh began to speak through Hosea. Certain particulars of his life become the subject of his commission, and these constitute a symbolic statement about the nature of the community. He is ordered to marry a whore (probably a woman who had once participated in the sex cult of the local Canaanite nature religion[25]) and the children born of this marriage are described as 'children of whoredom'. Their names (two sons, Jezreel and Lo' 'Ammi ['not-my-people'] and a daughter, Lo' Ruhamah ['not-pitied']) are symbolic of the condition and fate of the people of Israel. In his commission Hosea represents Yahweh, married to an apostate people, and the children represent a land doomed to destruction. The Canaanite motif of a marriage between the god and his people is used as the core of Hosea's message. The marriage imagery of his commission strongly influenced the language and imagery of two later prophets, Jeremiah and Ezekiel. A further account of a divine commission in Hos. 3 to love a woman who is unfaithful complicates the matter of interpreting Hosea's activities.[26] Again the action symbolizes the impending state of the nation. The precise relationship between these symbolic acts and Hosea's prophetic preaching is not clear, nor is there any attempt in the text to relate the two (except insofar as the one provided the means of illustrating the other, cf. Hos. 2). In the Hosea account, the pattern of the call narrative retains the elements of encounter with the divine, commission to *do* something and a variable of the sign element. What the prophet does *is* the message (amplified by numerous oracles). This element can be found in many of the prophetic traditions, though it is seldom associated with the commissioning to be a prophet.

Amos. Unlike the Hosea material, the call of Amos does not appear at the head of the collection but is inserted into a section of visions (Amos 7.1–8.3). The commission to be a prophet is given indirectly in the context of a dispute between the prophet Amos and the priest Amaziah (vv. 14f. in the pericope vv. 10–17). The fact that the section interrupts a series of four visions, appears to be in prose form (partly), and contains formidable translation and interpretation problems, has made the passage the subject of much dispute.[27] There are clearly some redactional problems associated with the section and there are justifiable suspicions about the genuineness of the piece in the Amos tradition. In a context of disputes about authenticity (the priest of Bethel versus the prophet of Tekoa) an oracle of commission looks like a formal defensive move by the editors. The call narrative pattern does not normally appear in the prophetic traditions in such an indirect way, but is usually given a prominence in the particular tradition. The matter is further complicated by the existence elsewhere in the biblical traditions of stories relating to prophetic disputes at Bethel or associated with authorities named Amaziah (cf. I Kings 13; II Chron. 25.14–16).[28]

Leaving aside these relevant but difficult issues the commission narrative is a very brief one: 'I am no prophet, nor a prophet's son; but I am a herdsman, and a dresser of sycamore trees, and Yahweh took me from following the flock, and Yahweh said to me, "Go, prophesy to my people Israel" ' (Amos 7.14f.). Apart from the defensive element in this account of the commission, it has the normative element of social context: Amos was taken to become a prophet from following the flock. There may be an echo here of a similar motif in the prophetic account of how the youth David was taken from following the flock to become king of Judah and Israel (cf. II Sam. 7.8).[29] While going about his normal duties as a herdsman Amos was commissioned to go and prophesy to Israel. This fits the pattern of the prophetic call. No vision of the divine is recorded, though the context of the passage is a series of visions, which elsewhere (e.g. Jer. 1.11–13) are associated with call narratives, so the redaction has made some normative connections.[30] The visions (7.1–9; 8.1–3; cf. 9.1) may have functioned in the way that signs do in other accounts. They confirm the prophet's sense of a commission and afford the basis of the preaching. In the redaction of Amos the commission, along with the visions, may have had the purpose of authenticating a prophet over whom there had been some dispute about legitimacy. Such an interpretation of Amos 7.14f. would correspond to the element of confirmation already delineated for so many call narratives.

The range and variety of call narratives associated with prophets and other community leaders indicate that the pattern of such narratives must be a very broad one. It cannot be allowed to be too rigid, or it will exclude more than it includes and so become too imprecise to be worth employing. The four main elements of the pattern are: encounter with the divine (an account of the circumstances of the individual concerned is usually included, though it is not necessary), commission (usually a sending to do or say something), response (this may consist of objection, arguments, acceptances or even passive responses) and sign/vision (either as part of the narrative [associated with call or the divine council motif] or as part of the redactional context). The pattern is basic, but the elements of it may vary or be transformed in the presentation of an individual prophet or leader. The distinctive features of any one call narrative are related to and constructed by the individual story, and such features are important for the interpretation of that story. Hence the need for taking notice of the variations within the pattern of a particular story, so as to be aware of the subtle hermeneutic points being made by that story. The occurrence of substantially modified call narratives should also be noted, as well as the fact that the majority of the prophetic traditions do not contain any form of a call narrative at all.

The call of Jeremiah

Now the word of Yahweh came to me saying,

> 'Before I formed you in the womb I knew you,
> and before you were born I consecrated you;
> I appointed you a prophet to the nations.'

Then I said, 'Ah, Lord Yahweh! Behold, I do not know how to speak, for I am only a youth.' But Yahweh said to me,

> 'Do not say, "I am only a youth";
> for to all to whom I send you you shall go,
> and whatever I command you you shall speak.
> Be not afraid of them,
> For I am with you to deliver you,
>   says Yahweh.'

Then Yahweh put forth his hand and touched my mouth; and Yahweh said to me,

> 'Behold, I have put my words in your mouth.
> See, I have set you this day over nations and over kingdoms,
> to pluck up and to break down,
> to destroy and to overthrow,
> to build and to plant.' (1.4–10)[31]

The pattern of the call narrative is well displayed in this opening oracle of the Jeremiah tradition. Variations in the pattern may be noted: the encounter element is limited to the use of a formulaic phrase from the prophetic traditions: 'The word of Yahweh came to . . .' No vision, event or experience is detailed in relation to this encounter, nor is there any information given about the circumstances in the life of Jeremiah when it may have happened. It may describe his becoming aware of being called to be a prophet, but at what point in his life this awareness developed we are not informed. So it is a variant form of the encounter element, but without circumstantial details. The only information afforded by the passage is the fact of Jeremiah's youthfulness. The term used (*na'ar*) is too imprecise to permit a deduction of what his age may have been. The word may describe an infant, a child, a boy, a youth, a person of marriageable age, a young warrior; it is also a technical term for a retainer, servant or squire.[32] Whatever information the term may convey about the historical Jeremiah, its function in the call narrative may belong to the response element (an objection), and also it may be part of a deliberate redactional ploy to make connections between the call of Jeremiah and the call of Samuel. For Samuel is the one prophet in the traditions whose call is related to his being a youth (cf. *na'ar* in I Sam. 2.11, 18; 3.1, 8). As deuteronomistic circles probably edited Jeremiah as well as the history of Israel (Joshua–Kings), the connection between Jeremiah and the early kingmaker prophet Samuel should be seen as deliberate. Furthermore, the great prophet for the deuteronomists was Moses (cf. Deut. 34. 10–12), and elements of the call of Moses narrative can also be found in Jeremiah's call. These two prophetic models, Moses and Samuel, are important influences behind the construction of the Jeremiah section (cf. Jer. 15.1). Taking the three prophetic figures together, we may note that, according to the biblical traditions, Moses was about eighty when he was commissioned to lead Israel out of Egypt (cf. Ex. 7.7), Samuel was a youth when he first received the prophetic vision and Jeremiah was called to be a prophet before he was born. Old man, youth and foetus – an interesting reverse progression spread through the biblical traditions about prophets.

The absence of information about the circumstances of Jeremiah's call may reflect the hyperbolic nature of its terms – known by God before he was conceived – hence there could be no circumstances or occasion for such a knowledge. However, the metaphor of v. 5 has to be recognized as hyperbolic, because before Jeremiah was conceived he did not exist, so there was nobody to be known. Nonsense predicated of God remains nonsense, so the language must be treated as metaphoric. Metaphor and hyperbole are typical of prophetic language, and often a succession of metaphors is used which can be confusing for the modern reader (e.g. Jer. 4.30f.).[33] Jeremiah's response shows that he became aware of his commissioning to be a prophet in his youth, unless this reference to his youth is a formal objection which should not be taken as a statement of a biographical nature. Moses objected that he was incapable of quick-witted speech, Samuel was too young and inexperienced to offer any objection whatsoever, and Jeremiah offers his inexperience as grounds for not accepting the commission. Whether these features indicate biographical material, as well as being formal features of the story-telling process, is open to debate. There is certainly a common element in the stories of Moses and Jeremiah. Both men object that they have no capacity for speaking, though each for different reasons. The influence of the Moses story on the Jeremiah passage may be the dominant constructing influence.[34] Whatever the precise nature of the story-construction may have been, the editors have provided no information about the circumstances under which Jeremiah became aware (whether gradually or suddenly) that he was called to be a prophet. The occasion did not interest them; it provided them (if they knew anything of it at all) with no useful information. So they placed the call narrative at the head of the collection and introduced it with a formal prophetic inspiration line 'The word of Yahweh came to . . .'

The four elements of the pattern – encounter, commission, response, sign – are all present in the Jeremiah material, though the sign element appears after the call narrative (vv. 11f.). It has been suggested that the sign of the almond rod vision has been inverted from its place at the beginning of the call narrative to its present position for rhetorical reasons, in order to provide a chiasmus in ch. 1 and an inclusio for chs. 1–20.[35] This view has the effect of providing a vision for the call of Jeremiah: he sees an almond rod and this becomes for him a symbol of Yahweh's watching over his word to perform it (the word-play of almond, šāqēd, and watching, šōqēd, is a classical instance of prophetic paronomasia). Accompanying this vision comes his call to be a prophet (vv. 4–10). Thus Jeremiah's commission is triggered by a vision just like Isaiah's and Ezekiel's. Such a rhetorical analysis makes ch. 1 consist of two events: a vision prefacing a call and a further vision prefacing a promise. The chapter as it now stands has been edited in a way that makes it misleading, but the writers (understood by practitioners of rhetorical criticism to be Jeremiah or Baruch) were more concerned with literary flourishes and clever devices than with comprehension. The approach of rhetorical criticism has much to offer by way of literary analysis, but it suggests a too sophisticated and Joycean approach to the editing of the literature to be persuasive (see below on v. 10).

If the encounter and sign/vision elements are only peripherally present in Jeremiah's call narrative, the elements of commission and response are integral to it. A wide range of terms is used to intimate

his appointment as a prophet. The deity says to him, 'I formed you
. . . I knew you . . . I consecrated you . . . I appointed you a
prophet.' He is to be sent to the nations, he is commanded to speak,
he is not to be afraid, the divine word is put in his mouth, and he
is set over (as overseer) the nations. Other call narratives may be
longer, but none have so many different terms utilized to convey
the sense of divine commissioning. Unlike the other prophets, Jeremiah is not sent to the people of Israel or Judah; at least such a
sending is not stated explicitly in the call narrative. This variation
in the call account separates it from those of Amos, Isaiah, Ezekiel
(cf. also Hosea) and links it more closely with the type of sending
in the stories of Moses (to the Pharaoh) and Gideon (against the
Midianites), and even Jonah (against Nineveh). Yet much of the
work of Jeremiah is directed to Israel and Judah, so too rigid and
narrow an analysis should not be imposed on the call narrative.
Pattern and variation construct a remarkably protean genre of narrative, and the exegete needs to be alert to the complex weaving of
pattern and variation in each individual call narrative.

The element of divine presence, already noted in the stories of
Moses and Gideon, appears in the Jeremiah account: 'Be not afraid
of them, for I am with you to deliver you, says Yahweh' (v. 8, also
v. 19). As in the Moses story, the divine presence motif is part of
the divine reassurance in response to the commissioned person's
objection to being singled out for such a difficult task. The role of
the opposition (the other), which plays such a large part in the
developed tradition of Moses in Ex. 3–6 (e.g. the Pharaoh, the
people, unbelief), also figures prominently in the editing of Jer. 1
(expanded in vv. 17–19; cf. 6.27–30; Ezek. 2.6f.; 3.7–9). Clearly
the editors are working with the Moses story as paradigm for the
presentation of a prophet in their edition of Jeremiah *the* prophet,
hence the repeated reassurance of the divine presence and the regis-
tering of popular opposition. Both men are presented as fighting
against feelings of inadequacy and self-doubts and also against fierce
public opposition.

One aspect of the Jeremiah story has links with the call accounts
of Isaiah and Ezekiel. 'Then Yahweh put forth his hand and touched
my mouth; and Yahweh said to me, "Behold, I have put my words
in your mouth" ' (v. 9). This shares with the Isaiah story the element of the touching of the prophet's mouth and with the Ezekiel
story the element of the words being put in the prophet's mouth.
But all three stories are presented in very different ways. For Isaiah
the touching (both accounts use the same phrase *wayyagga'* 'and he

touched') is done by a seraph, with a burning coal from the altar, and is done in response to Isaiah's awareness of his own uncleanness (Isa. 6.7). His commissioning follows after the incident. For Jeremiah the touching is done by Yahweh himself and symbolizes the putting of the divine words in his mouth. It is part of his commissioning, though it may be in response to his claim that he does not have the capacity to speak. For Ezekiel, the matter is part of his commissioning and conveys the divine words to him, but the metaphor is greatly extended. Instead of the divine words being put in his mouth, he is shown a scroll spread out before him and told to eat it (Ezek. 2.9–3.3). This consumption of the divine word of judgment is preparatory to preaching it to the community. There are common elements in the stories, but very different variations make for quite distinctive accounts.

The motif of eating the divine words found in Ezekiel also occurs in Jeremiah: 'Thy words were found, and I ate them, and thy words became to me a joy and the delight of my heart; for I am called by thy name, Yahweh, God of hosts' (15.16).[36] The sweetness of the divine word is a motif found in the Psalms (cf. Pss. 19.11; 119.103) and in Proverbs (cf. 16.24; 24.13f.) so its occurrence in two prophets of the exilic period may not be significant. Whether the Ezekiel usage is dependent on Jeremiah or both prophets dependent on a common circle which edited exilic prophecy must remain open to debate.[37]

Two further features of the call narrative should be noted: (*a*) the modified chiasmus in v. 10; (*b*) the motif of 'prophet to the nations' (vv. 5, 10). As both of these appear to be elements contributed by the redaction and to bear on the editing of the chapter they should be taken in conjunction with the analysis of the context (editorial) of Jeremiah's call (see below under 'function of call narrative'). The call narrative proper is in vv. 4–10, but the redaction of the chapter has provided, after the formal title to the collection (vv. 1–3), a number of additional features to that narrative. There are two visions (vv. 11f., 13f.), the almond rod and the overturned pot, and an expanded interpretation of the second vision which includes further reflections on the opposition to the prophet (vv. 15f., 17–19; cf. 6.27–30). The two visions are of the type found in Amos 7.1–9; 8.1–3 rather than the type of vision encounter with the divine found in Moses, Samuel, Isaiah and Ezekiel. The introductory form of the vision 'And the word of Yahweh came to me, saying, "What do you see . . ." ' (1.11, 13; cf. the formulaic 'the Lord Yahweh showed me [*hīr'anī*]' of Amos 7.1, 4, 7; 8.1; and 'Yahweh showed

me [*hîr'ani*]' of Jer. 24.1) presupposes that Jeremiah was already
a prophet and does not fit well with the suggestion that it was
originally before the commission (which would then be introduced
twice by the phrase 'and the word of Yahweh came to me, saying').
As the material stands it is more likely that the two visions were
originally independent of the call narrative and that, instead of the
almond rod vision being inverted for rhetorical reasons, the call
narrative was constructed and inserted before the two visions (hence
the use of '*a second time*', v. 13, to introduce the second vision).[38]
The call narrative would then provide the collection of Jeremiah
material with a much needed element from a pattern developed for
putting forward the claims of prophets and leaders. Again the matter
must be left open whether the elements of the call narrative originally came from the editors or, in any way, reflect the experiences
of the historical Jeremiah. The pattern of the prophetic calls is
established sufficiently to point to a common editing tradition rather
than to the particular experiences of unique individuals. This is not
to deny that such individuals may have had such experiences, but
to emphasize that what is going on in the traditions owes more to
the theological viewpoints and literary techniques and controls of
the editors. The redaction tells us what the editors wanted to say
more than it informs us of the original thoughts and words of the
name carrying the tradition.

The vision of the almond rod is understood to mean that Yahweh
is watching over his word to perform it. This probably means that
the word spoken to and against the nations will come to pass. Such
a meaning is in keeping with the fundamental dogma of the deuteronomists about history being the sphere of the fulfilment of the
creative word of Yahweh mediated by the prophets.[39] It might also
reflect the difficulties the prophet had over a long ministry during
which few people took seriously what he had to say and his word
did not appear to have any fulfilment (cf. 15.18; 17.15). In this
sense the vision may have strengthened his resolve to go on prophesying. Its original sense need not be the sense it has in its present
context. Given the exilic (or later) editing of Jeremiah's oracles and
life it may have indicated the faith of the (exilic) community or the
followers of Jeremiah that the words spoken against the nations
would yet be fulfilled. It is sufficiently vague to mean many things
by itself, but the range of its meaning probably should be controlled
by v. 10.

The second vision is an obscure one. The vision is of a pot turned
away from the north or overturned (tipped over) from the north or

possibly bubbling over from the north.[40] The image is imprecise but
the meaning seems to be clear: 'I see a boiling pot, facing away from
the north. Then Yahweh said to me, "Out of the north evil shall
break forth upon all the inhabitants of the land" ' (1.13f.). The
explanation of the vision is then expanded (vv. 15f.) to make it refer
to Judah and Jerusalem. This is the first intimation that Jeremiah's
work as a prophet has anything to do with his own people. No
wonder the vision had to be expanded. The vision simply identified
the fact of impending destruction and the direction from which it
would come. Such an invading force would certainly cause Judah
and Jerusalem trouble, but it would not be limited to their territory;
it would be an invasion of the whole near eastern territory down as
far as Egypt. To give the vague generality of the vision a specific
thrust, the editors have added a piece about Judah and Jerusalem
being the focus of this invasion. If this focus had been the intention
of the vision, the editors were not prepared to rely on its implicitness
being apparent to everyone. So they spelled it out. It is not surprising that they should have felt the need to make explicit the
target of this coming trouble. Nothing in the call account had
specified Judah as the object of Jeremiah's work; on the contrary,
it was to the nations he was appointed a prophet. Before the preliminary material gave way to the first collection of oracles (Jer. 2–
6) it was necessary to link the oracles with the prophet's commissioning material. Hence the first expansion. It specifies the target
and also provides a justification for the destruction (the first hint of
the theodicy motif in Jeremiah): 'I will utter my judgments against
them, for all their wickedness in forsaking me; they have burned
incense to other gods, and worshipped the works of their own hands'
(v. 16). Forsaking Yahweh, and the idolatry of worshipping other
gods, are the reasons for the trouble out of the north – precisely the
themes of the first cycle (cf. Jer. 2.9–13). Here the influence of
Jeremiah's oracles and the editorial concern with idolatry
(cf. Jer. 7.1–8.3) have been used to provide a prefatory comment
on the oracles by way of expanding the vision selected for the
introduction to the prophet's work.

The second expansion of the pot vision switches attention from
the people as idolaters to the people as opponents of Jeremiah
(vv. 17–19). This expansion looks like an explanation by way of
application of the phrase from the commission 'Be not afraid of
them' (v. 8). In the context of the commission, 'them' would appear
to refer to the 'nations', the only antecedent for it (v. 5, cf. v. 10).
However in the expansion 'them' clearly refers to Jerusalem and the

cities of Judah: 'I will utter my judgments against *them* . . . arise, and say to *them* everything that I command you. Do not be dismayed by *them*, lest I dismay you before *them*' (vv. 16f.; cf. vv. 7f.). It is a good example of the development of interpretation within the biblical tradition, where the use of terms already employed in the tradition has a meaning quite different from the original usage.[41] The expansion makes use of the motif of Jeremiah's obdurate opposition to the community from strands elsewhere in the Jeremiah tradition (cf. 6.27–30; 15.19–21). A similar motif also appears in the Ezekiel call narrative (cf. Ezek. 2.5–7; 3.7–9). This motif of the obdurate prophet and the rebellious people is used in the Jeremiah tradition to present the life of Jeremiah in terms of the violence he suffered at the hands of the community (cf. Jer. 11.21–23; 18.18; chs. 36–38). Such opposition could even lead to the killing of a prophet (cf. Jer. 26.20–23). The motif probably had its roots in the deuteronomistic view of history as Israel's rebellion against Yahweh, in particular its rejection of his prophets (cf. Jer. 7.13, 25f.; 25.3– 7), and as such tells us more about the views of the editing circles than about the lives of the prophets edited by them.[42]

Function of the call narrative in Jeremiah

The prophetic traditions are essentially *anthologies* of prophetic oracles, and by its very nature an anthology is a collection of various materials *selected* by somebody. Principles of selection operate in an anthology, and such principles lie behind the editing of the prophetic traditions. The selection and arrangement of the elements in any particular tradition indicate interpretation by presentation, and this interpretative factor is especially important in the three major traditions of Isaiah, Jeremiah and Ezekiel. In Jer. 1, a call narrative, two visions and two expansions of the second vision have been selected and arranged as the introduction (after the formal title of 1.1–3) to the work of the prophet Jeremiah. Given the range of possible presentations of prophetic work in the traditions (Hosea – Malachi), Jeremiah could have begun with 2.1 as the introduction to the early cycle of oracles (chs. 2–6) or prefaced 2–6 with 1.1–3. Instead the editors chose to use a call narrative with visions before the first cycle. Such a choice should be seen as having some significance for determining the intentions of the editors.

The use of a call account as a preface to a prophet's work occurs in Jeremiah and Ezekiel (the Ezekiel account is complicated by the expanded vision of Ezek. 1) but not in Isaiah or Amos (the Amos

account is complicated by the brevity of the call story and its setting
in a series of visions). All four accounts have some association with
visions, but four is too small a sample to indicate a definite pattern.
All that may be said of the four accounts is that the two exilic
prophets have the call narratives at the beginning of the collection
and the two eighth-century prophets have the call narratives interpolated into the work. Perhaps the distinguishing feature between
the two sets indicates that the exilic mode of presentation (i.e., call
narrative as preface) could not be used for collections of oracles
already begun for Isaiah and Amos, so call narratives were intruded
into their collections (Isa. 6.1–9.7 breaks up the critical oracles
sequence in Isa. 5 and 9, as does Amos 7.10–17 for the visions
sequence in Amos 7.1–8.3). It also may reflect the fact that a call
narrative was more important, hence was placed at beginning of
collection for the exilic prophets, because of the disputes about
prophetic authority in the time of Jeremiah and Ezekiel
(cf. Jer. 23.9–32; 28; Ezek. 13; 14.1–11). If the call narrative is
related to the problem of the authentic prophet, then it may be the
case that the call narratives in Isaiah and Amos come from the exilic
period and represent a claim for the authenticity of these prophets.
The need for demonstrations of the genuineness of certain prophets
arises from the conflict of prophets which disrupted the community.

The first function then of the call narrative in Jeremiah is to claim
for Jeremiah a genuineness and legitimacy that will be denied the
other prophets (cf. Jer. 2.8, 26; 4.9f.; 5.31; 6.13–15 [= 8.10b–12];
23.9–32). Against the other prophets the accusation is made that
they were not sent by Yahweh (23.21, 32; 27.15; 28.15; 29.31) and
spoke lying words not commanded by Yahweh (29.23). So it is
specifically said of Jeremiah that Yahweh sent him (1.7) and that he
is to speak to the people everything commanded him by Yahweh
(1.17). Thus his authenticity is shown at the beginning of the collection, and the oracles which follow may safely be taken as the
genuine word of Yahweh to the community. The call narrative is
therefore the public declaration of Jeremiah's status as a true
prophet of Yahweh in contrast to the false prophets who have misled
the community. Its structure and content are determined by the
need to distinguish between true and false prophets in a period
(exilic) when such differentiation was of prime importance for the
well-being of the people.

The two visions are associated with the call narrative (though
probably originally having no connection with it) in order to single
out two features about the work of Jeremiah. The vision of the

almond rod emphasizes the supervising control of Yahweh over his word and in association with the call narrative also stresses Yahweh's supervision over Jeremiah, the prophet who speaks his word. There may also be an element of editorial confidence (or hope) in the word spoken by Jeremiah in relation to the community's wellbeing (in the fully edited tradition of Jeremiah the book of consolation, Jer. 30–33, constitutes such an outlook). That is, the word which Yahweh performed through his servant Jeremiah, i.e., the destruction of the community, is a guarantee that Yahweh will also oversee his word and bring about the salvation of his people. The vision of the pot focuses on the destructive message of Jeremiah's oracles. The time of Jeremiah's activity is one of invading trouble from the north, a motif with various levels of significance for the community.[43] The early oracles are dominated by the image of destructive forces released against the community because of its offences. The expansion of the vision explains the reason for the trouble but adds little further by way of illumination of the obscure image. After the vision has been expanded by such an explanation, a second supplement is developed out of the reference to the people of Jerusalem and Judah. The wickedness of the community is identified as idolatry, a common motif in the deuteronomistic history. Another common motif in that history is the community's rejection of prophets. The two motifs are here associated; the second one probably was triggered by the use of the first one. So Jeremiah 1 has all the marks of deuteronomistic editing: the identification of the true prophet who is *sent* by Yahweh to speak his words, the divine watching over the word to perform it, the impending doom of an idolatrous nation and the community's opposition to the prophet (the prophet as a person usually sent *against* the community). These elements provide a characteristically deuteronomistic guide to understanding a prophet, and such a concern explains why these specific elements have been singled out in the construction of a call narrative.

The two features of the call narrative so far not analysed may be considered now in relation to the function of the narrative as an introduction to Jeremiah: the motif 'prophet to the nations' (vv. 5, 10) and the modified chiasmus in v. 10. Both elements have features about them which warrant scrutiny.

Prophet to the nations. In the initial statement of Jeremiah's call he is appointed 'a prophet to the nations' (*nābī' laggōyīm*, 1.5).[44] This is a very strange designation of a prophet, and there is nothing quite like it in the whole prophetic tradition; the nearest might be

Jonah, Nahum (against Nineveh) and Obadiah (against Edom), but
these are brief traditions hardly to be compared with the highly
developed Jeremiah tradition, which contains substantial material
on Judah. There is little warrant for the title in the contents of the
book because, with the exception of chs. 46–51 (cf. 25.15–38), they
refer to Israel, Judah and Jerusalem. That some of the oracles refer
to the invading foreign army (e.g., 4.13–17; 5.15–17; 6.1–8; 8.16f.;
cf. 27–29; 32; 34–40) hardly justifies the designation, because both
Isaiah (Assyria) and Ezekiel (Babylon) also speak of invading forces.
The inclusion of oracles against the nations is a standard feature of
the larger collections of prophetic material (e.g., Isa. 13–23;
Ezek. 25–32; cf. Amos 1–2; Zech. 9; 11.1–3), so Jer. 46–51 is unex-
ceptional. It should be noted, however, that the foreign oracles
section in Jeremiah (231 verses) *is* longer than those of Isaiah (189
verses) and Ezekiel (197 verses). The *Gestalt* of the material in the
three collections does not vary significantly from tradition to tradition. The fact that Jeremiah lived and worked during two Babylonian invasions of Palestine and experienced the destruction of
Jerusalem in 587, as well as being personally involved with the
Babylonian overlords (cf. Jer. 39.11–14; 40.1–6) and active in Egypt
(cf. 43; 44), may warrant the title 'prophet to the nations' (though
Ezekiel lived among the Babylonians most of his life). The title
may, of course, reflect the editors' sense of Jeremiah as a prophet
to the nations because of the circumstances of his life and work. As
such, the title should be treated as a variation within the call
narrative.

A further explanation for the title may possibly be found in the
situation of the deuteronomistic editors who shaped the book of
Jeremiah in relation to the exilic (and post-exilic?) community. The
recorded words and deeds of a prophet would only be of academic
interest (a modern concept) if unrelated to the life of the group to
whom they were directed. The preparation and editing of the Jeremiah tradition, with its complex growth of prose sections and
organization of oracle cycles, point to a development within the
community of the tradition long after the death of Jeremiah.[45] So
at the outset this reference to Jeremiah as a prophet to the nations
may have included an acknowledgment of the community's existence among the nations (the exiles) and have directed the tradition
at them. A feature of Deuteronomy (cf. Deut. 28–30) and the deuteronomistic history is the concern with the other nations, either as
spectators of Israel's fortunes or the scourge of their unfaithfulness
to Yahweh. Deuteronomy warns about the possibility of being exiled

among the nations as punishment for breaking the covenant. Is then Jeremiah appointed as a prophet to the nations because his tradition-ists intended their work to be directed to the exiles among the nations (and possibly the returned exiles)? Such an interpretation of the phrase would make a good deal of sense of it. The context of the editors' activity would have been 'among the nations'. This does not mean necessarily that they were among the Babylonian exiles, but that as long as their ideological group was not controlling the Jerusalem community the nations could be said to be ruling over the people of Yahweh.[46] Even after some exiles returned to Jeru-salem many exiles remained in Babylon (also in Egypt), so there must have been a very real sense of a community among the nations to which the continuing interpretation of the prophetic word was also addressed.

The argument here is inevitably difficult to sustain because of our complete lack of data about the period during which the book of Jeremiah was created and developed, and also because we know so very little about the circles which produced it. To posit a hint of benevolence in the phrase may be to go beyond the letter of the evidence, but a competent hermeneutic must take into account the possibility that the slightest indication in a text may be sufficient grounds for reading between the lines and attempting to take into account the context in which the text was produced. The hint of benevolence is suggested by the development of the nations motif in v. 10, and so the two elements ('prophet to the nations' and the modified chiasmus in v. 10) should be taken together to establish a faint word of hope to the community in ch. 1.

The modified chiasmus in v. 10. Chiasmus is a rhetorical figure by which the order of words in one clause is inverted in a second clause.[47] A chiastic structure is used in v. 10, but it has been frac-tured either by the editors or in the transmission of the text. It reads as follows:

> (See, I have set you this day over nations and over kingdoms,)
>> to pluck up (*lintōš*) and to break down (*welintōṣ*),
>> (to destroy [*ūleha'ᵃbīd*] and to overthrow [*welahᵃrōs*])
>> to build (*libnōt*) and to plant (*welinṭōʿa*).[48]

The superb chiasmus with assonance and paronomasia elements has been ruined in the transmission, but its force can be seen still. The chiastic elements are clear: pluck up – plant, break down – build; yielding the perfect *chiasmos* (diagonal arrangement):

    to pluck up   to break down

      to build   to plant

The disruption of the chiastic figure by the addition of the words 'and to destroy and to overthrow' is clear evidence of the editing of ch. 1 from elements contained within the Jeremiah tradition (cf. Isa. 1 as a similar presentation of elements from the Isaiah tradition). The six terms used in the present form of the verse can be found widely distributed in Jeremiah. In 18.7, 9 five of the words are present in a general statement about the principle of a nation turning: 'If at any time I declare concerning a nation or a kingdom, that I will pluck up (*lintōš*) and break down (*w⁽e⁾lintōṣ*) and destroy it (*ūl⁽e⁾ha'ᵃbid*) . . . and if at any time I declare concerning a nation or a kingdom that I will build (*libnōt*) and plant it (*w⁽e⁾linṭō'a*).'[49] The generality of the statement is then made specific by being referred to Judah (18.11). The occurrence of the words pluck (*ntš*) and build (*bnh*) in 12.14–17 shows a play on the words indicating a development of their reference in 1.10. In 24.6 (very similar to 42.10) it is said of the exiles by the deity, 'I will set my eyes upon them for good, and I will bring them back to this land. I will build them up (*ub⁽e⁾nītim*), and not tear them down (*w⁽e⁾lō' 'eh⁽e⁾rōs*); I will plant them (*ūn⁽e⁾ṭa'tim*), and not uproot them (*w⁽e⁾lō' 'etōš*).' 42.10 refers to the survivors of the fall of Jerusalem but uses the same four verbs (*bnh, hrs, nṭ', ntš*) to make the same offer to the community (only the pronoun is varied). In the book of consolation (Jer. 30–33) the six terms used in 1.10 occur in almost the same order (*hrs* precedes *'bd*): 'And it shall come to pass that as I have watched over (*šāqadti*) them to pluck up (*lintōš*) and break down (*w⁽e⁾lintōṣ*), to overthrow (*w⁽e⁾lah⁽ᵃ⁾rōs*), destroy (*ūl⁽e⁾ha'ᵃbīd*), and bring evil, so I will watch ('*ešqōd*) over them to build (*libnōt*) and to plant (*w⁽e⁾linṭō'a*), says Yahweh' (31.28). In the brief section about the rebuilding of Jerusalem (31.38–40) it is said of the whole area that it will be sacred to Yahweh and that 'it shall not be uprooted (*lō'-yinnātēš*) or overthrown (*w⁽e⁾lō'-yēhārēs*) any more for ever' (v. 40). The material in chapters 36–44 is supplemented by a brief piece giving an exchange of views between Jeremiah and Baruch, in which part of the divine message to Baruch uses some of these terms: 'Thus shall you say to him, Thus says Yahweh: Behold, what I have built (*bānītī*) I am breaking down (*'°nī hōrēs*), and what I have planted (*nāṭa'tī*) I am plucking up (*'°nī nōtēš*) – that is, the whole land' (45.4).[50]

These seven occurrences of the terms used in 1.10 indicate a number of interpretative developments within the construction of the Jeremiah tradition which led the editors to extrapolate them as a suitable summary of Jeremiah's work and so use them as an introduction to the tradition. Generally they are used in the latest strand of the tradition to anticipate the restoration of the exiles, so they have a positive meaning of salvation (e.g. 24.6; 31.28, 40; cf. 12.14–17; 42.10). In spite of 18.7–10 looking like a general principle of repentance directed at any nation, it is in fact directed at Judah (18.11). It may well also be the case that the generality ('if *any* nation will listen') of 12.17 is intended to refer to the exiles, but in its present context it appears to refer to the nations. The use of the different terms in conjunction with the motif of watching (*šqd*) in 31.28 may reflect the conjunction of vision and commission in 1.10–12, but which has influenced which is more difficult to determine. The motif of watching (*šqd*) occurs more frequently in Jeremiah than in any other prophetic tradition (1.12; 5.6; 31.28 (twice); 44.27). It is used in the metaphors of the animals destroying the community (5.6), but otherwise its use is in relation to the thematic terms of 1.10. In 44.27 the divine watching is a negative one in which he watches over the Judaean exiles in Egypt for evil rather than good. In 31.28 it is the two communities, Israel and Judah, which have been watched over for destruction that will, in the future, be watched over for reconstruction. So if the term *šqd* is used more often to express a destructive intent, in 31.28 it is polarized to encompass negative and positive aspects of the divine action. The breaking down and plucking up of the community is expressly identified as action against Judah, the community once planted and built by Yahweh (45.4), and the exiles in Egypt. But that apart, the only other negative uses of the terms are against the enemies of Judah (cf. 12.14–17; 31.40).

This lengthy analysis of the terms occurring in the modified chiasmus of 1.10 has been necessary in order to determine the meaning of 'the nations' in 1.5, 10 and to gain some insight into the way the Jeremiah tradition has been developed. As a prophet to the nations Jeremiah was seen as a traditional preacher of doom against the nations (cf. 25.15–38; chs. 46–51), but there are also elements of a more positive attitude towards the nations in the tradition (cf. 3.19; 12.14–17), and especially in relation to Babylon (cf. 25.8–14; 27; 29.1–9; 36–39). These elements might justify interpreting 1.10 as a reference to the nations if it were not for the way the terms of the verse are used throughout the tradition. In the light of the use made of them it has to be said that 1.10 is a reflection of the developed tradition and shorthand for the range of that development. The primary reference of the verse must be seen to be to Judah, in particular the exiles in Babylon, and the reference to the nations and kingdoms can only be a secondary meaning. In the circles which produced the Jeremiah tradition the resonance of the synonyms used in 1.10 would have conveyed a statement about the exiles (whether still in Babylon or returned from there to Jerusalem) and their positive future. Just as Yahweh had watched over his word to perform it by plucking up and overthrowing Judah, so he would go on watching over his word to perform it by planting the community and building it up again. Never again would it be destroyed (31.40). So the selection of material and motifs used by the traditionists in constructing the introduction to the Jeremiah tradition functions to create hope as well as give notice of punishment. The varied terms of 1.10 bring together the words of judgment and the words of restoration. Continuity and discontinuity are maintained in the creation of the call narrative as the way to understand the work of the prophet. That means the primary object of such a call account must have been the encouragement of the Judaean exiles to watch for the divine performance of their restoration in Jerusalem.[51]

3

Early Rhetoric:
Prophet against Community

According to the editorial information in 1.1, Jeremiah began work as a prophet in or around 627, the thirteenth year of Josiah's kingship.[1] It is generally agreed among scholars that his earliest work is to be found in chs. 2–6, though even these sections have been edited and expanded by the traditionists. As with all the major prophetic collections it is extremely difficult to separate original material from editorial additions and yet, if some account is to be given of a prophet's work and thought, a distinction must be made. Such a separation between primary and secondary material may be compared to musical analysis. Musicologists, when working on the canon of Mozart's music, attempt to distinguish between the work of Wolfgang Amadeus and that of his father Leopold or Süssmayer or other anonymous composers. The distinction is very important for the canon of his music and also bears on the enjoyment of *Mozart's* music; but for the enjoyment of music as such it is not very important. So it is with prophecy. To understand what Jeremiah said it is necessary to know what he said and to be able to distinguish between what he said and what others have added to his work. Yet it is extremely difficult to make such distinctions, especially for ancient literature. The prophetic traditions are such complicated collections of complex material that no two scholars are likely to be in agreement on any analysis of a particular section. This is particularly true of the accounting for the wide diversity of poetry and prose sections in the Jeremiah tradition.[2] Such disagreement is not a sign of a serious defect in scholarship, but a recognition of the lack of data for determining the matter conclusively, and also indicates the need for openness and toleration of ambiguity in approaching the biblical material. Fortunately for this book, the distinction between original prophetic word and later editorial or interpretative development is not as important as it might be, but it is still important that the distinction be maintained, otherwise it ceases to be possible to discern how the tradition has been developed along functional lines. The core of the distinction is the poetic structure of the prophetic word; the initial approach to the early oracles of Jeremiah must therefore be a brief consideration of the prophet as a poet.

The prophet as poet

The prophets were poets. The poetic nature of their oracles may be seen in English translations of the Bible (such as RSV or NEB) which set the poems out typographically so that they may be distinguished easily from prose sections. It is a working differentiation which generally achieves its aim, but occasionally there is room for disagreement over a piece which might be prose or poetry (e.g. Jer. 4.11f., which is treated as prose by RSV and as poetry by NEB).[3] As poetry the strophic analysis of prophetic oracles is important.[4] Where a poem is broken up by prose features or interpolated elements it is possible to posit secondary material indicating editorial activity. It may not be an inerrant method of determining primary and secondary levels but it is a good working method. Stylistic features and subject matter also provide guidance for distinguishing the prophet's work from that of his editors and traditionists. Despite a degree of dubiety about certain passages in a work, these differentiating techniques work adequately to provide a basis for interpreting a prophet's material. Of course the canonical form of the prophetic traditions is the creation of much more than the individual prophet's poetic oracles, and the interpretation of prophecy has to treat that development of each tradition. To interpret responsibly the afterlife (*Nachleben*) of a prophetic core which now constitutes the individual prophetic tradition requires a dialectical analysis of original poetic oracle and subsequent development into the tradition.[5]

Good examples of Jeremiah's poetry are to be found in the earliest collection of his oracles in chs. 2–6 (some further elements are to be found in chs. 8–10). The central themes of these oracles are the idolatrous nature of the community and the impending foreign invasion which will destroy community, city and countryside. The heavily edited and expanded material of the later chapters uses the same themes, but develops them into a complicated pattern of prophet versus society. It is probable that the early oracles were the ones collected for the scroll which Baruch is said to have prepared for the king (Jer. 36).[6] The influence of Hosea on Jeremiah's theology has long been recognized, and this is seen especially in the early oracles with their emphasis on the decline of the nation into idolatry (cf. 2.4–13). The fidelity and devotion of the bridal period has given way to involvement in the fertility cults of Baal, and Israel has changed its glory (Yahweh) for things which lack profit. The phrase 'things that do not profit' (2.8, *lō'-yō'ilū;* cf. *b'lō' yō'īl,* v. 11) is a play on the divine name Baal (*b'l-y'l*). Yahweh as the fountain of living waters is contrasted with these gods who represent cisterns, and broken ones at that, to the people – a graphic metaphor for the debilitating effects of idolatry. Some of the formal elements of the prophet's poetic style can be seen in the listing of terms for the desert in 2.6: 'who led us in the wilderness (*bammidbār*), in a land of deserts ('*ᵃrābāh*) and pits (*w'šūhāh*), in a land of drought (*ṣiyyāh*) and deep darkness (*w'ṣalmāwet*), in a land that none passes through, where no man dwells.'

No analysis of prophetic poetry can be adequate which does not pay some attention to that aspect of prophetic language which may be called 'bawdy'.[7] Bawdy language is a characteristic element in the Bible, and the prophets, being users of strong language and graphic metaphor, use it regularly. This is especially true of Hosea, Jeremiah and in particular Ezekiel.[8] In the cases of these prophets, the use of bawdy language arises out of the involvement of the community in the fertility cults of the local Canaanite religion. When condemning such involvement the prophets used the language appropriate to such a practice, so the terms employed are necessarily bawdy, though they may be intended as metaphors. The ambiguity of language arises here because it is the worship of false gods which is being condemned under the metaphors of adultery and whoremongering. The worship of these gods (the local numina represented manifestations of the one god Baal) may have included sexual activities, or the language describing the worship may have been derived from the breakdown of marriage (cf. Hosea's difficult marriage as a figure for the land polluted by abandoning Yahweh). In this latter case only the language is sexual; the behaviour described by it is (forbidden) religious ritual devoted to the cult of Baal, a cult which appears to have been practised 'upon every high hill and under every green tree' (Jer. 2.20; 3.6, 13; cf. Deut. 12.2; I Kings 14.23; II Kings 16.4; 17.10; Ezek. 6.13). The difficulty of determining whether the language is descriptive or metaphoric should not distract attention from its essentially bawdiness.

As one approach to Jeremiah's poetic language, the following bawdy images from his early work may be scrutinized:

> For long ago you broke your yoke
>> and burst your bonds;
>> and you said, 'I will not serve.'
> Yea, upon every high hill
>> and under every green tree
>> you *bowed down* (*ṣō'āh*)[9] as a harlot (2.20).

> Look at your way in the valley;
>> know what you have done –
> a restive young camel interlacing her tracks,
>> a wild ass used to the wilderness,
> in her heat sniffing the wind!
>> Who can restrain her lust?
> None who seek her need weary themselves;
>> in her month they will find her.
> Keep your feet from going unshod
>> and your throat from thirst.[10]
> But you said, 'It is hopeless,
>> for I have loved strangers,
>> and after them I will go.' (2.23–25)

The images are drawn from the Canaanite cult of sacred prostitution (2.20) and from nature (2.23f.), and the prophet, using strong language which includes obscene elements, depicts the community as wild animals in the desert feverishly sniffing the wind in search of satisfaction for their lust. It is a community driven on by lust which cannot be controlled, even though advised to restrain itself (2.25). This kind of activity is described as 'orgies on the mountain' (3.23), though again the language may be metaphoric and refer to crowded gatherings at the cult centres.[11]

Two similar pictures are drawn of the community in another couple of oracles.

> Lift up your eyes to the bare heights, and see!
>> Where have you not been lain with?
> By the waysides you have sat awaiting lovers
>> like an Arab in the wilderness.
> You have polluted the land
>> with your vile harlotry.
> Therefore the showers have been withheld,
>> and the spring rain has not come;

yet you have a harlot's brow,
you refuse to be ashamed. (3.2f.)

How can I pardon you?
Your children have forsaken me,
and have sworn by those who are no gods.
When I fed them to the full,
they committed adultery
and trooped to the houses of harlots.
They were well-fed lusty stallions,[12]
each neighing for his neighbour's wife. (5.7f.)

In both oracles the language is tantalizingly ambiguous and it is difficult to determine whether the prophet is attacking the community for its involvement in sexual activities or berating it for indulgence in the Canaanite cult. The strong emotions behind the language are apparent, and the oracles share the same atmosphere of outrage, pain and jealousy as may be found in Hosea. The roots of the metaphoric language are probably to be found in the cult of the incomparable Yahweh, the jealous God, who did not permit other gods to be associated with his worship (cf. Ex. 20.3; Deut. 5.7). As a man did not permit his wife to take lovers or go off after other men, so the deity did not permit the community to worship other gods. That is the force of the metaphors, but the precise interpretation of some of the metaphors is difficult. Although the statement 'they committed adultery and trooped to the houses of harlots' (5.7) may appear to be a straightforward description of brothel visitation after a good meal, it is not. The ambiguity occurs because in biblical language 'to commit adultery' or 'to play the whore' are also terms for involvement in religious cults other than that of Yahweh's. So the terms used may be metaphors for false religion rather than sexual practices. The translation of 'trooped' (*yitgodādū*) is also disputable; it could be taken to mean 'gashed themselves' (as it does in I Kings 18.28) which would make it a religious rite associated with Canaanite culture.[13] The phrase 'well-fed lusty stallions' is equally difficult to interpret, as well as being hard to translate. It may mean horses that are well hung (i.e., have large testicles = the written tradition of the text) or well-fed (hence sleek = oral reading of the text). It is a graphic image – but of what? Is the prophet (enviously?) abusing the citizens of the community who are handsomely equipped on their way to the brothel to participate in fertility rites? Or is he using bawdy images to ridicule their involvement in a heathen cult and describing the place of worship as a brothel? Common abuse is such a strong element in biblical descriptions of other groups' beliefs and practices that this may be another example of it. In spite of the indeterminacies of translation and meaning (always part of the problem of understanding metaphors) the verses are a good example of Jeremiah's use of bawdy images.

Jeremiah's other uses of metaphors are equally impressive. The image of the choice vine degenerated into a wild one (2.21) echoes the similar use of vine imagery in Isaiah (Isa. 6), though the vine as an image of Israel is too common in the Bible for direct borrowing to be necessary. Images of the approaching army threatening the life of the community abound in the oracles and graphically illustrate the growing encirclement of the city (cf. 4.5–7, 13–17, 19–21, 29; 5.6, 15–17; 6.1–6, 22–26; 8.16; 10.17f., 22). The invitation to the community, 'Run to and fro through the streets of Jerusalem, look and take note! Search her squares to see if you can find a man, one who does justice and seeks truth; that I may pardon her' (5.1), reminds the modern reader of the Greek Cynic philosopher Diogenes, whose reputation for unconventional views includes the story of his wandering about the city at midday holding up a lamp and searching for an honest man.[14] The image of death coming up into the windows, entering the palaces and killing the children in the streets is a powerful one (9.21).[15] Equally powerful is the way the prophet describes the coming invasion in meteorological terms: 'A hot wind from the bare heights in the desert toward the daughter of my people, not to winnow or cleanse, a wind too full for this comes for me' (4.11f.). An example of the way metaphor crowds on metaphor and the images change while making the same point may be seen in 4.30f.:

> And you, O desolate one,
> what do you mean that you dress in scarlet,
> > that you deck yourself with ornaments of gold,
> > that you enlarge your eyes with paint?
> In vain you beautify yourself.
> > Your lovers despise you;
> > they seek your life.
> For I heard a cry as of a woman in travail,
> > anguish as of one bringing forth her first child,
> the cry of the daughter of Zion gasping for breath,
> > stretching out her hands,
> 'Woe is me! I am fainting before murderers.'

How vivid these images are of a tart applying make-up before going out to meet her lovers, whose intentions are murderous, and a woman terrified by the experience of giving birth for the first time. The sense of doom carried by these metaphors is also conveyed by the image drawn from community reactions to a bad harvest: 'The harvest is past, the summer is ended, and we are not saved' (8.20).

Some of the criticisms the prophet makes of the community present a picture of a nation tearing itself apart by deceit, corruption and oppression. The falseness of the community is not to be explained as being due to the poor and ignorant who know no better, but is as much the fault of the leading elements in the community who know no better either (5.1–5). Social relations are so vicious within the community that the prophet wishes he could flee into the desert and take up lodging in a wayfarers' shack to escape from the people's treachery (9.2–6 [Heb. vv. 1–5]). This outburst against the corruption within the nation contains a fine piece of word-play on the name of the patriarch Jacob: 'for every brother is a supplanter (*'āqōb ya'qōb*), and every neighbour goes about as a slanderer' (9.4 [Heb. v. 3]). The force of the word-play could be brought out better in translation than it is in the RSV in order to indicate to the reader that here the prophet is alluding to Jacob (cf. NEB margin). Jacob's name (*ya'ªqōb*) is derived from a stem which can mean 'heel' (*'āqēb*) or, as a verb, 'overreach', 'supplant' (cf. Gen. 27.36; Hos. 12.4) and as an adjective (*'āqōb*), 'insidious', 'deceitful' (cf. Jer. 17.9). The nation has become a community of Jacobs![16] The various pictures of a community at war with itself and a leadership incapable of leading because they no longer know Yahweh (cf. 2.8; 5.30f.) indicate the social chaos of the period. The terrified responses to impending invasion deepen the picture of chaos.

A different vision of chaos is presented in one of the most striking pieces of the early collection. It is a description (or a vision) of the land devastated by terrible destruction which has reduced it to a state of primordial chaos and left it emptied of people.

> I looked on the earth, and lo, it was waste and void (*tōhū wābōhū*);
> and to the heavens, and they had no light.
> I looked on the mountains, and lo, they were quaking,
> and all the hills moved to and fro.
> I looked, and lo, there was no man,
> and all the birds of the air had fled.
> I looked, and lo, the fruitful land was a desert,

and all its cities were laid in ruins
before Yahweh, before his fierce anger. (4.23–26)[17]

There may be here an echo of the first creation account in Genesis
(cf. Gen. 1.2 where the same phrase *tōhū wābōhū* occurs) portraying a territory reduced to the disorder which prevailed before
creation and indicating the destructive, chaos-producing forces un-
leashed by the day of Yahweh (cf. Isa. 13.9–13).

These two senses of chaos, the chaotic disruptions of invasion
and the (metaphoric) chaos of social relations marked by cheating
and oppression, characterize the oracles of Jeremiah. The critique
of society underlines the impossibility of living in such a corrupt
state, and the invading armies of Babylon (the original referent of
the early oracles may have been a different invading force[18]) threaten
to reduce cities and countryside to chaos. Elements of internal chaos
(psychological) appear at certain points in the sections of the so-
called 'confessions' (mostly in Jer. 11–20), so that even the prophet
seems to inhabit an unstable (mental) world.[19] All these aspects
justify viewing Jeremiah as a prophet of chaos and warrant the use
of the term chaos in the title of this book. Living in a chaotic world
and witnessing the advance of forces which would reduce the territory to a state of chaos the prophet reflects his times in his life and
preaching.

The early material has been put together to emphasize the corruption of the community by its involvement in the Canaanite type
cults and the disintegration of the cohesive elements of justice and
goodwill which bind it together. It shows Jeremiah to have been a
prophet highly critical of the society in which he lived, and one who
continued the critique of Hosea against syncretistic religion. Various
rhetorical touches can be seen in the editing (cf. 6.12–15, which is
used again with slight modifications in 8.10–12) but the main question for this study is: what purpose did the editors have in presenting
this collection of Jeremiah's oracles?

Theodicy and the evil community

A general consideration of the early oracles and the other critical
oracles to be found scattered through the first part of the Jeremiah
tradition (chs. 8–10, 13–20) reveals an interesting feature of late
seventh-century prophecy. In the traditions of the eighth-century
prophets Amos, Isaiah and Micah (esp. Micah 1–3),[20] the gravamen
of the prophetic critique of the community is that elements within

society are oppressing the poor – 'grinding the faces of the poor' (Isa. 3.15). This is not a charge made by Jeremiah in the early oracles. However true it may be to say that there were still such elements in Judah in the time of Jeremiah, it is the case that Jeremiah does not single out such practices for condemnation. Instead he makes his charges against the whole of society: rich and poor alike are corrupt, evil and oppressive (cf. 5.1–5). The rhetorical flourish 'from the least to the greatest of them' (6.13; 8.10) is used to accuse everybody of being 'greedy for unjust gain'. It is 'this people' which 'has a stubborn and rebellious heart; they have turned aside and gone away' (5.23).[21] Not a single honest person can be found who practises justice and seeks truth (5.1).,

> They are all adulterers, a company of treacherous men. They bend their tongue like a bow; falsehood and not truth has grown strong in the land; for they proceed from evil to evil, and they do not know me, says Yahweh. Let every one beware of his neighbour, and put no trust in any brother; for every brother is a supplanter, and every neighbour goes about as a slanderer. Every one deceives his neighbour, and no one speaks the truth; they have taught their tongue to speak lies; they commit iniquity and are too weary to repent. Heaping oppression upon oppression, and deceit upon deceit, they refuse to know me, says Yahweh. (9.2–6 [Heb. vv. 1–5])[22]

The thorough gleaning of Israel as one gleans the grapes which remain on the vine (6.9) or the wind from the heights too hot for winnowing (4.11) are images of the destruction of the whole community. None are to be saved, but the wrath of Yahweh is to be poured out 'upon the children in the street, and upon the gatherings of young men, also; both husband and wife shall be taken, the old folk and the very aged' (6.11). In the coming doom of the community is the destruction of everybody, rich and poor, great and lowly, oppressor and oppressed. All have contributed to the corruption (cf. the deuteronomistic indictment of the family – children, fathers, women – in 7.18), so all must endure the catastrophe.

The same radical critique of the structures of society runs through Jeremiah's oracles in the description of the community's institutions as false (*šeqer*).[23] The worship is false because it is devoted to the Canaanite cults – 'as many as your cities are your gods, O Judah' (2.28) – a fact openly confessed in the liturgical response: 'truly the hills are a delusion (*laššeqer*), the orgies on the mountains' (3.23). The community's integrity is false because, though they swear, 'As

Yahweh lives,' yet they swear falsely (*laššeqer yiššābēʻū*, 5.2). The community's prophets prophesy falsely (*nibb'ū-baššeqer*) as well as being involved in the general false dealing (*'ōśeh šāqer*) in the community (5.31; 6.13). The scribes have perverted the divine torah with their activities and have made it false (*laššeqer 'āśāh*) with their lying pen (*'ēṭ šeqer*, 8.8). According to the deuteronomistic account of the temple sermon, the prophet also dismissed the community's trust in the temple as deceitful words (*dibrē haš-šeqer*) because their actions falsified their status (7.4). Such a comprehensive dismissal of community and institutions as false agrees with the indictment of the individual members of the community as thoroughly corrupt.

The intelligent reader of poetry, especially if the poetry is strongly metaphorical and imagistic, will tend to treat the strong language of Jeremiah as rhetorical in the sense of 'excessive use of ornamentation and contrivance in discourse' and tending towards the bombastic, rather like the talk of politicians. Rhetorical devices such as 'from the least to the greatest' or 'from prophet to priest', accusing *all* of behaving falsely, are hyperbolic statements rather than descriptions of literal truth. The failure to find one honest person in Jerusalem (5.1) would suggest a typical prophetic use of hyperbole. The fact that Jeremiah probably worked in and around Jerusalem for about forty years, and offended many people, because he was a man of such contentious and disputatious ways (cf. 15.10), yet stayed alive all those years (in contrast to Uriah ben Shemaiah, 26.20–23) with the support of his friends, confirms the hyperbolic nature of his language. If the community had been as vicious as his criticisms suggest (e.g. 9.2–6) then the false and corrupt leadership would never have protected him sufficiently to allow him such a long and active life. Like Mithridates, Jeremiah died old, having lived through sweeping social and economic changes, and having survived opposition, occasional beatings and imprisonment and experienced the Babylonian destruction of Jerusalem. The development of his tradition by followers and interested parties in the deuteronomistic circles also indicates the support he received from people who cannot have been as corrupt and vicious as the prophet accused the community of being. So stylistics, literary and social analysis and common sense demand that the rhetoric of the oracles be recognized as metaphor and hyperbole. Such recognition reduces the meaning of the oracles to more modest statements about corruption in the community and the falseness of certain beliefs and some people. It is not quite what the prophet appears to say, but in keeping with modern demands for the reasoned and reasonable approach to such matters. But who demands reason of a prophet? Who expects modesty and the balanced, judicious evaluation from an inspired seer? To analyse for rhetoric is to lose the flesh and blood approach of the prophet who sees things in terms of black and white, all or nothing. To quote T. E. Lawrence:

> Semites had no half-tones in their register of vision. They were a people of primary colours, or rather of black and white, who saw the world always in contour. They were a dogmatic people, despising doubt, our modern crown of thorns. They did not understand our metaphysical difficulties, our introspective questionings. They knew only truth and untruth, belief and unbelief, without our hesitating retinue of finer shades.[24]

The inappropriateness of our Cartesian perspective for analysing prophetic rhetoric may be one way of handling the difficulties of understanding Jeremiah's hyperbolic language. There is another way of treating the matter: the question *cui bono* (for whose benefit? or to what purpose?) needs to be asked of such literature. What function did these oracles have for the traditionists who put together the Jeremiah tradition? Were they simply recording the sayings of the prophet from the period before the fall of Jerusalem, or were they engaged in much more important tasks relating to the survival of the community? The destruction of Jerusalem and the various deportations of Judaean citizens to Babylon may have confirmed the critique provided by Jeremiah's oracles, but that did little to salvage a future for the community. To have survived the catastrophe was to be in a position not spoken to by these oracles. The later development of the book of consolation (Jer. 30–33) may have contributed to the demands of this exilic period,[25] but at this stage of my analysis I want to focus on two functions the oracles under discussion may have had in relation to the exilic period and the editing of the Jeremiah tradition.

The fiercest and, in the case of Ezekiel (cf. Ezek. 16; 20; 23), the most pathological denunciations of the Jerusalem community appear in the oracles of Jeremiah and Ezekiel. Judging by their statements (also to be found in the deuteronomistic editing of Jeremiah; cf. Jer. 7.23–26) the community which experienced the declining power of the Judaean state and the Babylonian invasions was the most corrupt, vicious and evil community which had ever lived in the history of Israel since the exodus from Egypt. Rhetoric and hyperbole, no doubt, but the language is more significant than that.

These two prophets experienced the invasions: Ezekiel was deported to Babylon in 597 and Jeremiah saw the final collapse of Judah and Jerusalem. Men of such passion must have been deeply affected by their experiences and, for Jeremiah, the inevitability of the decline and eventual destruction of the territory must have been particularly galling. To have watched the politics of the period lead to the inevitable invasion of the Babylonians, and then the further involvement with Egyptian power politics make the final catastrophe almost certain, would explain much of the bitterness and rancour to be found in Jeremiah's oracles. The outrageous entanglement with the Canaanite cults and the idolatrous practices associated with the temple (cf. Ezek. 8) allowed the prophets to make connections between the political fate of the community and the theology of the punishing deity. The harshness of the oracles should therefore be attributed to a number of factors associated with the notion of theodicy.[26]

The exile called forth a number of attempts at providing an explanation for the destruction of the community. Theodicy is the general term given to such attempts at explaining how physical and moral evil in the world are compatible with the existence of a sovereign deity who is good *and* involved in the affairs of the world. For Israel theodicy became a necessary activity in the exilic period because the loss of statehood, temple and (from the viewpoint of the deportees) land brought to an end the history of Yahweh's protective care of his people since the exodus. Centuries of history were wiped out with the onset of the exile and numerous theological dogmas were severely shaken by it. The sixth and fifth centuries BCE became a time of major literary productions (e.g., the editing and development of the books of Jeremiah, Ezekiel, Isaiah [mainly the oracles of Second Isaiah and his followers], Haggai, Zechariah, the deuteronomistic history, Job and probably the complete edition of the Pentateuch) which all seem to reflect the exilic experience or attempt to deal directly with it.[27] Such a period of creative response indicates the deep roots the exilic catastrophe put down into the consciousness of the communities in Palestine and Babylon. Much of this literary activity was concerned with providing the community with a justification of the disaster, in other words with producing a theodicy.

One explanation for the exile, favoured by the prophets and the prophetically influenced deuteronomists, was the sinfulness of the community in Jerusalem. The connection between human wrongdoing and political disaster may not be apparent to twentieth-century people, but in the ancient world (and probably up to the period of the industrial revolution as well) the connection was quite obvious. Some (by no means all) of the pre-exilic prophets had preached that the community was corrupt and oppressive and that the day of Yahweh would come and remove such a wicked community by means of foreign invading armies (e.g., the Amos, Isaiah, Jeremiah, Ezekiel traditions all maintain this viewpoint too often to require any references here). The collection of the oracles of Jeremiah therefore assisted the construction of the theodicy which would show how Yahweh remained a benevolent deity who ruled over everything, yet could punish his people for their sinfulness. The fact that the prophet had spent considerable time proclaiming this viewpoint before it happened singled his work out for preservation after the other prophets' work had been vitiated by the catastrophe. Beliefs about Yahweh could be protected from falsification by the prophetic preaching, which identified the community's wickedness as grounds for the exile. This emphasis on the community's sinfulness became necessary in order to produce a theodicy, as Yehezkel Kaufmann expresses it: 'It is the inner necessity of religious faith, of theodicy, that has produced the biblical doctrine of Judah's sin.'[28] Without this exaggerated sense of the sinfulness and corruption of the people it is difficult to see how a theodicy might have been constructed by the prophets (Job and Isa. 53 point in different directions away from the Jeremiah-Ezekiel-deuteronomistic theodicy). So one good reason for the rhetoric of Jeremiah's oracles and their preservation by the traditionists is the movement towards constructing a theodicy during the exile.

There is a second explanation which may contribute to an understanding of the fierceness and harshness of the oracles. They are directed against the whole community of Jerusalem and often depict the city as a woman suffering indignities, injury or bereavement (cf. Jer. 4.30f.; 7.29; 13.26). After the deportation of 597 what remains in the city is rotten and due for further destruction (cf. ch. 24; 13.1–11). The deportees become Yahweh's people but Jerusalem remains the target of his anger. Only in the exile, among the exiles, is hope to be found and can a future be expected (cf. 29.1–7). Although Jeremiah may have changed his mind about the possibility of hope for Jerusalem and its survivors after the fall of the city (cf. ch. 42), the editing of the tradition clearly shows that this was a forlorn hope (chs. 43–44).[29] Those who remained in Jerusalem, in particular the pro-Egyptian party, were corrupt, anarchistic (cf. ch. 41), and incapable of responding to Yahweh's word via his prophet. Only the patient exiles in Babylon were viewed with favour, only they constituted the future people of Yahweh who would be restored to Jerusalem. Those who survived the fall of Jerusalem and remained there during the exile (whether they went to Egypt or not is immaterial) were of no consequence for the future. They simply did not count.

To return to the important question *cui bono?* and apply it to this analysis, it should be evident that the beneficiaries of this view must have been the exiles in Babylon. The fierce polemic directed against the pre-exilic and exilic communities in Jerusalem was motivated by a desire to do down those who never went into exile and to bolster up the claims of the exiles to inhabit and organize the restored Jerusalem. The utter corruption of the old community, stated so viciously in the oracles, completely disqualified the survivors of that community from having any claim to reorganize life (cultic, political and intellectual) in the rebuilt city. The oracles have been maintained in their strong form and developed, as well as being illustrated in the prose sections (esp. chs. 36–42), so as to reinforce the claims of the exilic party. This does not necessarily mean that the editing of the Jeremiah tradition, with the incorporation into it of a very considerable prose tradition about the life of Jeremiah in Jerusalem, was done in Babylon by the deuteronomists among the exiles. On the contrary, it is more likely (the balance of probability is difficult to determine here) that the tradition was produced in Palestine among the deuteronomists of the returned exiles.[30] In the early reconstruction period (late sixth century to end of fifth century) there was a good deal of conflict and controversy in the Jerusalem community over who should do what and how.[31] Various parties had programmes for reconstruction (e.g., Ezek. 40–48) but had to compromise and pool resources in order to gain power and a shaping role in the new community. One of the arguments of this book is that the editing of the Jeremiah tradition was one of the elements in this power struggle. It was intended to legitimate the claims of the exiles by associating them with Jeremiah, the prophet of Yahweh, to whom had come the divine word before the exile and whose words they had preserved through the exile. With the dawn of the new age the prophetic tradition contained sufficient material (e.g., the new covenant idea and the book of consolation) to advance a programme for the new community. These claims need not be limited to the exiles in Babylon, but should include the returned exiles and those in Jerusalem who were prepared to accept the terms of this group. Apart from the legitimation aspect of the tradition, it also contained a virulent polemic directed against the old Jerusalem community (and, no doubt, its descendants). This constitutes guilt by association, but in political power struggles every polemical device may be used (cf. Ezek. 44 for a similar argument used to distinguish between priests in the new organization). The stark picture of the old community depicted in the oracles of Jeremiah points very much in the direction of this argument, and may help to explain just why there are so many bitter oracles in the first part of the Jeremiah tradition.

These, then, are the two elements in the development of the tradition which may explain why the rhetoric is to be taken at face value. The demands of the theodicy required an overemphasis on human sin in order to justify Yahweh's destructive activities (cf. Lamentations) and the fierce struggle during and after the exile by various political factions to gain and maintain power in the community required the denigration of the past and those who still had claims on the territory. The oracles of Jeremiah served such purposes admirably and contributed to the ideological struggles of the period.

Repentance in 3.1–4.2

An important element in the early material is the poem of Jeremiah on repentance, which has been expanded by the editors to incorporate their own views of repentance and the future. The analysis of the section is by no means an easy one, and different scholars have produced a variety of versions of the poem and its additions.[32] The original poem is most likely to be found in 3.1–5, 12b–13, 19f., 21–23; 4.1f. A rather different set of metaphors is found in 4.3f., which does not employ the important motif of repentance (*šūb*), so that brief section should be seen as a transition between the repentance material and the collection of judgment oracles in chs. 4–6.[33]

The poem begins with a characteristic rhetorical device of Jeremiah's: the rhetorical question followed by an indictment of the community (vv. 1–5; cf. 2.5ff., 14ff.). The disputation in vv. 1–5 appears to include a reflection on the legal ruling given in Deut. 24.1–4 about the proper treatment of a divorced wife.[34] The community is accused of having been unfaithful to Yahweh (the adulterous wife motif in Hosea) by frequent involvement with strangers, and also of having a superficial attitude towards Yahweh in that their words are not supported by their deeds (vv. 4f.). The force of the divorce law in Deut. 24.1–4 is that the husband cannot take his ex-wife back to be his wife again if she has married somebody else and then become free of that person. The use of it here in Jeremiah suggests that the prophet is saying that the community has been divorced by Yahweh and, having taken other lovers, *cannot* return to him. However, Jeremiah continues with an appeal to the community to return to Yahweh and be restored to the family. If the legal ruling is to have any point in the argument, it must be to set up a contrast between what is legally possible and what the deity is prepared to do for his people. It is therefore similar to Hosea's conviction that the deity would not behave in the normal human way but would spare Israel (Hos. 11.7–9). Then the prophet puts in the mouth of the people a liturgy of penitential response to the deity's invitation (Jer. 3.21–4.2). In response to this public confession ('truly the hills are a delusion, the orgies on the mountains. Truly in Yahweh our God is the salvation of Israel') the prophet warns the community that the return must be a genuine return, involving the removal of the pagan cult objects ('abominations', *šiqqūṣîm*, 4.1) and the development of genuine Yahwistic religion. The transitional piece in 4.3f. reiterates the appeal but with a stronger element of warning and uses two sets of different metaphors: the breaking up and ploughing of the land and circumcision. The circumcision metaphor (cf. 6.10) indicates the development of a symbolic meaning for that cultural practice, perhaps a necessary development because of the commonness of the practice (cf. 9.25f. [Heb. vv. 24f.]).

The strong emphasis on the possibility of returning to Yahweh (*šūb* is used in 3.12, 22; 4.1) implies an early period of the prophet's activity for the occasion of the poem. Whether it should be related to the prophet's involvement in the deuteronomic reform of Josiah's reorganization of the kingdom depends upon certain presuppositions held about that period and the interpretation of the few pieces of inconclusive evidence possibly bearing on the matter.[35] The editing of the poem associates it with Josiah's period (3.6) and develops some of its elements. A contrast is made between Israel and Judah in a very brief account of the destruction of Israel, using the divorce metaphor, and how Judah failed to learn from what happened to Israel her sister (cf. Ezek. 16; 23). Perhaps the most interesting feature of the deuteronomistic development is the notion of a false repentance: 'yet for all this her false sister Judah did not return (*lōʾ-šābāh*) to me with her whole heart, but in pretence (*bᵉšeqer*), says Yahweh' (3.10). Again it is debatable whether this is a reference to the deuteronomic reform or to such earlier reforms as Hezekiah's (cf. II Kings 18.4; II Chron. 29–31), but it makes better sense of the argument to relate it to the popular response to Josiah. Looking back on the events and reactions of that period, the deuteronomists could *now* see that the enthusiasm aroused (cf. II Kings 22–23) had little sustaining power behind it. Since that time the nation's fortunes had gone into sharp decline, the king had died (or been killed) and the abolished syncretistic practices continued as before. The return to Yahweh had proved to be false, hence the use of the poem to reinforce the appeal to repentance (probably now directed to the exilic communities). The evaluation of the earlier return as false helps to emphasize the prophetic appeal for a genuine turning to Yahweh (4.1f.): 'to me you will return'. This emphasis might account for 3.6–12a interrupting the poem. The piece contrasting the two adulterous sisters also uses the *šûb* motif, but in its negative sense of turning away from Yahweh and as an epithet for Israel – 'faithless Israel' (*mᵉšûbāh yiśrā'ēl*, 3.6, 8, 11f.). The redaction of the tradition has placed immediately after this expanded poem (the expansion in vv. 14–18 is about the reuniting of Israel and Judah in the restoration from exile, so does not concern this focus on the motif of repentance)[36] a series of judgment oracles which depicts a Jerusalem beset by invading armies and suggests that either the appeal to repent was a failure or the repentance (cf. 3.22) did not last too long. The only hint in these oracles that there might still be time to turn occurs in 6.8: 'Be warned, O Jerusalem, lest I be alienated from you; lest I make a desolation, an uninhabited land' (cf. 4.14).

There is no evidence in the tradition of when Jeremiah may have given up hope that the community would turn from apostasy and return to Yahweh, the fountain of living waters. That he eventually gave up believing in the possibility of such repentance is clear from the oracles. At some stage of his activities he became convinced that the community would not return and also that it could not return. The two elements of this conviction are to be found in the oracles. The refusal to return is expressly stated: 'They have made their faces harder than rock; they have refused to repent (*mē'ᵃnû lāšûb*)' (5.3); 'They hold fast to deceit, they refuse to return (*mē'ᵃnû lāšûb*)' (8.5; 8.4–5a is an impressive piece of word-play on *šûb*). The nation is also depicted as refusing to know Yahweh (9.6, Heb. v. 5), a phrase which, in Jeremiah, means the practice of justice within the community (cf. 22.15f.). There is an accusation that the community refuses to walk in the good (i.e., ancient) paths and ignores the warnings of the watchmen (i.e., prophets, cf. Hos. 9.8; Ezek. 3.17; 33.7): 'We will not walk in it . . . we will not give heed' (6.16f.). They are incapable of feeling ashamed for what they have done (6.15 = 8.12), none is aware of having done anything wicked (8.6) and, indeed, the community is convinced of its innocence: '. . . you say, "I am innocent; surely his anger has turned from me." Behold, I will bring you to judgment for saying, "I have not sinned" ' (2.35). These extracts from a number of the oracles show the refusal to turn to be a leitmotif in Jeremiah's preaching.

If the refusal to turn represents the community's will, there is another element in the oracles which suggests that turning was not possible because of the state of the nation. 'Though you wash yourself with lye and use much soap, the stain of your guilt is still before me, says the Lord Yahweh' (2.22). 'Woe to you, O Jerusalem! How long will it be before you are made clean?' (13.27). The metaphor of the choice vine which has degenerated into a wild vine (2.21) points to an irreversible change in the nature of the community (cf. Isa. 5.1–7). The hot wind sweeping in from the desert heights presages destruction rather than purification (4.11f.). Where the winnowing image is used, it refers to terrible destruction (15.7). That the community has reached a stage beyond redemption is clear from the statement 'Can the Ethiopian change his skin or the leopard his spots? Then also you can do good who are accustomed to do evil' (13.23; cf. 'They are skilled in doing evil, but how to do good they know not,' 4.22). Allowing some latitude for rhetoric and metaphor, the sense of these statements demonstrates the prophet's conviction that there was no hope for the community. This view is probably also to be deduced from the repeated use of the phrase 'do not pray for this people, or lift up cry or prayer for them, and do not intercede with me, for I do not hear you' (7.16; cf. 11.14; 14.11). Though the motif of the prophet not praying for the people (contrast 37.3; 42.2) may be derived from the editors,[37] it is in keeping with the tenor of the oracles. Jerusalem is a city doomed to destruction without the will to repent or the possibility of repenting.

At two points in the oracles of doom there occurs the odd phrase 'yet I will not make a full end' ($w^e k\bar{a}l\bar{a}h\ l\bar{o}$ ' $e^{cc}\acute{s}eh$, 4.27); 'I will not make a full end of you' ($l\bar{o}$'-' $e^{cc}\acute{s}eh$ '$itkem\ k\bar{a}l\bar{a}h$, 5.18). The difficulty with the occurrences of the phrase is determining whether they represent editorial modification of the harshness of the judgment or should be translated in such a way as to mean 'I will most *surely* make a complete end'.[38] If the second possibility is taken (it fits 4.27 better than 5.18) then it reinforces the exposition of the oracles given above:

For thus says Yahweh, 'The whole land shall be a desolation; and I will surely make a full end.
> For this the earth shall mourn,
> and the heavens above be black;
> for I have spoken, I have purposed;
> I have not relented nor will I turn back.' (4.27f.)

An asseverative force of *lō'* can be argued for in 4.27, but in 5.18 the whole phrase is set in a context of learning from the exile (a deuteronomistic motif, cf. 16.10–13; 22.8f.), so it is more likely to be a redactional insertion.

A coherent outline of Jeremiah's view of repentance would be: in his earliest period of public work he called on the community to turn from idolatry and evil ways; this preaching proved to be ineffective and his oracles (perhaps from the time of Jehoiakim onwards) became more negative, insisting on the refusal of the community to turn, until he became convinced that there was no hope at all for the community: it could not change, nor would the deity turn away its doom. That is a highly rational and simplified account, but it is a fair appraisal of the scanty evidence available for making a judgment on what the prophet's view might have been. Without glossing over the difficulties of establishing any prophet's view of an issue, given the complicated nature of the editing of prophecy, this account of Jeremiah on repentance may serve as a basis for a brief discussion of the development of the motif of repentance into a dogma of repentance in the Jeremiah tradition.

The deuteronomists, on the other hand, held a somewhat different view of the nature of repentance. The most complete statement of their dogma of repentance is to be found in Jer. 18.7–10, where it is set out in universal terms:

If at any time I declare concerning a nation or a kingdom, that I will pluck up and break down and destroy it, and if that nation, concerning which I have spoken, turns (*šāb*) from its evil, I will repent (*wᵉniḥamtī*) of the evil that I intend to do to it. And if at any time I declare concerning a nation or a kingdom that I will build and plant it, and if it does evil in my sight, not listening to my voice, then I will repent (*wᵉniḥamtī*) of the good which I intended to do to it.[39]

However, the universal rule has Judah and Jerusalem in mind be-

cause the conclusion drawn from the principle is the demand for
the men of Judah and the inhabitants of Jerusalem (cf. 4.3; 11.1)
to repent (*šūbū*, v. 11). An example of it applied to the nations
would be the story of Jonah. The deuteronomistic history uses the
principle to indict either king or community whenever he or they
failed to change their ways and thereby brought down upon the
community the wrath of God. The Chronicler uses it even more
dogmatically to deal with the limiting cases of Manasseh and Josiah.
Manasseh represents the evil king who, on one occasion, turned
from his evil and sought Yahweh's mercy (II Chron. 33.1–20). Josiah represents the good king who, on one occasion, turned from
doing good and disobeyed the divine word (II Chron. 35.20–27). In
the case of evil Manasseh, the turning to Yahweh effected his release
from Babylon and in the case of good Josiah his opposition to Neco,
king of Egypt, who spoke the words of God, resulted in his death.
The deuteronomists had not developed the dogma of repentance to
the point where they were able to deal with the limiting cases of
Manasseh and Josiah, so between their formulation of the dogma
and the Chronicler's use of it there was a further period of
development.

The catastrophe of the exile probably forced the circle which
produced Deuteronomy to modify their covenantal paradigm of the
relationship between Yahweh and Israel, in order to permit some
expression of the possibility of turning in exile (cf. Deut. 4.30;
30.10).[40] Such a modification of the covenant idea indicates some of
the inadequacies of the covenant paradigm for constructing the
community's way of life, though the weakening of the covenant
metaphor by permitting repentance to operate in relation to it also
broadened and strengthened a modified notion of covenant. The
motif of return-turning (*šūb*) is a fundamental element of the
theology of the deuteronomistic historians.[41] It was probably developed in the exile when covenant, salvation history and the other
regulative principles used in the presentation of Israel's history had
suffered a severe setback. The origins of the repentance motif are
unknown and there has been a fair amount of speculation among
scholars as to its source. The covenant motif is seen by many as the
source of the idea, but that seems less than likely, given the structure
of the covenant as an obligation which cannot be broken without
dire penalties coming into force against the community
(cf. Deut. 27.15–26; 28.15–68).[42] Yet repentance as a way out of
the dilemma of the broken covenant during the exile may point to
the development of the repentance motif among circles (e.g. the

deuteronomists) who had maintained the covenant motif before the exile. The deuteronomists were heavily influenced by prophecy and the levitical circles, so they may have developed a dogma of repentance which took the prophetic concept and made it into a formal rule. Where the prophets allowed the possibility that Yahweh might be gracious to Israel (cf. Amos 5.15f.), the deuteronomists grounded the divine graciousness in man's returning to him. Jeremiah might preach the possibility of returning to Yahweh, but he could also recognize a community for which there was no hope and a period after which repentance was just not possible. The deuteronomists took a rather different view of the grounds and application of repentance.

Here, then, is a common motif between Jeremiah and the editors of the tradition which allows for overlapping but also divides between the tradition and its development. The perspective of the editors is a different one from the prophet's, because most of his work was done before the fall of Jerusalem, but the deuteronomists worked through the exile. Jeremiah failed to turn the community of his time, but the deuteronomists were determined to use him in their scheme to turn the exilic community and to secure the future. The element of turning in Jeremiah's preaching was their focus for understanding him and for developing the tradition. So the prophet is presented in terms of the turning of the community (cf. 7.5–7; 17.24–27; 22.1–5; 25.1–7; 36.1–3). The overriding concern of the editors is with the community in exile, rather than with presenting a historically accurate account of the prophet. Jeremiah may have preached against the temple a message of absolute doom (7.8–15), but the presentation of the sermon includes a conditional version of it (7.5–7; cf. 26.1–6: 'it may be they will listen, and every one turn (*yāšubū*) from his evil way, that I may repent (*wᵉniḥamtī*) of the evil which I intend to do to them', v. 3). There is quite a difference between the two accounts of the sermon, but the presentation would have determined the meaning of the account for the exilic and post-exilic communities.[43] There is some distortion of Jeremiah in the shift from absolute to conditional message, but such distorting shifts are inevitable when material is taken from its original context and given a new context with a different meaning. However, because the traditionists are working with the concept of the word of God, the distortion does not register as such, and the word spoken on a particular occasion becomes a word for all occasions.[44] Thus the development of the Jeremiah tradition takes place in the develop-

ment of the deuteronomic doctrine of prophecy as Yahweh's word
to the community.

The theology of repentance is an obscure and difficult matter. It
had its roots in prophecy, particularly in the idea of broken and
mended relationships and metaphors of going astray and returning.
Because human relationships could be restored after breaches of
trust, it was posited of the deity that he would forgive and restore
the community which returned from its infidelity with foreign cults
to the proper worship of Yahweh. The difficulty with this extended
metaphor is that not only is it grounded in anthropomorphic (metaphorical) language but, further, it only makes sense when applied
to dealings between individuals or families. It loses substantive
meaning when applied to a whole community. That is why hand-
books on biblical theology tend to stress that repentance can only
mitigate punishment, rather than render it null and void. How a
community repents is a difficult concept. The Jonah story makes
repentance liturgical (fasting and wearing sackcloth), but the major
prophets tend to demand more than cultic reactions. However, such
changes as they demand tend to be long-term ones which can hardly
change things immediately (except for iconoclastic outbursts). In
fact it is so difficult to envisage what communal repentance might
consist of (i.e., the notion of *everybody* changing their behavioural
patterns immediately is too unrealistic to be entertained), that it is
not surprising to find that the prophets failed to persuade the community to repent. It also accounts for why the deuteronomists can
state the principle as an (abstract) universal and only use it as a
retrospective principle for treating the past history of the monar-
chies. It is, of course, greatly facilitated in meaning if posited of
representative individuals such as the king (hence it is Nineveh's
king who responds to Jonah's preaching and proclaims a national
fast), because a community may repent in terms of changing national
policy or instituting major fasts and festivals (cf. II Kings 22–23).
But without some such representative factor, it is hard to attach
meaning to it, and harder to imagine it ever occurring in reality.

The concept of repentance appears to have built into it the notion
of differentiation between individuals and groups. This differentiation factor breaks up a community into those who repent and those
who do not. In this sense repentance is analogous to the idea of the
remnant – those who are left or remain after a disaster. If those in
a community who repent may be said to form a group, then a
distinction can be made between the community (larger group) and
those who repent (smaller group). There are hints along these lines

in the prophetic traditions (cf. Isa. 1.27), but there is no formal doctrine developed of the idea. Perhaps the circles which developed the notion of the remnant pre-empted the need for such a development.[45] If this analysis has any weight, then perhaps it is the case that traditions which stressed the principle of turning (in particular the deuteronomistic) were developed by groups who did differentiate between the larger community and a smaller group within that community. The strong differentiation between Judah-Jerusalem and the deportees in the Jeremiah tradition (Jer. 24; 29; cf. Ezek. 11) points in that direction. Jeremiah's call to the community to return to Yahweh should be related to the *whole* community, but after the first invasion of 597 it became possible to differentiate between communities, and during the exile it was necessary to make such distinctions. The early post-exilic period of reconstruction was a time characterized by groups and factions, so the repentance principle provided the deuteronomists with a regulative principle and also a formal element for the development of the Jeremiah tradition (if it had not been developed during the exile).

The theological problems of repentance need not take up too much space here, but it is worth noting two specific problems. The anthropomorphism of the concept may not bother the hardy theologian, but the use of such metaphors in the construction of any theory or theology can lead to serious misunderstandings of what is going on in such language. All metaphors have limits, none more so than those applied to God. It may have been part of the prophetic leap of imagination (especially in the case of Hosea) to have posited of God that he would accept repentance as an effective means of changing the future. Insofar as the idea is flexibly held, it may be a useful way of doing theology, but its limitations should be recognized. The way the deuteronomists elevate the metaphor to a formal dogma (Jer. 18.7–10) can hardly be described as a flexible handling of a limited metaphor. It also underlines the second problem which concerns the rigidity of the deuteronomistic ruling. As stated, it commits the deity to acting in accordance with human behaviour. Divine action is determined by human action. Not only does that contravene the principle of divine transcendence; what is worse, it pre-empts divine initiative and makes the deity countersign human activity. Theologians who like to stress the freedom of God (Barth, Eichrodt, Zimmerli and many biblical theologians) should find that expression of repentance doctrine seriously defective. Not that I wish to elevate the *metaphor* of God's freedom to the absolutist level

which Barth and the Barthians do (the idolatry of metaphor), but
a properly dialectical theology should allow the freedom of God to
modify the doctrine of repentance and repentance to limit God's
freedom. What that envisages constitutes part of the theological
problem of repentance. Although the formulation of Jer. 18.7–10
leaves much to be desired, it would be unfair to the developed
Jeremiah tradition if the complete editorial context of the book were
not properly taken into account. The strong formulation of the
doctrine is intended to persuade the (exilic) community to repent,
so it uses typical prophetic (or biblical) hyperbole and then anchors
the statement in reality by referring it to Judah-Jerusalem. Elsewhere in the tradition it could recognize that repentance (communal)
might be false (3.10). Jer. 18.7–10 cannot be extrapolated from the
deuteronomistic development of the Jeremiah tradition in order to
formulate a universal principle of repentance. That is not how
theology works in the biblical traditions.

Whatever its origins or development in deuteronomistic circles
may have been, repentance developed in importance during the
period of early Judaism. For rabbinic Judaism it became a fundamental principle of reconciliation whereby, no matter what the sin
of Israel, the doing of repentance atoned for it. Thus it is written:

> And when Israel, under the heavy burden of sin, says, 'Master
> of the world, wilt thou receive us if we shall do repentance?' God
> answers them, 'I have received the repentance of Cain . . . the
> repentance of Ahab . . . the repentance of the men of Anathoth
> . . . the repentance of the men of Nineveh . . . the repentance
> of Manasseh . . . the repentance of Jehoiachin, against all of
> whom there were ordained heavy decrees, shall I not receive your
> repentance?'[46]

It would be difficult to exaggerate the importance of the repentance
motif in Jewish thought, and it may well be considered the fundamental soteriological principle of Judaism.[47] In spite of the possibility of false repentance,[48] the motif is woven through Judaism and
has even been developed in modern times into a philosophical principle.[49] This development from hesitant prophetic usage to full-
blown dogma in early Judaism was greatly assisted by changes in
belief about life after death and the shift in belief from communal
identity to individual soul identity. Communal repentance is difficult to determine, but repentance by the individual which affects
the post-mortem or resurrection state of the soul is much more
meaningful. It is in this Graeco-Roman cultural context also that

the proclamation 'Repent, and believe in the gospel' (Mark 1.15) gains its significance. The development of repentance as a formal doctrine was a lengthy process, but in that process we should recognize that some of the stages were developed by the traditionists working on the Jeremiah tradition.[50]

4

Temple Sermon and
Covenant Preacher

Jeremiah 1–25 as a complex series of blocks of prophetic material provides a good deal of evidence of editorial arrangement. The interpenetration of prose and poetry throughout and the tendency to bring together common thematic material indicate this redactional activity. In 14.1–15.4 there is a collection of material 'concerning the drought', in 21.11–23.8 prose and poetry sections are devoted to the kings of Judah, and in 23.9–40 a compilation 'concerning the prophets' takes up yet another theme. A number of prose pieces are associated together in 7.1–8.3 to form a substantive critique of the cult in Jerusalem (cf. Ezek. 8; 9). They deal with the falseness of the community's view of the temple cult, an illicit familial cult (7.16–20; cf. Jer. 44), the rebelliousness of the sacrificial system as practised by the people (7.21–26), a fire cult in the high place of Topheth (7.30–34), and a judgment against the astral cults of city and community (8.1–3). Together they constitute a formidable indictment of the religious life of Judah and Jerusalem and reveal the corruption of the cult of the period. However, an analysis of the language and substance of the section shows that it has been produced by the deuteronomistic school and represents their concerns more than it presents Jeremiah's thoughts.[1] It interrupts the collection of oracles in order to summarize the early oracles by way of focusing on the cult and denouncing the practices found there. It functions, therefore, as part of the deuteronomistic theodicy justifying the divine judgment of the exile and undermining the claims of the Jerusalem cult officials. The corruption and collapse of the Jerusalem temple cult are two elements to be found in the Jeremiah and Ezekiel traditions which are part of the exilic polemic and struggle about the nature of the cult and the legitimation of claims to reorganize it (cf. Ezek. 44). The temple sermon (Jer. 7.1–15), however, provides a number of interesting insights into the way the

Jeremiah tradition has been constructed and warrants specific consideration.

The temple sermon

The most important feature of the temple sermon in the Jeremiah tradition is the fact that there is a parallel account in ch. 26 which sets out the sermon and its aftermath.[2] As it now stands in 7.1–15, the account purports to be the story of Jeremiah preaching in the gate of the Jerusalem temple a sermon which warns the community that it must mend its ways or else the city will be destroyed like the older sanctuary at Shiloh. In ch. 26 more details are given: the sermon is dated in the beginning of Jehoiakim's reign (c. 609), the reactions of the leadership and the people are included, a trial of Jeremiah is staged, with details of some of the arguments used for and against him provided, and, after noting a dangerous precedent, the account concludes with a statement to the effect that Jeremiah escaped death at the hands of the people. The first version of the sermon (7.1–15) is part of the prophetic proclamation to the community and introduces a series of critical reviews of the cultic malpractices of that community. The second version of the sermon introduces the second half of the Jeremiah tradition (chs. 26–52) and belongs to a series of accounts of conflict between Jeremiah and the community's leaders. So different functions and contexts determine the significance of the accounts.

The deuteronomistic nature of the temple sermon is clearly evident in the use of the stereotypical introductory formula in 7.1 (cf. 11.1; 18.1; 21.1; 25.1; 30.1; 32.1; 34.1, 8; 35.1; 40.1; 44.1). It is even more evident in the conditional aspect of the sermon which is to be found on a number of occasions in the Jeremiah tradition (e.g. 7.3–7; 17.19–27; 22.1–5; 26.3–6).[3] The possibility of an amendment of life is stated, though this possibility need not presuppose a genuine offer to the pre-catastrophe community, because the deuteronomists may have been appealing to the exilic community as much as positing their own principles in the presentation of the prophet. Attention has been drawn to the fact that the sermon in 7.1–15 contains both conditional and absolute features.[4] In vv. 3–7 the community is given the option of amending its ways and being permitted to remain in the land. In vv. 8–15 an absolute statement (or prediction) of the destruction of Jerusalem is given, reinforced by using the destruction of Shiloh as an analogy for Jerusalem's fate. The summary of the sermon in 26.4–6 ignores the absolute element and makes the whole statement one of contingent judgment: '*If* you will not listen to me . . . *then* I will make this house like Shiloh.' Whether the absolute feature of the sermon represents the original statement of Jeremiah (so Skinner) depends upon taking the view that some original words of Jeremiah have been used at some point in the account. Controversy about Jeremiah's *ipsissima verba* in the prose sections may be modified by conceding that there are only quotations from Jeremiah used in the presentation or admitting that the sermons preserve no more than the gist of what the prophet may have said on any specific occasion.[5] On the other hand it must be acknowledged that there is as strong, if not stronger, a case to be made for the view that the deuteronomists present Jeremiah in their own words entirely. As a paradigm of prophecy they show him to have spoken and acted in the way the authentic prophet of Yahweh would have spoken and acted. Whether he did or not is beside the point and also beyond finding out now. Taking this line of approach, the absolute element in 7.8–15 should be interpreted in the light of the prefatory conditional element in vv. 3–7 and read as contingent in accordance with the version given in 26.4–6. It could be argued that the retention of the absolute element reflects the fall of Jerusalem in 587, but the strong emphasis on contingency illustrates the incorrigibility of the community and also carries the deuteronomistic appeal to subsequent generations (cf. 18.7–10).

The focus of the sermon is on the temple in 7.1–15, but in 26.2–6 the temple element only appears briefly (see vv. 6, 9, 12; cf. v. 18); the focus is really on the city and the redaction provides an account of the proper way to respond to a prophet. So, very different things are going on in the tradition in spite of the two accounts having the appearance of being one story. Redaction and function are the important elements to scrutinize when interpreting complex biblical material. In the context of ch. 7 the temple, and the practices associated with it, or cult rituals in general, are the concern of the editors because the temple was not only important for the deuteronomists; during and after the exile it was of vital importance to the community. What did Jeremiah have to say about the temple? Judging by the poetic oracles, he had virtually nothing to say about it. Indeed, few if any of the pre-exilic prophets said much about the temple. It became the focus for prophetic activity and comment (excluding the cult prophets normally found in the temple) from the time of the exile onwards (e.g. Ezekiel, Haggai-Zechariah, Ezek. 40–48). Before the exile it may have occasionally concerned the prophets, but little direct comment is included in the prophetic traditions. In the cult itself and among cult prophets the temple was the centre of divine activity, but such a perspective seems not to have been shared by the prophets for whom we have literary traditions. They could be critical of the activities associated with the temple (e.g., sacrifice), but generally the cult was not the focus of their attention.[6]

This being the case, the concentration on the temple and allied cultic activities in Jer. 7 should immediately alert the reader's attention to the fact that here we are dealing with something other than the prophet Jeremiah's concerns. The style and content of the temple sermon belong to a deuteronomistic presentation of the prophet as a preacher of Torah.[7] Standing at the gate, the prophet proclaims the conditions for the proper entry to the temple and denounces activities which would bar the community from access to the sacred house. In some ways the sermon is an entrance torah (cf. Pss. 15; 24). The use of the decalogue (v. 9) also indicates deuteronomistic influence (for the phrase 'other gods that you have not known' cf. Deut. 11.28; 13.3, 7; 28.64; 29.25; also Jer. 19.4; 44.3). The reference to the temple as 'this house, which is called by my name' (vv. 10, 11, 14) reflects deuteronomistic usage (cf. Deut. 12.11; 14.23; 16.2, 6, 11; 26.2; I Kings 8.43). The occurrence of the sanctuary place name Shiloh (vv. 12, 14) links the prophetic speech with the traditions about Shiloh associated with Samuel the prophet in the deuteronomistic history (I Sam. 1–4). Connections between the Samuel tradition and the editing of the Jeremiah tradition have already been noted in the call narrative (ch. 2 above). It is a moot point whether the text here refers to the fall of Shiloh during the Philistine opposition in the time of Samuel or during the Assyrian destruction of Israel in the late eighth century.[8] It is more probable that the deuteronomists are rounding off the pre-exilic history of Jerusalem by drawing analogies between it and the fate of Shiloh, the sanctuary it replaced, as well as making connections between the edited Jeremiah tradition and the deuteronomistic history.

The summary of the sermon (7.3f.) asserts the possibility of being allowed to remain in the sanctuary[9] and warns of the danger of paying attention to the deceptive words: 'This is the temple of Yahweh, the temple of Yahweh, the temple of Yahweh.'[10] The precise origin and significance of this enigmatic phrase are not included in the text. It may have been an expression of confidence in the temple buildings which represented for the people the nation's security under Yahweh. The presence of Yahweh's house symbol-

ized the protection of the land. It might have been a popular echoing
of the prophetic assurance 'Peace, peace . . . it shall be well with
you' (cf. 4.10; 6.14 [= 8.11]; 23.17). Whatever the exact meaning
of the phrase may have been, its function in the sermon is to
illustrate the misconception of the community in basing its security
on the presence of the sanctuary in its midst. The community
defines the nature of the sanctuary rather than the sanctuary defining
the nature of the community. In the words of a much later Christian
mystic (Johann Tauler), 'Men make places holy not places men
holy'. It is a different account of the sanctuary from the one given
by Ezekiel (the divine presence withdraws from the sanctuary, thereby exposing its devotees to the consequences of their own impurity),
but an important contribution to the exilic discussion about the
relation of the temple to the community. The conduct of the community determines the nature of the holy place, so that if thugs and
brigands worship there it becomes a 'den of robbers' (v. 11), rather
than it being the case that the holy place purifies the worshippers
and so delivers them. Behind the saying may have been a dogma of
trust in the temple derived from spectacular deliverances in the
past, associated with previous prophetic activities.[11]

One other deuteronomistic element should be noted in the sermon: 'And now, because you have done all these things, says Yahweh, and when I spoke to you persistently you did not listen, and
when I called you, you did not answer . . .' (v. 13). In the context
of the editing of the Jeremiah tradition, this is a statement about
the prophetic word in the history of Judah. The English translation
'persistently' is a rendering of a Hebrew phrase (*haškēm wᵉdabbēr*)
meaning 'rising early and speaking'.[12] It may stress persistence or
diligence. The strange phrase is used also in 25.3; 35.14 with variations in 7.25; 25.4; 25.5; 29.19; 35.15; 44.4 (*haškēm wᵉšālōaḥ*),
11.7 (*haškēm wᵉhāʿēd*) and 32.33 (*haškēm wᵉlammēd*). This
graphic metaphor (used often enough in the Jeremiah tradition to
border on cliché) describes the persistence with which the deity
sent his prophets to the people. That would appear to be the meaning of the phrase in spite of the variations of speaking, warning and
teaching. It is spelled out in 7.25; 25.3f.; 26.5; 29.9; 35.15; 44.4 –
'I persistently sent to you all my servants the prophets'. In the
conclusion of the first part of Jeremiah the prophet Jeremiah is
incorporated into that steady stream of prophets reaching back into
the past history of Judah (25.3f.). History is the medium of Yahweh's word through his servants the prophets. The occurrence of
the phrase, therefore, in the temple sermon indicates the influence

of the deuteronomistic view of history as prophetic history and strengthens the analysis of the sermon as a deuteronomistic creation. It should also be noted that a feature of this motif is the insistence on the fact that the long history of the prophetic witness is a long history of the rejection of that witness by the community. Again the deuteronomistic motif of the rejected prophet surfaces in the Jeremiah tradition. At the same time the motif contributes to the theodicy theme in Jeremiah by showing how the exile is justified as the cumulative divine reaction to persistent rejection of the word sent.

Before analysing the temple sermon as it appears in Jer. 26 there are a few points worth noting in the catalogue of cultic malpractices in 7.1–8.3. The image of the community rejecting the prophetic witness throughout history (a different image from that of the community being misled by the prophets in 23.9–32), developed from the temple sermon, is reinforced by a series of denunciations of false cults and false cultic perceptions. The enigmatic cult of the queen of heaven (7.16–20) is greatly expanded upon in ch. 44, so comment will be left until ch. 9 (below). The section against sacrifice (7.21–26) includes the deuteronomistic motif of the community being in rebellion against Yahweh since it came out of Egypt during the exodus (vv. 25f.). This is an element of the theodicy which can also be found in Ezekiel (Ezek. 16; 20) and is probably to be accounted for in terms of the need to explain and justify the horrors of the exile. As a deuteronomistic regulative principle it may have contributed greatly to such explanatory schemes, but it should not be taken to be descriptively accurate of the history of Israel or Judah. It also conflicts with the motif of Israel's period of bridal devotion in the wilderness period (Jer. 2.2f.). The two motifs only contradict each other if they are treated as facts of history, but, taken as ways of treating distinctive traditions for different purposes, and making due allowance for their different origins in discrete traditions, their presence in the Jeremiah tradition may contribute to understanding just how complex that tradition really is.[13] The emphasis on obedience rather than sacrifice is typically deuteronomistic, though a later generation made sacrifice the result of obedience (cf. Ex. 25–Lev. 16). The stress here clearly indicates that the sacrificial system of the temple could not warrant the well-being of the community if other factors were missing from the community's religion. The section on sacrifice concludes with poetic fragments reflecting the concern with theodicy. 'This is the nation that did not obey the voice of Yahweh their God, and did not accept discipline.'

Truth has perished;
it is cut off from their lips.
Cut off your hair and cast it away;
raise a lamentation on the bare heights,
for Yahweh has rejected and forsaken
the generation of his wrath. (7.28f.)

The attack on the fire cult practised in the valley of Ben-hinnom
(7.30–34) describes an obscure ritual which may have involved the
passing of children through fire in a rite of initiation or dedication
or may have entailed the sacrificing of children in fire (cf. Jer. 19.5–
12).[14] An interesting feature of the pericope is the contrast it affords
with Ezekiel's evaluation of a similar (the same?) cult involving the
offering by fire of the *first-born* (Ezek. 20.25f.). For Ezekiel the
deity is the moving force behind such an appalling cult: 'and I
defiled them through their very gifts in making them offer by fire
all their first-born, that I might horrify them; I did it that they
might know that I am Yahweh.'[15] The fact that one prophet could
envisage the deity being involved in an act of primitive aversion
therapy while another prophetic tradition could reject the notion
altogether ('which I did not command, nor did it come into my
mind', Jer. 7.31; cf. 32.35) helps to show that the nature of biblical
tradition is not the processing of information but the presentation
of diverse, and often mutually incompatible, stances and evaluations. What an Ezekiel could regard as an act of Yahweh the
deuteronomists rejected as an act of human folly. It would be comparable folly for the modern commentator to attempt to reconcile
the contradictory attitudes to be found in the prophetic traditions,
but the existence of such attitudes should be carefully noted and
used in the construction of any general account of prophecy in the
Bible.

The function of the material collected and presented in 7.1–8.3
is to show the cultic behaviour of the Jerusalem community to have
been so corrupt that the destruction of city and people was entirely
justified. Social behaviour, false familial cults, false priorities in
sacrifice rather than obedience, appalling practices involving children in the cult at Topheth, and the astral cults of the community
all warrant the rejection of Jerusalem. Provoking themselves to
confusion through their idolatry (7.19), the community is dismissed
as the generation of Yahweh's wrath (7.29) and an evil family (8.3).
The deuteronomists' obsession with correct worship (a leitmotif
running through the deuteronomistic history) is well harnessed in

this section to the quest for theodicy. If ever the destruction of a community was justified, then, in the deuteronomists' presentation of the matter, the Jerusalem of Jeremiah's time was that community. Ezekiel made a similar judgment with his presentation of cultic corruption in Jerusalem (Ezek. 8; 9). Whether the material in Jer. 7.1–8.3 and Ezek. 8; 9 represents to any degree an accurate picture of cultic life in the temple practices of the period must remain open to debate, because of the ideological factors at work in the traditions.[16] To justify the exile and dismiss the claims to legitimacy of the survivors in the Jerusalem community were the aims of the deuteronomists who edited and produced the Jeremiah tradition, and the presentation of material in 7.1–8.3 is well adapted to meeting these objectives.

Jeremiah 26. There are many subtle variations between the two accounts of the temple sermon: e.g., in 7.2 Jeremiah is to stand in the gate, whereas in 26.2 he is to stand in the court; 26.2 adds to the divine command the phrase 'do not hold back a word'; the sermon is greatly expanded in 7.3–15, including an extract from the decalogue, but only summarized in 26.4–6; 26.3 provides a purpose for the sermon which is notably absent in 7.[17] The main difference is the subsequent account of the priestly and popular response to the sermon (26.7–24), which has no equivalent in 7.1–15. A brief description of the contents of that account will help to clarify what the traditionists were doing in their construction of this story. Jeremiah's sermon is heard by the priests, prophets and all the people in the temple area. When he finishes what he has to say, the priests, prophets and all the people seize him, saying 'You shall die!' This reaction is caused by his having spoken in the name of Yahweh: 'This house shall be like Shiloh, and this city shall be desolate, without inhabitant.' The story now changes slightly, because the princes of Judah come up from the king's house when they hear about the matter and the parties to the dispute are realigned. There are now four parties as well as the prophet involved in the argument: priests and prophets on one side, princes and all the people on the other side – Jeremiah in the middle (v. 11). Again it is asserted that Jeremiah is worthy of death because he has spoken against *the city* (v. 12). In vv. 12–15 Jeremiah reiterates the sermon and adds a section about his own position in the dispute to the effect that he has spoken Yahweh's words; he is in their hands, but if they kill him they will bring innocent blood upon themselves and the city. In response to this the princes and all the people accept his claim to be a prophet sent from Yahweh and assert, against the priests and the prophets, 'This man does not deserve the sentence of death' (v. 16). As the story now stands in its final redactional form note how the group 'all the people' have changed from the side demanding Jeremiah's death (v. 8) to the side demanding his release. A fifth group is now introduced; 'certain elders of the land arose and spoke to all the assembled people' (v. 17). This group produces an argument from precedence for the release of Jeremiah. They cite a prediction from the prophet Micah, who preached in the days of Hezekiah, king of Judah (v. 18):

> Thus says Yahweh of hosts,
>> Zion shall be ploughed as a field;
>> Jerusalem shall become a heap of ruins,
>> and the mountain of the house a wooded height.[18]

On the basis of this citation from Micah (3.12), the elders posit Hezekiah's reaction to such a dire threat to have been one of entreating Yahweh for favour with a concomitant repentance (*nhm*) on Yahweh's part. To increase the suspense, the editors then insert a piece of information about how King Jehoiakim, on a different and presumably later occasion, had had the prophet Uriah ben Shemaiah, who also prophesied against Jerusalem and the land 'in words like those of Jeremiah', brought back from Egypt, whither he had fled, executed and his body flung into a common grave (vv. 20–23). The account ends with a note to the effect that with the assistance of Ahikam ben Shaphan Jeremiah was not handed over to the people for execution (v. 24).

Despite having the appearance of being a simple story about a dispute between Jeremiah and various parties in the temple, the account in Jer. 26 is a very complex piece of tradition building. My brief description of the story's contents is intended to focus on the different parties to the dispute and to note the way the role of the people changes throughout. Five groups are portrayed in the account: priests, prophets, all the people, the princes of Judah, certain elders of the land. The priests and the prophets throughout the story are intent on killing Jeremiah; the princes, supported by the elders, regard him as innocent of any capital offence because he has spoken in the name of Yahweh; but the attitude of the people varies in the telling of the story. To begin with, all the people join in seizing the prophet and demanding his death (v. 8); then they become the audience, along with the princes, for the priestly-prophetic insistence on the death penalty (v. 11); then, with the princes, they exonerate Jeremiah (v. 16); and finally, Ahikam prevents Jeremiah being handed over to the people to be put to death (v. 24). There is clearly no consistent representation of the people's role in the story as it now stands. The force of that inconsistency is made stronger if v. 24 is read immediately after v. 19 where it properly belongs.[19] It might be arguable that the people changed sides when the princes became involved and then, perhaps, changed back later, but it is more likely that the inconsistency belongs to the way the tradition was constructed. The phrase 'all the people' is the term used throughout the story to indicate one of the parties to the dispute (vv. 7, 8, 9, 11, 12, 16, cf. 'all the people of Judah' v. 18). However, v. 24 simply refers to 'the people', so it might be an additional verse concluding the story and possibly taken from a different kind of conflict account. It introduces Ahikam ben Shaphan (cf. II Kings 22.12, 14), who assists Jeremiah, and it seems to be more influenced by the account of Uriah's execution (vv. 20–23) than the attitudes described in vv. 16–19. So the original story might have been a simple one of hostile reaction to the prophet which might have led to his being lynched by the mob, if Ahikam had not helped him to avoid that fate. Then the story was developed in order to make a number of points about the nature of prophecy and the proper response of the community to a genuine prophet speaking in the name of Yahweh. This development takes Jer. 26 away from the category of temple sermon and relates it much more closely to the material in chs. 27–29, which is concerned with prophetic conflict and the nature of the authentic prophet of Yahweh.

Even as brief a treatment of Jer. 26 as this analysis should demonstrate the complexities involved in the interpretation of any single strand of the Jeremiah tradition. It should also reinforce the view that the function of the material must be sought if the interpretation of it is to make any progress. The simple question 'What is going on in this text?' is a primary hermeneutical move. The surface similarities between the temple sermon in 7.1–15 and the account in 26.1–19 allow for a common treatment, but the more the texts are scrutinized, the greater the dissimilarities appear. Starting from roughly the same point, the different traditionists have utilized the temple sermon to say different things within the Jeremiah tradition about the community. In 7.1–15 the content of the sermon is the focus, whereas in 26 the prophet's fate and the response of elements within the community to him are the foci. The redactional setting of both pieces also determines the significance of the accounts. The first occurrence of the sermon should probably be seen as editorial reflection on and summary of the cycle of oracles condemning the community (chs. 2–6). The second use of the sermon (in summary form) is as a preface to the material on Jeremiah in controversy with the prophets, and should probably be seen as making a contribution, along paradigmatic lines, to that issue.

This assessment means that ch. 26 need not be analysed too closely at this juncture in terms of detail because it can be dealt with in the chapter on prophetic conflict (see ch. 7 below). Elements in the account also bear on the subject of repentance: the purpose of the sermon in the first place ('It may be they will listen, and every one turn ($w^e y\bar{a}\check{s}ub\bar{u}$) from his evil way', v. 3; cf. 25.3–6) and the use of the citation from Micah. The Micah quotation is interesting in a number of ways which impinge more fully on the question of genuine prophet versus 'false' prophet, but a few points may be noted. Such a quotation from prophecy in the course of an argument is very unusual in biblical narratives. There are many examples of pieces of other prophetic traditions appearing in a particular tradition (e.g., Isa. 2.2–4 = Micah 4.1–4), but not as part of the argumentation of the context. It is also remarkable that Micah 3.12 should be quoted, because the harsh judgments of Micah 1–3 (of which 3.12 is a fair summary) belong to a prophet whose work was, in many ways, a singular failure in its time.[20] Nothing in the Micah tradition (i.e., Micah 1–7) warrants the view that Micah preached repentance or believed such repentance would obviate the destruction of the community. The expectations of Micah were not realized in his time and Jerusalem survived the invasions and sieges of the Assyrian period. So Micah could be viewed as a false prophet. However, the deuteronomists worked with the principle that prophetic preaching was designed to turn the community from its wicked ways (a principle used throughout the Jeremiah tradition), so their reading of Micah and the history of his period understood his work to have been a resounding success rather than a complete failure. There is no evidence in the deuteronomistic history for Hezekiah's response to Micah, but the reference to his cult reform (II Kings 18.4) might have been the basis for this view.[21] Traditions about Hezekiah entreating Yahweh appear elsewhere (cf. II Chron. 29–32; Isa. 37–38), so the use of the motif in Jer. 26.19 may reflect a stage in the development of that tradition. For the deuteronomists prophecy always carried an implicit, if not explicit, element of repentance, and the proper response to a prophet was for the community to pay attention and mend its ways. So for the traditionists working on this account of the temple sermon, the issue was not the failure of Micah but the correct communal response to a prophet.[22]

The use of the Hezekiah example may also have been intended to make a comment on the proper behaviour of kings in relation to prophets. This would fit the redactional context afforded by chs. 25 and 27 which deal with kings, Jehoiakim (25) and Zedekiah (27), who are not prepared to change their political policies in response to the preaching of Jeremiah. However, this point should not be overstated because the role of the king (Jehoiakim) is not a part of the story. Jehoiakim appears in the editorial dating of the passage 'In the beginning of the reign of Jehoiakim' (26.1) and also in the parenthetical section on Uriah (vv. 20–23), but he has no part to play in the story at all. He is not one of the actors in a story which incorporates a good deal of role playing (e.g., priests, prophets, people, princes, elders). The structure of the story has no place for him, yet the conflict between Jeremiah and Jehoiakim is an important element in the Jeremiah tradition (cf. 22.13–19; ch. 36; see ch. 6 below). It may be the case that originally the story was simply a conflict account between a prophet (unnamed?) and the various strata of society, but it has been developed in the Jeremiah tradition into an imperfectly realized story about Jeremiah as a passive object of arguments between social strata. The Jehoiakim element comes more into focus when the editors wish to point out how dangerous the situation could have been for Jeremiah, but as the king is not involved at all in the trial it contributes very little to the story. So again there is some evidence for the complex nature of the way the story has been constructed.

To conclude this examination of some of the complexities of the temple sermon, a functional interpretation of ch. 26 bearing on the main argument of this book may be included here. Throughout the story of Jeremiah's trial the priests and the prophets remain his fiercest opponents. This opposition is a constant feature of the Jeremiah tradition. The priests and prophets here represent the Jerusalem community which opposed the word of Yahweh and brought upon itself the judgment of that word. The princes and the elders represent those leading citizens who supported Jeremiah and who, after they had gone into exile (cf. 24.4–7; 29.1–7), constituted the hope for the future (they may also have been the addressees of this deuteronomistic version of the Jeremiah tradition). The ambiguity about the role of the people may represent an equivocal view of the people taken by the deuteronomists or be due to unconcealed seams in the construction of the story.

The covenant preacher

In 11.1–14 Jeremiah is presented as a preacher of the deuteronomistic covenant. The language and substance of the section are so
clearly deuteronomistic that there can be no denying the involvement of some members of the deuteronomistic schools in the editorial processes which produced the Jeremiah tradition.[23] The
complete pericope is made up of three pieces: a command to Jeremiah to proclaim the words of this covenant to the men of Judah
and the inhabitants of Jerusalem, a command to which Jeremiah
responds willingly (vv. 1–5); then a further command to proclaim
the words of this covenant in the cities of Judah and the streets of
Jerusalem, but this time in the light of the rejection of the covenant
by the community's fathers and the resultant destruction of the
community (vv. 6–8); and finally a third passage in which the rebellion of the community is condemned and the broken covenant
made the grounds for coming destruction (vv. 9–14). This section
includes a condemnation of the community's idolatry and the rejection of the prophet's role as intercessor (vv. 12–14). Taken together
the pieces constitute the most direct statement implicating Jeremiah
in the deuteronomistic programme and presenting him as a peri-
patetic covenant preacher. The sense of v. 8 is best understood as
a reflection on the exile, and so should be related to the theodicy
theme in the tradition. The expression 'this covenant' (vv. 2, 3, 8)
may refer to the covenant enacted by Josiah (cf. II Kings 23.2f.) or
be a more general reference to the covenant associated with Sinai
(cf. Ex. 19–24; Deut. 5–9).[24] However, the distinction between the
two senses of covenant should not be overstressed, as the covenant
motif in the work of the deuteronomists is essentially a regulative
principle for shaping history and the community in relation to the
Sinaitic event.[25] The account of Josiah's reform has been heavily
shaped by the use of the principle of covenant and even made to
confirm the importance of the deuteronomic lawbook.[26]

The Skinnerian approach to the Jeremiah tradition would see in
the presentation of the prophet as a supporter of the deuteronomistic
covenant evidence for determining the issue of whether Jeremiah
approved of the reform movement in Josiah's time or disapproved
of it. This conventional approach accepts the *ideological* material in
the deuteronomistic history as fact and so the question does arise:
what was Jeremiah's attitude to the reform? As the prophet began
his work c. 627/6 and the reform was in progress c. 621, then the
young prophet must have taken a stance in relation to what the

deuteronomists were trying to do. It is inconceivable that he would have ignored it or, even worse, opposed it. In a neatly rationalized account Skinner shows how the young Jeremiah went part of the way with the deuteronomists (just as a woman may sometimes need to be engaged to a man to discover that she cannot marry him), but eventually realized that his spirit was quite different from theirs.[27] This approach, then, involves the prophet in the reform, perhaps even as an eager advocate of the radical changes envisaged in the national religion by the main terms of the reforming party. At first, the prophet went about the towns and villages of Judah proclaiming the terms of the reformers' covenant, a happy disciple of the reforming zeal sweeping through the countryside. The superficiality of the reform only became apparent with the passage of time, and on reflection Jeremiah began to withdraw from involvement in the movement. Skinner outlines its defects as 'its superficiality, its inability to cope with prevalent immorality, and the surviving tendencies to polytheism and superstition', and comments: 'Jeremiah began to suspect the inherent impotence of the legal method of dealing with national sin. At a later time he detected a worse evil in the new-born spirit of self-righteousness based on a formal acceptance of the Covenant and an outward compliance with its demands.'[28]

This account of the matter appeals to the approach which favours the historical and biographical interpretation of the book of Jeremiah and also is profoundly Protestant in its treatment of religion. Jeremiah emerges as a Luther opposing the Catholic Church's devotion to rituals, images and superstitions and preaching an alternative religion of the heart. Because this is the image of Jeremiah which will appeal to many readers, it is worth devoting a few paragraphs to a consideration of some of the issues involved in the argument before treating the matter in terms more consistent with the general approach of this book.

Taking the account in II Kings 22–23 (cf. II Chron. 34–35) as the starting-point and at face value, the reform may be described as follows. Josiah in the course of renovating the temple was informed about a lawbook found therein which purported to be the word of Yahweh, and which warned of divine wrath directed against the community for its failure to obey the terms of the lawbook. The king's reaction to this discovery was to make a covenant before Yahweh with all the people and to institute a destructive programme against all the cult centres and shrines in Jerusalem and the cities of Judah. The iconoclastic enthusiasm and violence created by this

programme involved murder and pillage throughout the country.
Towns and temples were ransacked, priests and acolytes butchered
and tombs desecrated. Wizards, mediums and idols were driven out
of the land and the terms of the lawbook followed explicitly. Such
is the account in the deuteronomistic history. The chronicler's
account has variations which suggest that Josiah's activities were
already under way when the lawbook was found. This account
suggests that the reform was really a political policy of Josiah's
designed to monopolize cultic power in Jerusalem. The destructive
features of the reform achieved such a monopoly of power and
advanced Josiah's scheme for a reunited Judah-Israel with himself
reigning over it as a latter-day David-Moses.

Would a prophet such as Jeremiah have been party to such a
movement of political-religious empire building and fanaticism?
Skinner pleads his youthfulness as an excuse for his having accepted
a view of religion which thought legal forms could structure inward
spirituality. The impossibility of the state authority enforcing a
national conversion was something the young Jeremiah would have
to learn through experience. So he joined in the fervour with which
the reform was enforced and thereby earned the hostility of his
kinsfolk (cf. Jer. 11.18–23). His commitment to the reform led to
his family losing their family shrine in Anathoth. He weathered
these storms of opposition because he really believed that good
would come from the fierce iconoclasm of the reformers and threw
himself into preaching the demands of the covenant throughout the
land. The lack of permanent success the reform movement achieved
was concealed by initial success and nationalistic celebrations. However, as he matured, Jeremiah came to see that the reformers'
ideology and methods were inadequate to the task of national reform, and his own inner development convinced him of its inevitable
failure. The life of the community after the death of Josiah demonstrated the utter superficiality of the reform movement. The reform
also produced new problems for Judaean religion which Skinner
analyses as 'a new class of professional religionists, the scribes, in
whose hands religion was divorced from the essential and the spiritual, and resolved into a routine of sumptuous ritual and priestly
ceremony'.[29]

Skinner's dichotomy of spirituality and ritual, i.e., prophetic and
priestly-scribal religion, is a heavily biassed and grossly inadequate
account of religion. It may represent an individualist's account of
what genuine piety may be like, but it is not an accurate account of
any known religion in human history. The spirituality of the indi-

vidual is cradled in the religion of the community. No religious urge or spirit can survive without a superstructure of communal rituals patterned by time and place. Nor can the piety of the individual have any influence without a community to nourish it or provide a foil for it to develop against. The reformer emerges out of the community's religion and proceeds to create another communal structure. Without some such communal structure no reforming movement or spirituality could survive for any length of time. The reformers who fail to create alternative communities to the ones they oppose will fail (contrast Luther with Spartacus or Lenin with Kerensky). An alternative to forming new communities would be the complete or partial transformation of the larger society by the reforming or revolutionary group. Whichever possibility is undertaken, the net result relates to communal structures. Skinner's contrast should be between movements which successfully transform the community (or elements in it) and those which fail to make any impression whatsoever. Spiritual elements will be found in both sets of movements, and should not be used to contrast prophet and priest or scribe.

There is, however, a real tension within the struggle to change and shape society which might loosely be described in terms of spirituality and ceremony. The revolution may fail, be betrayed, become revisionistic, be sidetracked, or whatever, and what survives may be a hollow mockery of the revolutionists' aims and programmes. Some commentators would say that in fact the revolution had succeeded only all too well and the resultant state of affairs should be seen as an exposure of the falseness of the programme. The tension arises out of the problems of maintaining revolutionary fervour against the inexorable passage of time and the inevitable emergence of further and greater problems. In religious language such problems would be described as the problem of permanent reformation (cf. Trotsky's permanent revolution) – how to maintain the same level of commitment, enthusiasm and fidelity to the original programme as time passes and the reforms are formally accepted and enacted. When the king has been deposed, how can 1688 be prevented? Indeed, when the king has been deposed, how is the community to prevent any of its members assuming a similar role, though without using the same title? The problem exists for all human institutions: how can the passion of love be maintained throughout a long marriage? How can the freshness of a ritual, experience or event be sustained over years of repetition? How is routinization avoided? The distinction between ritual and experience is a false one, if posed in terms of spirituality and ceremony, because both terms may describe meaningful, open experiences or static experiences. In popular religious discussions spirituality conceals as many corpses as ceremony does. Without ceremony and ritual, spirituality cannot be maintained in the community and without spirituality (whatever may be meant by the term) ceremony and ritual can easily become dull and meaningless. The relationship between the two is a dialectical one and, as with dialectical matters, tension is inevitable. The routinization of ritual is a danger which has to be guarded against permanently, but the rejection of ritual is not a method of protecting the structures of religion. Ritual is endemic in religion and society, and it is only a misconception of its nature which permits commentators to suggest that it can be avoided. The Quaker meeting house gathering is as ritualized as a pontifical Requiem Mass (with music by Verdi, if permitted). The individual devotee who says grace before every meal, reads the Bible twice daily and goes to church at least once a week pursues a life of ritual. That ritualized existence may also be regarded as a genuinely spiritual life, thus indicating that the terms ritual and spiritual may be commutative, depending upon definitions and stances. It may be the case that *our* religion is spiritual and *their* religion consists of (empty) ritual (legalism is the preferred Christian term of abuse), but such a chauvinistic evaluation of the matter contributes nothing to analysing the problem.

The problem, then, is not a contrast between prophetic and organized religion, but resides in the very nature of social behaviour with its inbuilt ritualized forms. In religious terms the problem arises because such ritualized forms may very easily be substituted for ethical practices. Instead of loving my neighbour I may be content to pray for him – an example of ritual replacing ethics (though, given the wide variety of religious traditions and practices, it is less than clear which activity benefits my neighbour more). Judaeo-Christian forms of religion are inevitably command structured, so the practice of ritual forms of behaviour tends to have dominated the history of the multiple variations of those traditions. Within the formal structures of such religious traditions there has been a very strong ethical element informing and structuring the communities, but the various essences of Judaism and Christianity have entailed that religious identity should be determined in terms of adherence to the ritualized community – you may be declared a heretic for having an unorthodox view of the deity (e.g., Spinoza) but not for hating your neighbour. So tensions cannot be avoided,

given the nature of such religious communities. As the philosopher
R. G. Collingwood observed:

> Religious morality is . . . a morality of commandments, a for-
> malistic morality, one in which the spirit in which an act is done
> cannot be separated from the act itself. This is illustrated by the
> fact . . . that religion requires us to go to church not because
> hating God in church is preferable to loving him anywhere else,
> but because religion identifies the service of God with the outward
> act, namely churchgoing, which symbolizes it: an identification
> against which the highest religion . . . struggles but struggles in
> vain.[30]

To relate this abstract discussion to the Jeremiah tradition, it
should be noted that Jer. 8.8 has been seen as bearing on the issue
of Jeremiah's view of Deuteronomy and the reform movement.[31] In
the midst of a harangue directed against the community for its
inability to be natural and turn back to Yahweh there appears this
statement.

> How can you say, 'We are wise,
>   and the law of Yahweh is with us?'
> But, behold, the false pen of the scribes
>   has made it into a lie.

It looks like a public objection to the assertion 'my people know
not the ordinance of Yahweh' (8.7), a counter-assertion which
affirms: 'We are wise, we have Yahweh's law'. The law (*tōrāh*)
here referred to may be the recently promulgated law of Deuteronomy (cf. Deut. 4.6, which associates the law with the community's wisdom). The prophetic rejection of this counter-assertion
accuses the scribal authorities of having falsified the law or of having
a false law. The Skinnerian approach would make 8.8 a rejection of
Deuteronomy by a later and more mature Jeremiah. Disappointed
by the outcome of the reform, the prophet revised his judgment
because the law had become the community's fetish. The law had
fallen into the hands of a professional class, and they had developed
its teaching in such a way as to falsify it. No longer did it constitute
the community's wisdom; it had become yet another example of its
falseness. Along with all the other structures (priests, prophets,
sacrifice, temple, community behaviour, worship), the divine word
was also false. The element of false repentance (3.10) should perhaps
be associated with this interpretation, only in terms of a redactional

awareness that the reform movement had been false because it had been superficial.

Now from the viewpoint of a general abstract and static view of religion, this Skinnerian interpretation is very appealing. Its picture of a radical prophet dismissing the community's bible with a few well-chosen words as false is attractive for anybody living or working among fundamentalists. The notion that the divine law is no better than the people handling it (cf. Jer. 2.8), that the human interpretation of the divine word can falsify it, is an idea which is extremely powerful and encouraging for those who perceive in Judaeo-Christian structures a trenchant critique of all power groups and ideological positions. It is a prime example of the Jewish critical spirit which has radically opposed political and religious ideologies over millennia.[32] It also asserts a fundamental truth about social structures vis-à-vis politics and religion, namely that truth can become fossilized through ideological activity and thereby falsified. There can be no static account of truth which preserves truth free of corruption through time and human activity. (Indeed, on the contary, truth may often be 'the daughter of time'.) Even entities designated 'the word of God' can be false or become falsified by institutional handling. No prophet would accept subjection to a *written* divine law, for how could the recipient of the immediate, direct and spontaneous vision, revelation or divine word allow other people to dictate through documents limits and controls on inspiration and imagination. Jer. 8.8 suggests such an argument between prophetic speaker and scribal school over the nature of the divine word. Against the written word the prophet opposes the spoken word. As a document the divine word is false, has become frozen within the text and trapped in a social construction of the community. Nobody living in today's world, where the idolatry of fundamentalism is rampant,[33] could fail to be moved by such an argument, nor fail to see in the long history of Jewish, Christian and Muslim communities the constant temptation facing synagogue, church and mosque to make idols of the written word. The struggle within theology (and politics *mutatis mutandis*) has always been a struggle against such idolatry, a struggle to keep the community open towards the future rather than closed and facing the past. The matter has been expressed superbly by Arend van Leeuwen in his Gifford Lectures given at the University of Aberdeen in 1970, of which only a fragment can be quoted here to illustrate the problem in terms far superior to anything I may write:

The '*written heaven*' may, in itself, be very much a novelty as compared with the visible heaven which represented the ultimate horizon of antiquity; yet it is still a closed horizon. Visible nature has been replaced by audible Word; but this Word remains imprisoned in a written text which can be possessed, manipulated, a text which has, in fact, become an instrument of tyranny and suppression of spiritual freedom. The Word, as distinguished from nature, may bear testimony to the spirit; it still remains sealed. The true work of the spirit still lies ahead, therefore; but the intensity of its activity now appears to have assumed a new and higher quality. Whereas within the world of antiquity the struggle was directed against the ascendancy of natural bondage, now the front is directed against the powers of spiritual bondage. It is the sealed Word, the '*written heaven*', which this time has become the antagonist. The arena in which the battle is to be fought is no longer the realm of nature but the realm of the spirit itself. The sealed Word has to be unsealed, the 'written heaven' has to be 'pulverized', the palpable, reified text of a canonized Bible, a frozen creed, a congealed tradition, has to be reduced to ashes, to be melted down and transformed in the devouring fire of the spirit.[34]

The truth and importance of the general discussion here should not be ignored, but its bearing on the exposition of Jer. 11.1–14 is very limited. Jer. 8.8 is too brief and enigmatic to formulate a critique of institutional religion on the strength of it. It may reflect a conflict with wisdom circles in the community of the period (cf. 9.12, 23, Heb. vv. 11, 22), but the precise period and the parties to the dispute remain unknown. The redactional employment of 8.10–12 as a refrain (cf. 6.12–15) suggests that the proper way to treat the passage is to see in it an editorial polemic against the community, in particular against the wise men. This approach does not rule out the possibility that the statement might originally have been about some dispute over a document, but, as it now stands, its function and meaning belong to the redaction of the tradition. That it might even have been about the lawbook found in the temple depends upon whether the incident regarding the finding of such a lawbook (II Kings 22.8) is treated as a historical fact or, what is much more likely, an ideological move on the part of the deuteronomists to anchor their presentation of history in reality by constructing such a story. If no such book was ever found, except in the imagination of the deuteronomists (theological history is history

written in the way it *should* have happened rather than in the way
it did happen), then it is pointless trying to make Jer. 8.8 yield
evidence of Jeremiah's rejection of the lawbook's claims.

A similar line of argument may be pursued for the subject of the
deuteronomistic reformation in the time of Josiah. That Josiah in-
stituted wide ranging changes in his territory as part of his campaign
to extend his rule over areas of northern Israel need not be denied,
though to what extent he attempted to monopolize worship by
limiting it to Jerusalem is open to debate. The deuteronomistic
account of Josiah's activities may therefore be ideologically slanted
to provide a legitimation of their theology. One of the main difficulties in taking the account of the reform in II Kings 22–23 at face
value is the fact that prophets such as Jeremiah and Ezekiel condemned the post-reformation community and temple for blatant
idolatrous practices (cf. Ezek. 8). This difficulty has been noted in
biblical scholarship, and it has been suggested that either the
prophets were exaggerating (i.e., typical prophetic rhetoric) or the
material more accurately describes the pre-reformation period of
King Manasseh.[35] Those who are not prepared to face the fact that
biblical accounts have a strong ideological factor present in them
usually resort to weak and vague arguments about the failure of the
reform movement after the death of Josiah. No sooner had the good
king died than the old ways returned, the old priests came back into
power and the destroyed cults were resurrected. Presumably the
reformers who had taken over the cult gave it back or revised their
theology to accommodate syncretistic practices. This is so unlikely
an explanation and so unconvincing an argument (it is comparable
to arguing that the communities founded and ruled over by Luther,
Calvin and Zwingli returned to Catholicism in the later years of the
reformers' lives) that it will only serve those who wish to evade
thinking about the difficult problem entailed in taking *all* the biblical
reports seriously. A more likely explanation involves distinguishing
between the political reforms of Josiah and the deuteronomistic
ideological account of them, accepting the prophetic critique about
pagan practices in the temple and developing a more sophisticated
theory about the relation between ideology and history in the biblical
writings.[36] It took the destruction of the temple, a lengthy period
of exilic desolation and a long post-exilic period of intense ideological
conflict to produce a monolatrous cult in the Jerusalem temple.
Such an account, though not without serious problems of its own,
makes more sense of the evidence about syncretistic cults in the
temple right up to the destruction of the city than the deuteron-

omistic account of a pure Yahwistic cult from the beginning which
was regularly disrupted by pagan cults.

It is as part of the ideological presentation of history by the
deuteronomists that Jer. 11.1–14 should be interpreted. The logic
of their view of Josiah's reformation demanded that their account
of Jeremiah, the prophet active in Josiah's reign, should also be an
account of an active supporter of the reformation. If Josiah celebrat-
ed a great covenant-making ceremony, and used the terms of the
covenant to reshape the territory, then Jeremiah should be presented
as a prophet of that covenant, travelling around the countryside
preaching the terms of the obligations laid on the community. The
account in ch. 11 then represents an interpretation of the life of the
prophet rather than a description of his real activities. It is an
interpretation or presentation of Jeremiah in terms of deuteronomistic theology. The prophet behaves as a perfect deuteronomist
because to the deuteronomists that is how a prophet working in
Josiah's time should behave. Ideology shapes and creates the representation of the prophet, and helps to explain why the deuteronomists produced the Jeremiah tradition.

In editing and expanding Jeremiah's oracles, the deuteronomists
have taken the opportunity to present a number of accounts and
pictures of the prophet which set him forth as a deuteronomist.
This activity places the prophet in a tradition-building stream, and
also helps to legitimate the deuteronomistic ideology by associating
it with the prophet who had been so active in Jerusalem before the
destruction of the city. Thus the deuteronomists could claim continuity links between their time and pre-exilic Jerusalem, and also
between their ideology and the preaching of Jeremiah. It is no
longer possible to determine what the historical Jeremiah might
have said and done, because the evidence we have in the Jeremiah
tradition is more indicative of what the deuteronomists said and did
than what Jeremiah may have said or done. The deuteronomistic
ideology is the shaping principle behind the tradition, so we see
Jeremiah through deuteronomistically ground lenses. Whether there
were natural links between Jeremiah and deuteronomistic thought
(i.e., common holdings in beliefs and practices) or the deuteronomists have distorted completely the figure of Jeremiah in so presenting him cannot now be determined. As in all such presentations,
the elements in it tell us much more about the deuteronomists than
they do about Jeremiah. Without the presentation we would not
have a prophet, so it is not possible to strip away the deuteronomistic
elements and then argue that what remains must be the historical

Jeremiah. We must accept the interpretation as it is, and attempt to discern in that presentation what elements we can of the exilic and post-exilic activities of the traditionists.

5

The Confessions of Jeremiah:
Towards an Image of the Prophet

Scattered through chs. 11–20 are a series of poems and poetic fragments which have come to be known as the 'confessions of Jeremiah'.[1] The term 'confessions' is not a precise one, and owes more
to its association with Augustine and Rousseau than to an analysis
of the Jeremiah tradition. A better term might be 'soliloquy' (the
act of speaking alone or to oneself), a theatrical word associated
with some of the speeches of Hamlet – though it is also a term used
of Augustine's work.[2] It is unlikely, however, that scholars will stop
using the term confessions and start using the word soliloquies, so,
recognizing the limitations of its application, I shall retain the traditional word for describing the category of the poems.

The confessions are a popular focus for the pietistic approach to
the Jeremiah tradition, for, as Skinner says,

> They lay bare the inmost secrets of the prophet's life, his fightings
> without and fears within, his mental conflict with adversity and
> doubt and temptation, and the reaction of his whole nature on
> a world that threatened to crush him and a task whose difficulty
> overwhelmed him. There is nothing quite like them in the range
> of devotional literature . . . we shall find here a certain expansion
> or sublimation of the prophetic consciousness into the larger
> relationship which is properly called religion – a relation of which
> one term is God, and the other is the human soul, in its desolation
> and weakness and need, and its irrepressible craving for assurance
> of its worth to the God who made it.[3]

Here is mystical religion whereby the *individual* escapes the re-
straints of institutional religion and, alone with God in prayer,
focuses on itself as the victim of an unkind and harsh world. Treating the confessions in this way secures them as a contribution to the
construction of paradigms of personal religion based on prophecy,

and is in keeping with the Skinnerian approach to Jeremiah as biographic portraiture. It facilitates the use of the text as a handbook for spirituality and encourages the reader to pursue an imitation of Jeremiah. It is not, however, the only way the confessions may be read, and an alternative reading of the tradition will be offered in this chapter.

The delineation of the confessional material is a difficult task, but whilst scholars are not in full agreement about the precise division of each section, there is general agreement that the confessions are to be found in 11.18–12.6; 15.10–21; 17.12–18; 18.18–23; 20.7–18.[4] Throughout the poems there is a strong sense of complaint or lament (*Klage*), hence they might be better entitled 'Jeremiah's laments' than 'Jeremiah's confessions'. The careful reader of the sections will be struck by the similarity between the language of the confessions and the language of the book of Psalms. This similarity is an important feature of the analysis and argument in the following treatment of the poems, and points to redactional influences in the Jeremiah tradition.

The poems

Yahweh made it known to me and I knew;
　　then thou didst show me their evil deeds.[5]
But I was like a gentle lamb
　　led to the slaughter.
I did not know it was against me
　　they devised schemes, saying,
'Let us destroy the tree with its fruit,
　　let us cut him off from the land of the living
　　that his name be remembered no more.'
But, O Yahweh of hosts, who judges righteously,
　　who triest the heart and the mind,
let me see thy vengeance upon them,
　　for to thee have I committed my cause. (11.18–20)

A divine response is provided for this prayer in vv. 21–23, and it announces judgment against the men of Anathoth, who are seeking the life of Jeremiah in order to stop him prophesying. This redactional element, which explains the setting of the poem, probably justifies interpolating 12.6 between v. 18 and v. 19: 'For even your brothers and the house of your father, even they have dealt treacherously with you; they are in full cry after you; believe them not, though they speak fair words to you.' The motif of sheep led to slaughter as a metaphor for the persecution of the righteous by the wicked occurs in Ps. 44.11, 22 (Heb. vv. 12, 23), a psalm which is usually categorized as a collective lament.[6] One of the more common motifs in the Psalms is the conspiracy of the nations against Israel, designed to wipe out the people of Yahweh (e.g., Ps. 83.1–8 [Heb. vv. 2–9]; cf. Pss. 2.1–3; 21.8–12 [Heb. vv. 9–13]; 56.5–7 [Heb. vv. 6–8]). Equally common is the motif of the king, community or individual as the target of such plots (e.g., Pss. 35.1–8; 41.5–7 [Heb. vv. 6–8]; 56.1f., 5–7 [Heb. vv. 2f., 6–8]; 64.1–6 [Heb. vv. 2–7]; 140.1–5 [Heb. vv. 2–6]). So common are these motifs in the Psalms that we must see in their occurrence in the Jeremiah tradition the strong influence of liturgical language from cultic sources. The linking of the formal lament style with the men of Anathoth (Jer. 11.21–23) suggests either a redactional attempt to relate such motifs to the life of Jeremiah (on the analogy of the psalm titles, which relate formal cultic elements to the life of David the king) or an association of two approaches to the life of Jeremiah. These two approaches are a construction of his inner life from the language and motifs of the cult, thus making him analogous to Israel and his enemies the enemies of the nation, and a development of the motif of the persecuted prophet constantly opposed by the community (cf. 1.17–19; 6.27–30; 18.18). The two approaches may well overlap with one another. Is the prophet in the process of becoming identified with the nation so that the relationship between Israel and Yahweh has become a relationship between prophet and deity? This would seem to be the image emerging from this particular lament.

> Righteous art thou, O Yahweh, when I complain to thee;
>   yet I would plead my case before thee.
> Why does the way of the wicked prosper?
>   Why do all who are treacherous thrive?
> Thou plantest them, and they take root;
>   they grow and bring forth fruit;
> thou art near in their mouth
>   and far from their heart.
> But thou, O Yahweh, knowest me;
>   thou seest me, and triest my mind toward thee.
> Pull them out like sheep for the slaughter,
>   and set them apart for the day of slaughter.
> How long will the land mourn,

and the grass of every field wither?
For the wickedness of those who dwell in it
    the beasts and the birds are swept away,[7]
    because men said, 'He will not see our latter end.'
'If you have raced with men on foot, and they have wearied
        you,
    how will you compete with horses?
And if in a safe land you fall down,[8]
    how will you do in the jungle of the Jordan?
For even your brothers and the house of your father,
    even they have dealt treacherously with you;
    they are in full cry after you;
believe them not,
    though they speak fair words to you.' (12.1–6)

I have included v. 6 with this poem in order to allow the difficulty of its positioning to become apparent. As it stands in the MT, it may represent the explanation of the obscure metaphors in v. 5. They seem to make the point that if the prophet (?) had experienced difficulties in normal circumstances (competing on foot and dwelling in a secure land) then a fortiori he would be in trouble in extraordinary circumstances. But what does that refer to? Had the prophet had trouble in some ordinary situation but could now look forward to even more difficult times? Could the formal discussion of vv. 1–4 really be described as ordinary compared to opposition from his family? If v. 6 is shifted to a position after 11.18, part of the problem is resolved, but the difficulty of the MT presentation of the passage should be noted.[9] Taking the MT as the redactional account of the poem, it may be the case that v. 6 is to vv. 1–5 what 11.21–23 are to 11.18–20 – prosaic explanations of the prophet's troubles. Such an explanation, though not resolving all the problems, avoids having to reverse the order of the two pieces (i.e., 12.1–6 before 11.18–23)[10] because it focuses on the independence of the poems and their explanations.

The poem of 12.1–4 reflects on the problem of why the wicked prosper, a theme of the Job story and of a number of psalms (cf. Pss. 37; 49; 73). The reference to 'our latter end' (12.4), in view of the different Greek rendering, might be a redactional reflection on 'their latter end' of Ps. 73.17. The problem of the prosperity of the wicked or the suffering of the righteous is essentially the theodicy motif, a problem which developed for the Judaean community during the exile. Why had Yahweh punished Judah and spared the wicked nations? The prophet here stands for the nation and pleads the nation's cause over against the prosperity of the nations. Perhaps 12.5 should be taken as indicative of further trouble to come (cf. the deepening problems of Job), though it could also be a link verse between the poem and the more prosaic explanation in v. 6. Again there are the two motifs of the nation as victim and the prophet as target of his family. A different explanation is offered by Reventlow, who focuses on the drought motif of v. 4 (cf. 14.1–15.4) and, associating the poem with 10.19–22; 15.10ff.; 17.12ff. (cf. 8.14ff.; 14.17f.), sees it as a collective lament of the nation.[11] The 'how long?' of v. 4 is certainly part of a lament formula,[12] and the general argument of the poem is similar to the psalms already mentioned (e.g., 10; 64; cf. 73.11; 94.7; Job 21.14f.). Forensic elements can also be seen in the poem: Yahweh is right, the speaker pleads a case (*rīb*), the guilty prosper. The poem is an elegant plea for judgment to be given on behalf of the righteous against the guilty who prosper in spite of their wilful dismissal of the deity. In formal terms the piece suggests the laments of the community, though not necessarily over the drought (which has come into the poem at some stage in the development of the text from 14.1ff.).

The two lament poems in 11.18–20 and 12.1–4 represent liturgical compositions designed to express the community's response to the catastrophe of the destruction of Jerusalem and the exile of the nation (cf. 3.22b–25 for a similar liturgical composition representing the community's response). In the redaction of the tradition they have been combined with the motif of the persecuted prophet, and so the laments are partly transformed into personal statements of the prophet's. This transformation of statements in the Jeremiah tradition due to the influence of presentational motives is common in the book of Jeremiah (note how the vision of the pot in 1.13 is developed in the redaction into a statement about Jeremiah's opposition from the community [vv. 17–19]). The motif of opposition to the prophet is a dominant one in the tradition and it keeps recurring. Yet the strong influence of cultic-liturgical language on the poems should warn against treating the laments as biographical statements about the prophet. Whether the overlapping motifs of national lament bewailing the exile and the prophet as persecuted figure and representative figure of the community come from different stages of the redaction or belong to different groups (different groups of deuteronomists or deuteronomists and non-deuteronomists?) cannot be determined with any certainty. All that may be

said with any certitude is that the redaction of the Jeremiah tradition
was an extremely complex affair.

> Woe is me, my mother, that you bore me, a man of strife and
> contention to the whole land! I have not lent, nor have I bor-
> rowed, yet all of them curse me. So let it be,[13] O Yahweh, if I
> have not entreated[14] thee for their good, if I have not pleaded
> with thee on behalf of the enemy in the time of trouble and in
> the time of distress! Can one break iron, iron from the north,
> and bronze?[15] (15.10–12)

The first section of the 15.10–21 confession is difficult and confirms
the general impression that few of the (so-called) confessions have
had a smooth history of transmission. Nor can the units be isolated
with any ease. Some commentators would exclude v. 12 (an echo of
1.18/6.28 or 17.1?), others treat vv. 10–21, others divide it into
vv. 10–12, 15–21, or vv. 10–18, 19–21 or even vv. 15–20. So little
agreement between commentators is a sure indication that there are
problems in the text as well as problems in the analysis. I am
inclined to take vv. 10f. as the piece for analysis and to see in v. 12
a further echo of the opposition motif taken from 6.27 (with the
north element coming from 1.14f.). Yet the element of punishment
and deportation in vv. 13f. could explain the north element in v. 12
(cf. 10.22). The use of similar phrases in vv. 13f. and 17.3f. indicates a complex pattern of editorial activity (very common in the
Jeremiah tradition) whereby phrases and even verses are employed
more than once. This means the elements do not have any single
context, so meaning cannot be determined by context. Such features
of the Jeremiah tradition demand a hermeneutical approach to Jeremiah which focuses primarily on the redactional aspects of the
text.[16] The final redaction of the text broke up sequences of thought
by reiterating other motifs for reasons beyond our comprehension,
but the fractured sequences have to be recognized as part of the
redactional technique employed. More force may be given to
vv. 10f. if vv. 15–18 are used as a counterpoint before interpreting
the pieces.

> O Yahweh, thou knowest;
>   remember me and visit me,
>   and take vengeance for me on my persecutors.
> In thy forbearance take me not away;
>   know that for thy sake I bear reproach.
> Thy words were found, and I ate them,[17]

and thy words became to me a joy
and the delight of my heart;
for I am called by thy name,
O Yahweh, God of hosts.
I did not sit in the company of merrymakers,
nor did I rejoice;
I sat alone, because thy hand was upon me,
for thou hadst filled me with indignation.
Why is my pain unceasing,
my wound incurable,
refusing to be healed?
Wilt thou be to me like a deceitful brook,
like waters that fail? (15.15–18)

This complaint is then followed by a piece which may be regarded as the divine response to the prophet's lament.

Therefore thus says Yahweh:
'If you return, I will restore you,
and you shall stand before me.
If you utter what is precious, and not what is worthless
you shall be as my mouth.
They shall turn to you,
but you shall not turn to them.
And I will make you to this people
a fortified wall of bronze;
they will fight against you,
but they shall not prevail over you,
for I am with you
to save you and deliver you,
says Yahweh.
I will deliver you out of the hand of the wicked,
and redeem you from the grasp of the ruthless.'[18]

(15.19–21)

The material in 15.10–21 is probably the most complicated and ambiguous of the lament sequences. Neither its division nor its interpretation can be set out with any confidence, so my analysis is aimed at drawing out some of the layers of meaning to be found in the sections. In the opening piece (vv. 10f.) the prophet laments his birth and his role as a contentious and litigious person (the Hebrew terms *rīb* and *mādōn* have strong forensic connotations) to the whole land. He is the object of the community's cursing in spite of having given no cause for this treatment. On the contrary, he has entreated the deity on their behalf against the enemy. Which enemy is this? The MT is unclear at this point.[19] The most likely interpretation is 'the enemy from the north', moving *miṣṣāfōn* 'from the north' from v. 12 to v. 11 for the purpose of clarifying both verses. The time of trouble and distress probably refers to the sweeping judgment of Yahweh (cf. 4.11). Triggered by this reference to divine judgment, the redaction has added a few lines (vv. 13f.) which are a variation on 17.3f.[20] The variations in the use of what is essentially the same piece of Hebrew may be significant. In 17.3f. the sin of Judah is punished by exile in an unknown land: the meaning of 17.1–4 is determined by the initial statement, 'The sin of Judah is written with a pen of iron' (v. 1). However, in 15.13f. there is not a similar determining interpretative indicator. This may account for the variation between 'I will make you serve your enemies in a land which you do not know' (*haʿᵃbadtikā ʾet-ʾōyᵉbekā bāʾāreṣ ᵃšer lōʾ-yādāʿtā*, 17.4) and 'I will drive away your enemies into a land you do not know' (*haʿᵃbartī ʾet-ʾōyᵉʾbekā bᵉereṣ lōʾ yādāʿtā*, 15.14).[21] Such a variation suggests that 15.13, 14 may have been added in an attempt to assure the exiled community that Yahweh would yet defeat its enemies.

The complaint begins with the figure of the contentious prophet pleading on his own behalf that he has interceded for the people in the time of trouble. The image of Jeremiah as the nation's intercessor is a common one in the Jeremiah tradition (15.11; 18.20; 37.3; 42. 2–4; cf. 27.18; implied by the prohibition in 7.16; 11.14; 14.11) and there are a number of liturgical passages which present the prophet as speaking the laments of the community (e.g., 3.22–25; 14.7–9, 19–22). The strong resemblances between the language of the complaints and the lament psalms in the Psalter increase the likelihood that the editors of the tradition were intent on presenting Jeremiah as an intercessor for the nation.[22] The motif of the intercessor, however, has to be balanced with the motif of the nation as the prophet's enemy. Running through the tradition is a complicated strand of tension between the prophet's proclamation of absolute judgment intended against the community by the deity and the motif of the intercessor, standing before the deity to speak good for the nation. The element of repentance also adds to the tension between these motifs. The opposition of the nation to the prophet, a dominant element in the confessions, complicates the notion of the prophet as the community's intercessor (cf. 37.3). The presentation of the prophet in the tradition oscillates between these various motifs without settling for a consistent view of the prophet. The repeated command, 'Do not pray for this people' (7.16; 11.14; 14.11) indicates the redactional element at work and is intended to denounce the Jerusalem community as beyond redemption. After the communal confession of sins with its appeal to the deity to save the nation (14.7–9, 19–22), the editors include a piece denying the possibility of effective intercession (15.1–4). If the prayers of Moses and Samuel cannot save the nation, then Jeremiah's will be no more successful. Hence the lament in 15.5 introducing a description of the terrible consequences of invasion and siege (15.6–9):

> Who will have pity on you, O Jerusalem,
>   or who will bemoan you?
> Who will turn aside
>   to ask about your welfare?

Then after this section comes the first element of the confession pericope (15.10–21), and once more we have the prophet presented as an intercessor entreating Yahweh on the people's behalf. This redactional arrangement suggests that the answer to the question asked in 15.5 (assuming it is not a rhetorical question) is Jeremiah. So did Jeremiah go on interceding before Yahweh in spite of the interdict on such intercession? To ask the question of the historical Jeremiah is to fail to see that the issue arises from the redactional handling of the tradition. It is the deuteronomists who operate with a paradigm of the prophet as intercessor (cf. I Sam. 12.23), so it is they who have constructed the images of the prophet Jeremiah as the nation's intercessor. At the same time they have to present not only a picture of Jeremiah as the man standing between Yahweh and the nation, but also a picture of a community beyond prayer. The intercessor motif successfully achieves this because the negative aspect of the divine prohibition of intercession is stressed in three occurrences. Each occurrence is placed after a statement about the community's wickedness (7.1–15; 11.1–13; 14.10) and introduces a further statement about its offences (cultic in 7.17–20; 11.15–17; 14.12(?); false prophecy in 14.13–16). Here is an excellent example of the redactional control of the material in the Jeremiah tradition.

The intercessor motif is combined in the confessions with the motif of the community's opposition to the prophet. Again the interpretation of the confessions shows how the redactional approach wished to present Jeremiah as the victim of persecution in order to develop the theme of the history of prophecy in its public reception as the history of prophecy rejected and the prophet persecuted.

Each complaint has at its heart the sufferings of the prophet at the hands of the community. In this way further justification for the destruction of the community is provided, in that its fate is linked to its attitude to the prophetic word. In 15.15–18 the motif of the enemy in vv. 11, 14 is transformed from the enemies of Israel to the enemies of Jeremiah. The prophet prays for vengeance to be taken on those who persecute him. The elements of request, complaint and reproach in vv. 15, 17, 18 all have parallels in the Psalms. The appeal to Yahweh to remember the suppliant and to recognize that the worshipper bears reproach for Yahweh's sake is a common appeal in the lament psalms (cf. Pss. 6.1f. [Heb. vv. 2f.]; 44.23–26 [Heb. vv. 24–27]; 59.1.f. [Heb. vv. 2f.]; 69.7 [Heb. v. 8]; 89.50f. [Heb. vv. 51f.]). The complaint about sitting alone in great anguish because the hand of Yahweh is against the petitioner can be found in the Psalms (cf. Pss. 55.12–14 [Heb. vv. 13–15], where the cause of the trouble is the psalmist's friend; 88.8, 13—18 [Heb. vv. 9,14–19]) and the book of Job (cf. Job 19.13–22; 30.9f.). The reproach about the incurable nature of the wound in v. 18 is directed at the deity and evokes the question 'Wilt thou be to me like a deceitful brook, like waters that fail?' This identification of the deity as the cause of the trouble, with an underlying sense of grievance against and censure of the deity, also appears in the lament psalms (cf. Pss. 44.9–14 [Heb. vv. 10–15]; 89.38–45 [Heb. vv. 39–46]; cf. Job 10.18). The cause of the prophet's troubles is depicted in motifs drawn from the language of the worshipping community in the cult, and it makes the interpretation of the passage much more difficult, because conventional language tends to destroy precision of reference in favour of making formal connections between different sets of circumstances. Just as the interpretation of the Psalms involves a good deal of ambiguous material, which yields very little in the way of concrete meaning and relation to specific events and periods in time, so the interpretation of the confessions of Jeremiah is equally imprecise and difficult to relate to specific occasions in the life of the prophet.[23] The construction of the confessions out of language and motifs at home in the temple cult is indicative of the redactional origins of the material, and renders them less open to being construed as events in the life of Jeremiah.

The finding and eating of the words motif in v. 16 may be a reference to the reception of the prophetic word (cf. the notion of finding the prophetic vision from Yahweh in Lam. 2.9). In the Ezekiel tradition, part of the prophet's commission account includes the motif of Ezekiel eating a scroll covered with words of lamentation and woe (Ezek. 2.8–3.3). The joy and delight of Jeremiah's eating may be comparable to Ezekiel's scroll tasting as sweet as honey. On the other hand, the word of Yahweh need not be limited to meaning the prophetic word. In the Psalms Yahweh's word refers to his commands or precepts (cf. Pss. 17.4; 33.4; 56.4, 10 [Heb. vv. 5, 11]; 105.8; 107.20; 130.5; 147.15, 18f.) and Ps. 119 demonstrates the importance of the divine word in the worship and meditation of the community. As the vocabulary of the passage is fairly stereotyped, too precise a meaning for the motif cannot be sustained (for 'joy and delight' in v. 16 cf. Jer. 7.34; 16.9; 25.10; 31.7, 13; 33.9, 11; Ps. 51.8 [Heb. v. 10]).

The phrase 'for I am called by thy name' (*kī-niqrā' šimkā 'ālay*, v. 16b) is formulaic, though not usually used with reference to an individual.[24] The sense of ownership conveyed by the phrase is clear (cf. II Sam. 12.28; Isa. 4.1), but the theological notion of something belonging to God is not used of individuals except in this case. As a theological formula it is used of the people of Israel (Deut. 28.10; Jer. 14.9; Isa. 63.19; II Chron. 7.14; cf. Amos 9.12), the ark (II Sam. 6.2 = I Chron. 13.6), the temple in Jerusalem (I Kings 8.43 = II Chron. 6.33; Jer. 7.10f., 14, 30; 32.34; 34.15), and the city of Jerusalem (Jer. 25.29; Dan. 9.18). It is used in Isa. 43.7 with reference to the exiles who belong to Israel. Now a formal element such as this which normally refers to a place, object or collective suggests a formal significance in v. 16b. Either it reflects the late exilic usage to indicate a member of the chosen nation, and therefore confirms the formal piety of the confession, or it indicates a theological move by the redactors to see in Jeremiah (as they present him) the representative figure of the community. Jeremiah speaks as Israel, the people and possession of Yahweh.[25]

The image of the prophet sitting alone, nursing his misery and full of indignation (v. 16), has contributed a good deal to the popular image of Jeremiah as a solitary figure in opposition to everybody. In this way he becomes the model for the prophet as trenchant critic of his society and his times. As a popular image it can be maintained on the strength of a number of such verses, but it is derived from a rather literal reading of the whole tradition. It is part of the redactional presentation of the prophet, designed to contrast the singular figure of Jeremiah with the corrupt Jerusalem community which justly deserved the destructive wrath of Yahweh. It is certainly an image the redactors wished to convey (how well they succeeded!), but it needs to be balanced with other images presented of the prophet in the tradition. Images of the prophet in discussion

with the king (e.g. Jer. 38) or supported by the princes, elders and
people (e.g. Jer. 26) or protected by court officials (e.g. Jer. 26.24;
38.7–13) give a different account of the prophet. It may be the case
that the historical Jeremiah was an awkward and disruptive figure
in the community (we cannot be sure to what extent the redaction
reflects a real or imaginary Jeremiah), a figure regularly protected
by his friends, supporters and sympathizers, but such protection
must be assimilated into our reading of the tradition. Even this
protected figure is part of the redactional projection of the prophet.
It produces an image of Jeremiah similar to the picture of Pyrrho,
the Greek sceptical philosopher, drawn by Diogenes Laertius, which
depicts him as 'going out of his way for nothing, taking no precau-
tion, but facing all risks as they came, whether carts, precipices,
dogs or what not . . . but he was kept out of harm's way by his
friends who . . . used to follow close after him.'[26] The lonely,
isolated figure, suffering greatly because of the community's rejection and the heaviness of Yahweh's hand upon him, is too stereotyped a biblical picture (e.g., in the Psalms and in Job) to allow us
to assert confidently the historicity of the portrayal of Jeremiah in
the confessions. He is more likely to be a construction of the redactors drawn from liturgical sources in order to produce a figure
representative of prophet and community.

The complaint 'Why is my pain unceasing, my wound incurable,
refusing to be healed?' (v. 18a) uses a motif common in the Jeremiah
tradition.[27] The description of the wound as being incurable
(*'ᵃnūšāh*) and the pain permanent (*neṣaḥ*) includes the motif of
incurableness (*'ānūš*). Apart from its use to describe Job's condition (Job 34.6) and its occurrence in this complaint, *'ānūš* is
normally used in a more general and metaphorical way. In Jer. 17.9
it refers to the incurable deceitfulness of the human mind.[28] Its
sense in the phrase 'day of disaster' (*yōm 'ānūš* 17.16) is similar
to that depicted in Isa. 17.11, 'yet harvest will flee away in a day of
grief and incurable pain (*kᵉ'ēb 'ānūš*)'. In Jer. 30.12, 15 the term
is used to describe the community's brokenness:

> Your hurt is incurable (*'ānūš lᵉšibrēk*)
>   and your wound is grievous.
> There is none to uphold your cause,
>   no medicine for your wound,
>   no healing for you.
> Why do you cry out over your hurt?
>   Your pain is incurable (*'ānūš mak'ōbēk*). (30.12f., 15)

This representation of the community bemoaning its incurable state (cf. Micah 1.9 for a similar use of *'ānūš* to describe the corruption of the community) suggests that the role of Jeremiah in 15.18a might be as a representative of the community. The community's wound is incurable, so the prophet's wound is incurable. Standing for the community, the prophet assumes the role of the people.[29] In the earlier oracles the motif of the wounded community is an important element in the depiction of the prophet's great grief (e.g. 8.18–9.1 [Heb. vv. 18–23]).[30] The prophet is represented as the community grief-stricken at the sudden catastrophic destruction of the land (e.g. 4.19f.; 10.19f.; cf. the image of the community as Rachel weeping for her lost children, 31.15). The accusation that the priests and prophets failed to treat the wounded community adequately (cf. 6.14 = 8.11) is also part of this metaphor cluster. Illness or wounding as metaphors for the state of the community, whether of corruption or disintegration, are quite common in the prophetic traditions (apart from the Jeremiah tradition cf. Hos.5.13; Isa. 1.5f.; 53.5; Micah 1.9) and function as descriptions or evaluations of the life of the nation.[31]

The final element in vv. 15–18 introduces an ironic touch to the confession: 'Wilt thou be to me like a deceitful brook, like waters that fail?' (v. 18b). The image here is of a wadi which runs dry in the summer heat and so cannot be relied upon for water. In an early oracle the deity had been described as a source of living waters and the community had been castigated for its rejection of such a fountain in order to find water in broken cisterns (2.13). Now the prophet accuses the deity of being an unreliable source of water, like a failed wadi. The force of this accusation may be that, as in the lament psalms, the community regarded its misfortunes at the hands of the Babylonians to have resulted from the failure of divine protection (cf. Lam. 2). The element of divine deception can be found in the Jeremiah tradition (cf. 4.10; 20.7), so the confession of such a possibility here may be part of that strand in the redaction. The incurable wound of the community (prophet as community?) is to be accounted for in terms of the unreliability of the deity. This enigmatic element in the confession should not be overemphasized, but it is of a piece with the lament psalms.

The final section of the lament (vv. 19–21) represents the deity's response to the prophet's complaint. The emphasis here is on the prophet as victim of the community's opposition, and uses the image of the prophet as a bronze wall (cf. 1.18; contrast 6.28). Responding to the accusation that the deity may have become like a deceitful

stream, the prophet is accused of having gone astray and is counselled to return to Yahweh. There is a skilful word-play on *šūb* in
v. 19b, d:

> If you return (*tāšūb*), I will restore you (*waʾašībᵉkā*) . . .
> They shall turn (*yāšubū*) to you,
>   but you shall not turn (*lōʾ-tāšūb*) to them.

There is the turning of the prophet followed by divine restoration,
then the turning of the people to the prophet but unmatched by the
prophet's turning to them: a series of reciprocated and unrecipro-
cated turnings. The turning of the people to the prophet is probably
to be understood in the light of v. 20 (cf. 1.19) as the opposition of
the community focused on the prophet. In such a context his not
turning to them must mean his not yielding to or being influenced
by them. The image of the prophet as a bronze wall besieged by the
people but not prevailed over by them reintroduces the motif of the
divine presence (cf. 1.8, 19) and deliverance. The similarity between
1.19 and 15.20 (v. 20 has the additional 'to save you') is such that
they should be considered the same verse (with the inevitable slight
variations characteristic of biblical stylistics) used redactionally in
different contexts, but making the same point. The additional verse
in 15.21 makes more or less the same point as v. 20, but it may
have a more general application to the nation. That is, the addition
applies the promise of divine protection of the prophet to the nation
in exile against its oppressors (for *ʿārişīm*, 'the ruthless', as a term
applied to the Babylonians cf. Isa. 13.11; 25.3; Ezek. 28.7; 30.11;
31.12; for the more general sense of the enemies of the pious sup-
pliants cf. Ps. 54.3 [Heb. v. 5]; Job 6.23). The oscillation in the
confessions between the redactional presentation of the prophet as
the victim of the community's oppression and the prophet as the
personification of the oppressed community (in exile?) appealing to
Yahweh for deliverance is sustained in this particular confession.
The call to return to Yahweh is applied by the Skinnerian approach
to some occasion in the life of Jeremiah when he lost heart.[32] It is,
perhaps, better applied, in the light of 3.1–4.2, to the prophet *as*
community – standing for the community, the prophet is invited to
return to Yahweh, so hope is held out to the exiled community.[33]
The deuteronomistic redaction of the Jeremiah tradition seldom
misses an opportunity to insist on the constant possibility of repentance for the community. This confession, spread over 15.10–

21, should be interpreted in the light of that principle.

The next confession is to be found in 17.12–18, though commentators vary in making it begin at v. 12 or v. 14, and some wish to include vv. 9f. in the confession.[34] By starting with vv. 12f. the cultic nature of the confession is brought out more clearly:

> A glorious throne set on high from the beginning
> > is the place of our sanctuary.
> O Yahweh, the hope of Israel,
> > those who turn away from thee[35] shall be written in the earth,
> > for they have forsaken Yahweh, the fountain of living waters.
> Heal me, O Yahweh, and I shall be healed;
> > save me, and I shall be saved;
> > for thou art my praise.
> Behold, they say to me,
> > 'Where is the word of Yahweh?
> > Let it come!'
> I have not pressed thee to send evil,[36]
> > nor have I desired the day of disaster,
> > thou knowest;
> that which came out of my lips
> > was before thy face.
> Be not a terror to me;
> > thou art my refuge in the day of evil.
> Let those be put to shame who persecute me,
> > but let me not be put to shame;
> let them be dismayed,
> > but let me not be dismayed;
> bring upon them the day of evil;
> > destroy them with double destruction! (17.12–18)

Problems of section division, translation and interpretation, so characteristic of the confessions, also abound in this particular confession. The central theme, however, appears to be a meditation on the day of evil and the possibility of escaping it.

The liturgical fragment in vv. 12f. (for Yahweh as the hope of Israel in v. 13 see also the liturgical use of the phrase in 14.8; cf. 50.7) predisposes the interpretation of the confession to be in terms of a prayer for the deliverance of the community.[37] As the redactional presentation is a fundamental element in determining the meaning of the text, the shaping of the pericope must be taken seriously as a guide in the difficult task of elucidating these enigmatic poems. The prayer for healing in v. 14 echoes a common motif in the Psalms (e.g., Pss. 6.2 [Heb. v. 3]; 41.4 [Heb. v. 5]; 60.2 [Heb. v. 4]; cf. 30.2 [Heb. v. 3]; 107.20) and one also to be found in the Jeremiah tradition (e.g., 3.22; cf. 30.17; 33.6). Such occurrences of the healing motif in Jeremiah are either liturgical or consolatory, and are addressed to the community rather than the individual. So the use of the motif in 17.14 should be understood as a prayer for the community's healing. Again, the prophet is presented as the community engaged in prayer for restoration. The community's request for the divine word is addressed to the prophet, and his response is to dissociate himself from the day of disaster. The meaning of the question 'Where is the word of Yahweh? Let it come!' is ambiguous. Taken as an example of communal scepticism about the prophet's preaching, it indicates the delay in the fulfilment of the prophetic word.[38] However, the redactional shaping of the passage has made the quest for salvation the contextual meaning of the confession (e.g. vv. 12, 14), so the question should be treated in relation to the community's expectation of salvation. Such an expectation of deliverance may be pre-exilic in origin, but probably should be seen here as the prayer of the exiled community awaiting divine restoration (cf. 30.17; 33.6). The question then is about the existence of a prophetic word (*dābār*) of salvation addressed to the community and declaring its imminent deliverance from the exilic day of evil. The divine word is the word of deliverance from suffering and from the enemy (cf. Pss. 56.8–11 [Heb. vv. 9–12]; 107.20; 130.5). Impatience with the prolongation of the exile gives rise to the question, and it is addressed to the prophet because the word of hope (i.e., oracle of deliverance) comes from the prophet in the cultic community. The prophetic dissociation from wanting the day of disaster to befall the community confirms this understanding of v. 15, and is part of the redactional presentation of the prophet's identification with the community. Accused, perhaps, of being party to the destruction of the nation (cf. 38.4), he here makes the necessary protestation of innocence required for acquittal from such a charge. The prayer in v. 17a, 'Be not a terror to me', identifies the deity as the source of the trouble and is in keeping with the sentiments already expressed in 14.8f.; 15.18b. If there is evil in the community, it is Yahweh who is behind it (cf. Job 2.10; Amos 3.6). The contrast between 'I' (*ᵃnî*) and 'them' (*hēmmāh*) in v. 18 is probably between the exiled community and the foreign nations. This interpretation is supported by the generality of references to the enemy or the evildoer in the Psalms[39] and the attitude taken to the nations in the Jeremiah tradition (e.g. 10.25; 25.15–38; 46–51). It could also include those elements in the community (the exilic inhabitants of Jerusalem as opponents of the exiles?) considered to be hostile to the prophet.

Throughout my interpretation of the confessions there is a double sense of reference and application to the prophet and the community. This interpenetration of the individual and the collective is very characteristic of the way the Psalms work, and illustrates the common bond between the reflection upon and expression of experience in the Psalms and in the Jeremiah tradition.[40] Elements of the prophet as object of opposition, as intercessor for the community and as preacher of the word of deliverance are combined with elements of the community's expressions of despair about the destructiveness of the exile and its communal laments seeking divine restoration. These combined elements are best seen in 17.12–18. The interweaving of so many elements using so much of the traditional lament language makes it very difficult to interpret precisely what the confessions are about, and compels the interpreter to allow for a wide range of possible meanings in every individual confession. The overall impression of the confessions illuminates the condition of the community in exile, and shows how the construction of the Jeremiah tradition utilized many elements from the life of the community in its presentation of the life of a prophet.

In 18.18–23 the conflict between prophet and community is at its strongest, and the introductory statement in v. 18 makes it clear that the whole leadership of the community is against him. The rejection of the prophetic word could not be stated more explicitly, so v. 18 should be seen as contributing to the motifs of theodicy and the rejection of the community. Close parallels between the confession and the Psalms also underline the liturgical nature of the poem.

> Then they said, 'Come, let us make plots against Jeremiah, for the law shall not perish from the priest, nor counsel from the wise, nor the word from the prophet. Come, let us smite him with the tongue, and let us not heed any of his words.'[41]
>
> > Give heed to me, O Yahweh,
> > > and hearken to my plea.[42]
> > Is evil a recompense for good?
> > > Yet they have dug a pit for my life.[43]

Remember how I stood before thee
  to speak good for them,
  to turn away thy wrath from them.
Therefore deliver up their children to famine;
  give them over to the power of the sword,
let their wives become childless and widowed.
  May their men meet death by pestilence,
  their youths be slain by the sword in battle.
May a cry be heard from their houses,
  when thou bringest the marauder suddenly upon them!
For they have dug a pit to take me,
  and laid snares for my feet.
Yet, thou, O Yahweh, knowest
  all their plotting to slay me.
Forgive not their iniquity,
  nor blot out their sin from thy sight.
Let them be overthrown before thee;
  deal with them in the time of thine anger. (18.18–23)

The complaint of this confession is typical of the conflict between
the righteous and the godless in the lament psalms (cf. Pss. 10; 21;
35; 36.4 [Heb. v. 5]; 41; 56; 140). One feature of some of these
psalms (e.g. Pss. 35.11–16; 109.1–5) is the suppliant's claim to be
receiving evil for good done to the enemy. At two points in the
confessions Jeremiah is represented as standing before Yahweh to
speak good for the community (15.11; 18.20). It is a stereotypical
factor in the lament that the doer of good should be the victim of
evil (the same factor plays a large part in the story of Job). So the
presentation of the prophet as the innocent victim of vicious con-
spiracies by men on whose behalf he has spoken good to the deity
is too formal a convention to throw any light on the life of the
historical Jeremiah. It is more informative about the ways in which
the Jeremiah tradition was constructed and sheds some light on
what the redactors were trying to do in that presentation. The
relation of the confession to the life of Jeremiah is provided by the
redactors in v. 18 where they show the prophet to be the target of
the animosity of the three major social institutions – priests,
prophets, wise men. The whole leadership of the corrupt society is
ranged against the righteous prophet.

The final set of confessions appears in 20.7–18 with the usual
problems of section division, translation and interpretation.[44] The
occurrence of a brief hymn of praise to Yahweh for delivering the

needy from evildoers (v. 13) indicates the liturgical redaction of the section (cf. Pss. 6.9 [Heb. v. 10]; 22.24 [Heb. v. 25]). In order to facilitate my treatment of the confession I will divide it into three sections.

> O Yahweh, thou hast deceived me,
>   and I was deceived;
> thou art stronger than I,
>   and thou hast prevailed.
> I have become a laughingstock all the day;
>   every one mocks me.
> For whenever I speak, I cry out,[45]
>   I shout, 'Violence and destruction!'
> For the word of Yahweh has become for me
>   a reproach and derision all day long.
> If I say, 'I will not mention him,
>   or speak any more in his name,'
> there is in my heart as it were a burning fire
>   shut up in my bones,
> and I am weary with holding it in,
>   and I cannot. (20.7-9)

The motif of divine deception (cf. 15.18b) opens the confession and reveals a lament of bitter impotence in which the suppliant complains about the divine machismo. The word used here for deceiving is *pittitani*, from the stem *pth*, meaning 'to be simple' and, in the form used in 20.7, 'to be deceived, enticed, seduced'. It can have the legal sense of seducing a virgin (Ex. 22.16 [Heb. v. 15]) or the ordinary sense of a woman enticing a man to do something through the use of her sexuality (cf. Judg. 14.15; 16.5; for a metaphorical sense of a husband enticing his wife cf. Hos. 2.14 [Heb. v. 16]). One of the major uses of *pth* is for the divine deception of prophets (cf. I Kings 22.20, 21, 22 = II Chron. 18.19, 20, 21; Ezek. 14.9). So there are two main lines of interpretation available for Jer. 20.7. It is a reference to the divine seduction of the prophet or it refers to the prophet's sense of being a false prophet, deceived by the deity. In the first view, the association of the seduction motif with terms indicative of the superior strength of the deity ('you are stronger than I and you prevailed') suggests that the metaphor is one of rape rather than seduction.[46] The psychoanalytical approach to biblical interpretation (insofar as there is such a thing) would see in the strong bawdiness of Jeremiah's language (cf. 2.20-25; 3.1-3, 23; 5.7-8), his hostility towards those participating in the sex cults of Canaanite religion, and his own state of celibacy (16.1–4) clear pointers to a sense in 20.7 of divine rape (an internalization of the prophet's hostility towards his own sexuality). Psychoanalysis might be right in so reading the Jeremiah tradition, but sufficient prima facie evidence is not available to sustain such an interpretation. The sense of outrage at being raped with a concomitant sense of being humiliated in public may be retained as the meaning of the verse without accepting the infrastructure of the psychoanalytical position. Whether the text should then be interpreted of the prophet or the community (or both) is harder to determine. The second possibility is to see in the accusation of rape a reference to the divine deception of prophets. The prophet is conscious of being deceived in his proclamation of 'violence and destruction' because nobody is paying him any attention. The terms used (*ḥāmās wāšōd*) can refer to the violence of invasion by national enemies (Jer. 51.35; Ps. 74.20; cf. Ps. 18.48 [Heb. v. 49]) as well as the violence of oppression and injustice within the community (cf. Jer. 6.7; Ezek. 7.11; 8.17; 12.19). So the preaching could be directed against the injustices of the community, warning it about impending invasion for such viciousness, or it could reflect the later view (cf. Jer. 15.11–14; 25.15–38) that the enemy nations would soon be destroyed by Yahweh. Either interpretation fits the context, which refers to the general rejection of such prophetic announcements (cf. 18.15). Both expectations were delayed sufficiently to produce a sense of failure and bitter disappointment within the community.

The image depicted in vv. 8f. is of a prophet who, when he speaks, is mocked and when he keeps silent burns up inside himself. He can neither speak nor can he be silent. Is this an image of the community in exile or is it part of the redactional presentation of the struggles of the prophet? If the latter, what bearing does the divine deception have on the prophet's experience? Is it part of the dispute between prophet and deity already delineated in 1.4–10? The silence enforced by terrible suffering (cf. Job 2.13) may be a representation of the community reduced by the exile to silence about the deity (cf. Ps. 6.5 [Heb. v. 6]; 137.4). However, the two levels of meaning in the confessions, that of community in exile and presentation of a prophet, are very difficult to separate from one another, so these questions must remain unanswered.

> For I hear many whispering,
>   Terror is on every side![47]
> 'Denounce him! Let us denounce him!'

> say all my familiar friends,
>> watching for my fall.
> 'Perhaps he will be deceived,
>> then we can overcome him,
>> and take our revenge on him.'
> But Yahweh is with me as a dread warrior;
>> therefore my persecutors will stumble,
>> they will not overcome me.
> They will be greatly shamed,
>> for they will not succeed.
> Their eternal dishonour
>> will never be forgotten.
> O Yahweh of hosts, who triest the righteous,
>> who seest the heart and the mind,
> let me see thy vengeance upon them,
>> for to thee have I committed my cause.[48]
> Sing to Yahweh;
>> praise Yahweh!
> For he has delivered the life of the needy
>> from the hand of the evildoers. (20.10–13)

If the first part of the confession focuses on the divine source of the prophet's trouble, the second part concentrates on the human sources of his difficulties. The two pieces constitute a parallel account of the same matter. Both begin with the motif of the prophet's deception, but each has a very different account of that deception. The phrase 'terror is on every side' (*māgōr missābîb*) is used in a number of different ways in the Jeremiah tradition. It refers to the dangers of leaving the city to go about the roads during the invasion (6.25). In a similar way it refers to the defeat of the Egyptians by the Babylonians (46.5) and the destruction of Kedar and the kingdoms of Hazor (49.29). It is also the name given by Jeremiah to Pashhur the priest after he released Jeremiah from the stocks (20.3). In Ps. 31.11–13 (Heb. vv. 12–14) it occurs in a context very similar to the Jeremiah confession:

> I am the scorn of all my adversaries,
>> a horror to my neighbours,
> an object of dread to my acquaintances;
>> those who see me in the street flee from me.
> I have passed out of mind like one who is dead;
>> I have become like a broken vessel.
> Yea, I hear the whispering of many –

> terror on every side! —[49]
> as they scheme together against me,
>   as they plot to take my life.

Clearly it is an important redactional phrase used to construct a number of elements in the tradition. Its appearance in the lament psalm indicates the liturgical nature of the conspiracy complaint. The motif of the conspiracy is too common in the Psalms to need documentation here, but its occurrence in the Jeremiah tradition is part of the confessions material (e.g. 11.21–23; 12.6). The image of the prophet wounded in the back by his friends is to be found in the latest strand of the prophetic traditions (Zech. 13.6).[50]

As in the Psalms, the resolution of the complainant's problem is the presence of Yahweh. This motif has already been noted in the call material in the Jeremiah tradition (Jer. 1.8, 19) and in the confessions (15.20). Yahweh as a terrifying warrior defends the suppliant and his opponents are crushed. The element of 'eternal dishonour' (v. 11) is equivalent to the 'double destruction' of 17.18. Because v. 12 is virtually the same as 11.20 (the variation is not semantically significant) we should see in the occurrence of the verse in two confessions the activity of the redactors building up the tradition of liturgical confessions as part of their presentation of Jeremiah. The hymnic piece in v. 13 is a common feature of lament psalms whereby the worshipper (or worshipping community) thanks the deity for deliverance from the enemy (cf. Ps. 6.9 [Heb. v. 10[4]]; 22.24 [Heb. v. 25]).

Given the number of formal similarities between the confessions and the Psalms, it is very difficult to limit the interpretation of the confessions to plotting the life of Jeremiah or even to isolating an opposition to the prophet motif. Such limitations fail to explore the intentional connections between the life of the cultic community as expressed in the Psalms and the life of the exilic community as put forward in these confessions.

The final piece in the confession abruptly changes the mood of triumph expressed in vv. 11–13 and reverts to the gloomy pessimism of vv. 7–10 and some of the other confessions. In some ways it makes an inclusio with the equally gloomy elements of the call narrative and accompanying extended visions (cf. 1.4–12, 13–19).[51]

> Cursed be the day
>   on which I was born!
> The day when my mother bore me,
>   let it not be blessed!

> Cursed be the man
>   who brought the news to my father,
> 'A son is born to you,'
>   making him very glad.
> Let that man[52] be like the cities
>   which Yahweh overthrew without pity;
> let him hear a cry in the morning
>   and an alarm at noon,
> because he did not kill me in the womb;
>   so my mother would have been my grave,
>   and her womb for ever great.
> Why did I come forth from the womb
>   to see toil and sorrow,
>   and spend my days in shame? (20.14–18)

The bitterness of this self-cursing is only matched (in fact it is bettered) by the longer, more intensely expressed lament of Job, spoken on breaking his seven days' silence (Job 3).[53] Although both poems curse the day of birth and wish for non-existence, the linguistic differences between the poems show that they are not directly related to each other. They clearly belong to a circle where such laments were given expression.[54] It is hardly surprising that the Jeremiah and Job traditions should share such a concern with the lament form (also with the Psalms), because both traditions focus on major tragedies and were developed (most likely) during the exilic period when the Judaean community suffered such extreme losses.[55] The poem of Job was constructed to deal with the most extreme exigencies a man could face, and the formation of the Jeremiah tradition incorporated the terrible exigencies faced by the community into its presentation of the prophet.

Lament psalms, the speeches of Job and the confessions of Jeremiah are all concerned with suffering in human life. That suffering could concern the individual or the community. In spite of appearances the real problem of such suffering was the fact that it came from Yahweh. All the laments identify this as the source of the destruction. At times the community can hide behind its own sins as the cause of the trouble, but the poem of Job, the occasional lament (e.g. Ps. 44) and the confessions of Jeremiah recognize that the murdered child and raped virgin point to a deeper horror than the consequences of self-determining actions (cf. Lam. 5). In fusing the life of Jeremiah with the communal lament, the traditionists expressed the darkness at the heart of the exile and contributed towards a resolution of that horror. The vengeance motif in the confessions is conventional, but is used to express the conflict between prophet and community in terms of the divine vindication of the innocent against the false accusations and persecution of the godless. It also may reflect the exilic community's attitude to the national enemies responsible for the destruction of city and community. It is more difficult to determine whether it includes an element of conflict between the Jerusalem community and the exiles, but such a function of the confessions would be in keeping with the ideology of some of the redactors. The combination of elements from the individual and communal laments in the construction of an image of the prophet Jeremiah allows for a complex interpretation of the confessions reflecting the various levels of meaning and function. No interpretation of the confessions can dogmatically insist on only one strand of meaning being taken from the material, but the liturgical nature of the poems should warn against using the poems too precipitately to reconstruct a biographical account of the life of Jeremiah. Too many factors and features are at work in the poems to facilitate such an approach, and the only adequate interpretative method is to develop a multiplex hermeneutic of the confessions. Such a hermeneutic will focus on the complex factors involved in the social, political, theological and apologetic movements of the exilic period and will attempt to relate the material in the confessions to such a polyvalent background. In developing the thesis of this book about the uses of prophecy in the Jeremiah tradition, the interpretation of the confessions makes an important contribution to the general argument.

The prophet as actor

Numerous accounts are given in the Jeremiah tradition of the prophet performing actions which constitute an important aspect of his work. These accounts include symbolic and dramatic actions, acted parables and extended metaphors, and are intended to convey some of his teaching. The representation of a prophet performing such actions is a common feature of the prophetic accounts in the deuteronomistic history (e.g., the Samuel and Elijah-Elisha sagas) and also is to be found in the Isaiah and Ezekiel prophetic traditions.[56] It is necessary, therefore, to consider briefly the extensive range of such accounts in the Jeremiah tradition in order to see how the image of the prophet is developed by such means.

Jer. 13.1–11. Jeremiah is commanded to buy a linen waistcloth and to wear it without washing it. Then he is commanded to hide it in a cleft of the rocks at the Euphrates. After a period of time he is again commanded to go to the Euphrates and dig up the waistcloth. By this time the garment is ruined and useless. The interpretation of the action (vv. 8–11) shows the waistcloth to have represented Judah-Jerusalem and the spoiling of the garment to be Yahweh's ruining (*šḥt*) of the community. The rest of the interpretation (vv. 10f.) is a deuteronomistic comment on the idolatry of the nation.[57]

As with so many biblical parables and symbolic actions (e.g., the parables of Jesus), it is difficult to match the interpretation and the parable or symbolic action of the waistcloth. The action itself seems to imply that the nation will be ruined by exile to Babylon, but this is not the interpretation offered in vv. 10f. There the focus is on the figure of the ruined waistcloth: its ruination is not caused by exile in Babylon but by idolatry within the community. The interpretation is therefore an example of the redactional concern with the false cults of the doomed city, and so belongs to the motif of the fall from grace seen in 2.4–13, 21. The original sense of the action may have stressed the inevitability of exile to Babylon.

The account in vv. 1–7 is not without difficulties itself. What is meant by the prophet going to the Euphrates? The distance between Jerusalem and the Euphrates is around 400 miles, and to undertake the round trip twice would have taken Jeremiah a good deal of time; Ezra, in the company of a number of officials, took four months to do the journey from Babylonia to Jerusalem (Ezra 7.7–9). Furthermore, unless Jeremiah took witnesses with him, his journey would have been wasted on the community. Some scholars have tried to lessen the problem of distance by treating the word *pᵉrāt*, normally used in the Hebrew Bible to indicate the Euphrates, as a reference to Parah (modern Khirbet el-Farah), a town in the neighbourhood of Anathoth.[58] However, this suggestion depends upon treating the account as a description of a literal journey made by the prophet. It would be better to see the story as a parable (acted or spoken) or the report of a vision.[59] If taken as an acted parable it might have involved the prophet in a set of dramatic actions involving the community as audience or spectators and marking out on the ground areas representing the Euphrates, with himself obtaining and wearing the waistcloth. Details of such a performance are not given in the text, so this interpretation of the prophet as actor must remain reasonable but speculative. The deuteronomistic understanding of

the prophet's action/parable may give grounds for the interpretation
of vv. 1–7 as the spoiling of Judah by its political and religious
alliances with Mesopotamia (so Hyatt; cf. Jer. 2.18), but the simplest view of the matter is to see in the ruination of the garment by
the Euphrates the ruin of Judah through exile there.[60]

Jer. 16.1–4. In this brief piece, heavily developed by deuteronomistic editing,[61] Jeremiah is commanded not to take a wife because
it is not a time or a situation into which children may safely be
brought. So the prophet's celibate life carries the message of his
preaching destruction against the community (cf. his sitting alone
in 15.17). The prophetic traditions carry a number of examples of
the prophets' marital status as part of their work (the medium is
the message): Hosea's unhappy marriage to a whore, Isaiah's pro-
genitive involvement with a prophetess (Isa. 8.1–4; as well as
accounts including reference to his children, e.g., Isa. 7.3), Ezekiel's lack of reaction to the death of his wife (Ezek. 24.15–27). All
these accounts function as ways of stating and reinforcing the
preaching of the prophets. Presumably the editors understood Jeremiah as explaining the significance of his celibate status to the
community, though in 16.1–4 it is more a part of their construction
of the prophet's image than an integral part of Jeremiah's life. The
symbolic nature of the prophet's activities is continued in vv. 5–7,
8f., where the prophet's abstention from entering the house of
mourning or the house of feasting also convey similar messages of
impending communal doom.[62]

Jer. 19.1–2a,10–11a. The visit to the potter's house, which produced the extended metaphor of Yahweh as potter and Israel as clay
(18.1–11), has a redactional echo in the symbolic action associated
with the purchase of a potter's earthen flask (presumably the editors
linked the sections because the purchase may have involved a visit
to the potter). A good deal of redactional activity has expanded, and
obscured, the symbolic action by interpolating a deuteronomistic
sermon against Jerusalem (or Topheth) into the material.[63] The
prophet is commanded to buy a flask (*baqbuq*: a water decanter), to
take with him some elders and senior priests and to go out to the
valley of Ben-hinnom. There he is to break the flask in the presence
of the elders and priests and to announce to them the divine word
of judgment: 'Thus says Yahweh of hosts: So will I break this
people and this city, as one breaks a potter's vessel, so that it cannot
be mended' (v. 11a). In this example action and interpretation are

fairly clear, but the redaction has broken up the account of the act and used it as an occasion for developing its own polemic against the Topheth cult (cf. 7.30–34). However the nature of the prophet's symbolic act is to be interpreted (either as a gesture symbolizing Yahweh's destruction of the city or an act effecting the city's devastation[64]), the incident is a good example of the motif of the prophet as actor.

Jer. 25.15–29. The concluding section of chs. 1–25 contains a strange account of the divine command to Jeremiah: 'Take from my hand this cup of the wine of wrath, and make all the nations to whom I send you drink it' (v. 15). Jeremiah obeys the command: 'So I took the cup from Yahweh's hand, and made all the nations to whom Yahweh sent me drink it' (v. 17). There then follows a listing of the nations to whom the cup is sent (vv. 19–26).[65] It is highly unlikely that the prophet trudged from nation to nation with a very large goblet of wine and forced each nation (or its representatives) to drink from it. So what kind of account is this? As with the incident in ch. 13, Rudolph treats this section as an account of a vision.[66] Alternatives to this approach are to see in the chapter a literary working of an original poem[67] or to posit an acted parable or dramatic action account by the editors. Such an approach would see in the presentation here a view of the prophet which cast him as an actor performing, with ritualized gestures, a drama in which he went around selected members of the crowd watching him (having designated them to be representatives of the nations) and offered them a goblet of wine. The explanation of the significance of the actions would then be given after the performance. It is a similar treatment of the text as is offered for the linen waistcloth incident and is suggested by the dramatic action of breaking the flask in 19.10 (cf. 51.59–64). This treatment would make sense of the text, though it is not based on information provided by that text. It would, however, be in line with the presentation of the prophet as an actor found elsewhere in the Jeremiah tradition.

Jer. 27.1–3, 12; 28.10f. Set in a lengthy account of conflict between Jeremiah and the court of Zedekiah is a brief treatment of Jeremiah making, at the divine command, yoke-bars to symbolize the coming domination of the Babylonians over Judah and the nations. Wearing them, the prophet invites the king and the neighbouring states to put themselves under the yoke of Babylonian hegemony voluntarily. Opposing his viewpoint, the prophet Hananiah breaks the yoke-bars worn by Jeremiah as a symbol of Yahweh breaking the Babylonian domination (28.10f.). In these accounts the symbolic play-acting of the prophets represents dramatic actions accompanying and underlining the viewpoints of the prophets. For once in the tradition the dramatic action is unequivocal and what it symbolizes is also self-evident.

Jer. 32.1–15. Just before the Babylonians finally breached the walls of Jerusalem and took the city, Jeremiah is presented as having the opportunity to buy some property in Anathoth which belongs to his family (vv. 6–8; cf. Lev. 25.25–28). Going through the proper legal procedures, the prophet buys the field and stores the deeds of purchase in an earthen jar (vv. 9–14). Whether the account represents a real legal transaction involving Jeremiah and family property or is a story created by the redactors in order to develop a theme in the book of consolation (32.1–15 *is* set in the context of the larger book of consolation in ch. 30–33) is unimportant. The editors are concerned with the story as a symbolic gesture. Jeremiah's act of faith in buying property at a time when it probably could not be given away free is a pledge for the future. 'For thus says Yahweh of hosts, the God of Israel: Houses and fields and vineyards shall again be bought in this land' (v. 15). The symbolic nature of Jeremiah's action gives hope for the future, and the redactors develop that point in a series of lengthy additions (vv. 16–44). Here then is an ordinary action which is given further symbolic meaning in the context of the tradition.

Jer. 43.8–13. This symbolic action is set in Egypt, after the fall of Jerusalem and after the prophet Jeremiah was taken to Egypt. The prophet is commanded to take large stones and hide them in the pavement at the entrance to Pharaoh's palace in Tahpanhes, in the sight of the Judaeans (v. 9).[68] The hidden stones mark the place where the invading Nebuchadrezzar will set up his throne, after having destroyed the gods and temples of Egypt (vv. 11–13). The symbolic nature of the action is clear, though the precise details are not. Whether the action was carried out literally (would the Egyptians have taken kindly to immigrants digging up their palace grounds?) or in some symbolic way must remain open to debate.

Jer. 51.59–64. The final symbolic action relating to the prophet in the Jeremiah tradition concerns something which happened before the collapse of Jerusalem.[69] The prophet is represented as writing in a book all the evil predictions against Babylon and giving it to Seraiah ben Neriah. Seraiah is to take the book to Babylon, read its contents there (presumably he is to read it aloud), bind a stone to it when he is finished reading, and then cast it into the Euphrates. The meaning of this ritual is clear from the words accompanying the hurling of the book into the river: 'Thus shall Babylon sink, to rise no more, because of the evil that I am bringing upon her' (v. 64).[70] The only distinctive element in this account of a symbolic action is the fact that Jeremiah does not perform it but instructs somebody else to do it. It is, however, a good example of how the redactors used the notion of symbolic actions to put across elements of the tradition. Oracles accompanied by dramatic actions show Jeremiah to have been as much an actor as a speaker; at least, that is the image of the prophet conveyed strongly and graphically by the series of symbolic actions enumerated above.

6

Conflict I:
Concerning the Kings of Judah

The deuteronomistic history of the kings of Israel and Judah uses as one of its central motifs the conflict between the kings and the prophets. Each prophet is shown, on occasion, to be in conflict with the king, or kings, in whose reign(s) he worked. This conflict is marked by a severely critical attitude towards the king, either as general policy (e.g., Elijah against Ahab) or on specific occasions (e.g., Nathan against David). Throughout the history of the kings, the prophets represent the deuteronomistic ideology and mark carefully how far short of it a particular king may fall. The importance of this conflict motif can be seen in the fact that the reign of so many kings is punctuated by the appearance of angry prophets denouncing some act or attitude of a king. For example, Samuel hounds Saul, Nathan severely criticizes David (II Sam. 12), Ahijah legitimates Jeroboam's disruption of Solomon's kingdom (I Kings 11.26–40; note how no prophet *confronts* Solomon, but the divine word informs the king of his faults, vv. 9–13), an anonymous prophet speaks against Jeroboam in favour of Josiah (I Kings 13.1–10), Elijah hounds Ahab and speaks against Ahaziah (I Kings 17 – II Kings 1), Elisha's legitimation of Jehu completes the destruction of the house of Omri (II Kings 9–11). The only kings in the history who do not attract severe censure are Hezekiah and Josiah, though Jehoash (II Kings 12, cf. v. 3) is also highly commended. Most of the prophetic traditions do not have accounts of the prophets speaking out against kings (except insofar as they speak against the community's leadership), but the few traditions which include so-called biographical material also have stories of conflict between the prophet and the king. In Amos the clash between prophet and Amaziah the priest is related to the prophetic proclamation, 'Jeroboam shall die by the sword' (Amos 7.10–13), and in the Isaiah tradition the prophet attacks king Ahaz for his lack of faith in

Yahweh (Isa. 7.1–17). The Ezekiel tradition does not have any
specific king identified as the recipient of the prophet's critique, but
then Ezekiel worked in exile in Babylon, so there were no opportunities for such an encounter.

Such an impressive collection of conflict stories in the deuteronomistic history makes it inevitable that the Jeremiah tradition
should include a conflict motif. This is especially the case if the
theory that the tradition was edited and produced by deuteronomists
is accepted as a reasonable account of the construction of the tradition. Theoretically we should expect to find in the Jeremiah tradition a strong presence and use of the prophet versus king motif. It
is therefore hardly surprising that a perusal of Jeremiah, the longest
of the prophetic traditions, should reveal a large amount of material
on conflict, in particular conflict with the kings and also with the
prophets. Such conflict would appear to have been dominant in the
closing decades of the Judaean state, and the prophetic traditions of
Jeremiah and Ezekiel contain a good deal of criticism of the other
prophets. The presentation of Jeremiah as a prophet active during
the reigns of the final kings of Judah is partly constructed around
the motifs of prophet and king and prophet against king.

In the oracles there are the usual general criticisms of the community's leadership which can be found in most of the traditions of
the eighth- and seventh-century prophets (e.g., Amos 7.9; Hos. 5.1;
7.3–7; 9.15; Isa. 3.1–15; 9.14–16 [Heb. vv. 13–15]; 28.14–22; Micah 3; Ezek. 17). However, it must be stressed that these prophets
more often criticized the whole community for its oppression and
corruption (see especially Amos). So with the oracles in the Jeremiah
tradition the community is identified as the source of injustice and
immorality (cf. Hos. 7.4: 'they are all adulterers'), but there are a
number of statements which specify the leadership as particularly
corrupt. It is the priests, the rulers and the prophets who do not
know Yahweh (Jer. 2.8).[1] Priests and prophets rule falsely and are
encouraged by the people to do so (5.31). The false dealings of the
priests and prophets have failed to heal the community's wounds
because these leaders take too superficial a view of the damage done
to the nation (6.13–15 = 8.10–12). Because the wise men have
rejected the divine word they lack true wisdom and are therefore of
no use to the people (8.8f.). In all these statements there is no
specific reference to the kings nor is the royal house singled out for
criticism (cf. 13.18f. for passing reference to the effect of the exile
on the king and the queen mother). The reference to shepherds in
2.8 may include the kings, but in the context of the verse the ruling

aristocracy is not singled out but included in the classes of leaders offending the deity. So the oracles in the Jeremiah tradition have no particular bias against the Judaean kings.

The deuteronomistic edition of Jeremiah, however, has put together a number of oracles and statements about kingship and the kings in a formal pattern. The tendency for the editors to put into blocks of material elements having a common theme has already been noted (e.g., cultic abuses in 7.1 – 8.3; liturgical elements relating to the drought in 14.1 – 15.4; material associated with the potter in 18.1–11 – 19.13; oracles concerning the prophets in 23.9–40), so it is in keeping with this redactional policy that a substantive amount of material devoted to the Judaean kings should be associated together in 21.1 – 23.8. This is the longest cycle of thematic material in the first half of the tradition and is made up of diverse and discrete elements.[2]

The cycle of texts on kings

The material is not presented in chronological order, but appears to be developed from one of the latest pieces (21.1–10 associated with the siege of Jerusalem in 589–587) and then proceeds to deal with the various kings in order. The cycle probably starts with Jeremiah's response to the king's inquiry mediated through Pashhur and Zephaniah (21.1f.) because of the similarity between the names of the officials involved in two incidents: *Pashhur* ben Immer, the priest who beat Jeremiah over the earthen flask business (20.1–6), and *Pashhur* ben Malchiah, who was sent to Jeremiah by King Zedekiah (21.1). The material in 21.1–10 is clearly part of the redaction of the tradition, because it is virtually the same as various accounts in the second half of Jeremiah. 21.2 is equivalent, with variations, to 37.3–5, with 21.3–7 parallel to 37.6–10 and 21.8–10 a variation on 38.2f. (21.1 is similar to 38.1). The main variations between the parallel passages are due to the different settings: in 21.1–10 the concern is with the presentation of Jeremiah's preaching, whereas in 37.1–10 and 38.1–6 the context is the representation of the prophet's life in the final days of the Judaean state. The difference may not be that great, but in the Jeremiah tradition distinctions should be drawn between the concern with what the prophet had to say and the desire to depict the life of the prophet in the context of an antagonistic community. Different things are being presented by the tradition. There is nothing in 21.1 – 23.8 that contributes to the redactional biography of Jeremiah, whereas that is the main concern of chs. 37–40.

The gist of the two distinctive traditions may be the same, but the variations permit a good deal of scope for developing the stories, and demonstrate the way the redaction built up the tradition. In 21.1 it is Pashhur and Zephaniah who convey the king's inquiry to Jeremiah: 'Inquire of Yahweh for us, for Nebuchadrezzar king of Babylon is making war against us; perhaps Yahweh will deal with us according to all his wonderful deeds, and will make him withdraw from us.' Is there here an echo of the providential withdrawal of Sennacherib from the siege of Jerusalem in the time of Isaiah (cf. II Kings 19.36)? In 37.3 Zephaniah is sent by King Zedekiah along with Jehucal ben Shelemiah to Jeremiah: 'Pray for us to Yahweh our God' (Jehucal = Jucal in 38.1). Pashhur is missing from this account because, for the editors of this part of the tradition, he is hostile to Jeremiah (his hostility is clearly indicated in 20.1–4), and so he appears in 38.1–6, where the prophet is maltreated for his condemnation of resistance to the Babylonians. The futility of the mission of Jehucal and Zephaniah in 37.3 is indicated by the redactional preface to the account in 37.2, which states that king, courtiers and people paid no attention to the divine word spoken by the prophet. The theme of chs. 37–38 is the opposition of the court to Jeremiah, so the main concern of the material is with the mistreatment of the prophet, though the message delivered by the prophet is essentially the same as it is in 21.1–10. The later chapters focus on the prophet as the bearer of the rejected word and, therefore, as the rejected prophet he suffers beatings and imprisonment. This motif is quite different from the other motif used in the tradition of the prophet as the fighter against opposition who triumphs over it (e.g., 26; 28; 29).[3] These different motifs are important elements in the variegated tradition of Jeremiah created by the redactors.

The language of 21.1–10 is strongly deuteronomistic (e.g., 'with outstretched hand and strong arm' in v. 5, cf. Deut. 4.34; 5.15; Yahweh's great wrath against the people in v. 5, cf. Jer. 32.37; Deut. 29.27; for 'I set before you the way of life and the way of death' in v. 8 cf. 'I have set before you this day life and good, death and evil', Deut. 30.15; cf. also Deut. 11.26). In response to the king's inquiry about the possibility of a divine action making Nebuchadrezzar withdraw his siege, the prophet declares that no amount of resistance will work against the Babylonians, because it is Yahweh himself who is fighting against the city. All will be destroyed, man and beast, king, counsellors and people. Those who survive pestilence, sword and famine will become prisoners of the Babylonians, who will show no mercy. One possibility of survival is offered the beleaguered city: those who surrender to the Babylonians shall escape with their lives (vv. 8f.). But the city is doomed because Yahweh is against it. It will be burned with fire (21.10; cf. 34.3; 37.8, 10; 38.18; 39.8). In 21.1–10 the opportunity to escape from the siege and surrender to the Babylonians is only made to the people (vv. 4–7 is the message to the king and his followers, vv. 8–10 is the message given to the people). Elsewhere the possibility of escape is offered to King Zedekiah (cf. 34.1–5; 38.17–23).[4] The inconsistency between the different traditions may reflect distinctive stages of the growth of the Jeremiah tradition, with 21.1–10 constituting a deuteronomistic rewriting of some of the later traditions (loosely attentive to detail) intended as an introduction to the cycle of kings texts. It prefaces the material on the kings with a note that the royal house is doomed and that in the days of Zedekiah the Babylonians captured the city, fired it and executed the king's sons and his nobles. Now read on!

The opening oracles of the collection (if 'to the house of the king of Judah', v. 11, is a heading to the collection[5]) are general statements lacking any specific details which would enable an exegete to locate them in a particular context of time and place. The giving of oracles by prophets to kings is a traditional feature of the biblical presentation of royalty and prophecy (cf. II Sam. 7; Isa. 9.2–7 [Heb. vv. 1–6]; 11.1–9; Ps. 2). In the preface to this cycle Zedekiah sought such an oracle, but received instead a word of doom. The oracle in v. 12 is a general appeal to the royal house to practise justice in the morning, i.e., to maintain the rights of those involved in legal disputes, which were adjudicated in the early part of the day.[6] Failure to execute such justice will lead to the wrath of Yahweh breaking forth like fire. The elements of the oracle reflect the central concerns of the cycle, namely the danger of divine wrath being directed against the royal city and the need for the practice of justice by the kings. The oracle in vv. 13 is obscure.[7] It might be directed against Jerusalem (under the image of a dweller in the valley, the rock of the plain[?]), but it seems to be made up of fragments referring to other places (cf. the oracles against Moab in Jer. 48.8, 21, 28). However, in its present context it should be taken as applied to Jerusalem and warning that city against destruction by fire (the fire motif appears in vv. 10, 12, 14 and is probably the linking motif in the editing of the sequence).

The next stage of the cycle consists of a deuteronomistic sermon (22.1–5), an oracle of judgment (vv. 6f.), and the conclusion of the sermon (vv. 8f.). The deuteronomistic conventions and terminology in the sermon are obvious (cf. Jer. 7.1–15; 17.19–27 for sermons of a similar type). As with the other sermons the redactors present a situation where the community or its leaders are given the choice between practising justice, and thereby securing the future of the city, or ignoring the warnings, and thereby bringing destruction upon the city. The three sermons make the city's future dependent upon proper worship in the temple (conditioned by the practice of justice), sabbath observance and the maintenance of justice by the royal house and the people. Implicit in all these sermons may be the lesson for the exiles: that community failed to do any of these things so it was destroyed (let that be a lesson for you!). It is assumed that Jeremiah is addressed in v. 1, but throughout the cycle of texts about the kings (from 21.11 – 23.8) Jeremiah is never mentioned by name. Such an omission would justify the view that the collection is made up of anonymous royal oracles gathered together and attributed to Jeremiah by the redactors. However, in the absence of evidence either way the question of attribution may be left open. In 22.1 the command to '*go down* to the house of the king of Judah' (*rēd bēt-melek yᵉhūdāh*) implies that the prophet is in the temple (hence a cult prophet as presented by the redactors?) and goes down to the royal palace (for the descent from the temple to the palace cf. 26.10; 36.12). The threat of destruction of the city is emphasized by incorporating a brief oracle comparing the city (or the land?) to other territories:

> You are as Gilead to me,
>> as the summit of Lebanon,
> yet surely I will make you a desert,
>> an uninhabited city.[8]
> I will prepare destroyers against you,
>> each with his weapons;
> and they shall cut down your choicest cedars,
>> and cast them into the fire. (22.6f.)

The motif of fire (v. 7) makes a further link between various sections (e.g., 21.10, 12, 14). The final section of the sermon is a characteristically deuteronomistic redactional technique of presenting the nations as spectators of the life and fate of Judah-Israel (cf. Deut. 9.27–29). It imagines the nations passing by the (burned out) city and asking each other, 'Why has Yahweh dealt thus with this great city?', to which question they also provide the answer 'Because they forsook the covenant of Yahweh their God, and worshipped other gods and served them' (how theologically articulate the nations can be in the deuteronomistic texts!). This device is used in a variety of ways in the Jeremiah tradition (cf. 5.18f.; 9.12–14 [Heb. vv. 11–13]; 16.10–13; 22.8f.; see also Deut. 29.22–28; I Kings 9.7–9). The cutting down and burning of the choicest cedars may refer to the destruction of the palaces with their massive cedar pillars (cf. 'the house of the forest of Lebanon', I Kings 7.2–5; also Isa. 22.8; Jer. 21.14; 22.15), rather than the forests of the land. The sermon begins with a warning about the practice of justice but finishes with a reference to idolatry, indicating the deuteronomists' real belief that it was false worship and idolatry which caused the exile rather than simply the practice of injustice.

The next element in the cycle (22.10–12) is a brief oracle plus prose comment on the fate of King Jehoahaz, Josiah's son, who succeeded to the throne when his father was killed at Megiddo (II Kings 23.29–34). His personal name was Shallum (cf. I Chron. 3.15), but after a reign of only three months the Egyptians deposed him, took him to Egypt where he died, and put an older son of Josiah, Jehoiakim, on the throne. The terse oracle transfers a lament motif from Josiah ('him who is dead') to the deported Shallum ('him who goes away'):

> Weep not for him who is dead,
>   nor bemoan him;
> but weep bitterly for him who goes away,
>   for he shall return no more
>   to see his native land. (22.10)

The prose accompaniment (vv. 11f.) spells out the meaning of the oracle, which is clear as its stands. Such an explanation may have been necessary at the time of the tradition's redaction, when many may never have heard of the young ruler who was king for three months and then went cruelly into exile, there to die. It is sometimes argued that the death of Josiah must have been an insuperable problem for the deuteronomists' theology.[9] It may have been, but there is little evidence here that it constituted a real problem for theology; instead the redactors focus attention away from the dead Josiah to the living but exiled Shallum (using his personal name rather than his throne name because he was no longer the effective king).

The longest of the oracles in the cycle (22.13–19) is generally regarded to be an attack on the reign of Jehoiakim, who succeeded the deported Shallum and was king c. 609–597 (v. 18 probably justifies seeing Jehoiakim as the object of the oracle). It is therefore the one clear denunciation of that king in the Jeremiah tradition. Some of the more general attacks on society in the tradition may have belonged to the period of Jehoiakim's regnancy but, the incident in ch. 36 apart, this is the only direct criticism of that king. Jehoiakim was put on the throne by the Egyptians, and as their vassal he had to pay heavy tribute to Egypt (II Kings 23.34f.). To meet the tribute demands he had to tax the nation (as kings have ever done since time immemorial). Like his father, he also believed that building programmes and political expansion were the marks of kingship, but unlike Josiah he chose the wrong period for such schemes. The pro-Babylonian party in Judah (to which Jeremiah is presented throughout the tradition as belonging) was strongly opposed to the pro-Egyptian faction (to which Jehoiakim necessarily belonged). Josiah had opposed the Egyptians (he most likely met his death in confrontation with them at Megiddo) so it is possible that the Egyptians removed Shallum in order to install a more sympathetic member of Josiah's family, namely Jehoiakim. Being the son of such a dominating father, whose megalomaniacal schemes had led to his death, may have turned Jehoiakim away from such policies. It is not possible to determine these matters now, but the reader of the Jeremiah tradition is warned about a too facile acceptance of the deuteronomistic ideological shaping of the tradition which makes Josiah almost an ideal king and Jehoiakim an irredeemable scoundrel (should Bibles carry a Government warning: *Caveat lector?*).

The oracle in vv. 13–17 does not mention by name the king charged with the follies outlined in the oracle but as in the oracle of v. 11 obliquely refers to 'him who builds his house by unrighteousness, and his upper rooms by injustice; who makes his neighbour serve him for nothing, and does not give him his wages' (v. 13).[10] The charge against the king is splendidly stated in an ironic treatment of his building programmes.

> Do you think you are a king
> because you compete in cedar? (22.15a)

There can have been few kings in the Bible (or elsewhere in the world for that matter) against whom such a charge could not be made. Solomon is a prime example of a king who saw kingship in terms of massive building projects, crushing and taxing the people to achieve such symbols of self-glorification. Here it is Jehoiakim who is accused of confusing royal ostentation with authentic kingship. In this charge can be heard a constant criticism of kingship which is presented throughout the biblical traditions dealing with the monarchy (cf. I Sam. 8). It is the ancient protest of the independent tribal groups which opposed kingship because it centralized authority and legitimated imposed taxation and exploitation. The function of the oracle for the redactors is the contrast it permits between the behaviour of Jehoiakim and his father Josiah.

> Did not your father eat and drink
>   and do justice and righteousness?
> Then it was well with him.[11]
> He judged the cause of the poor and needy;
>   then it was well.
> Is not this to know me?
>   says Yahweh. (22.15b–16)

The reference to Josiah's 'eating and drinking' should be understood as a statement about the king's ability to live well and enjoy himself. It is unnecessary to see in it a reference to covenant making (as in II Kings 23.3), for there must have been occasions when biblical characters ate food or drank wine without making a covenant by doing so.[12] The contrast is not between sensual enjoyment of life and the doing of justice but between a combination of both and the failure to practise justice in spite of enjoying material well-being. Knowledge of Yahweh is here defined as the vindication of the poor and needy (cf. Hos. 6.6; Micah 6.8; applied to the king cf. Jer. 21.12; Ps. 72.4, 12–14). The king is then accused of seeking only violent gain, the shedding of blood and the practice of oppression (v. 17). Some commentators have seen in the reference to 'shedding innocent blood' an oblique comment on the killing of prophets by Jehoiakim (cf. Jer.26.20–23).[13] As this is a general charge made against the community elsewhere in the tradition (cf. 2.30, 34; 5.26–29), it is more likely to be part of the rhetoric of the oracle than a specific accusation against the king. In Jehoiakim's reign such oppression and injustice was tolerated by the royal house. Insofar as the redactors identified Jehoiakim as a particularly vicious king, and this point is open to serious criticism, then their use of this oracle may indicate such opposition to the king expressed in the traditional terms of the prophetic critique of kingship carried by the deuteronomistic tradition (cf. the view of Ahab in I Kings 17–22).

A further oracle directed against Jehoiakim (vv. 18f.) is introduced by a prose statement indicating that the following oracle is the divine word of Yahweh against Jehoiakim. By implication it suggests that the previous oracle (vv. 13–17) is also about Jehoiakim. It is a lament for the death of a king presented as a prediction about Jehoiakim's death:

> They shall not lament for him, (saying)
>   'Ah my brother!' or 'Ah sister!'
> They shall not lament for him, (saying)
>   'Ah lord!' or 'Ah his majesty!'[14]
> With the burial of an ass he shall be buried,
>   dragged and cast forth beyond the gates of Jerusalem.
>   (22.18f.)

The intent of these verses is clear, but there are problems with their interpretation because what evidence there is suggests that Jehoiakim's burial followed the normal procedures for the burial of kings (cf. II Kings 24.6; II Chron. 36.8).[15] This oracle may have influenced the treatment of the burial notices in the histories, because they are curiously reluctant to give any details of Jehoiakim's burial. The phrase 'to sleep with one's fathers' is a biblical circumlocution for 'being buried in the family grave', so II Kings 24.6 indicates that Jehoiakim was buried in the family tomb. The problem of an unfulfilled prediction in Jer. 22.18f. should not be allowed to weigh too heavily on the interpretation of the text, because the biblical writers did not always match predictions and fulfilments.[16] If the oracle is taken as an emotional outburst against an unpopular king (unpopular, that is, with certain sections of Jerusalem society), threatening him with an ignominious treatment after his death, then the predictive aspect of the threat should be treated as subordinate to the emotion released. Predicting the future is always a very tricky business, and the biblical traditions contain a number of failed predictions specifically about the deaths of kings. Thus Huldah's prediction that Josiah would be gathered to his grave in peace (II Kings 22.20) was falsified by his being killed by Pharaoh Neco (II Kings 23.29).[17] The strange statement attributed to Jeremiah (Jer. 34.4f.) predicting the peaceable death of Zedekiah is similar to Huldah's prediction: 'You shall not die by the sword. You shall die in peace.' Perhaps the blinded, bereft Zedekiah (Jer. 39.6f.; II Kings 25.7) did die in peace, but it is a curiously perverted sense of peace so to describe his condition. Taking the three strange predictions together, it may be the case that part of the conventional prophet's duties included laments on the death of a king and oracles during his life assuring him of a peaceful end and a traditional burial. This would explain the inversion of convention in 22.18f. and the conventional forms of 34.4f. and II Kings 22.20 (cf. Elijah's treatment of Ahab in I Kings 21.17–19).

The next oracle in the cycle (vv. 20–23) does not deal with a king but addresses Jerusalem (personified as a woman). It may belong to the period c. 597, when Jehoiachin surrendered to the Babylonians, and as such is an appropriate poem to place between the sections dealing with Jehoiakim (vv. 13–19) and Jehoiachin (vv. 24–30).[18] The poem bears on the theme of kingship because the city's alliances with other groups would have been organized by the kings and their nobles. There is also a word-play on the leadership in v. 22, 'the wind shall shepherd your shepherds', meaning your leaders will be swept away (as well as the city's allies).

The final oracle in the sequence is made up of prose and poetic elements relating to Jehoiachin the son of Jehoiakim, using his personal name Coniah (cf. I Chron. 3.16) rather than Jehoiachin, his throne name. The prose introduction to the oracle (vv. 24–27) is a deuteronomistic statement about the hopelessness of Coniah's future.[19] The argument of the material seems to have as its background community speculation about the future of the deported king. Exiled to Babylon, he was replaced on the thone by Zedekiah, who was the vassal of the Babylonians (II Kings 24.17). So the Jerusalem community consisted of those who supported Jehoiachin, the king in exile, and those loyal to the new king, the Babylonian puppet(?). Would Yahweh restore Jehoiachin to the throne along with the return of the temple vessels (cf. Jer. 28.1–4)? Such a hope appears to have been prevalent in Jerusalem after 597. It may have led to conflict within the community; it certainly split loyalties among the people. During the last decade of Jerusalem's existence, before the catastrophe of 587, one of the political issues was the hope that Jehoiachin would return, hence the partisan question: 'Is this man Coniah a despised, broken pot, a vessel no one cares for?' (v. 28).[20] To this popular question an oracular answer is given:

> O land, land, land,
>   hear the word of Yahweh!
> Thus says Yahweh:
> Write this man down as childless,
>   a man who shall not succeed in his days;
> for none of his offspring shall succeed[21]

> in sitting on the throne of David,
> and ruling again in Judah.' (22.29f.)

The oracle comes from a source hostile to Jehoiachin and dismisses the future hopes of that king. Whether it comes from a source sympathetic to Zedekiah or reflects the subsequent failure of Jehoiachin's line is more difficult to determine. The claim that Jehoiachin would be 'childless' should not be taken literally, because I Chron. 3.17 lists seven sons of his. The term here indicates that no children of his will succeed to the throne, therefore he and his family should no longer be counted among future prospects for the throne. In the tension between the supporters of the former king and the followers of the current king the oracle comes out on the side of Zedekiah and his circle. This factor suggests that the oracle was produced by the circles supporting Zedekiah (the deuteronomists and therefore Jeremiah as they present him?).

An interesting feature of this oracle against any future succession to the throne of a member of Jehoiachin's family is the fact that after the exile there was a movement to place a member of that family on the throne. The abortive attempt to restore the Judaean monarchy c. 520, involving Zerubbabel, Jehoiachin's grandson, came from supporters of the family, including the prophets Haggai and Zechariah, who did not belong to the group which produced this oracle. Even the association of the oracle with Jeremiah gave it no weight against a movement supported by the prophets Haggai and Zechariah. This ideological clash of prophets is characteristic of biblical prophecy, where no two prophets ever agreed with one another without substantive conflict between them.[22] The different prophetic attitudes to Jehoiachin and his family indicate the involvement of prophets in the conflicting political ideologies of the communities in which they worked.

The cycle of texts dealing with kingship is completed by a series of oracles and pronouncements on kingship, Zedekiah and the future hopes for the community (23.1–8). The false leaders of the community are condemned as shepherds who have failed to care for the people but have scattered the flock (vv. 1f.). The remnant of the flock will be gathered from the various countries to which they have been scattered and brought back to the fold (i.e., the land of Judah). Over this fold will be set shepherds who will care properly for the sheep (vv. 3f.). This hope for good leaders in the future is clearly an exilic element in the tradition because it presupposes the exile and probably belongs to a redaction which also included 3.15–

18 in the tradition. It is placed here to make a contrast between the false shepherds who scattered the people (v. 2, though v. 3 makes Yahweh the one who scattered the people) and the future leaders who will make sure that none of the community is missing.

The last king of the Judaean state was Zedekiah, and he now appears in a brief oracle expressing hope for the future (vv. 5f.). The general interpretation of the piece has been complicated by the problem of whether Zedekiah or a future (idealistic) king is referred to in the terms used.[23] If the lines originally were spoken in the time of king Zedekiah then there is no good reason for not applying them to him. The phrase 'Yahweh is our righteousness' (*yhwh ṣidqēnū* v. 6) is a word-play on the name Zedekiah (*ṣidqiyyāhu*), so the oracle might have arisen out of an original oracle spoken by a prophet on the accession of Zedekiah to the throne in 597. This interpretation would fit the conventional oracle forms in the cycle. However, it is equally possible that the redaction of the tradition should be made responsible for the shaping and placing of the oracle. In that case it represents an element of the exilic hope for a restoration of the Davidic monarchy which would contribute to the well-being and security of Judah-Israel. Elements of this movement are to be found in Jer. 33.19–26 and Ezek. 37.24–28 (cf. the extended metaphor treatment of shepherds and sheep in Ezek. 34). The source of this hope would have been those elements among the exiles who maintained the royal ideology associated with the house of David, including those who were behind the moves to make Zerubbabel king in the early reconstruction period. To what extent Jeremiah held any beliefs about the future of the monarchy cannot now be reconstructed from the Jeremiah tradition because of the overwhelming influence of the redactors on the presentation of the prophet.

The concluding verses (7f.) reflect the exilic period and express the hope that in the future Yahweh will bring back to their own country the descendants of the exiles. They are virtually the same as 16.14f. (where they are out of context) and link the restoration of the exiles to the future monarchy.[24] The presence of such hopes in the tradition reveals the exilic redaction of the material and demonstrates the way the Jeremiah material was made to carry various elements of exilic thought.

The main connection between Jeremiah and the cycle of texts on the Judaean kings is the redactional presentation of the material as coming from the prophet (this is an implied rather than explicit connection). The conflict theme is not used to construct the elements of the cycle, though some of the oracles are highly critical of certain kings. The prophet Jeremiah is presented as an official speaker of oracles on royal occasions, usually the death or deportation of a king. He is also presented as an intercessor on behalf of the king and the city (21.2) and as a preacher of the call to righteous behaviour by the community. All these elements are concerns of the deuteronomistic redactors, so it is impossible to assert with any confidence that these are the kinds of things which Jeremiah went about doing rather than that these are the types of behaviour expected from a prophet by the deuteronomists and, therefore, Jeremiah is shown to have behaved as a conventional prophet. The standard deuteronomistic view of the prophet ranged against the king and in conflict with him is the informing principle behind the redaction of the Jeremiah tradition. For a much fuller exposition of the tradition in terms of this principle it is necessary to consider the narratives in the second half of the tradition.

The cycle of conflict narratives

The isolation of a conflict motif in these narratives is only one way of interpreting them. As they now appear in the Jeremiah tradition, they represent a complex structure of redactional activity which has incorporated a number of different motifs into the presentation of the material. Elements of conflict appear in many of the stories, though some of the stories are designed to emphasize motifs other than the conflict one. Furthermore, I have divided the narratives into stories of conflict between prophet and king and accounts of conflict between prophet and the other prophets. Both sets of stories should be read together in order to see how much the conflict motif has been used in the presentation of Jeremiah as a prophet. This isolation of the conflict motif is only intended as a regulative probe for analysing the tradition in order to lay bare the redactors' reliance on it as a way of handling the discrete material relating to the prophet.

The conflict between Jeremiah and the various kings is not presented as a cycle of material (unlike the elements in 21.1 – 23.8) but occurs in two different blocks of material (chs. 26–29 and 36; 37–43).[25] The image of Jeremiah is somewhat different in these complexes in that in the first series (chs. 26–29 and 36) he triumphs over the opposition and demonstrates the superiority of the true prophet against whatever opponents may confront him. In the second series (chs. 37–43) he is a much more passive figure and requires assistance from various sources in order to escape the predicaments into which he has fallen. Furthermore in ch. 43 he is presented as being taken down to Egypt against his wishes so that he ends his life in exile away from Jerusalem. The two sets of traditions then present the prophet as actor and as acted upon. Such distinctive features of the different blocks of material used in the Jeremiah tradition should be noted carefully, because they indicate the distinctive elements shaping the tradition.

Although conflict is a dominant motif in the stories in chs. 26, 27–28, and 29, the kings are hardly involved in any of the stories. The redactors relate the stories to specific periods in the reign of various kings (cf. 26.1; 27.1;[26] 28.1; 29.2), but the kings are *not* participants in the conflict between the prophet and his opponents. The concern of the stories is with a presentation of *the truth of the preaching of the prophet Jeremiah*.[27] The element of conflict is at its strongest in the temple sermon sequel in ch. 26 where, as already noted, various classes of people oppose the prophet and other classes support him. The outcome of the clash of opinions seems to be the triumph of Jeremiah (i.e., the vindication of his message). Elements in the story suggest that Jeremiah was arraigned before a tribunal and charged with a capital offence.[28] The only role the king (Jehoiakim) plays in the story is in the redactional comment on that king's attitude to prophets who oppose him (26.20–23). For the redactors, his presence is implicit in the story, but the story itself concerns a debate among the leaders and people about the nature of the divine word. In ch. 27 the prophetic action is directed to the kings of the neighbouring nations (v. 3), to Zedekiah (v. 12), to the priests and the people (v. 16), but the king has no role to play in the story. In ch. 28 the conflict, though set in Zedekiah's reign, is strictly between Jeremiah and Hananiah. The conflict in ch. 29 is between Jeremiah and the exiled prophets, with elements of a potential conflict between Jeremiah and Zephaniah the priest (29.24–29), but again the king (assumed to be Zedekiah) is not an active element in the story. Only in ch. 36 is there an open conflict involving the king, and then Jeremiah has only an indirect role to play in the story, because he is not party to the encounter with King Jehoiakim. Being barred from the temple (36.5), he is represented by Baruch and has the scroll read to the king. It is the content of the scroll which is important, rather than the person of the prophet.

The account in ch. 36 provides a cluster of problems for the interpreter of the Jeremiah tradition.[29] It introduces the figure of Baruch as Jeremiah's amanuensis who, at the prophet's dictation,

ch 36

writes the scroll of Jeremiah's words spoken between 627–605 (from the time of Josiah to the fourth year of Jehoiakim – 36.2). A similar account in ch. 25 (dated in the fourth year of Jehoiakim) makes no mention of Baruch. Much ink has flowed on identifying Baruch and the contents of the scroll he wrote for Jeremiah.[30] My own inclination is to regard the figure of Baruch as a deuteronomistic creation in order to carry certain elements in the tradition (cf. the finding of the lawbook in the temple as a similar invention, in order to legitimate the deuteronomistic position, in II Kings 22.8). The scribal figure probably stands for the traditionists who worked on the Jeremiah tradition and in that sense represents something real – after all, the tradition was created and transmitted by real people who were sympathetic towards the original figure of Jeremiah and used his work to develop the longest (and possibly the most formidable) volume in the prophetic traditions. However the data available on Baruch underdetermine any argument towards a conclusive account of the matter. Baruch appears at a number of points in the second half of the tradition: he is party to Jeremiah's purchase of the family field (32.12f., 16); he writes the scroll of Jeremiah's words (or as the text presents it 'the divine word') at the prophet's dictation (36.4–32); he is accused of being the source behind Jeremiah's advocacy of surrendering to the Babylonians (43.3); for his pains he is taken off to Egypt along with Jeremiah (43.6); and he is the recipient of a special oracle assuring him of his survival in the disastrous times ahead (ch. 45; note the similarity of v. 3 to the confessions of Jeremiah).

In the dictation of the scroll account Baruch is called in because, for unstated reasons, Jeremiah is barred from access to the temple (36.5). The parallel account in ch. 25 indicates no lack of access to the public, and throughout the tradition Jeremiah regularly proclaims in the hearing of the community a summary of his preaching (cf. 26.1ff.; 27.1ff.), so this feature of ch. 36 may be there to justify the invention of the figure of Baruch. Other explanations have been offered for Jeremiah's inability to go to the temple: Jehoiakim had barred him after the temple sermon (cf. 7.1–15; 26); after the beating by Pashhur he was excluded from the temple (cf. 20.1–6); perhaps he suffered from some ritual impurity and could not go to the temple (given the period of time which lapsed between 36.1 and 36.9 this seems unlikely); he was in hiding because of bad feeling between him and the court officials. Whatever is behind the statement, it serves to make Baruch indispensable. The purpose of the scroll reading is to persuade the nation to turn from evil so that

Yahweh's anger will be avoided (36.7). This is the deuteronomistic account of all the great public statements of Jeremiah's words – time after time the prophetic word is proclaimed in order to turn the nation back to Yahweh. On this occasion the reading of the scroll is given on a fast day (vv. 6, 9). Such a ritual indicates the general piety of the nation, but whether the fast had been called because of the drought (cf. 14.1ff.) or because of approaching danger from the Babylonians (the fifth year of Jehoiakim was 605, the year the Babylonians defeated the Egyptians at Carchemish on the Euphrates) is not indicated in the text. After reading the scroll in the hearing of all the people, Baruch was invited to read his scroll to the princes, and they in turn informed the king of its contents (vv. 11–19).

A third reading of the scroll now takes place in the hearing of the king. The scene is graphically described: it is winter time (the ninth month); the king, with his princes standing beside him, is sitting in the winter house in front of a brazier; Jehudi reads the scroll to him, column by column, and as he finishes with three or four columns the king cuts them off with a penknife and throws them into the fire (vv. 21–23). Some of the officials urge him not to burn the scroll, but he ignores them and orders the seizure of Jeremiah and Baruch; however, Yahweh hides them (vv. 24–26). Then it starts all over again! Another scroll is taken; Jeremiah dictates his words again, but adds a special word for Jehoiakim: 'Thus says Yahweh, You have burned this scroll, saying, "Why have you written in it that the king of Babylon will certainly come and destroy this land, and will cut off from it man and beast?" ' (v. 29). Jeremiah predicts that none of Jehoiakim's family will inherit the throne, and that his own dead body will be cast out (v. 30, cf. 22.19). So Baruch writes another scroll containing all the previous scroll's contents and adds many similar words to it (v. 32).

It is a brilliant story of conflict between the prophetic word and the king in which one of the protagonists is absent. It is therefore a story of conflict focusing on the divine word which cannot be defeated. Whether Jehoiakim was showing contempt for that word, destroying its power by his action (the power of the king versus the power of the prophet), or acting in the light of a different theological position, cannot now be determined, but from the redactional viewpoint the function of the story is to show the effective word overcoming the power of the king. The theological presuppositions of the traditionists are shaped by a theology of the word, and the story is designed to state that theology. Hence the element of conflict between prophet and king is subordinated to that end. Conflict is on the surface of the stories, but theology is the depth structure informing the tradition. Nothing can effectively oppose that word, and its burning by a king is a futile gesture because it will be recreated and will survive the ignominious death of that king.

The other sequence of conflict stories (chs. 37–43) presents the prophet suffering at the hands of various officials during Zedekiah's reign. If Jeremiah resists and fights back in various ways in chs. 26–29 and 36, in this sequence he suffers passively and does not escape harm (cf. 20.1–6).[31] A significant difference between the two sequences is the tendency of one set of traditions to make Jehoiakim the villain of the piece (this is, strictly speaking, only true of ch. 36, though it is hinted at in ch. 26), whereas the other set of stories tends to acquit Zedekiah of any involvement in the prophet's sufferings. Zedekiah is sympathetically portrayed in the stories, so that between him and Jeremiah there is a muted relationship of trust. This distinction between the kings serves the theological purposes of the redactors, who are busy in the tradition creating paradigms of the proper relationship between the king and the word of Yahweh mediated through the prophet.

In spite of Zedekiah's sympathetic attitude towards Jeremiah, the stories in chs. 37–39 show the prophet at the mercy of members of the royal court. Yet Jeremiah does not give way to such pressures, but maintains his fidelity to the divine word and continues to proclaim the same message: surrender to the Babylonians and save your lives. A temporary lull in the siege, caused by a Babylonian withdrawal to deal with the Egyptian army which had come out of Egypt, allowed Jeremiah to give Zedekiah a further assurance that the Babylonians would destroy the city (37.3–10). Zedekiah is presented as a pious king regularly seeking the prophetic word (cf. 21.1f.) but incapable of responding to it because his officials controlled him (curiously, Jeremiah is presented as having received more sympathetic treatment from some of Jehoiakim's officials; cf. chs. 26; 36). His attitude is correct, but his power is lacking, so he appears as a vacillating king. So Jeremiah suffers more physical harm under his rule than he did under Jehoiakim's regime. No doubt the traditionists saw in the declining days of Judah a more determined effort by the forces opposed to their theology, so they present the prophet as suffering more in the final days of Zedekiah. During the Babylonian withdrawal Jeremiah takes the opportunity to visit the field he had purchased, but is arrested leaving the city and accused of deserting to the enemy (37.11–14). The outraged princes beat him and imprison him (v. 15). After some time Zedekiah summons him, seeks an oracle from him and accedes to his request not to be sent back to prison (vv. 16–21). The king's intervention guarantees Jeremiah a food supply during the harsh siege.

A second account of the story is given in ch. 38 and it develops the same themes but in different ways.[32] Although both accounts present an image of Zedekiah as being afraid of the princes, he does in fact act effectively in both stories, so that Jeremiah's fate is decided by the king and not the princes. In spite of the fate of Uriah (cf. 26.20–23), the traditionists seem to be saying, the true prophet will always be protected by Yahweh (cf. the statement in 36.26, 'but Yahweh hid them'). The divine word remains inviolable and the bearer of it is a protected species. In the first account Jeremiah's message asserts the inevitable destruction of the city (37.7–10), but the second account uses a different form of message, which offers to the community the opportunity of escaping the siege by surrender to the Babylonians (38.2f.; cf. 21.8–10). Such a call to surrender must have constituted treasonable behaviour to those who were defending the city, and such an accusation is made against Jeremiah: 'Let this man be put to death, for he is weakening the hands of the soldiers who are left in this city, and the hands of all the people, by speaking such words to them. For this man is not seeking the welfare of this people, but their harm' (38.4).[33] Zedekiah hands over the prophet to the princes, because he is powerless against them, but they do not kill Jeremiah. Instead, they put him in an empty cistern where presumably he is left to starve to death (38.6). Although the weakness of Zedekiah is emphasized, it should be noted that the princes, in spite of the charge of treason, do not kill the prophet. The cistern incident is equivalent to the imprisoning of Jeremiah in Jonathan's house, which had been turned into a prison with dungeons (37.15f.).

The second account of Jeremiah's conflict with the princes introduces a new character into the story – Ebed-melech the Ethiopian (38.7–13; cf. 39.15–18).[34] It is the intervention of this official which rescues Jeremiah from the cistern and secures him a place in the court of the guard until the siege is over (38.13, 28). The incident uses a number of motifs common in the construction of the tradition. There is a king's official who is sympathetic towards Jeremiah (cf. 26.24; the Baruch material; the officials in 36.12, 25), Zedekiah is anxious to help the prophet (38.8–10), and the association of Ebed-melech with Jeremiah is instrumental in sparing the Ethiopian's life in the aftermath of the siege (39.15–18; cf. Baruch in

45.5; see also 21.9). This motif probably explains the promise of
peaceful death to Zedekiah in 34.4f. To be associated with the
prophet, either by helping him or listening to him sympathetically,
is to protect one's own life. Thus is the prophetic word presented
throughout the second half of the Jeremiah tradition as the source
of life and protection in the community. To reject that word is to
be doomed. Because Zedekiah oscillates between sympathy towards
Jeremiah and inability to follow him (cf. 37.1f.), his fate at the
hands of the Babylonians is uncertain in the tradition (cf. 34.4f.;
39.7; 52.11 [cf. II Kings 25.7]). He dies in peace but blinded and
in prison.

The sequel to Jeremiah's rescue by Ebed-melech is a summons
from the king, who wishes to discuss his prospects with the prophet
(38.14–26; cf. 37.16–20). The discussion is essentially the same as
the first account, but it is given at greater length and with more
details. Pacifying the prophet with promises that his life will be
spared (vv. 15f.), the king presumably asks for a word from Yahweh
(cf. 37.17; the account in ch. 38 does not contain this information).
The message from Jeremiah is a reiteration of previous elements in
the tradition (38.17f.) promising the king his life if he surrenders
to the Babylonians. The king responds to this offer with an expression of fear about the designs the deserters to the Babylonians may
have on his life (v. 19). Again the prophet reassures the king that
his life will be spared, but warns him about the consequences of
not surrendering by means of a vision (vv. 20f.). The vision is of
the women of the king's house being led into captivity and
lamenting:

> Your trusted friends have deceived you
>   and prevailed against you;
> now that your feet are sunk in the mire,
>   they turn away from you. (38.22)

The formal shape of this lament and the gap between the terms
expressed in it and the actual events they anticipate should convince
the reader that such laments are devices used by the redactors to
tell their story, rather than literal descriptions of events
(cf. Obadiah 7). Such a conviction is important for understanding
the same gap between the terms used in the confessions of Jeremiah
and the attempt to match them to events in the life of the prophet.
Formal devices heighten awareness but do not necessarily teach
history!

The spelling out of Zedekiah's fate (38.22f.; cf. 37.17) is followed by a strange exchange between king and prophet (38.24–28). The king assures the prophet that he will not die, *provided* he does not tell the princes about what has passed between the two of them (vv. 24–26; cf. v. 16). All these references to the prophet's possible death suggest a shaping motif in the redactors' creation of these stories, but one which is at odds with any realism in the accounts. In order to escape death the prophet must tell the king the truth, but may lie to save himself from the princes who already have tried to kill him. Why should the princes simply question Jeremiah (v. 27) instead of returning him to the cistern or promptly killing him on the spot? To ask such a question is to demand of the account a correlation with reality, whereas it is really only a story intended to convey the theologoumena of the redactors. So also to focus on the white lie Jeremiah tells in order to escape death and not to embarrass the king, and to denounce the prophet as a liar, is to take the story too seriously and at the wrong level.[35] To the absolute moralist (e.g., Sissela Bok) any form of lying, be it white or whatever colour, is morally wrong and indefensible,[36] but realism demands that distinctions be drawn between forms of polite social behaviour, truth-telling and the defence of one's life. However, to concentrate on Jeremiah's prevarication is to miss the point of the story, which is that once again Jeremiah escaped death, yet remained faithful to his uncompromising vision of Jerusalem's destruction if the king did not obey the divine word. Zedekiah's role in protecting Jeremiah (and himself?) should not be ignored as a feature of the story.

The other elements of conflict in the narratives are better treated in relation to the material dealing with the aftermath of the fall of Jerusalem (see ch. 9 below). The final statement on the kings in the Jeremiah tradition appears in ch. 52, where the redactors have used a version of the material in II Kings 24.18–25.30 (mainly omitting 25.22–26 on the assassination of Gedaliah, which is more fully dealt with in Jer. 40.7–43.7) to link the book of Jeremiah with the final section of the deuteronomistic history. This makes an inclusio type connection between II Kings and Jeremiah.[37] As the concluding chapter is taken from other sources, it does not display the conflict motif of the tradition, but ends the Jeremiah tradition by focusing on the special treatment afforded the exiled king Jehoiachin (Jer. 52.31–34 = II Kings 25.27–30 with slight variations, including the phrase 'until the day of his death' in the concluding clause). Whether this ending should be seen as a word of hope to the house of David about a brighter future or constitutes the final scene in the history of the doomed house on its way to extinction is a matter for much debate.[38]

The importance of the conflict cycle of oracles and stories is the way it allows the redactors to present their ideology of the relationship between kings and prophets as the context of the operation of the divine word. No matter how kings may act or even persecute prophets, the word remains sovereign. The only hope for the kings is that they bow to that word and respond to the prophet. The history of the last kings of Judah is presented as the failure of those kings to respond correctly to the preaching of Jeremiah, and it is therefore the history of the destruction of community and city. Throughout the period Jeremiah faithfully proclaims the word and, through much opposition and suffering, survives the collapse of Jerusalem. The redaction of the tradition maintains fidelity to that word.

7

Conflict II:
Concerning the Prophets

The second element of conflict which has a thematic role in the Jeremiah tradition is that between Jeremiah and the prophets. The closing decades of political life in Judah before the fall of Jerusalem saw a considerable amount of prophetic activity. In the first instance the expansionist programmes of Josiah set against the decline of Assyrian power greatly increased the nationalistic fervour of the community and so encouraged the chauvinism of its court prophets. The continued decline of Assyria, which led to the special redaction of the Isaiah tradition, strengthened belief in the divine protection of Jerusalem. The death of Josiah in 609 may have been cause for concern in some quarters, but there is little evidence to suggest that it in any way undermined confidence in the inviolability of Judah-Jerusalem. The emergence of Babylon in 605 as the new effective power in the struggle for hegemony was vigorously opposed by the pro-Egyptian forces in Jerusalem, and throughout the period 605–587 such forces held the balance of power in Judaean internal politics. The pro-Babylonian opposition party was not nearly as effective in determining Judaean policy of the period, and its failure created the conditions for the eventual destruction of Jerusalem. In such a period of political struggle, conflict between the prophets was inevitable.

The traditionists who created the Jeremiah tradition knew from experience and hindsight that the failure of the Judaean community to implement pro-Babylonian policies had led to its destruction, and so throughout the tradition (apart from the conventional oracles against the nations, e.g., Jer. 50–51) the Babylonians are favoured against the Egyptians. Zedekiah, the Babylonian choice of king, is presented in as favourable a light as possible and Jehoiakim, the Egyptian choice of king, represented as a vicious, evil king. The exiles in Babylon are the good people (cf. Jer. 24.4–7; 29.1–14) and the community remaining in Jerusalem after 597 the bad people (cf. Jer. 24.8–10). Supporters of the Egyptian line and opponents of the pro-Babylonian attitudes are therefore condemned throughout the tradition. Among such condemned parties must be included the various prophetic groups who advised, supported or encouraged the kings to resist the Babylonian menace. This is the political background to the conflict between the prophets, a conflict which concerned the deuteronomists in a number of ways and led to their production of controlling rules for prophets (cf. Deut. 13.1–5; 18.15–22). In the clash between prophets (I Kings 22 is a classical instance of such a conflict) the deuteronomists took the opportunity to delineate the features of the authentic prophet of Yahweh by means of their redaction of the Jeremiah tradition. The issue was an important one in the exilic period because it exposed the weaknesses of prophecy as a means of mediating the divine word, and the deuteronomists needed to develop a more sophisticated ideological treatment of the controversy in order to maintain their advocacy of prophecy as a divine instrument. The substantial amount of material on prophetic conflict in Jeremiah should be seen as the deuteronomists' contribution to resolving the problems raised by the warring prophets in the post-Josiah period. Material bearing on the issue can also be found in the Ezekiel tradition (e.g., Ezek. 13.1 –14.11).[1] There has been considerable interest in the problems raised by prophetic conflict in recent biblical studies, so this anlysis of the relevant Jeremiah material is intended to be a clarification of some of the issues involved in that discussion.[2]

The fact that the bulk of material on prophetic conflict and matters relating to the determination of the authentic prophet is to be found in the Jeremiah tradition reflects the deuteronomists' involvement in the redaction of Jeremiah, and also makes the book of Jeremiah fundamentally important for such a discussion. Some of the elements of prophetic conflict are scattered throughout the material in Jeremiah 2–14, but the main features of the argument have been collected and organized into two sections in 23.9–40 and chs. 27–29. So these three areas of the tradition will be scrutinized in turn in order to formulate a general treatment of the subject.

Against the prophets: fragments

The strong current of criticism directed against the leaders of the community in the oracles of Jeremiah has already been noted and analysed. Rulers (often referred to under the term 'shepherds',

cf. 2.8; 10.21; 23.1–4), priests, wise men and prophets are all included in the leadership condemned for its incompetence, corruption and wilful misleading of the community. Each category may
have had a different role in society – the ruler determined political
policy counselled by the wise men, the priests provided instruction
in the divine torah, and the prophets conveyed to the community
the divine word (cf. 18.18 for the tripartite division of duties between priest, prophet and wise man) – but in the prophetic critique
the *whole* leadership was corrupt and one of the root causes of the
community's state of disintegration. (The other root cause, as we
have seen, was the corruption of the people in the community;
cf. 5.1–5; 6.7, 19; 9.2–9 [Heb. vv. 1–8]). The priests, not knowing
Yahweh, had involved the community in meaningless sacrifice
(cf. 6.20) and the wise men had falsified the divine torah (cf. 8.8f.),
so both groups were part of the problem rather than the way to
resolve the community's problems. The prophets were equally part
of the problem. In a number of places the tradition includes them
in the enumeration of the corrupt elements in the community's
leadership. The prophets prophesy by Baal, i.e., either gain their
inspiration via baalistic techniques or prophesy in the name of Baal,
and in pursuit of worthless things reduce the worth of the community (2.8). They are also accused of being involved in the Canaanite nature cults, along with the kings, princes and priests (2.16).
In countenancing the corruption of the community, the prophets
have (falsely) reassured the people that Yahweh will not act against
such evil practices: 'He will do nothing; no evil will come upon us,
nor shall we see sword or famine' (5.12). Hence they are described
as 'wind' – 'the prophets will become wind' is a word-play on wind/
spirit (*rūaḥ*) (cf. Hos. 9.7 for the prophet as a man of the spirit,
'*îš hārūaḥ*) and accuses the prophets of being just wind (a Hebrew
equivalent to our windbag?) – and they will suffer precisely what
they said would not happen (5.13). The false prophesying of the
prophets is described as 'an appalling and horrible thing . . . in the
land' (5.30f.).[3]

The prophets are included in the general condemnation of the
community's corruption in the formal phrase 'from prophet to
priest' (6.13 = 8.10), which in its context probably means 'all the
leaders' (just as the other formal phrase in the verse, 'from the least
to the greatest', means 'everybody'). The repetition of the section
(6.13–15 = 8.10b–12), but in different contexts, indicates redactional activity and should be seen as a formal device concluding
sections which describe the hopeless state of the nation. In 6.9–12

the whole community will be punished and their houses, fields and wives given over to the invaders (then vv. 13–15 summarize the corruption of all the elements in society). In 8.8–10 it is the folly of the wise men which is singled out for comment, and their wives and fields will be given to the invaders (then vv. 10b–12 apply the general summary to the wise men, but retain the social criticism implicit in the statement). The section is probably better suited to its position in ch. 6 than in ch. 8, but in the latter case it does incorporate the wise men into the categories (prophet and priest) criticized. The charge against the prophets and the priests is false dealing: 'they have healed the wound of my people lightly, saying, "Peace, peace," when there is no peace' (6.14 = 8.11). It is a charge better made against the prophets than the priests, as it is the prophets who proclaimed the well-being of the community (cf. 4.10; 23.17). But the formal use of the piece as a redactional element has removed its specific meaning and given it a rhetorical function in the tradition.

The final two fragments for consideration are much more substantial pieces, and bear more directly on the subject of prophetic conflict in terms of making a contribution to the general discussion. They are 4.9f. and 14.13–16, and are both probably interpolations into their present contexts.

> In that day, says Yahweh, courage shall fail both king and princes; the priests shall be appalled and the prophets astounded. Then I said, 'Ah, Lord Yahweh, surely thou hast utterly deceived this people and Jerusalem, saying, "It shall be well with you"; whereas the sword has reached their very life.' (4.9f.)[4]

The coming destruction of Jerusalem will shatter the leadership which has blindly carried on without the slightest understanding of the real nature of the political changes taking place on the international level. The prophet (or the people according to a couple of Versions) sees in this shocked reaction to disaster the hand of God making the community blind to reality. The blindness is due to divine deception: 'you have completely deceived (*haššē' hiššē'tā*) this people' (for *nāšā'*, 'beguile', 'deceive', cf. Jer. 29.8; 37.9; 49.16; Gen. 3.13; Obad. 3, 7). Whether this statement should be interpreted as 'God permitted the community to be deceived by listening to its prophets' or 'God deliberately used the prophets to mislead the community' is difficult to determine because of its brevity. The notion of Yahweh using a lying spirit in the mouth of the prophets is one the deuteronomists used in the story of Micaiah in conflict with the court prophets (I Kings 22.13–23). The lying spirit (*rūaḥ šeqer* vv. 22f.) is sent by Yahweh to be in the mouths of the king's prophets in order to entice him (the word used in vv. 20, 21, 22 is *pātāh*, 'deceive', 'entice', 'seduce', 'persuade', the same word as in Jer. 20.7; Ezek. 14.9) to go to battle where he will meet his death. Even lies, deception, corruption and falseness serve the purposes of Yahweh and confirm the sovereignty of the divine word. That the deity might use false prophets or dreamers to tempt (test) the community into apostasy is a possibility recognized by the deuteronomists (cf. Deut. 13.1–3).[5] Ezek. 14.6–9 also admits that Yahweh may deceive a prophet in relation to an idolater and destroy both. From these examples it would appear to be the case that Jer. 4.9f. reflects deuteronomistic theology, and should be treated as an additional element in the tradition coming from its redactors, and designed to deal with the problem posed by false prophets in the community. The prophets misled the community into believing sword or famine would not come upon the nation (cf. 5.12; 14.15) and in this false security the nation perished. It is an explanation which makes a virtue of necessity, but is not in fact used in the bulk of material on prophetic conflict in Jeremiah (it is notably absent from 23.9–40; chs. 27–29). Hence it must come from sources outside the mainstream arguments in the Jeremiah tradition and should be attributed to the deuteronomistic redactors. It is simply there in 4.10 and is neither used again nor developed in the rest of the Jeremiah tradition.

The liturgy dealing with the drought (14.1–15.4) is interrupted in a number of places by the redactors, and one such interruption is constituted by a piece criticizing the prophets (14.13–16). Its position here may be accounted for by the occurrence of the threat made by Yahweh in 14.12: 'but I will consume them by the sword, by famine, and by pestilence.' To which the prophet replies: 'Ah, Lord Yahweh, look, the prophets say to them, "You shall not see the sword, nor shall you have famine, but I will give you assured peace in this place" ' (14.13). So here we have the essential distinction between Jeremiah and the other prophets as presented by the tradition. Jeremiah warns the nation that sword, famine and pestilence are coming (cf. 15.4; 21.7, 9; 27.8; 38.2), whereas the other prophets are going about the land assuring the nation that sword and famine will not come, but that Yahweh will give the people true peace (*š*lōm *'*met).[6] The central motif of the other prophets' preaching certainly seems to have been peace (*šālōm*), to judge by the number of allusions to the term in the tradition: the prophets

say, 'It shall be well with you' (*šālōm yihyeh lākem* 4.10); 'they
have healed the wound of my people lightly, saying, "Peace, Peace,"
when there is no peace' (*šālōm šālōm w^e'ēn šālōm*, 6.14 =
8.11); they say 'It shall be well with you' (*šālōm yihyeh lākem*,
23.17). The battle line is drawn around this motif. Peace (or well-
being of the community) is proclaimed by the court prophets whose
function it is to encourage the king and his counsellors in their task
of providing firm political rule in the land. Against all their enemies
the prophets announced *in Yahweh's name* (cf. 14.13, where the 'I'
of '*I* will give you assured peace' is the deity speaking; 14.14; 23.25,
30f.) real peace in their time. The charge that the prophets were
prophesying by Baal (2.8, 26–28) is not made here. This feature of
the opposing prophets *all* speaking in Yahweh's name is one of the
most important and central issues in the problem created by
prophetic conflict. Prophets speaking in the name of other gods may
be dismissed without much argument (cf. Deut. 13.2), but the
prophet who announces 'Thus says Yahweh . . .' is a different
matter altogether.

The interpolated passage continues, using a number of themes
which are explicated more fully in the cycle of oracles in 23.9–40.
Here they are expressed very briefly:

> And Yahweh said to me: 'The prophets are prophesying lies
> (*šeqer*) *in my name*; I did not send them, nor did I command
> them or speak to them. They are prophesying to you a lying
> vision (*h^azōn šeqer*), worthless divination, and the deceit of their
> own minds. Therefore thus says Yahweh concerning the prophets
> who prophesy *in my name* although I did not send them, and who
> say, 'Sword and famine shall not come on this land': By sword
> and famine those prophets shall be consumed. And the people to
> whom they prophesy shall be cast out in the streets of Jerusalem,
> victims of famine and sword, with none to bury them – them,
> their wives, their sons, and their daughters. For I will pour out
> their wickedness upon them. (14.14–16)[7]

The deuteronomistic terminology of this section should not distract
attention from its resolution of the problem, which constitutes the
other central issue in the debate about criteria for determining the
authentic prophet. From the redactors' viewpoint the other prophets
are false because, in spite of preaching in the divine name, they
have not been sent by Yahweh, nor have they been commanded by
him nor has he spoken to them. The importance of these terms in
the call narratives of prophets has already been stressed in the

chapter on the call of Jeremiah (cf. 1.4–10, especially the elements of divine sending, speaking and commanding in that section). That is the negative side of these prophets. On the positive side they prophesy *lies* in the divine name, lies which come from their own deceitful minds. What they have to say is made up of their own words, which are worthless divinations. From the vantage point of hindsight, such an analysis is very convincing, but that is precisely the problem. The falseness of these prophets is apparent to anybody who holds a different view of prophecy or who analyses the political situation differently from them or who is looking back on the fate of Jerusalem from the exilic period. *Now* it is clear who was right and who was wrong but now is too late! That is the problem with this analysis – it does not help determine which prophet is true and which false at the time when both are speaking in the divine name but offering different visions of the future. Jeremiah says that terrible trouble is coming (doom and gloom), other prophets say that a wonderful time of divine salvation and peace is coming. Who is to be believed? Who has made the right analysis of the conditions prevailing at the time of speaking? How does what is said relate to the dominant ideology current in the community? Because it is *not* obvious to the audience which prophet is speaking lies from the deceit of his own mind, and which prophet is really speaking the divine word (assuming one is and the other is not, rather than that both are not), the judgment made by the redactors (through hindsight and out of their own ideology) is not available to the audience. It is a matter of shared norms and values – norms and values which were still being constructed by the deuteronomistic circles when Judah was plunged into the Babylonian crisis which destroyed its independent existence as a state.

This brief analysis of the fragments relating to prophetic conflict in the early chapters of Jeremiah has isolated two of the most important issues in the current debate about authenticity in prophecy. The lines of the arguments in the Jeremiah tradition also have been picked out in these fragments. For the deuteronomists, with their heavy emphasis on the divine word as mediated by the prophets, the débâcle of the exile required reflection and explanation, and they saw in the activity of the prophets of the period one of the chief causes of the community's failure to change its course. They were also concerned with creating a framework of reference which would provide norms and values for the exilic community (and all future communities) and which would deal with the problem of prophetic conflict. In their redaction of the Jeremiah material they built into their presentation of the *true* prophet at work a significant number of features bearing on the subject of the prophet in society. It had not been obvious to the community which experienced the fall of Jerusalem which prophet was true and which false (it is in the nature of the case that such determining factors are usually not apparent at the time when they are required), but a society constructed on deuteronomistic principles would be in a much better position to make such judgments. That was part of the task the deuteronomists set themselves in creating the book of Jeremiah.

The cycle of oracles concerning the prophets

The organization of the Jeremiah material into sequences of related themes is a marked feature of the redaction of the Jeremiah tradition. In 23.9–40, following the sequence of texts on the kings, there is a cycle of oracles entitled 'concerning the prophets' (*lann^{e}bi'im*).[8] The cycle is made up of poetic and prose pieces, not all of which directly relate to the prophets (e.g., vv. 9–12 are a soliloquy about the state of Jerusalem with only a passing reference to the prophets; vv. 33–40 are a prose expansion of a prophetic saying in v. 32). The focus on the prophets of the cycle is in vv. 13–32, where poetry and prose sections set out a number of attacks on the prophets. The value of the cycle is the contribution it makes to determining the redactors' views on what distinguishes the genuine from the false prophet. As with so many of the collections of oracles in the Jeremiah tradition, no dates or circumstances are provided for the occasions on which these oracles were preached, so it is not possible to relate them to specific events, reigns or disputes in the life of Jeremiah. Most commentators regard the oracles as genuine utterances of Jeremiah with little or no evidence of deuteronomistic editing.[9]

Jer. 23.9–12. The introductory oracle describes the prophet's emotional and mental state over the condition of the community. He is like a drunk because of Yahweh's words. The land is full of adulterers (v. 10; cf. 'they are all adulterers', Hos. 7.4), though whether adultery here refers to sexual practices or illicit cults, whose evil way of life has corrupted the territory, is a moot point.[10] Priest and prophet are godless, and their godlessness has been discovered in the temple (this particular statement in v. 11 is spoken by Yahweh himself, *n^e'um yhwh*). This may be a reference to pagan cults in the temple (cf. II Kings 23.7), in which case the 'adultery' of the passage is involvement in the Canaanite rituals of the fertility cult. For slippery paths (*ḥᵃlaqlaqqōt* v. 12) as a mode of divine punishment cf. Pss. 35.6; 73.18.

Jer. 23.13–15. The oracle here does focus on the prophets exclusively and relates the corruption of the community to their actions and attitudes. The prophets of Samaria had led Israel astray by prophesying by Baal (v. 13; cf. 2.8). Such a charge in contrast to that made against the prophets of Jerusalem suggests that the reference to prophesying by Baal in 2.8 is to the Israelite prophets rather than the Judaean prophets (this would fit the context, though as 2.4 indicates the charge is a very general – and introductory – one and intended to apply, in general terms, to Israel and Judah). In 23.13–15 the point of referring to the northern prophets is to provide a contrast with the southern prophets. The Samarian prophets were bad but the Judaean prophets are worse.

> But in the prophets of Jerusalem
>   I have seen a horrible thing:
> they commit adultery and walk in lies;
>   they strengthen the hands of evildoers,
>   so that no one turns (*lᵉbiltī-šābū*) from his wickedness;
> all of them have become like Sodom to me,
>   and its inhabitants like Gomorrah. (23.14)

The main thrust of this statement is the accusation against the prophets of being the source of encouragement for the community's corruption. Hence the statement in v. 15b: 'for from the prophets of Jerusalem ungodliness has gone forth into all the land'. An exaggeration no doubt, but it conveys well the emotions of the charge: the corruption of the community has been led, encouraged and deepened by the behaviour of the prophets. The meaning of the sentence 'committing adultery and working in falsehood' (v. 14b) is not clear. As in v. 10, it may refer to involvement in pagan cults and maintenance of the false views about the nation's security criticized elsewhere in the Jeremiah tradition, though some commentators think literal immorality is referred to here (cf. 29.23).[11] In that case the charge might be: by committing adultery themselves the prophets encourage others to maintain their adulterous relationships. They thereby strengthen the hands of evildoers (cf. 38.4 for the opposite metaphor of 'weakening the hands'). Implicit in this interpretation is the notion that the prophets ought to have been exemplars of morality for the community. The reference to Sodom and Gomorrah (v. 14) is presumably to the community ('all of them' and 'its inhabitants' must then refer to the 'evildoers' rather than the prophets) and reflects a popular tendency in the prophetic traditions to use the names of the famous cities of the plains (cf. Gen. 19.1–29) as a metaphor for the judgment of Yahweh (cf. Amos 4.11; Isa. 1.9; 13.19; Jer. 49.18; 50.40; Zeph. 2.9; also Lam. 4.6; Deut. 29.23 [Heb. v. 22]) and as a metaphor for the corrupt Jerusalem community (cf. Isa. 1.10; 3.9; Ezek. 16.46–56; Deut. 32.32; the use of the metaphor sometimes is limited to referring to Sodom, but its meaning is not changed by such an omission of Gomorrah).

The word of judgment against these prophets is:

> Behold, I will feed them with wormwood,
>   and give them poisoned water to drink;
> for from the prophets of Jerusalem
>   ungodliness has gone forth into all the land. (23.15)

Wormwood (*la⁽ᵃ⁾nāh*)[12] is a bitter substance, and is used in Amos to describe what the community has turned righteousness and justice into (Amos 5.7; 6.12), and in the Jeremiah tradition to designate the judgment of Yahweh as a bitter thing (Jer. 9.14; 23.15; cf. Lam. 3.15, 19). It is the prophets who corrupted the community, who will be poisoned by the divine judgment. As idolatry is described in Deut. 29.18 (Heb. v. 17) as 'a root bearing poisonous and bitter fruit' (*rōʾš wᵉla⁽ᵃ⁾nāh*), there might be a reflection of the crime in the punishment (if idolatry is the charge of adultery made against the prophets). In this oracle the well-being of the community is made the responsibility of the prophets, so their profaneness has corrupted the nation and they must be punished for such corruption. This view of the prophets is most likely a deuteronomistic one, as that was the circle which valued prophecy as a community factor most highly. Motifs of profanation and comparison between Israel and Judah found in 23.13–15 (cf. 23.11) are also to be found in Jer. 3.1, 9. Idolatry (under the figure of adultery) profanes the land (makes it godless); the prophets by their behaviour (idolatrous?) have profaned the land and so will experience the bitterness of their idolatrous ways (cf. Deut. 29.18) and be destroyed by Yahweh's judgment.

Jer. 23.16f. The proper division of the next section is probably vv. 16–22, but the mixture of poetry and prose in vv. 16–17 war-

rants a brief treatment of them in isolation from what follows. The
RSV puts v. 16 in prosaic form: 'Thus says Yahweh of hosts: "Do
not listen to the words of the prophets who prophesy to you, filling
you with vain hopes; they speak visions of their own minds, not
from the mouth of Yahweh." ' It might be rendered strophically:

> (Thus says Yahweh of hosts)
> Do not listen to the words of the prophets,[13]
> They are deluding you.
> They speak the vision of their own minds,
> Not from the mouth of Yahweh.

The meaning of the verse is quite clear. The prophets who address
the community use only their own visions, not words given them
by Yahweh. These self-induced visions delude (the verbal form
mahbilim means 'become vain') the community, just as idolatry
deludes the nation; the noun *hebel* (Qoheleth's word) is used in the
Jeremiah tradition to dismiss idolatrous practices (e.g. Jer. 2.5;
8.19; 10.3, 8, 15 [v. 15 = 51.18]; 14.22; 16.19). The delusions of
the prophets constitute another form of idolatry in the community.
In v. 17 there is evidence of deuteronomistic redactional influence:
the phrase in 17a, 'it shall be well with you' is identical with a
phrase in 4.10, and in 17b the phrase 'no evil shall come upon you'
is virtually the same as a phrase in 5.12 ('us' for 'you'). The phrase
'the stubbornness of his mind' (*šᵉrirūt libbō*) reflects the idiom
'stubbornness of the mind' (*šᵉrirūt lēb*) used frequently in the
Jeremiah tradition (cf. 3.17; 7.24; 9.14 [Heb. v. 13]; 11.8; 13.10;
16.12; 18.12; 23.17). It may be a deuteronomistic term
(cf. Deut. 29.19 [Heb. v. 18]) which has been used almost exclusively in the editing of the book of Jeremiah.[14] The charges against
the prophets in vv. 16f. are: filling the people with empty hopes,
speaking visions out of their own minds, encouraging those who
despise Yahweh's word and reassuring the wayward. These last two
elements are the equivalent of 'strengthening the hands of evildoers'
in v. 14.

Jer. 23.18-22. The attack turns in these verses to consider the
relation of the prophets to the divine council (vv. 18, 22).

> For who among them[15] has stood in the council of Yahweh
>   to perceive and to hear his word,
>   or who has given heed to his word and listened? (23.18)

As the MT stands the question is a more general one than this.

'Who has stood in the council of Yahweh?' It could be understood as a rhetorical question with an implicit 'no one' as the answer. However, in view of v. 22 the question is probably directed against the prophets and, in question form, accuses them of never having had access to the divine council chamber where all the important decisions about the fate of human communities are made. John Bright thinks the question should be understood as: 'Who is it that has stood in Yahweh's council? How can you tell him?'[16] Taken this way, the verse contributes to making a definite distinction between the prophets and Jeremiah. The true prophet (in this instance, Jeremiah) is the one who has stood in the divine council, and the false prophet is the one who has not had access to that august body. How do you know which prophet has stood in the council? Of course the deuteronomists knew who the genuine prophet was, so the discussion is really about the negative features of the other prophets. In Jeremiah's time (as history proved) the prophet with access to the council was the one proclaiming destruction and gloom.

> Behold, the storm of Yahweh!
> Wrath has gone forth,
> a whirling tempest;
> it will burst upon the head of the wicked.
> The anger of Yahweh will not turn back
> until he has executed and accomplished
> the intents of his mind.
> In the latter days you will understand it clearly. (23.19f.)

The vision of Yahweh's storm bursting upon the wicked community is what access to the council reveals, and those prophets whose work does not consist of preaching such a disastrous outburst of divine anger have clearly not stood in the council. These two verses also appear in 30.23f., but are more suited to the context here in ch. 23 than in ch. 30. The two occurrences of the same piece in the tradition point to redactional activity, and the editors may have put vv. 19f. in here in order to spell out the significance of being party to the council's decisions. If the prophets had had access to the council they would have known what was on the agenda for the community and would have acted accordingly. Their ignorance of the true nature of the community's condition and future was proof that they had no such access.

After spelling out the information which could only have been acquired by having participated in the divine council, the redactors

return to the implications of the absence of the prophets from the
council.

> I did not send the prophets,
>   yet they ran;
> I did not speak to them,
>   yet they prophesied.
> But if they had stood in my council,
>   then they would have proclaimed my words to my people,
> and they would have turned them from their evil way,
>   and from the evil of their doings. (23.21f.)

The charges in v. 21, that the prophets were not sent by Yahweh
nor did he speak to them, appear in 14.14. Had the prophets stood
in Yahweh's council, they would have had his words to speak to the
people and would have been sent by him. Evidence of possessing
the divine words would be their turning (*šūb*) the people from evil.
The motif of turning from evil is a deuteronomistic one
(cf. I Kings 13.33; II Kings 17.13) and is used in the redaction of
the Jeremiah tradition (cf. Jer. 18.11; 25.5; 26.3; 35.15; 36.3, 7).
For the deuteronomists the call to turn from evil is the mark of the
genuine prophet: 'Yet Yahweh warned Israel and Judah by every
prophet and every seer, saying, "Turn from your evil ways and
keep my commandments and my statutes, in accordance with all
the law which I commanded your fathers, and which I sent to you
by my servants the prophets" ' (II Kings 17.13). By this standard
the prophets were false; Jeremiah, on the other hand, as the redaction presents him (cf. 7.3–7; 18.11; 25.5f.; 26.3; 36.3), constantly
sought to turn the community from its evil ways. Throughout the
traditions influenced or redacted by the deuteronomists the prophets
are presented in Yahwistic terms as 'my servants the prophets'.[17]
Occasionally in the deuteronomistic history other prophets appear
(cf. I Kings 22), but they are invariably presented as in conflict with
the genuine Yahwistic prophet. This clash of prophets is particularly
dominant in the Jeremiah tradition: the references to Yahweh's
servants the prophets (e.g. Jer. 7.25; 25.4; 26.5; 29.19; 35.15; 44.4)
should be contrasted with the wide range of references to the other
prophets, of which the bulk appear in 23.9–40; 27–29 (Ezek. 13.1–
14.11 is the only other area where there are a number of statements
about such prophets). That the exilic traditions of Jeremiah and
Ezekiel are the two foci of the material on prophets against prophets
(the motif of prophetic conflict only appears occasionally in the

other traditions) is a pointer to the problem of prophecy in the period just before the collapse of the Judaean state.

The statement in 23.22b is put very strongly: 'they would have turned them from their evil way, and from the evil of their doings'. The testimony of the whole deuteronomistic history is that in spite of the continual divine sending of the prophets and their constant call to the nation to repent of its evil ways, neither Israel nor Judah ever actually repented. The destruction of Israel in 721 and Judah in 587 were ample evidence of the failure of the long history of genuine prophetic preaching. Only Jer. 26.19 knows of a prophet persuading a king to entreat Yahweh to repent of threatened evil and only the Chronicler knows of a king seeking Yahweh's favour (i.e., Manasseh, and that without prophetic assistance, II Chron. 33.10–13). The singular failure of all the prophets, including Jeremiah, to persuade the communities addressed to change their ways is a remarkable comment on their incompetence. Perhaps part of their defence is (though not stated in the traditions) the incredible effectiveness of the other prophets' preaching. The tradition about the long history of the communities' refusal to listen to the prophets is part of the deuteronomistic view of history. The prophets were faithful in their preaching of repentance, but the communities of Israel and Judah were more effectively unfaithful in their disobedience and so were destroyed by the divine wrath. It is therefore rather hard on the prophets criticized in 23.9–32 that they should be accused of failing to turn the people when the genuine prophets failed to achieve that turning too. Both sets of prophets, true and false, achieved the same result. The summary of Jeremiah's first twenty-three years of preaching includes the notice that he singularly failed to change the people's attitudes (Jer. 25.3–7). Now given the fact that all the prophets failed to change the people (whether because they did not try to turn the nation or tried and failed), what kind of criterion is having stood in the divine council for determining the genuine prophet of Yahweh?

The problem goes still deeper. We have already noted the motif of the divine deception of prophets (cf. Jer. 4.10; Ezek. 14.9; Deut. 13.3; I Kings 22.19–23). Such a motif complicates the matter by introducing the notion of Yahweh sending false prophets whose task it may be to deceive the people and bring about their destruction (cf. Isa. 6.9f.). The sons of Eli refused to listen to their father's restraining advice against their evil ways 'because Yahweh desired (*ḥāfēṣ*) to kill them' (I Sam. 2.25).[18] Yahweh's will cannot be thwarted, even by repentance, so individuals, communities or nations may go to destruction if he wills it so. Such is the biblical doctrine of divine sovereignty and, though prophetic and deuteronomistic tendencies may have overvalued the notion of repentance, in the end nothing could prevent the terrible destructive forces annihilating man and beast. Micaiah's vision of the lying spirit sent by Yahweh into the mouths of the king's prophets, in order to entice the king into battle and so to his death, shows how deadly access to the divine council can be. The decrees handed down from that council are final, and all a prophet may do when so commissioned is to inform the community of its impending destruction (hence the account given in Isa. 6.9–13 in the light of the exile). The true prophets announced the destruction of the nation, the other prophets assisted in making that announcement come true:

> Your prophets have seen for you
>   false and deceptive visions;
> they have not exposed your iniquity
>   to restore your fortunes,
> but have seen for you oracles
>   false and misleading. (Lam. 2.14)

In the light of the failure of the genuine prophets to turn the people from destruction (i.e., in practical terms, to persuade them to adopt different political policies) and the refusal of the other prophets to challenge the people to change at all, how may Jer. 23.22 be used as a criterion of authenticity? Some would modify it to mean: the genuine prophet is the one who preaches repentance and *tries* to turn the nation from its evil ways. This is the slippery slope down to the death by a thousand qualifications, but it is necessary to slide down it a little if the criterion is to be retained in any sense as a criterion. The modification has become necessary in the light of the performance of the genuine prophets rather than because of the other prophets. It is perhaps a symptom of the bias or prejudice of the redactors against the other prophets that 23.22 should demand of them more than is demanded of the genuine prophets. Neither group prevented the disaster of the exile; the most that may be said in the defence of the deuteronomistic prophets is that they tried and failed. The lack of cogency in the argument from having access to the divine council typifies the enormous difficulties involved in producing a criteriology which would demonstrate the authenticity of one group of prophets and the falseness of another group.[19] The deuteronomists had cast-iron proof of which group was which, because they lived in the aftermath of the fall of Jerusalem and, gifted with hindsight, could clearly determine each by empirical means. For doing history the criteriology works very well, but for the more important task of determining the truth when it really matters (i.e., before the community is plunged into destruction) prophecy was a complete failure. No amount of editing the traditions could conceal that colossal failure.

The divine council motif appears in a number of traditions relating to the prophets and influenced by the deuteronomists.[20] The motif is essentially metaphoric, drawn from mythology and international court life. It is one of the biblical pictures of how the prophets receive the divine word and has elements of the messenger motif in it.[21] The prophet has access to this heavenly court, and may convey its decisions to the community or describe the vision (e.g. I Kings 22) or proclaim the message received (e.g. Isa. 6.8–13). It is but a way of speaking about the activities of the prophets, and should not be taken literally nor overemphasized in the interpretation of prophecy. The late dogma, 'surely the Lord Yahweh does nothing, without revealing his secret to his servants the prophets' (Amos 3.7), only asserts a belief about the prophets from within the framework of an already accepted belief system relating to prophecy. It has no authenticating factor outside that framework. The claim that only prophets who had access to such a council were true prophets, and knew what was going to happen in and to the community, could only be confirmed after the expectations had been realized. Thus the authentication of prophecy could only be a post hoc matter, as indeed it is in Jer. 23.22. Given the subsequent facts about the exile, Jeremiah was a true prophet, but, when he was alive and preaching to the community, whatever claims might be made about or by him were without substantiation. Therein lies part of the accounting for the failure of prophecy, and also what made prophecy so important in the life of the post-exilic community, when all the prophets were safely dead and their traditions in the process of being committed to writing.

Jer. 23.23–32. The final important section (vv. 33–40 are interesting but unimportant in this respect) for analysing the deuteronomists' criteria of inauthentic prophecy is essentially a prose passage with the occasional piece of poetry. The opening question (v. 23) is rather enigmatic: 'Am I a God at hand, says Yahweh, and not a God afar off?' Is this asserting that Yahweh is both near and far, or not near, only far? If the other two questions are taken in conjunction with it (v. 24), then it is an assertion of Yahweh's distance. The

sense of the questions is that Yahweh can see everything that is
going on (i.e., v. 25, 'I have heard what the prophets have
said . . .'). But this would be equally true if he were a deity who
was near. Perhaps the first question has to do with a view of the
deity among the prophets which saw Yahweh as a friendly god ready
to connive at their schemes and, opposing this belief, asserts the
distance of Yahweh.[22] General assertions among the commentators
that God is both immanent and transcendent may be true, but these
are theological clichés which add nothing to the argument. The
great distance between Yahweh and the prophets is such that their
activities will not be tolerated. God is not their pal. He is distant
yet sees all, fills all and is against the prophets.

In vv. 25–32 a series of prophetic activities is listed; these contribute to the deuteronomistic picture of what an inauthentic
prophet is like. The kind of prophet opposed by Yahweh uses
dreams (v. 25), prophesies lies out of the deceit of his own mind
(v. 26), causes the people of Yahweh to forget the divine name by
such dreams (v. 27; cf. Deut. 13.1–3), steals the divine word from
other prophets (v. 30), uses his tongue to say the correct formula
'says Yahweh' (*neʾum yhwh*, v. 31), and leads the people astray by
his lies and recklessness. Apart from the pejorative elements in that
list, there are one or two substantive issues raised which are worth
discussing briefly. The rejection of dreams is strange, because biblical religion has a place for dreams and associates a number of
heroic figures with important dreams: e.g., Jacob (Gen. 28.10–17;
31.10–13), Joseph (Gen. 37.5–20; 42.9), Solomon (I Kings 3.5–15),
Daniel (Dan. 7.1–15; he is described as having 'understanding in
all visions and dreams', 1.17), and in the future, when the divine
spirit is poured out on all flesh, the sons and daughters will prophesy, the old men will *dream dreams* and the young men see visions
(Joel 2.28 [Heb. 3.1]). Visions and dreams are the media appropriate to prophets (cf. Num. 12.6), though in some circles there
may have been a tendency to downgrade dreams and visions in
favour of the word (e.g., Num. 12.6–8; Deut. 13.1–3). The editors
of the Jeremiah tradition may reflect such circles, especially given
the influence of Moses as a paradigmatic model for the presentation
of Jeremiah.[23] Perhaps Jeremiah did not sleep well, so either he did
not dream or could never remember his dreams, but it is more likely
that the redactors wished to distinguish between the word and
dreams as one way of differentiating between the two kinds of
prophets in conflict. Given the dream as an important medium of
revelation (even in the New Testament, dreams, visions or trances

have a role to play in revealing the divine will, cf. Matt. 1.20–24;
27.19; Acts 10.1–8, 9–29; 16.9) in the religions of the ancient world,
it is odd that it should be rejected in the argument with the prophets,
but the polemical tone of the debate may account for this rejection
of one of the normal channels of divine revelation. The twentieth
century has reinstated the dream as an important aspect in understanding the human mind and its imaginative-creative powers (this
is particularly the case in Freudian psychology), so it is even odder
to contemplate this rejection of the dream as an important and
creative element in the output of a prophet. Some have regarded
the dismissal of dreams as a move from the irrational to the rational,[24] but, as prophecy is so determined by irrational and imaginative forces in man, such a view reduces the prophet to being
a philosopher and only half a person. The alternative modern view
of the behaviourists that 'the content of dreams may be totally
devoid of "meaning" ', being but assemblages of thought-elements
conveying no information whatsoever, mere noise, may appeal to
those who feel that the redactors of Jeremiah were correct to reject
the dreamers of dreams.[25] Coming from a period of prophetic conflict, when too many prophets were declaring too many different
things, the editors wished those with dreams to declare them *as*
dreams and not as the divine word, because, in the words of a
slightly later age (Zech. 10.2),

> the dreamers tell false dreams,
> and give empty consolation.

The stealing of the divine words from one another (v. 30) is an
enigmatic charge, because it asserts that the prophets do have the
divine word, but are stealing it from one another. Now throughout
the polemic so far, the main charge has been that the prophets do
not possess the divine word at all. Yet here they are charged with
stealing it from each other! How can that be? Perhaps the simplest
way to explain it would be to see it as a characteristic feature of
argument where opponents are accused of doing something and also
doing its opposite: 'you do not have the divine word' and 'you speak
the divine word which you have stolen'. Fairness and reason seldom
survive for long in heated arguments between bitter opponents, and
one of the strongest features of biblical arguments is the tendency
to abuse the opponent – in fact, abuse is more often used than
argument (cf. in particular the polemic against idols to be found in
the Psalms, Second Isaiah and the Jeremiah tradition, e.g., Jer. 10.
1–16). So any stick will do with which to beat the prophets. As the

background of the oracles is a period of intensive struggle between prophets during grave political crises, the sweet voice of reason (exemplified by Socrates) must not be expected among the practitioners of the mantic art. Fierce struggles, abusive onslaughts, *ad hominem* arguments and the hurling of whatever functioned in those days as the Hebrew equivalent of *Anathema sit* – such were (and always have been) the stock-in-trade of the accomplished polemicist. Given this structuring factor behind the oracles, the small details of the argument should not be too closely examined. The more significant charge is that of stealing each other's oracles. This presumably means that there was a tendency among the busy prophets to use each other's work without due acknowledgment of its source (infringement of copyright or, in academic terms, without the copious use of footnotes). Rather than work out their own oracles, waiting on inspiration, thought or whatever was required to produce such oracles, the unscrupulous prophets simply borrowed (pejorative description would call it stealing) the oracles of their fellow prophets and spoke them *as their own*. A despicable practice, but understandable, given the troubled times and the difficulty of always having to have fresh material. Even prophets can run out of inspiration.

What is more disturbing about the substance of the charge is the fact that few of the canonical prophets can be absolved of that charge if the present state of their traditions is taken at face value. The use of common oracles, quotations and sayings is to be found in all the major prophetic traditions (e.g., Isa. 2.2–4 = Micah 4.1–4; Amos 1.2; Jer. 25.30; Joel 3.16 [Heb. 4.16] all share the same element; similarities are to be found between Isa. 10.27b–32 and Micah 1.10–15; Isa. 5.8–10 and Micah 2.1–3; Jer. 49.7–22 and Obad. 1–9).[26] The strong influence of the language and ideas of Hosea on the Jeremiah tradition also indicates the difficulty of separating a speaker from his influences, and warrants a charitable estimate of what is original and what derivative. Perhaps the editors had in mind the more specious practice of people parroting other people's opinions and oracles because they are too superficial to have any ideas of their own and too shallow to be able to distinguish good from worthless ideas. Specific social practices of the period might have been in mind, but the more general charge is difficult to sustain against any prophet without upholding it against the major prophets as well. The reference to the prophets manipulating their tongues to say 'says Yahweh' (v. 31) suggests that it is the mimicry of authentic behaviour which the redactors deplore because it misleads the community into thinking 'here are real prophets'.

The lies, loose talk (*paḥᵃzūt* has the force of 'wantonness', 'extra-vagance', 'recklessness'), dreams, and mimicry of genuine ecstatic utterances, all contributed to deceiving the community and brought no benefit whatsoever to the nation (v. 32).

Included among the charges are a number of points which indicate the position of the speakers: 'What has straw in common with wheat? says Yahweh. Is not my word like fire, says Yahweh, and like a hammer which breaks the rock in pieces?' (vv. 29f.). The contrast between the word and the dream is analogous to the contrast between wheat and straw. Because the word of Yahweh is like fire, only what burns, destroys or refines can be the authentic word. Like a hammer the genuine word only smashes and destroys. Those prophets whose words do not burn and destroy are therefore (by definition) false. Such arguments are fine from the viewpoint of the word as fire and hammer or wheat to the others' straw. But such terms are not objective descriptions; they occur within a framework of reference which accepts the definitions without question. What if, on occasion, the word is not like fire or hammer? What if, under different circumstances, straw is needed? What about prophets like Second Isaiah, whose word did not function as fire or hammer? Indeed his image of the servant (Israel) is of one who 'will not cry or lift up his voice, or make it heard in the street; a bruised reed he will not break and a dimly burning wick he will not quench' (Isa. 42.2f.). What kind of prophet could legitimately cry out 'Com-fort, comfort my people, says your God. Speak tenderly to Jerusalem . . .' (Isa. 40.1f.)? Where is the fire or the hammer here? The framework of reference sets limits and outlaws by definition what under other circumstances can be the word of Yahweh. As such, the attacks on the prophets in the cycle of oracles do not constitute a criteriology of authentic prophecy, but indicate how such a cri-teriology might be constructed from within a given position. Accept the framework and the criteria operate adequately, but not to share the framework entails rejecting the criteria as underdetermining the problem of authenticity. From the deuteronomists' viewpoint pseu-doprophecy (cf. the Greek term *pseudoprophētēs* used in the Jere-miah tradition) was a pseudoproblem.[27] It was this because they knew it to be wrong, and therefore did not need to provide a criteriology demonstrating its falseness. Such a criteriology could only function historically as an account of the behaviour of prophets in the past and as a demonstration of what was false about them. History and hindsight had dismissed these prophets, but it was necessary to put certain arguments into the mouth of Jeremiah which would vindicate their theology and show him to have been a good, practising deuteronomist. Had the criteriology needed to be functional it would never have worked, because it could only demonstrate that it was true to those who already believed it (in this sense the tradition is preaching to the converted). The relativity of the positions isolated the participants from each other and allowed no common ground between them. The exile made the debate academic, and before the exile there was no telling (at least from the viewpoint of the audience) which view was correct. Only hindsight could provide an adequate criteriology, and such a validation theory is useless if the function of prophecy is to forewarn.

How could a member of a Jerusalem prophet's audience, listening to different accounts from different prophets about the immediate future of the community, tell which prophet (if any) was speaking the truth? The question is real rather than academic (in modern times it could be applied to political parties or ideologies to indicate the range of possible answers). If the evaluations in Jer. 23.9–32 are used as criteria, it must be remembered that they were constructed from the position (confirmed by the exile) that Jeremiah was the authentic prophet. The audience did not have that information, and when they did have it it did not matter any more, because the city was wrecked and the community destroyed. The community could not know that some of the prophets were lying. Indeed it is questionable whether any of them were lying. To lie is deliberately to state what one *knows* to be untrue. A prophet who is wrong or mistaken is not necessarily a lying prophet. To predicate lying of someone else requires evidence that they know that what they are saying is wrong. They may be wrong, but that is different from lying. The man who assures me that by the next decade Britain will once again have a dominant Liberal parliamentary party with a majority in the House of over three hundred may be an idiot, but he is hardly a liar. So the prophet who declared between 609 and 597 (or 597 and 587) that Yahweh would save his people, as he had in the time of the exodus or in the time of Hezekiah, could have been wrong, but to accuse him of lying is to be committed to an ideological notion of truth. Given the deuteronomistic ideology, of course he was lying – we speak the truth, our opponents lie! This is the language of ideological conflict, which substitutes abuse for argument and insult for understanding, but it only demonstrates the truth of assertions to those who already believe them. It is incapable of sustaining argument between different ideologies or parties because it is a closed system of thought.

My intention here is not to show that the prophets who disagreed with Jeremiah were right or innocent of folly, but to argue that the real problem of prophecy was the difficulty it had in convincing the community which view, among the many prophetic opinions on offer, was the analysis which would benefit the community the most. There was no authenticating criteriology available at the time the prophets were preaching, and so the community had to choose whichever view it thought was most likely to be right. They opted for the wrong view and the community was destroyed. That is too simple an analysis to be useful, but space does not permit a detailed argument which would show the reasonableness of the course the community followed.[28] The rage against the prophets, characteristic of the oracles in the Jeremiah tradition, indicates the impotence felt by the redactors that the community should follow such scoundrels. How could they not see what was going to happen? The destruction of Jerusalem was obvious after 587! Only a few thought it was obvious before then (just as only a few percipient people could see, *before* the team went to Argentina, that the Scotland football team would perform disastrously in the 1978 World Cup), but after the catastrophe it was plain how events had been developing. So, if the community did not foresee it, they must have been blind and vicious (the argument of the first half of the Jeremiah tradition) and/or misled completely by those who should have known better (the argument of the oracles and narratives against the kings and the prophets). The material in the cycle contains various attempts to account for the disaster, and if rage and emotion get the better of reason and argument, it is hardly surprising, given the collapse of city and community. Among the attempts to account for the destruction are the accusations against the prophets and the age-old sense of conspiracy compounded by betrayal, which has always demanded scapegoats and always found them. The oracles against the prophets should be seen in the light of these normal ideological reactions to disaster, and treated as standard sociological responses to the crisis in ideology brought about by the exile and the need to rebuild the community in closer harmony with the group's (i.e., the deuteronomists') belief system.[29] As such the accusations of immorality and deception can be understood as part of a complex argumentation within the group, designed to subsume the disaster of the exile under an ideology of prophecy which would make sense of the whole business without undermining the foundations of deuteronomistic theology.

Jer. 23.33–40. The final element in the cycle is a heavily worked
prose piece based on a pun in v. 33. 'When one of this people, or
a prophet, or a priest asks you, "What is the burden (*maśśā'*) of
Yahweh?" you shall say to them, "You are the burden (*maśśā'*),
and I will cast you off, says Yahweh." '[30] The word 'burden'
(*maśśā'*) is a technical term in the prophetic traditions for an
oracle (cf. Nahum 1.1; Hab. 1.1; Mal. 1.1), often an oracle of doom
and destruction. It is, perhaps, a weight given to the prophet by
Yahweh with instructions to pass it on to the nation. So when
anybody asks 'What is Yahweh's word/burden?', the reply is to be
'You!' and 'You are such a weight on him that he will throw you
off'. It is good, ironic prophetic word-play. But an unimaginative
commentator has developed the pun into a turgid piece of work on
the word *maśśā'*, using the word six times in vv. 34–38.[31] The gist
of the addition seems to be a prohibition against using the phrase
'the burden of Yahweh'. Nobody may ask a prophet 'What is the
burden of Yahweh?' They may ask 'What has Yahweh answered?'
or 'What has Yahweh spoken?' but they must not use the phrase
'the burden of Yahweh'. If they do they will be lifted up (*nś'*) and
cast out, people and city, and 'I will bring upon you everlasting
reproach and perpetual shame, which shall not be forgotten' (v. 40).
Such strength of feeling over the use of a phrase suggests some local
feud between prophets of which only traces are left in this oracle
(cf. Zech. 13.2–6).[32] Prophecy has disintegrated into warring factions, and this echo of battle has survived in the addition to the
cycle of oracles concerning the prophets.

The charges against the prophets in the cycle of oracles may be
summarized briefly as (1) some of them prophesied by Baal rather
than Yahweh (the Samarian prophets); (2) the prophets were of low
moral character; (3) they proclaimed peace rather than doom, and
thereby encouraged the community in vain hopes; (4) they had not
stood in Yahweh's council, so did not know what was going on; (5)
they were guilty of deception by using dreams, stealing each other's
oracles and aping genuine prophetic techniques. Being false people,
they were false prophets and led the community astray. In the
destruction of the city they would be swept away and their shame
would remain as a perpetual memory of the false prophets who had
helped to destroy the community. A number of these charges also
appear in the next section, on prophetic conflict, so they may be
dealt with there.

Jeremiah against the prophets

After Jehoiakim's death the Babylonians came up against Jerusalem
and besieged it. King Jehoiachin surrendered to them and was taken
captive to Babylon along with his chief officials and the city's
treasures, and the Babylonians installed his uncle Mattaniah, re-
named Zedekiah, in his place as king (II Kings 24.6–17). This
change of fortunes in Judaean politics led to opposing factions
quarrelling over whether allegiance should be given to the Babylonians or the Egyptians. Hostility against the Babylonians broke out
in the fourth year of Zedekiah's reign because of the pillage of
temple and court, and a wave of optimistic prophecies declared the
imminent return of the exiled king and the city's treasures.[33] Jeremiah, as a pro-Babylonian, is depicted in three narratives as responding to the national hysteria about an imminent return of the
exiles. The three narratives (Jer. 27–29) afford further insights into
the redactors' analysis of genuine prophecy and prophetic conflict.

Do not listen to the prophets (Jer. 27). The chapter has been edited
heavily by the deuteronomists and the MT is quite different from
the Greek version.[34] It describes the prophet's symbolic performance
with yoke-bars as a warning to Zedekiah against involvement with
the neighbouring states in a revolt against the Babylonians. Envoys
had been sent to Zedekiah from Edom, Moab, Ammon, Tyre and
Sidon to persuade him to revolt or to plan with him an agreed
strategy of revolt (v. 3). Jeremiah's performance is intended to dissuade Zedekiah from such revolt, because the Babylonian hegemony
is sanctioned by Yahweh (v. 6). To rebel against Nebuchadrezzar
is to rebel against Yahweh, incur his wrath and bring down destruction upon the nation (vv. 8, 10). To serve the Babylonians
(symbolized by submitting to wearing the yoke-bars) is to dwell
securely in one's own land (v. 11). This message is addressed to the
nations, to Zedekiah the king and to the priests and all the people.

The opposite message is coming from the prophets associated
with the court; they say 'You shall not serve the king of Babylon'
(v. 9). So it is a simple clash between prophets: Jeremiah proclaims,
'Serve the king of Babylon' and the other prophets announce, 'Do
not serve the king of Babylon'. The story reflects a political struggle,
and the purpose of the narration is stated a number of times: 'Do
not listen to the (your) prophets' (vv. 9, 14, 16, 17). The prophets
are denounced as diviners, dreamers, soothsayers, sorcerers (v. 9)
who are prophesying a lie (*šeqer*) to the community (v. 10). The

result of this deception will be the destruction of the community by
deportation (v. 10), sword, famine and pestilence (v. 13). These
prophets have not been sent to the community by Yahweh, but are
prophesying falsely in the divine name (*w^ehēm nibb^e'īm bišmī
laššāqer*, v. 15). It is a lie (*šeqer*) they are prophesying (v. 14),
and it can only lead to destruction for people and prophets. A
further account of the prophets' message relates it to more specific
topics (vv. 16–22): 'Behold, the vessels of Yahweh's house will now
shortly be brought back from Babylon' (v. 16). The word used for
'vessels' (*k^elē*) refers to the temple objects, valuable for their metal
content, which are listed in the MT as the pillars, the sea, the
stands, and the rest of the temple furnishings (v. 19;
cf. I Kings 7.15f., 23–26, 27–37). The return of the valuable objects
would have been a reversal of the Babylonian plundering of the
temple and the first stage of the hoped-for defeat of Babylon by
Yahweh (for the enthusiasm of nationalistic hopes for Babylon's
defeat see the oracles against the nations, Jer. 50–51; cf. Isa. 13–14;
47). This also is dismissed as a lie (*šeqer*). The prophetic advice is:
'Do not listen to them; serve the king of Babylon and live. Why
should this city become a desolation?' (v. 17). The section ends with
the threat that the vessels left in the temple by the Babylonians
(i.e., the pillars, the sea, the stands) will also be taken into captivity
and will not be brought back until Yahweh is prepared to restore
them (vv. 19–22). This statement is odd, in that it is highly unlikely
the Babylonians would have left such valuable material behind in
their first plundering of the temple.[35] The differentiation between
the vessels taken in v. 16 and those left in v. 19 (the Greek tradition
simply refers to 'the remaining vessels which the king of Babylon
did not take') is probably a later redactional attempt to introduce a
note anticipating the restoration of the people to Jerusalem (or even
an anticipation of rebuilding the temple).

The charges against the prophets already noted in the other oracles are again made in this narrative: the prophets are telling lies in
order to deceive the people, they are prophesying falsely in the
divine name, they have not been sent by Yahweh, and the net result
of all this deceitful posturing will be the destruction of the community. The repeated admonition 'do not listen to the words of the
prophets' (vv. 9, 14, 16, 17) indicates that the narrative is designed
to put a good deal of the blame for the Babylonian destruction of
the city on the prophets. It is because the king and his people
believed the lie which the soothsayers, diviners, sorcerers, dreamers
and prophets told them that the Babylonians returned and sacked

the city. Those prophets encouraged the community to believe that Yahweh would act soon against the king of Babylon, and in that false hope the community acted to its own destruction. The one feature in the polemic which is not to be found in the cycle of oracles is the suggestion in v. 18 that, if the prophets were really prophets and possessed Yahweh's word, they would 'intercede with Yahweh of hosts, that the vessels which are left in the house of Yahweh, in the house of the king of Judah, and in Jerusalem may not go to Babylon'. It is the motif of the prophet as intercessor on behalf of the city's welfare. If they were true prophets they would be seeking the well-being of the community and not encouraging it to get involved with the harebrained schemes of the neighbouring states to fight the Babylonians. It is a variation on the charge made in the earlier oracles that priest and prophet had healed the wound of the people too lightly, only here they are making too light of the danger posed by the might of Babylon. But the warnings against the folly of the prophets failed and, as v. 22 states, the temple vessels would go to Babylon and there await Yahweh's pleasure to return them to Jerusalem.

Jeremiah and Hananiah (Jer. 28). Associated with the general attack on the prophets for encouraging false hopes about the brevity of the Babylonian hegemony is a narrative which focuses on one such prophet and which presents Jeremiah in conflict with that prophet. The clash between Jeremiah and Hananiah is a narrative which has attracted much attention in recent discussion of prophetic conflict, because it clearly functions as a paradigm case for the deuteronomistic presentation of prophecy and its authentication.[36] All the texts so far have been concerned with Jeremiah against the prophets in general, but in ch. 28 one of the other prophets is introduced by name, Hananiah ben Azzur, both sides of the argument given and the sequel appended. It is as interesting and as unusual a feature of the prophetic traditions as is the account of the clash between Micaiah and the prophets, where one of them is named and contributes briefly to the discussion (i.e., Zedekiah ben Chenaanah, I Kings 22.24–25). Where the story of Jeremiah's conflict with Hananiah over the matter of the return of the temple vessels differs from the conflict of ch. 27 is the presentation of Jeremiah in the third person in ch. 28.[37] The redactor is an observer of the scene and presents the two prophets in discussion as representatives of the two opposing viewpoints. Hananiah is a preacher of well-being (*šālōm*) and Jeremiah a preacher of woe. Two ideologies are in conflict, and each has a spokesman who sets out the case for treating the question in hand in terms of that ideology. The common topic of concern is that raised in 27.16–22 – what about the temple objects plundered by the Babylonians? Will Yahweh return them soon? The discussion there is used by the redactors as a lead-in to the story of Jeremiah and Hananiah, which is a further treatment of the same debate. It is not, however, an academic report of a discussion between two prophets; it is a demonstration of an encounter between the true prophet and a prophet not sent by Yahweh. The Greek tradition makes this point even more clearly by referring to Hananiah *the false prophet* (*Ananias ho pseudopro-phētēs*), a term it also uses for the prophets referred to in chs. 27 and 29.

The prophet Hananiah declares the divine word in the temple in the presence of the priests and all the people:

> Thus says Yahweh of hosts, the God of Israel: I have broken the yoke of the king of Babylon. Within two years I will bring back to this place all the vessels of Yahweh's house, which Nebuchad-nezzar king of Babylon took away from this place and carried to Babylon. I will also bring back to this place Jeconiah the son of Jehoiakim, king of Judah, and all the exiles from Judah who went to Babylon, says Yahweh, for I will break the yoke of the king of Babylon. (28.2–4)[38]

It is essentially the prediction of the prophets discussed in the previous chapter, except that it adds a piece about the return of the exiled king (contrast Jer. 22.24–30). Its connection with the preceding chapter is also pointed, in that the breaking of the yoke motif is intended to reject the significance of Jeremiah's making and wearing yoke-bars. Hananiah accompanies his oracle with a symbolic gesture: he takes the yoke-bars from Jeremiah's neck and breaks them (v. 10), reiterating his message, 'Thus says Yahweh: Even so will I break the yoke of Nebuchadnezzar king of Babylon from the neck of all the nations within two years' (v. 11).

Jeremiah's reactions to this oracle are given in two stages. Firstly, he responds to Hananiah's statement with words of encouragement: 'Amen! May Yahweh do so; may Yahweh make the words which you have prophesied come true, and bring back to this place from Babylon the vessels of the house of Yahweh, and all the exiles' (v. 6). It is a most remarkable exchange between prophets in the biblical traditions. Normally two prophets could be expected to hurl abuse at each other and incorporate each other into their next oracles

of doom. Yet here Jeremiah expresses a hope that things will turn
out as Hananiah has predicted. Perhaps it is the intention of the
editors to show that Jeremiah really did care about the community
and wished it well. Jeremiah's reply continues with a statement of
the deuteronomistic view of prophecy:

> Yet hear now this word which I speak in your hearing and in the
> hearing of all the people. The prophets who preceded you and
> me from ancient times prophesied war, famine, and pestilence
> against many countries and great kingdoms. As for the prophet
> who prophesies peace, when the word of that prophet comes to
> pass, then it will be known that Yahweh has truly sent the
> prophet. (28.7–9)

So although he wishes Hananiah well with his prediction he does
point out that the general tradition of prophets has been to predict
'war, famine, and pestilence' (the Greek tradition limits it to 'concerning war').[39] That means that a prediction of well-being is unusual and therefore requires further corroboration, such as actual
fulfilment. This is an application of the rule in Deut. 18.21f., but
limited to positive predictions, where the deuteronomic text makes
it a general test of all predictions. So the community will have to
wait two years to find out if Hananiah has been speaking the word
of Yahweh or telling lies. This need for a waiting period to verify
the prediction is then incorporated into the story after the symbolic
gesture of breaking the yoke-bars.

Jeremiah goes away to think about Hananiah's prediction, and
'sometime after' (MT simply has 'after', v. 12) the word of Yahweh
comes to Jeremiah and denies the truth of Hananiah's prediction.
The *wooden* yoke-bars broken by Hananiah are to be replaced by
iron yoke-bars, indicating the inevitability and severity of the Babylonian hegemony (vv. 13f.). Then Jeremiah confronts Hananiah
with the declaration: 'Listen, Hananiah, Yahweh has not sent you,
and you have made this people trust in a lie' (v. 15), and, in accordance with Deut. 18.20, pronounces the divine death sentence on the
unfortunate prophet. 'Therefore thus says Yahweh: "Behold, I will
remove you from the face of the earth. This very year you shall die,
because you have uttered rebellion against Yahweh" ' (v. 16). The
account ends with the redactional note: 'In that same year, in the
seventh month, the prophet Hananiah died' (v. 17; for a similar
incident in the Ezekiel tradition cf. Ezek. 11.1–13). The prophet
whose prediction was false died and Jeremiah's prediction of his
death was confirmed, thus indicating that Jeremiah was a genuine

prophet on two scores: his predictions come to pass, and those predictions belong to the good old tradition of prophesying doom (cf. v. 8). The would-be peacemaker dies and the deuteronomistic paradigm of prophecy is complete.

The narrative is full of interesting insights into how the deuter-onomists viewed prophecy. On the basis of the datum that Jeremiah was a true prophet of Yahweh, it followed that all prophets who either opposed him or took a different view from his were false. Yahweh had not sent them (there is a nice word-play on 'sent' [*šlḥ*] in vv. 15, 16 – 'Yahweh has not sent you [*lō'-šᵉlaḥᵃkā*]' and 'I will remove you [*mᵉšallēḥᵃkā*, lit. "send you"]'), nor had he spoken to them, yet they went and spoke in his name, and this constituted rebellion against Yahweh. Such rebellion was punishable by death, so Hananiah the (false) prophet dies. Because the account is a paradigm case, the death is simply recorded and no public reaction to it is included in the narrative. It is an ideal account (ideal in the Weberian sense of existing only as an idea) rather than a historical record of a conflict between two prophets, and is intended to spell out in dramatic terms the nature of the prophetic task and the way an untrue prophet may be shown to be false. The starkness of the encounter between the two prophets illustrates that Semitic use of black and white categories (without any grey areas) already noted above in ch. 3. One prophet is true, the other false, and how the false one is detected is demonstrated in the account. What makes Hananiah's viewpoint a *lie* is not that he is lying but the fact that his view is false, and therefore, on a scale containing only black and white, the objective account (from the deuteronomists' subjective viewpoint made objective by hindsight) of his position is that it is a lie. If what made the other prophets false was their false lifestyle, in the case of Hananiah it is the failure of his prediction which falsifies him. How Jeremiah determined that Hananiah was wrong is not stated in the text. The interval between the encounter and Jeremiah's second response may have been spent in reflection, analy-sis and meditation, but we are not told. Eventually the divine word came to Jeremiah and he denounced Hananiah. Here the account adds a new dimension to the uncovering of false prophecy: the true prophet in the community stands as a source for the detection of untrue prophets because he has access to the divine word. It is analogous to the genuine prophet having stood in the divine council and therefore knowing what is going to happen (cf. 23.18–22). Be-cause Jeremiah, for the redactors, is the true prophet, he may also pronounce the death sentence on the false prophet (cf. the reversal of roles in I Kings 13.20–25). If the material in ch. 27 is concerned to blame the other prophets for the encouragement of the community in its revolt against Babylon, ch. 28 concretizes the discussion with a portrayal of one such prophet, but in order to set out a paradigm case of prophetic falsification, using the rules set out in Deut. 18.20–22.

Hananiah's statement in vv. 2–4 is couched in the language of the authentic oracle speaker and its theology is impeccably Yahwistic. It was, therefore, impossible for the audience to distinguish it from the utterance of a true prophet. However, the redactors' interest is not in audience participation or response (it is merely the context of the utterances, cf. vv. 1, 5), so the question which interests the modern reader – how could anybody listening to any of these prophets distinguish true from false? – is never broached. Writing from the context of the exile, the presenters of the Jeremiah tradition did not need to determine which prophets were true and which false; they already knew. Such knowledge was not available to the prophets' audiences, but we are not dealing with historical reconstruction in the tradition, so it is futile to try to use the material on the prophets to create a criteriology of prophetic validation. It represents ideological reconstruction and informs us about the deuteronomistic perspective on prophecy.

Jeremiah's counter to Hananiah's proclamation of divine restoration of temple objects and king is a deuteronomistic account of the prophetic tradition. That tradition consists of prophets prophesying 'war, famine, and pestilence' (v. 8; for this phrase as a leitmotif in the Jeremiah tradition cf. 16.4; 18.21; 21.7; 24.10; 27.13; 29.17f.; 38.2), so any prophet speaking outside that tradition requires further justification for his utterance. The only sufficient justification for such a departure from tradition is the fulfilment of the prediction. This deuteronomic criterion (Deut. 18.21f.) requires a period of time to elapse before the prophet can be deemed to be a genuine speaker of the word of Yahweh. Such a criterion presents a view of prophecy as a predictive activity to be checked against possible fulfilment and therefore as something which is retrospectively reacted to as true or false. It is a rather static view of prophecy, and does not see the prophet to be a speaker demanding immediate response from the community on questions of vital importance to its well-being. Of course the criterion can be limited to predictive statements, but it is a strangely narrow view of prophecy and one which fits the deuteronomistic movement towards producing canonic forms of torah governing the community, to which has been

added (hastily?) a brief, but inadequate, guideline for determining
authentic prophecy. The use of the criterion in Jer. 28.9 is limited
to predictions of a positive nature rather than all predictions in
general. Because there is a good deuteronomistic tradition of
doom-preaching prophets (from I Kings 13 onwards), it is unnecessary to provide criteria for such prophets. The use of the tradition
here is a concealed legitimation of Jeremiah as a traditional prophet,
standing in a long line of prophets prophesying war, and hints at
Hananiah being an innovator. There is nothing radically new or odd
in Jeremiah's preaching; it is the time-honoured role of a prophet
of doom. Hananiah, on the other hand, is engaged in something
unconventional and innovative and therefore must be subject to
more stringent checks. Those theologically inclined commentators
on the problem of false prophecy who have accused Hananiah of
being too tied to the old ways of Yahwistic theology and, unlike
Jeremiah, of being incapable of imagining Yahweh doing something
new, have completely misread the treatment of the matter in
Jer. 28.[40] The criterion of fulfilment may have a place also in the
presentation of the encounter, because the deuteronomists worked
with another model of prophecy as well, the prophets as Yahweh's
servants calling the community to the amendment of its ways (23.22;
cf. 7.3–7, 22–26; 18.11; 25.3–7; 29.19; 36.3). The preaching of
doom could carry (explicitly or implicitly) that call, so was not
subject to the fulfilment criterion in the same way as preaching
which had no such possibility of response built into it. Where the
community was not expected to change its ways, then it became
necessary to scrutinize the predictions by means of waiting for their
fulfilment. This explanation is not provided by the traditions, but
it would make sense of the limitation of the deuteronomic criterion
to positive oracles in the Hananiah story.

The subordination of the prophet to a tradition of prophets prophesying war (28.8) may have assisted the deuteronomists in their
production of a paradigmatic presentation of prophetic conflict, but
it does raise problems about the individuality of the prophets so
presented. The individual prophet's relation to and dependence
upon tradition is a very important aspect of the interpretation of
prophecy.[41] However, to allow tradition to determine the performance of a particular prophet is to limit that prophet's individuality
and spontaneity.[42] It is a failure to incorporate into the account of
prophecy the innovative elements in a prophet's work or to take
account sufficiently of the transformational aspects of a prophet's
activity. Prophets work within traditions, but also over against trad-

itions. There is a dialectical relationship between prophecy and tradition which can produce negation of some traditions, transformation of others and enhancement of still yet others. So the presentation of Jeremiah as a representative of a particular tradition of prophets, in order to legitimate his position against Hananiah's innovative stance, is an undialectical treatment of a complex issue by the deuteronomists. As an account of prophecy, the deuteronomistic approach is too simplistic, functional and inadequate. It is, however, concerned to present a canonical view of prophecy as a norm from which deviations must be thoroughly checked before they can be permitted as legitimate prophetic activities. The criterion which falsified Hananiah would also have falsified Second Isaiah, and that is an example of how inadequate the deuteronomistic view of prophecy is. But in the exilic period there was a movement in the production and editing of prophetic traditions which aimed at making certain collections authoritative and therefore normative (cf. Isa. 8.16–20).[43] An element of this movement can be seen in the presentation of the conflict between Jeremiah and Hananiah.

Jeremiah's letter to the exiles (Jer. 29). The narratives in Jer. 27–29 present Jeremiah speaking in general against a particular scheme of the prophets (ch. 27), in conflict with an individual prophet, Hananiah, over that scheme (ch. 28), and now in ch. 29 in conflict at a distance with the Judaean prophets exiled to Babylon over, presumably, the same issue. I am assuming the three narratives are all concerned with the one topic, though ch. 29 does not specify the issue of contention (it is probably implied by v. 28). The narrative in ch. 29 is disrupted by extraneous pieces which have been incorporated into it during the history of its transmission (e.g., vv. 16–20).[44] Heavy deuteronomistic editing is also evident in the letter (cf. vv. 10–14), and it is rather difficult to be certain about the precise contents of the letter (probably vv. 4–9, 15, 21–23). It is followed by material on the reception of and response to the letter which results in Jeremiah sending a second letter (vv. 24–32). In spite of the difficulties of sorting out what belongs where in the chapter, there is an underlying theme of prophetic conflict in it, which justifies its being linked with the other two chapters.

Jeremiah's concern in the letter is to assure the exiles that their exile will be a long one and therefore they should settle down to a normal life in Babylon (vv. 5f.). They should also seek the welfare (*šālōm*) of the city to which they have been exiled, because only in its well-being will they be able to live well (v. 7). This is one of the most remarkably irenic attitudes to foreign nations expressed anywhere in the Bible, and is in striking contrast to the usual oracle howling for the painful destruction of the enemy nations. The other important element in the letter is a warning against being deceived by the exiled prophets (vv. 8f.). If the letter is written to convince the exiles that it will be a long exile and that they must not be fooled by the prophets, who deceive with lies and dreams, then it is reasonable to assume that the prophetic deception concerns the length of the exile. The context provided by chs. 27, 28 strengthens that assumption, and the reaction of Shemaiah to the letter (vv. 24–28) confirms the argument in favour of seeing the conflict as one between prophets over the precise duration of the exile. Hananiah had suggested 'within two years', so clearly there was a feeling, if not a movement, among the exiles and also in the Jerusalem community, that the recent Babylonian intrusion into Judah (in 597) would soon be repulsed by Yahweh and the temple objects, the king, and the deportees restored to the homeland. It was not to be. So the redactors present Jeremiah as the spokesman for the opposing viewpoint (the viewpoint of history?) and focus a good deal of attention, through the three narrative blocks, on the issue. The real guilty men in the situation, which was having a most unsettling effect on the community and especially the exiles, were the prophets, notably Hananiah (though his death diminished his interest in the controversy). One curious feature of the material is the condemnation of Hananiah for making a prediction which would only have taken two years to verify or falsify, yet Jeremiah is represented as predicting a *seventy year* exile (v. 10; cf. 25.11f.) without any need for verification of such a safe prediction.[45] This contrast is a further illustration of the redactors' standpoint in relation to the two prophets.

The standard charges of prophesying a lie, dreaming dreams, deceiving the community and not being sent by Yahweh are all made against the prophets in 29.8f. Two prophets, Ahab ben Kolaiah and Zedekiah ben Maaseiah, are singled out in the letter for special comment (vv. 21–23). They are involved in the general deception of the exiles by speaking lying words in Yahweh's name, but they are also condemned for committing adultery with their neighbours' wives (it did not take the exiles long to settle down to normal civilized life in Babylon!), which practice is described as 'folly in Israel' (v. 23; for the term as a technical description of illicit sexual acts, cf. Gen. 34.7; Deut. 22.21; Judg. 19.23f.; 20.6, 10; II Sam. 13.2). As the consequence of their activities the two prophets will be killed by Nebuchadrezzar, so that the exiles will use as a curse the saying 'May Yahweh make you like Zedekiah and Ahab, whom the king of Babylon roasted in the fire' (v. 22; judging by Dan. 3, roasting people in the fire seems to have been one of Nebuchadrezzar's predilections!).[46] There may be elements of word-play in vv. 21f. in the terms 'ben Kolaiah' (*qōlāyāh*), 'curse' (*qᵉlālāh*), and 'roasted them' (*qālām*); if there are, then it is very much a case of gallows humour in the Bible. The charge of immorality here is not a reference to involvement in Canaanite religious practices but clearly refers to sexual neighbourliness. The prophets are condemned for it as well as for their lying words, but presumably the Babylonians burned them because of their seditious oracles.

The rest of the narrative is directed against Shemaiah of Nehelam (the dreamer? cf. 27.9; 29.8) who apparently did not like Jeremiah's letter, and wrote a few of his own to important people in the Jerusalem community (vv. 24–32). The text is confused, but the main points may be as follows: Shemaiah wrote to the priest in the temple in charge of prophesying madmen (v. 26; for *mᵉšuggāʿ*, 'madman', as a description of prophets, cf. Hos. 9.7; II Kings 9.11) demanding to know why he had not punished Jeremiah for prophesying a long exile for the deportees. The letter was read in the hearing of Jeremiah, who promptly arranged for a reply to be sent to Shemaiah. The reply consists of the usual condemnation of a prophet for not being sent by Yahweh and for causing the people to trust in a lie; punishment will follow.

The narrative therefore contains what now must be regarded as the standard deuteronomistic critique of the prophets, including the specific condemnation of named prophets (Ahab, Zedekiah, Shemaiah), and the continued presentation of Jeremiah as the true prophet and spokesman for the reality of a long exile because of a lengthy period of Babylonian domination. The redaction presents Jeremiah as a letter-writing prophet, exercising his prophetic ministry in Babylon as well as Judah (for the motif of a prophet communicating by letter see Elijah's letter to King Jehoram in II Chron. 21.12–15; it also must have been a very nasty letter to receive!). But his message remains the same, no matter where he is working: the scheme to revolt against the Babylonians is futile, and expectations that the deportees will soon be returning home are equally fanciful. Whatever the circumstances, the true prophet does not change his message but maintains it against all opposition. Further confirmation of the true prophet's status is afforded by the fate of his opponents (Hananiah's death and the roasting of Ahab and Zedekiah). Everything confirms Jeremiah as *the* prophet of Yahweh in the community.

The true prophet

It is an axiom of the redactors that Jeremiah is *the true prophet*, so the problem of criteriology does not arise for the tradition. Throughout the presentation he functions in opposition to lying, deceiving prophets, vicious and vacillating kings, obdurate princes and corrupt priests. The corollary of this view is the falseness of all who oppose him or who differ from him. That is the linchpin of the tradition, confirmed by the experience of the exile and necessary to the deuteronomists' handling of the material. The modern concern with a criteriology of validation which would allow any community to determine the truth or falsity of the prophets in its midst is not one shared by the deuteronomists. They already knew who the true prophet was, and working from that position constructed the accounts of his relationship with the other prophets, whom they knew to be false by definition. The gap between the shadowy figure behind the poetic oracles and the transparent form of the prophet in the narratives is to be explained by the redactors' construction of a true prophet to carry their account of prophecy. The deuteronomic rulings on prophets (Deut. 13.1–5; 18.15–22) may point in the direction of an inchoate criteriology (even used in places in the Jeremiah tradition), but the formulation of Moses as the greatest prophet (Deut. 34.10–12), and the development of Torah as the controlling system of thought and behaviour in the post-exilic community, prevented the need for a fully worked out criteriology. The repudiation of prophets in the later period (cf. Jer. 23.33–40; Zech. 13.2–6) assisted the controlling influence of Torah over prophecy, and the hardening of prophecy into a distinctive tradition (cf. Zech. 1.4–6; 7.7) tended to make past prophecy the bearer of the divine word, a process which helped to modulate the tensions between canonic Torah and the spontaneous outbursts of mantics in the community.[47]

The growing literature on the subject of prophetic conflict and the complicated nature of the issues involved in the discussion warrant a book-length treatment of the subject. However, within the limited space available here a few comments on the main features of recent discussions may be justified. There is general agreement among scholars that there are no objective criteria for distinguishing true from false prophets.[48] All the criteria which may be extrapolated

from biblical sources produce rules which would falsify even
prophets accepted in the traditions as true. Rules which outlaw
everybody are not useful rules for any society. For example, if the
preaching of repentance is the *sine qua non* of the true prophet
(cf. Jer. 23.22), then Second Isaiah and some of the cult prophets
in the traditions are false. The same applies to the rule about being
a prophet in the tradition of prophets prophesying war. The fulfilment of predictions is not a useful criterion because it would falsify
virtually all of the prophets in the traditions whose work contains
salvation oracles which had no fulfilment (i.e., the three major
traditions of Isaiah, Jeremiah, Ezekiel most notably). The immorality issue raised by Jer. 23.13–15; 29.21–23; is hardly more feasible,
in spite of the conventional view, 'You will know them by their
fruits' (cf. Matt. 7.16).[49] Such a rule may have some use in eliminating the grotesquely immoral from certain advisory positions:
e.g., one might not accept a dinner invitation from the Macbeths or
appreciate the advocacy of the sanctity of marriage by a much-
married Hollywood personality, but beyond this range of examples
it is difficult to formulate a persuasive case for excluding truth from
the statements of immoral people.

The immorality criterion takes us into the heart of one of the
major problems of the quest for a criteriology of validating prophecy. To what extent is the truth of a statement determined by the
lifestyle of its proponent? Can an immoral person (whatever may be
meant by immoral here must be left open to question) tell the truth?
The simple answers to these two questions are 'Not a lot' and 'Yes'.
To unpack these answers would require a complex series of examples
for discussion, but only a few questions can be posed here to indicate
the lines along which the discussion might proceed. Is the music of
Wagner bad because he was an antisemite? Must Frege's philosophical work be dismissed as false because he too was antisemitic? Are
the theological systems and insights of Tillich or Barth to be rejected
on the grounds that both men had relationships with women other
than their wives? Would you rather have your shoes mended by a
good cobbler or a good man? What about the view expressed by
some people: 'I would rather be operated on by a first-class Christian
who is a second-rate surgeon than by a first-class surgeon who is
not a Christian at all'? Given the number of first-class Jewish sur-
geons in modern surgery the last question sounds absurd, yet it is
a claim made by some people. No doubt there are connections
between people's lifestyles and the attitudes we may take towards
them, but that is not the point of this discussion. It concerns the

relationship between truth and lifestyle. In religious circles certain practices are considered to be bad form, and their indulgence by theologians is seen to be problematic.[50] The same attitude might apply to prophets, but it would not make what they say any the less true. The application of strict moral rules to the prophets would make some of the canonical prophets appear less than perfect, and that would have the effect yet again of producing a criterion which helped to falsify everybody.[51] The matter is even more complicated, because to set up norms of behaviour to which everybody must conform is also to miss the possibility that truth may come through breaches of those norms, or via people outside such norms. In the prophetic traditions this point is made strongly in the enigmatic story of the prophet and the man of God in I Kings 13.[52] The same 'crushing of truth by conformity' principle operates for the imposition of a tradition on the prophets: it not only kills the imagination, it outlaws the outsider and produces 'yes men' who always confirm the past and never disturb anybody. Both criteria constitute the castration of prophets, and this is a much more serious offence against prophecy than even the production of a criteriology (though perhaps it is only the logical outcome of such a criteriology).

If there is so much difficulty extrapolating a criteriology from the material in the Jeremiah tradition, and if the attainment of such a structure would be a bad thing, what then is going on in the traditions which may be analysed? A few comments may be warranted on this aspect of the subject as a way of concluding the discussion. The strong element of polemical opposition in the narratives is so evident that a sociological analysis is required to do justice to the material. The conflict between two groups of prophets displaying the intensity of opposition shown in the narratives indicates the strongly ideological nature of the deuteronomistic presentation. Ideology tends to make conflict fiercer, as analysts of social conflict have suggested:

> Conflicts in which the participants feel that they are merely the representatives of collectivities and groups, fighting not for self but only for the ideals of the group they represent, are likely to be more radical and merciless than those that are fought for personal reasons.[53]

Non-realistic conflicts also tend to be occasioned by the need for tension release, and require antagonists in order to exist rather than to resolve problems.[54] Prophetic conflict fits into this analysis of conflict quite well. The frustrations of the exile were partly alleviated by creating various targets on which to blame exile, and abusing them mercilessly. This would account for the failure to produce a criteriology from the material: it was not aimed at providing such a criteriology but designed to give vent to rage and to display the redactors' ideological views. Blaming the prophets for the exile, and showing how that exile could have been avoided if only the community had followed the ideology of the deuteronomists, are some of the intentions behind the production of the Jeremiah tradition and represent a very strong ideological position. As part of that ideological struggle the abuse of the other prophets was inevitable. Just as in a later period accusations of witchcraft characterized the political ideologies of Christian Europe, so in the exilic period accusations of being a false prophet were an effective means of countering opponents' claims.[55] The charge of immorality made against the prophets may be attributed to the same ideological strategy. Slogans hurled against opponents accusing them of adultery, deception, lying, dreaming, scheming falsehood, sorcery or divination are all excellent ways of discrediting opponents. The twentieth century has seen too much of 'guilt by accusation' manipulated as a weapon against others in ideological struggles (e.g., Stalin, Hitler, McCarthy have all demonstrated its power) to fail to recognize it when it occurs in other ages. How do you distinguish between prophets? You do not even try, you abuse, accuse and denounce. The presentation of the Pharisees in the gospels illustrates the principle sufficiently to show how effective a method it is for destroying the reputation of good men. Whether the prophets opposed in the Jeremiah were good men we will never know (Hananiah does not appear as a vicious man) because the dominant ideology has removed virtually every trace of what they were like and presented them as the conspirators who, by their deceit, lies and immorality, destroyed the people of God.

Some analyses of prophetic conflict have sided with the deuteronomists and have seen in the other prophets the manipulators of ideology in the sense of maintaining the current power structures. Thus, in Henri Mottu's analysis, Hananiah is a spokesman for the dominant royal ideology of power of the king's house and the rulers of Judah.[56] Mottu's treatment of the matter is a sensitive and extremely useful analysis, using Marxian and sociology of knowledge concepts and, in my opinion, contributes to advancing the discussion. However, a reading of Jer. 28 which carefully scrutinizes the text for ideological factors will find that they are virtually all coming from the deuteronomists and not from Hananiah. Not enough attention has been paid to the redactional construction of the account. It is a clash of ideologies, with one ideology providing a critique of a viewpoint (Hananiah's) which might be the output of an ideological position. It might not, and therefore the ideological element in the chapter may be the deuteronomistic one entirely. Ideology can, of course, function in a critical way, but in Jeremiah's encounter with Hananiah it is very much a case of the deuteronomists imposing their own ideology in terms of a paradigmatic account of prophecy. Detecting ideologies at work in the text is not a way of sorting out the prophets, though it is a way of producing a deeper analysis of the text.

Reading the extensive coverage of prophetic conflict in the Jeremiah tradition, one is reminded of Thoreau's observation made about the political climate of life in his own times: 'The spirit of sect and bigotry has planted its hoof amid the heavens.'[57] The conflict between prophets suggests such warring sects of opinion and grouping that the matter may in fact be a case of different groups bolstering their own identity by abusing their opponents. To be a false prophet is to be a member of a different prophetic guild. *Our* prophets are good, *their* prophets are bad. If a prophet is not 'one of ours' then he is, by definition, false. This is to view the prophets purely in social terms, rather like the supporters of the Rangers and Celtic football clubs of Glasgow. The sensible, intelligent person in Glasgow supports Partick Thistle, but the fanatics and hooligans support Rangers or Celtic. Nobody supports Rangers *and* Celtic. That is to state the matter in very simple terms. Yet social conflict can be described in such simple terms. To the supporter of one side the other side is inevitably and necessarily wrong. The Samaritan Chronicle illustrates the attitude very well in its description of the Judaean prophets as 'soothsayers, sorcerers, diviners', a description which covers the canonical prophets.[58] Of Jeremiah it says, 'In the thirteenth year of Josiah's reign he began to claim for himself that he was a prophet of the Lord, the god of Israel, but many of the people of Judah conspired against him, stoning him to death.'[59] However inaccurate or prejudiced that brief report may be, it epitomizes the attitude of a particular group to the heroes of an opposing group. There is no such thing as a prophet recognized by all groups, because prophets are very much figures within their own group and speak solely to that group. One group's prophet is another group's deceiver, just as one group's messiah may be another group's magician (or antichrist).[60] Some critics of this kind of religion might even go so far as to dismiss all prophets out of hand, agreeing with Bishop Butler's famous dismissal of certain types of religious experience: 'Sir, the pretending to extraordinary revelations and gifts of the Holy Ghost is a horrid thing – a very horrid thing.'

Horrid it may be, but there has been a long history of such claims (or pretensions), and the social historian or literary critic must deal with them sympathetically in order to understand them and to discover what they reveal about the communities in which they appear. For the deuteronomists the prophets were false and Jeremiah true. What had been needed between 609–587 was political cooperation with the empire, which became the norm after 520. Jeremiah epitomizes this attitude and so can be used by the redactors to construct their norms of prophecy. In some senses the only true prophet is a dead prophet, because then his work may be assessed and used to produce paradigms. Yet there is no criteriology available for prophecy; each generation must work that problem out for itself, or move away from a reliance on prophets towards a canonic notion of Torah, as Judaism was to do.

8

The Book of Consolation and the New Covenant

The book of Jeremiah has sufficient problems of interpretation to
warrant a series of books and commentaries on it, and one of the
more difficult issues is the relation of the salvation oracles to the
oracles of judgment in the tradition. The main concerns of the
tradition are with the poetic depiction of a corrupt society about to
be destroyed and the lengthy narratives intent on showing the
prophet representing the divine word in court and among the
prophets during the closing decades of the Judaean state. However,
there is a distinctive block of material made up of poems and
narratives which may be described justifiably as a book (cf. 30.2) of
consolation. These poems and stories set out a bright future for the
nation, a future of restoration and *permanent* salvation (for the note
of permanence cf. 31.36, 40; 33.18). City and palace will be rebuilt,
kingship restored with a Davidic figure on the throne, the land
reoccupied with justice and righteousness flourishing in it, levitical
priests permanently offering sacrifice, a new covenant between Yahweh and people and a reunification of the two nations. It is a dream
made up of all the elements of the past which disintegrated under
the onslaught of the Assyrians and the Babylonians. But it is a
dream at odds with the Jeremiah tradition of trenchant criticism
and condemnation of society. How is the realism of the critical
material, the acceptance of the destruction of city and community,
to be squared with the proclamation of permanent security in the
future?

One way of dealing with the problem would be to recognize no
integral connection between the Jeremiah behind the poetic oracles
of destruction and the oracles of salvation. The Jeremiah tradition
is simply the carrier of such oracles. They have been built into the
tradition by the redactors to bring it up to date with the development
of thought in their own time, and by being attributed to Jeremiah

they gained greater credibility. The figure of Jeremiah thereby legitimates the salvation element by underwriting it. It is an explanation which makes a good deal of sense and may well approximate to what really happened. However, there are a number of other ways in which the connections between the salvation material and Jeremiah can be made, and various suggestions have been advanced by scholars in recent studies.[1]

The alternation of judgment and salvation oracles is a feature of the prophetic traditions, especially the Isaiah tradition, so the problem is very much one related to the interpretation of prophecy in general. One approach is to deny the salvation elements to the original prophet and regard them as secondary features of the various traditions.[2] If, however, a dialectical account of prophecy is to be maintained, then there should be some connection between the different elements in the traditions, even if only to ground the possibility of some future for the community.[3] Thus an Amos might admit the remote possibility of divine favour (Amos 5.15), an Isaiah warn Assyria of future divine judgment (Isa. 10.15), a Hosea insist that Yahweh could not let his people be destroyed (Hos. 11.8f.). They might all be wrong, but the presence of such elements in their traditions provides grounds for later redactors and traditionists building upon their insights. To use metaphorical language: the prophets provided a few seeds which later gardeners supplemented with many more seeds, tending the seedlings and nurturing the gardens. It is all very vague, but, again, it is a reasonable hypothesis, and it does have the advantage of suggesting connections between the origins of the traditions and their later developments.

To apply this approach to the Jeremiah tradition is more difficult because of the very strong ideological features of the redaction. If, as seems most likely, the tradition was developed during the latter part of the exile, then the inclusion of a cycle of salvation oracles (some of them rather similar to the material in Second Isaiah) would reflect the growing hopes of restoration. To what extent the tradition was further developed after the fall of Babylon is not known, but some of the material may have been directed at the reconstruction of community life in Jerusalem (the new covenant perhaps). Whether the salvation oracles ought to be attributed to Jeremiah or not is partly dependent upon a number of framework arguments which I am not going to rehearse here. If the figure detected behind the poetic tradition of the judgment oracles is at all a reliable one (a very large if), then it is very difficult to see how a man who proclaimed judgment against all false senses and objects of security could subsequently with equanimity reinstate those objects within a permanent restoration of the community to its land. The climate of the salvation oracles would suffocate a Jeremiah, or send him into paroxysms of rage against such smug belief in the perfectibility of human society. Although sophisticated theological arguments may be advanced to show how only a Jeremiah could have authorized such hopes, and how the catastrophe of the exile radically altered his thinking on the matter, I suspect that the Jeremiah of the early oracles would have been appalled at the chauvinistic optimism of the salvation oracles.[4] The development of the tradition in particular directions dictated by the needs of the exilic community may have taken it further away from the position of the critical poet around whom it had been built.

To justify a dialectical account of prophecy, and also in order not to offer too negative a view of the salvation oracles in their association with Jeremiah, the following position will be taken in this chapter. On the basis of the call to return addressed to *Israel* in Jer. 3.12–14a, the early preaching of Jeremiah may have included promises of restoration to the remnants of the northern kingdom. It was the period of Assyrian decline, there were great hopes in some circles that Assyria would be crushed soon by Yahweh (see the late redaction of the Isaiah tradition in this period), and the prophet, heavily influenced by Hosea's language and thought, proclaimed expectations of restoration for Israel. Elements of such hopes are found in Jer. 31.2–6a, 16–20.[5] Of course the connection could be between the development of the Hosea tradition and its subsequent maintenance in deuteronomistic circles, using the Jeremiah tradition as its carrier. The interconnectedness of the Hosea and early Jeremiah traditions is such that it is very difficult to separate them out into their constituent strands. However, taking the influence of Hosea on Jeremiah to be a genuine part of the Jeremiah tradition, rather than an extension of the Hosea tradition, permits an element of salvation hope to be seen in Jeremiah's preaching. This might be no more than the view 'There is hope for your future, says Yahweh, and your children shall come back to their own country' (31.17), but it makes a connection between the early poetic Jeremiah and the later development of the tradition signified by the book of consolation. That connection may be explicated further. As it stands in the early preaching the word of hope is addressed to Israel rather than Judah. Israel had been dispersed for almost a century and could be considered to have expiated its offences by prolonged suffering at the hands of the Assyrians. As the

Assyrian empire declined, the expansionist policies of Josiah made the way clear for a restoration of Israel. Hence the call to return is directed to it. The inclusion of such oracles in the book of consolation is a redactional reapplication of them to the situation of Judah in the exile. The justification for such a reapplication is probably to be found in the view that the destruction and exile of Judah was analogous to the destruction and exile of Israel, so the same proclamation of restoration could be used to address the exiled nation. Such a reinterpretation of Jeremiah's oracles is paralleled in the tradition in the case of the 'foe from the north' cycle of oracles, which was probably originally proclaimed in a different context from its later reapplication to the Babylonians. Some of the oracles in the book of consolation may come from Jeremiah, even though their use in the tradition owes more to the traditionists. Such an explanation meets the demand for a connection between the origins of a tradition and the ways in which it may have developed.

There are a few elements of hope outside the book of consolation which may be worth noting briefly before we analyse the material in chs. 30–33. It should be emphasized at the outset of any analysis of the positive elements in the Jeremiah tradition that they do constitute a very small proportion of the tradition. About ten per cent of the book of Jeremiah may be said to be devoted to expressions of future hope for the community. That is not a very large amount of material, though it is large enough to warrant a separate chapter. In comparison to the positive elements in the Isaiah tradition, or even to the Ezekiel tradition, the Jeremiah tradition is rather poor in salvation oracles. That is to be expected, given the deuteronomistic redaction of Jeremiah, because the whole outlook of the deuteronomists, as displayed in their history of the kings of Israel and Judah (as well as in Deuteronomy), is a cautious, anxiety-ridden one. They hope and look for the future well-being of the community, but they are aware of the possibility that the community may not make the most of its opportunities. The salvation oracles are incorporated into the tradition and given some distinctively deuteronomistic features (e.g., the new covenant in 31.31–34), but the tradition as a whole is more obsessed with the causes and consequences of the exile than with grandiose schemes of restoration (unlike the Isaiah tradition).

Jer. 24. The vision of the two baskets of figs placed in front of the temple has a bearing on the hope motif in the tradition. One basket of figs is described as very good, and the other basket of figs as too rotten to eat (v. 3). The interpretation of the vision (vv. 4–10) makes the good figs representative of the deportees taken into exile by Nebuchadrezzar in 597. Yahweh will regard them as good, and wills for them a good future in which they will be restored to their own land (vv. 5f.). Not only will they return to their own land, but they will return to Yahweh also (v. 7), and so become his people. The bad figs, on the other hand, are representative of Zedekiah the king, his princes and the remnant of Jerusalem, who will be destroyed by sword, famine and pestilence (vv. 8–10). They will be exiled to many places and will become to other nations 'a reproach, a byword, a taunt, and a curse' (v. 9). It is a vision designed to replace the Jerusalem community associated with Zedekiah in Yahweh's affections with the exiles associated with Jeconiah, so it clearly emanates from that group.[6] Jeremiah is made to legitimate the exiles in Babylon, and not those who remained behind, as the true inheritors of the land (for a similar discussion cf. Ezek. 11.14–21). Although the chapter gives a brief statement of future hope for the exiles of the first deportation, the main intention of the passage is to praise the exiles and vilify the Jerusalem community. That is a motif already clearly established in the redaction of the poetic oracles of judgment, i.e., the presentation of the community as too wicked for words, only here the full significance of such a motif becomes clear – it is done in order to bolster the hopes of the exiles and to invalidate the claims of the Jerusalem community to divine approval (contrast Jer. 42.1–12).

The hopes of a future for the Davidic house (23.5f.) have been noted already, and they are too conventional a feature of the royal ideology to warrant detailed exegesis. The Jeremiah and Ezekiel traditions contain a number of such elements expressing confidence in the revival of the royal house, so it is fair to see in the motifs a persistence of belief in and hope for the monarchy throughout the exile and later.[7] Fragments of the belief in the restoration of the dispersed people are also to be found in 23.3, 7f. (vv. 7f. = 16.14f.), though it is highly unlikely that in the post-exilic period such returning exiles replaced the exodus motif with a return from dispersion motif in their confessional statements about Yahweh. The rise of Judaism was to see even greater emphasis on the exodus from Egypt due to the canonization of the Torah.

Jer. 29.10–14. The letter of Jeremiah to the exiles after the deportation of Jeconiah warning them of a protracted exile has been further developed in the redaction to include a note of hope for the exiles. The piece therefore bears on the future hope motif in the tradition. It is based on a divine promise to restore the community (v. 10), a promise for which there is no basis given in the tradition but which must have arisen out of this redaction of Jeremiah (applying the early oracles of restoration for Israel to the exiles in Babylon). The divine intention is one of well-being (*šālōm*) rather than evil in order 'to give you a future and a hope' (v. 11). As already seen in 24.7, the exilic community will seek Yahweh with all its mind and will find him (v. 13; the language is that of Deut. 4.29; cf. I Kings 8.46–53 for a much fuller exposition of the deuteronomistic principles involved). The promise of restoration in v. 14 (for *šūb š°būt*, 'restore the fortunes', cf. Deut. 30.3) reflects the later dispersion, and is not limited to the Babylonian exiles.[8] Perhaps the most interesting element in the addition to the letter is the reference to the length of the exile as 'seventy years' (v. 10).

The seventy years of exile. The statement about the duration of the exile is given in 29.10 and 25.11f. (cf. the three generations of Babylonian rule in 27.7). What makes it remarkable is the wide range of possible interpretations available for the phrase, rather than the fact that it looks clearly like a piece of writing from hindsight (what is usually called *vaticinium ex eventu*). Seventy could be a round figure without reference to a specific length, it could be the conventional figure for a life-span (cf. Ps. 90.10), or it could be a variation on the three generations of 27.7. If taken literally, it is a question of when the seventy-year period should be dated: from what event to when? Should the rise of Babylon as an empire be the starting point? From the fall of Nineveh in 612 to the fall of Babylon c. 539 yields just over seventy years. From the defeat of the Egyptians at Carchemish in 605 (also the year of Nebuchadrezzar's accession) to the fall of Babylon is just under seventy years. If related to the Judaeans, then there are a number of further possibilities: from the first deportation (597) to the edict of Cyrus (539) is about sixty years; from the fall of Jerusalem (587) to the rebuilding of the temple (c. 516) is seventy years; with a careful selection of starting and finishing points seventy years' duration can be contrived. The conventional nature of the figure seven may indicate a metaphorical, rather than a literal, understanding of the number. This seems to be the case with the Chronicler's interpretation of the exile as punishment related to the sabbath:

He took into exile in Babylon those who had escaped from the sword, and they became servants to him and to his sons until the establishment of the kingdom of Persia, to fulfil the word of Yahweh by the mouth of Jeremiah, *until the land had enjoyed its sabbaths. All the days that it lay desolate it kept sabbath, to fulfil seventy years.* (II Chron. 36.20f.)

Apart from seventy years being a term used to describe a period of divine judgment against a nation (cf. Isa. 23.15–18 for the seventy years during which Tyre will be forgotten, at the end of which it will return to playing the whore), there is evidence of similar numerical typology used by Assyrian scribes. An Esarhaddon inscription refers to a seventy-year period when Babylon shall be desolated:

Seventy years as the period of its (Babylon's) desolation he (Marduk) wrote . . . Until the time becomes full (malū) and the heart of the great lord Marduk shall become quiet and with the land which he punished he shall become reconciled (iršū salīmu), seventy years shall be completed (malū).[9]

The redactors of the Jeremiah tradition have used a conventional scribal element drawn from the world of the ancient Near East to indicate the wrath of the deity against their people. The fact that the duration of the exile can be made to fit into almost a seventy-year period complicates the interpretation by increasing the alternative possibilities for explanation, but the most reasonable approach to the motif is to treat it as a conventional figure for a period of divine judgment. Later traditions developed the seventy-year figure (cf. Zech. 1.12; 7.5; II Chron. 36.21; Dan. 9.2, 24–27), and the lunatic fringe of Christian sects, in the medieval and modern periods, has made it into a happy hunting ground.

The book of consolation

Technically the book of consolation consists of chs. 30–31 only. The narratives in chs. 32–33 include material on the positive future of the community, but they belong to the narrative redaction of the second part of the Jeremiah tradition. They are included in this section because of their positive content, but 30–31 are distinctive in being a collection of oracles, from discrete sources and different periods, designed to set out the future hopes for the community. The chapters have been linked together redactionally (30.1 = 32.1a; cf. 33.1), so that all the material is presented as the divine word mediated to the community through Jeremiah. Some of the linking elements in chs. 30–31 can be seen clearly: the book is to be written because 'days are coming' (30.3) when the fortunes of Israel and Judah will be restored (using the phrase *šûb š³bût*) – this motif of the coming days (*yāmim bā'im*), with variations of the phrase used, links a number of pieces. Sections introduced by the phrase 'days are coming' appear in 31.27–30, 31–34 and 38–40.[10] In 30.8 'in that day' (*bayyōm hahû'*) relates to 'that day' (*hayyōm hahû'*) in v. 7. The phrase 'at that time' (*bā'ēt hahî'*) in 31.1 has probably introduced or influenced the statement in 30.24, 'in the latter days (*b³'ah³rît hayyāmīm*) you will understand this'.[11] The oracles have been collected together because they mainly (there are some exceptions) focus on the future prosperity of the nation. This common focus makes it unnecessary to provide a detailed analysis of each oracle.[12] What follows will be a brief treatment of the material to show how the tradition has been developed to present Jeremiah as a major preacher of future salvation.

Jer. 30.1–4. A redactional introduction to the oracles which presents them as the contents of a book written by Jeremiah at Yahweh's command. A summary of the book's message is given in v. 3: 'For behold, days are coming, says Yahweh, when I will restore the fortunes of my people, Israel and Judah, says Yahweh, and I will bring them back to the land which I gave to their fathers, and they shall take possession of it.' The motif of the gift of the land to the fathers is probably deuteronomistic in this context (cf. Deut. 6.10, 23; 7.8; 8.1, 18; 9.5; 10.11; 11.9, 21). Verse 4 is the introduction to the complex which follows.

Jer. 30.5–7. Although the collection is intended to be a book of consolation, there are elements of a different kind of oracle contained in the anthology. These elements are to be found in 30.5–7 and 30.12–15 and are essentially the same kind of oracles as are found in the early collection of Jeremiah's poetry (cf. 8.18–22; 10.19–21; 14.17f.). In the earlier oracles the prophet is presented as weeping over the incurably wounded community. Here it is the community's lament over its state which is incorporated into the collection and edited together with a prose piece (vv. 8f.) which effectively transforms it into an expectation of salvation. The oracle depicts the community in a state of great pain, the men are clutching themselves and everyone is pale.[13] It is the day of Yahweh, a day of terror and panic (cf. Amos 5.18–20; Isa. 2.12–21; Zeph. 1.14–18), especially for Jacob. The last phrase 'yet he shall be saved from it'

(v. 7d) is a transition from the horror of the day of Yahweh to a piece promising salvation to Jacob.

Jer. 30.8f. A prose insertion anticipates the salvation oracle in vv. 10f. (originally introduced by the last clause in v. 7). It abrogates the dominion of the Babylonians over Judah and promises independent freedom for the community. The only sovereign they will serve 'in that day' will be Yahweh their God and David their king. It is an exilic piece coming from the circles which maintained future hope for the restoration of the Davidic monarchy (cf. the similar gloss on the Hosea tradition in Hos. 3.5; see also the Ezekiel tradition at 34.23f.; 37.24f.). For the motif of Yahweh breaking the yoke and bonds of foreign domination cf. Nahum 1.13.

Jer. 30.10f. These verses also appear in 46.27f., at the end of the oracles against Egypt (Greek omits them, as it often does for the repetition of a piece already used, in 36.9/12). Echoes of Second Isaiah (cf. Isa. 44.21; 45.4; 48.20) can be heard in this oracle, as might be expected in what is probably a priestly oracle announcing deliverance to the community.[14] There are also echoes of the Jeremiah tradition in the phrases 'for I am with you to save you' (v. 11; cf. 1.8; 15.20), 'I will not make a full end' (v. 11; cf. 4.27; 5.10), and 'chasten . . . in just measure' (v. 11; cf. 10.24). That the deity will punish Israel but not make a complete end of it is balanced by his complete destruction of all the nations (hence the appearance of this piece in the context of the oracles against the nations in 46.28). Salvation for Israel, destruction for the nations – that is the way the Jeremiah tradition developed away from the views of Jeremiah on the nation and the nations. The priestly oracle has transformed the early oracle into a later statement of deliverance. Talk about the day of Yahweh as a day of judgment against Judah (as developed by the Amos tradition against Israel) does not feature significantly in the Jeremiah tradition, though there are references to 'the day of slaughter' (12.3) and 'the day of their calamity' (18.17). The more conventional day of Yahweh language (i.e., Yahweh's day, so referred to, as the day when Israel's enemies are to be wiped out by Yahweh) appears in the oracles against the nations (against Egypt in 46.10, 21; and against Philistia in 47.4).[15] So 30.7, expanded by vv. 8f., should be seen as a modification of the original oracle describing Judah's bitter condition, by means of the conventional view of the day of Yahweh as a time of suffering for the nation's enemies.

Jer. 30.12–17. The first part of this piece (vv. 12–15) uses the language normally associated with Jeremiah's genuine oracles (cf. 8.18–22; 10.19–21; 14.17f.) to describe the incurable state of the community. The motif of sickness or wounding as a metaphor for the terrible state of the nation has already been noted as a feature of the prophetic traditions (cf. Hos. 5.13; Isa. 1.6; Micah 1.9). In this oracle Yahweh is the nation's enemy (cf. Isa. 63.10) and the other peoples are described as the nation's lovers (v. 14; cf. 3.1f.; 22.20–22; Lam. 1.19). Then in vv. 16f. there is a sudden and sharp transition from an oracle of lament to a proclamation of salvation for the community accompanied by destruction of the enemy. Here the enemy is identified as the national foes, rather than Yahweh. Without insisting that the prophets were rigid practitioners of Aristotelian logic, we can still see, in the switch from Yahweh as enemy destroying the community to Yahweh the defender of the community against the enemies destroying it, a movement from one speaker to another, both using rather different conceptions to describe what is going on and speaking at different periods of time. The promise of the restoration of the community's health in v. 17a is also to be found in 33.6a (cf. Isa. 30.26).

Jer. 30.18–22. A further piece promising restoration of Israel, in particular the city (presumably Jerusalem) and royal palace, population increase and the establishment of the religious assembly. The terms used suggest that it is from a hand later than Jeremiah, and so belongs to the exilic (or conceivably the post-exilic) period when hopes for the future tended to focus on the institutions of the past. The restoration of the nation's fortunes is a common motif in the salvation oracles (for *šūb š^ebūt* see Jer. 29.14; 30.3, 18; 31.23; 32.44; 33.7, 11, 26; cf. Lam. 2.14; Ezek. 16.53; 39.25; Deut. 30.3; Ps. 126.1; applied to the foreign nations it is used of Moab (Jer. 48.47), the Ammonites (Jer. 49.6), Elam (Jer. 49.39), and Egypt (Ezek. 29.14)). Again the motif of the punishment of the nation's enemies appears in this passage (v. 20). However, the reference to 'their congregation' (*^adātō*) in v. 20 uses a technical term which does not appear elsewhere in the Jeremiah tradition (the occurrence of *^edāh* in 6.18 indicates a textual distortion).[16] As the term is normally used by priestly writers (very rarely elsewhere cf. I Kings 8.5; 12.20), either the whole section or this verse should be attributed to priestly circles at work in the exilic or post-exilic period. The punishment (*pqd*) of the enemies (v. 20b) uses a term normally used in the Jeremiah tradition for the destruction of Judah (cf. 5.9, 29; 6.15 = 8.12; 9.9, 26 [Heb. vv. 8, 25]; 11.22; 14.10), though it is also used to describe the overthrow of the national enemies (cf. 25.12; 50.18, 31; 51.44, 47, 52) and to refer to Yahweh's gracious visits to individuals or the nation (cf. 15.15; 27.22; 29.10; 32.5). The move away from Jeremiah's application of the term to the nation's destruction to the more conventional one of the punishment of the nations confirms the view that the section belongs to the post-Jeremianic development of the tradition. In v. 21 the royal leader is presented as a 'prince' rather than as a 'king' (contrast 30.9; cf. 23.5); this leader (*mōšēl*) will come forth from the nation itself, rather than from a foreign source. Such an expression probably reflects a similar concern in Deut. 17.15, and some of the language suggests a common origin for the piece with the oracle in Micah. 5.2–4 (Heb. vv. 1–3).[17] A priestly role seems to be posited for the ruler in v. 21b. The section is completed with the redactional addition of v. 22, 'and you shall be my people, and I will be your God' (LXX omits). As the couplet appears in various places in the Jeremiah tradition, it may represent the final stages of the redaction (cf. 7.23; 11.4; 24.7; 31.33; 32.38), though it is possible that its intrusive position here (the change of person, 'you' for 'their', is awkward) may be no more than the glossing of the tradition by a pious hand.

Jer. 30.23f. The presence here of a piece already encountered at 23.19f. indicates the freedom with which the redactors shifted pieces around to build up the tradition, but why it should appear here is rather difficult to explain. It is arguable that the piece is as out of place in 23.19f. as here, but it is used here along with 31.1 to hint at the future restoration of Israel in spite of the present context of divine anger.

Jer. 31.2–6. This is generally regarded by scholars as a genuine oracle of Jeremiah. There is some discussion as to whether it should be dated to the early period of his preaching (i.e., the time of Josiah) or to the latest period (i.e., during the governorship of Gedaliah).[18] The strong influence of Hosea is evident, especially in vv. 2f. (cf. Hos. 9.10; 11.1, 2f., 8–11).[19] The thematic elements of return and rebuilding appear in the oracle and, as it is the northern kingdom which is addressed, it is probable that it was uttered during the period of Assyria's decline, when the possibility of Israel's restoration may have been an element in Josiah's expansionist plans. To bring the oracle up to date the redaction may have added v. 6b or modified the oracle so as to relate it to Judah's restoration hopes, though some have argued that as Gedaliah's centre was at Mizpah it might reflect cult movements of that period (cf. 41.5) and therefore be part of the original piece.

Jer. 31.7–9. This is a difficult oracle to analyse, as elements of Jeremiah's preaching to the northern exiles (cf. v.9b) are mixed with elements of the exilic hope for restoration from the land of the north. Some of these elements are to be found in the Isaiah tradition (cf. Isa. 35; 40.3–5, 11; 41.18–20; 42.16; 43.1–7; 44.3f.; 48.20f.; 49.9–13), though the motif of the return from the north also appears in the developed Jeremiah tradition (3.18; 16.15; 23.8; cf. 23.3; 32.37). The reference to the remnant of Israel in v. 7 is a positive one, indicative of the exilic context of the statement. In other parts of the Jeremiah tradition, 'remnant' refers to what is left of Judah-Jerusalem due to be destroyed (cf. 6.9; 15.9; 24.8) or, in the material often attributed to Baruch, to the survivors of the fall of Jerusalem who remained in Judah (cf. 40.15; 41.10, 16; 42.2, 15; 43.5, 44.28). Because the exilic group came to be identified with the remnant, a term designating the recipients of the future salvation, during the exile, the application of the divine deliverance to the remnant of Israel in v. 7b reflects the development of the remnant motif in the later exilic period. The restraint of the promised restoration in v. 8 should be noted, as it contrasts with numerous other statements which depict the return in more grandiose terms. The statement in v. 9, 'for I am a father to Israel, and Ephraim is my first-born' is possibly out of place in this oracle, though where it might have come from is disputed (some, e.g., Bright, would place it after vv. 2–6, others, e.g., Peake, after v. 20).

Jer. 31.10–14. Addressed to the nations and among the coastlands (v. 10; for a similar form of address to the nations and the earth cf. 6.18f.) this oracle has elements in common with the prophecies of Second Isaiah. The piece is hardly a unity, because in vv. 10–12 the deity appears in the third person but in vv. 13f. is in the first person. The motif of the shepherd in the Jeremiah tradition refers to the political leaders of the community (cf. 2.8; 6.3; 10.21; 12.10; 25.34–36); here, however, the shepherd is Yahweh. Such a metaphor for the deity is very common in the Psalms (too common to give exhaustive references, but cf. Pss. 23.1–3; 28.9; 80.1 [Heb. v. 2]; and numerous psalms which refer to the people as Yahweh's sheep) and also in Second Isaiah and other exilic writings (cf. Isa. 40.11; Ezek. 34.11–22; Micah 7.14). It would appear to be a metaphor much used in lyrical settings (hence its appearance in Jacob's very moving blessing of his grandchildren, which contains the line 'the God who has been my shepherd all my life long to this day', Gen. 48.15), so its occurrence in 31.10 probably reflects the cultic songs of the exilic period which looked forward to Yahweh's great shepherding of his people back to their own land. The terms 'ransom' (*pdh*) and 'redeem' (*g'l*) in v. 11 are not concepts used by Jeremiah, but are very common in Second Isaiah (cf. Isa. 43.1; 44.22–24; 48.20; 50.2; 51.10f.; 52.9). For the triple items 'the grain, the wine and the oil' (*dāgān tīroš yiṣhār*, v. 12) see Hos. 2.8, 22 (Heb. vv. 10, 24), Deut. 7.13; 11.14; 12.17; 14.23; 18.4. They are elements of the fertility of the land of Canaan associated with Yahweh's bountiful provision for his people, and indicate the exilic idealization of the homeland. The perspective of the oracle changes slightly with the change of person in vv. 13f., and divine promises are given which will make the community merry (with dancing and wine drinking, no doubt) and the priests well fed. In the transformation of the community's mourning into joy the deity will comfort them (*niḥamtīm*), a term usually used in the tradition to describe the deity's repentance or lack of it (cf. 4.28; 15.6; 18.8, 10; 20.16; 26.3, 13, 19; 42.10; also occasionally used of men, cf. 8.6; 16.7; 31.19); here it has more in common with Second Isaiah than the Jeremiah tradition (cf. Isa. 49.13; 51.3, 12; 52.9; see also Isa. 12.1; Zech. 1.17; Lam. 2.13). The final element in the oracle (v. 14) is a promise to the priests and the people of satiation with divine goodness. How ironic it is to see such approval of the priests in a tradition more noted for its trenchant and unending criticism of priests, but as the passage comes from a very late exilic period (or even post-exilic, as the phrase 'like a watered garden' (v. 12) may be derived from Isa. 58.11), it demonstrates how the transformation processes at work in the prophetic traditions could, on occasion, produce elements diametrically opposed to other elements in the traditions (cf. Ezek. 8–9 with Ezek. 44.9–16).

Jer. 31.15–20. Another oracle generally agreed to be from Jeremiah and related to the northern kingdom.[20] It may be dated to the same period as the oracle in 31.2–6 and probably represents Jeremiah's early preaching of hope for Israel. The introductory formula 'thus says Yahweh' in v. 15 may only indicate the beginning of a new section (so Bright) because the verse is better understood as a description of the community rather than a divine statement (that begins in v. 16 with the same formula). The image of Rachel weeping for her children is a graphic metaphor for the desolation of the community (cf. 20.14 for the reference to the community's [?] mother in a lament over bitter suffering). The ancestress of the nation (cf. Gen. 30.1–24) refuses to be comforted because of the loss of her children. So in vv. 16–20 the deity speaks and attempts to comfort her. The reassurance is modest: 'There is hope for your future, says Yahweh, and your children shall come back to their own country' (v. 17). What follows in vv. 18f. is probably a liturgy of repentance placed in the mouth of the people by the prophet (cf. 3.21–23; 14.7–9; see also Hos. 6.1–3; 14.2f.). The importance of the repentance motif in Jeremiah has already been stressed, and here is a good example of how the prophet is able to announce restoration because the community has repented. Yahweh's strong feelings for the nation are expressed in v. 20 and made the grounds for divine mercy.

Jer. 31.21f. A difficult piece to interpret, with v. 22b constituting perhaps the most incomprehensible saying in the whole book of Jeremiah. As vv. 15–20 refer to Ephraim and vv. 23–26 refer to Judah, vv. 21f. may be a redactional addition attempting a transition from one to the other. The exiles are called upon to return to their cities (*šûb* as a reference to journeying back rather than repentance?), having noted the route by which they went into exile – a figurative statement rather than a literal one. The change of gender (from son in v. 20 to virgin Israel in v. 21) indicates the redactional break in the sequence of vv. 15–20, 21f. Elements of vv. 21b, 22a are similar to 3.14, which is part of the secondary material in the tradition. However, the reference to 'highway' (*mᵉsillāh*) suggests a link between this piece and Second Isaiah, where the motif of the highway is an integral part of the restoration preaching (Isa. 40.3; 49.11; cf. Isa. 11.16; 19.23; 35.8). The reference to the divine creation of a new thing in v. 22b (*bārā'*, 'create', only used here in the Jeremiah tradition) also has links with the Second Isaiah tradition (*bārā'* is used frequently in Isa. 40–45; for the creation of new things see Isa. 48.6f.). The word-play on *šûb*: 'return . . . return' in v. 21b and 'faithless daughter' (*habbat haššōbēbāh*) in v. 22a is a feature of the Jeremiah tradition. If vv. 21–22a are a mixture of elements from circles associated with Second Isaiah and bits of the Jeremiah tradition producing a brief piece whose meaning is fairly clear, then v. 22b is quite different. The new thing created by Yahweh is described as 'a woman protects a man' (*nᵉqēbāh tᵉsōbēb gāber*) – whatever that may mean![21] The difficulties are created by the obscure meaning of the statement, finding a precise meaning for the verb and determining whether the line refers to men and women in a generic sense or is a figurative reference to the relationship between Yahweh (the man) and Israel (the woman).

Space does not permit a full consideration of the range of possibilities and suggestions available for the interpretation of the line, but a few points are worth making. Responsible scholarship can no longer dismiss the problem of meaning by rejecting, like George Adam Smith, the couplet as an exilic addition to the section.[22] Whether it be additional or part of the original piece does not exempt the modern commentator from having to explain (or attempt to explain) its meaning. The line is certainly not a gloss, because glosses have explanatory purposes and this line obscures more than it clarifies. The normal senses of the verb *sbb* include 'surround', 'encompass', 'enclose', 'march around', 'turn around'. Here the meaning may be 'to encompass (with protection)', though if referred to a reversal of the normal relations between men and women (i.e., the new thing is that a woman will protect a man) it is difficult to see how such a meaning fits the context of vv. 21–22a. If taken as an addition to vv. 21–22a, then it may be a saying (popular during the exile?) indicative of the radical reversal of fortunes in the future, of which women protecting men or courting men will be a divine sign.[23] In the future women will be supportive of men rather than the normal practice of men supporting women. The alternative interpretative approach is to take it with vv. 21–22a and treat it as a figurative statement about the relations between Yahweh and Israel. The faithless daughter (v. 22a) will become a supportive woman (v. 22b) and will turn to Yahweh instead of turning away from him.[24] Given the context provided by the piece and the setting of that piece within the book of consolation, an approach along these lines may be the most reasonable way to handle a difficult interpretative issue. But there are many different suggestions in the commentaries and I would not undervalue the newness of this special creation by advocating a simple answer to a complex problem. The commentators are agreed that there is no agreement about the meaning of the phrase, only guesses at what it might mean.[25] Such agnosticism will have to serve here by way of explaining v. 22b.

The approach taken by rhetorical criticism would see in 31.22b a conclusion to the collection in 30.5 – 31.22 formed by inclusio: the collection begins with 'man' (*geber*) in 30.6 and ends with 'man' (*geber*) in 31.22 (reinforced by the symmetry of 'male' [*zākār*, 30.6] and 'female' [*n^{e}qēbāh*, 31.22]).[26] What follows in 31.23–40 is most likely an appendix to the book of consolation, expanding the more positive elements in the collection. Such an expansion is probably warranted, because the material in 30.5 – 31.22 is by no means devoted entirely to hope and salvation. It is a mixed complex of judgment oracles modified by additional elements of hope and salvation pieces. Such a mixture means that the interpretation of any one element in the complex may be ambiguous, and the general impression of hope is gained by ignoring the details and focusing on certain aspects of the material. These aspects are developed in greater detail by the additional material in 31.23–40.

Jer. 31.23–26. This piece most likely comes from sources other than Jeremiah and probably was produced by a Judaean who looked forward to the restoration of Judah, its cities, its farmers and shepherds (v. 24; contrast 14.4). The reference to the temple mount in the lines quoted in v. 23b reflects a conventional cultic view of the city, emphasizing the temple complex (for a similar view cf. 17.12). It is highly unlikely that a prophet so critical of the nation's institutions as Jeremiah would have taken such a view of the city. The statement in v. 26 is most odd: 'Thereupon I awoke and looked, and my sleep was pleasant to me.'[27] It seems to suggest that the vision of a restored Judah (if not the whole complex of salvation material in chs. 30–31) was a dream, though whether a dream of the kind dismissed in 23.25–28 is more difficult to determine. It could be a dismissive comment of a sceptical annotator, whose remark has been incorporated into the tradition (another irony in the book of Jeremiah). Like 31.22b, it could be a citation of a well known song or saying, but without further information it is not possible to give an adequate explanation of its meaning here.

Jer. 31.27–30. One of a series of additions introduced by the phrase 'Behold, the days are coming . . . ' (cf. vv. 31, 38) and devoted to depicting the nature and extent of the divine restoration of the nation. This addition focuses on the theme of the repopulation of Judah and Israel (the Babylonian campaigns had depopulated the territory). The motifs of repopulation (cf. Ezek. 36.8–15; Hos. 1.10 [Heb. 2.1]; 2.23 [Heb. v. 25]) and reunion of Judah and Israel (cf. Jer. 3.18; 50.4; Isa. 11.11–14; Ezek. 37.15–28; Hos. 1.11 [Heb. 2.2]) are elements to be found in other prophetic traditions of the exilic period (contrast Zech. 11.7–14, which announces the disruption of the nations). The promise of building and planting in

v. 28 is a deuteronomistic element in the piece and reworks elements used throughout the tradition (cf. Jer. 1.10; 12.14–17; 18.7, 9; 24.6; 31.40; 42.10; 45.4). The popular proverb quoted in v. 29 is also to be found in Ezek. 18.2 (cf. Lam. 5.7). Its occurrence in the Ezekiel tradition is part of a very lengthy polemic against the popular use of the proverb (cf. Ezek. 14.13–20; 18.1–32), whereas in Jer. 31.29–30 the argument seems to be that in the future it will no longer apply, so presumably it applies in the period of its popular use. It echoes the popular account of theodicy: '*others* have sinned, *we* have suffered', but is used here to indicate a coming end to its applicability.

Jer. 31.35–37. Two brief pieces of poetry assert the eternal permanence of the restored nation. They argue, from the fixed permanence of nature (i.e., sun, moon, stars, sea), the immeasurability of the heavens, and the inaccessibility to exploration of the foundations of the earth, that the descendants of Israel will always be a nation protected by Yahweh (for a similar kind of argument see 33.20–26). In many ways this very strong nationalistic conviction is precisely the kind of belief opposed by the early oracles of Jeremiah the prophet. The irony of the developed tradition carrying views so antagonistic to his spirit should not be overlooked by the modern analyst of the book of Jeremiah.

Jer. 31.38–40. A brief extract celebrating the rebuilding of the walls of Jerusalem and the transformation of the accursed valley of Ben-hinnom (cf. 7.31f.; 19.2, 6; 32.35; II Kings 23.10) into an area sacred to Yahweh. Never again will the city be uprooted or overthrown. This is a nationalistic outlook from sources which had learned virtually nothing from the exilic experience.

The collection of chs. 30–31, with its mixture of pessimistic oracles, modest hopes for the future along conventional lines, and occasional fantasies about the future, is followed by a couple of chapters which develop the salvation expectations of the exiles further in the direction of the permanent restoration of the people to their own land. There is little in the material that requires major analysis as most of the themes have appeared already in chs. 30–31. The permanent covenant of 32.40 adds a detail to the new covenant of 31.31–34, and the divine covenant with the levitical priests of 33.21f. (cf. 33.18) spells out more fully the fragmentary references to priests already analysed. There is a much greater focus on David's descendants as occupants of the royal throne (33.14–26), but the expectation has been noted in the tradition already (cf. 23.5f.; 30.9). A dominant motif in ch. 33 is the divine promise 'I will restore their fortunes' (*šûb šᵉbût* with grammatical variations in vv. 7, 11, 26; also in 32.44). The purchase by Jeremiah of a field belonging to his family has been discussed above in the treatment of symbolic actions of the prophet (see ch. 5), so it is unnecessary to go over it again here. The narrative of the purchase has been expanded greatly in the redaction and now includes sections on the restoration of the exiles and the permanent covenant to be made with them (32.36–41, 42–44). Other relevant sections on salvation hopes for the future in the Jeremiah tradition can only be noted, as space does not permit the detailed analysis they may warrant. The sermon on sabbath observances leading to a permanent royal house in a city inhabited for ever (17.19–27), the commendation of the Rechabites for their fidelity to a teetotal policy with the promise of survival as a reward for such perseverance (ch. 35), Ebed-melech's reward of having his life as a prize of war for trusting Yahweh, by saving Jeremiah (38.7–13; 39.15–18), a similar reward to Baruch, though without any statement of why he should have his life as a prize of war during the impending destruction of the city (ch. 45): all these accounts posit salvation hopes for certain groups and individuals, and the sabbath observance sermon sets out a paradigm of possible salvation coming from the deuteronomists (for similar emphasis on the sabbath cf. Isa. 56.2–6; 58.13f.; Neh. 13.15–22). Trust in Yahweh or fidelity to past commitments or even loyalty to Jeremiah (and hence to the divine word) qualifies an individual or a group for survival in a period when to survive was everything. Like the priest who lived through the French Revolution, these individuals, if asked 'What did you do during the great catastrophe which befell Jerusalem?', could reply, 'I survived!' All things considered, that was some achievement!

The new covenant

I have isolated Jer. 31.31–34 for special consideration, not because it is of any particular importance in the tradition, but because for so many Christian commentators it is the high point of prophecy, if not of the whole Hebrew Bible. It is certainly an important passage for the New Testament, indeed it is probably responsible for the titular distinctions *Old* and *New* Testaments. Such terminological generalizations are essentially a Christian issue and have no bearing on the interpretation of the Jeremiah tradition (for the

importance of Jer. 31.31–34 in the New Testament cf. Heb. 8.8–
12; 10.16f.; the 'new covenant' is related to the last supper in
Luke 22.20; I Cor. 11.25). However, because the motif of a new
covenant is rated so highly by many Christian writers, there has
been a tendency among commentators to insist that the passage
comes from Jeremiah himself and is one of the mountain peaks of
the Bible. John Bright is even moved to write: 'As regards its
authenticity, one can only say that *it ought never to have been questioned.* Although the passage may not preserve the prophet's *ipsissima verba,* it represents what might well be considered the high
point of his theology. It is certainly one of the profoundest and most
moving passages in the entire Bible.'[28] It would be foolish to attempt
to list the scholars who have asserted its importance and authenticity, or to name those other scholars who have *argued* that it is
secondary and, possibly, not as important as many imagine.[29] A few
general remarks, however, are warranted on this controversial issue.
Whether it comes from Jeremiah, one of his followers or one of the
redactors does not affect its importance or lack of significance.
Granted that in religious contexts the authority issuing a statement
can contribute to the significance of that statement (e.g., the Pope
outranks everybody), but the meaning of texts is not changed by
regarding them as secondary. If the new covenant passage is a
fundamentally important concept, then it remains an important
concept no matter who penned it or when it was written. On the
other hand, if the concept is uninteresting and not very important
it hardly becomes vital by being attributed to somebody important.
It then becomes part of a great man's ephemera. The old practice
of dismissing as unimportant (or not warranting exposition) the
secondary material in the biblical traditions is on the wane, and a
more responsible attitude is beginning to be taken towards all the
elements in the text. This is a positive and welcome move in biblical
interpretation. It is equally important, however, that the recent
concern with the history of exegesis and interpretation of biblical
texts should not be allowed to read back into the text later developments in the interpretation of that text. From the Christian viewpoint the idea of a new covenant is a very important element in
early Christian thought, but that should not entail reading
Jer. 31.31–34 as if it were Jeremiah's plan for and approval of the
rise of Christianity. Within the context of the development of the
Jeremiah tradition there are other ways of handling the passage, and
to some of these I now turn.

Jer. 31.31–34. This is the second of a series of three appendices to the book of consolation (30.5–31.22) introduced by the phrase 'Behold, the days are coming' (31.27, 31, 38). They are all written in prose, have many elements alien to the Jeremianic core, and tend to include deuteronomistic phrasings. The reference to covenant in v. 31 immediately signals a close connection between this passage and the deuteronomistic redaction of the tradition (cf. 11.1–11; 34.8–22). The poetic oracles of Jeremiah do not contain any reference to the covenant, but use virtually every other description of the relationship between Yahweh and the nation (e.g., son, bride, wife, house, meadow, darling, vine, field, people, virgin, daughter) except covenant. Covenant is a term and a concept at home in the deuteronomistic writings and ideology.[30] Jeremiah is presented as a preacher of the covenant because, for the deuteronomists working during the exile, that is what he must have been, and so he is made to perform such a role. The sense of obligation built into the notion of covenant (obligation on the deity's part, cf. Ps. 74.20; 89.39 [Heb. v. 40]) could hardly have made it palatable to the prophets.[31] For Jeremiah, the only grounds for national deliverance is the return of the people to Yahweh; for the deuteronomists the answer lies in a *new* covenant. The old covenant had been broken, hence the catastrophe which befell Jerusalem. It was too late to go on pretending that that covenant still functioned adequately – the city was in ruins, the people dispersed and the covenant shattered. That is all conceded in this passage: '*not* like the covenant which I made with their fathers when I took them by the hand to bring them out of the land of Egypt, *my covenant which they broke*, though I was their husband, says Yahweh' (v. 32). Indeed, according to the deuteronomistic history, that covenant was broken with a regularity which almost beggars the imagination (cf. Judg. 2.1–3, 20; the preface to the deuteronomic work also focuses on the broken covenant as an event right at the beginning of the nation's escape from Egypt, Deut. 9.6–21). If ever an institution was created which was a complete failure from the beginning it must be the deuteronomistic covenant! Yet here in Jer. 31.31–34 the redactors are proposing yet another covenant, a new one. What a triumph of hope over experience! It is a good example of a certain kind of ideological thinking which, when in trouble, retreats to advocating the principle: 'If something has failed, what is required for its success is more of the same.' A few alterations and modifications will produce a new model and *that* will be an unprecedented success.

The inability of the deuteronomists to escape from thinking in

terms of making and implementing covenants has produced this
appendix to the collected material on the future hopes of and for
the community. The new element in this version of the covenant is
stated in v. 33: 'I will put my law (*tōrātī*) within them, and I will
write it upon their hearts; and I will be their God, and they shall be
my people.' It is the notion of internalization; the stipulations and
content of the divine torah will be internalized in the minds of the
people. Whereas the original version of the covenant had the conditions externalized in the form of inscribed stones, this version will
do without such objects. The effect of such an internalization move
will be: 'And no longer shall each man teach his neighbour and each
his brother, saying, "Know Yahweh," for they shall all know me,
from the least of them to the greatest, says Yahweh' (v. 34). A
further effect of such an arrangement will be the divine forgiveness
of the nation's sins. The only difference between the old and new
forms of the covenant would appear to be the internalization principle employed in the new covenant. The stipulations, effects and
purposes remain the same for both models. Presumably the deuteronomists felt that the only thing wrong with the constantly broken
covenant was the fact that its instructions were externalized in rules
and regulations which to be taught to the community by teachers
(priests who handled torah, cf. 2.8). If the teachers were corrupt or
ignorant, then the covenant failed because the community was not
taught properly (this point is not made in the text, but it does
furnish an argument in favour of internalizing the rules). So in the
future the people would automatically keep the covenantal regulations, only there would be no more teachers in the community.
Because everybody would already know Yahweh – 'know' in the
sense of 'be intimate with' Yahweh or the practice of justice?
(cf. 22.16) – there would be no need for religious teachers, and
because the community's sins had been forgiven already there would
be no more sinning and therefore no more sacrifice (again these
implications are not spelled out in the text, so it is not possible to
determine precisely what the deuteronomists envisaged or had in
mind).

    This analysis of the text in terms of its constituent elements raises
a number of interesting points, though they are not always discussed. Space is lacking for an adequate discussion of them here,
but a few are worth mentioning. I have stressed the effect of the
new covenant as abrogating the need for teachers in the community.
Yet the subsequent history of Judaism is shaped at many points by
formidable teachers, and the great rabbinic tradition is a teaching

one. Christianity, when it developed away from its Jewish roots, also produced an equally formidable tradition of teachers which contributed to the emergence of the magisterium of the church. In no sense can either of these religions be regarded as fulfilling (or being the fulfilment of) this passage (treating it as predictive, as befits its presentation). The singular lack of influence this motif of the new covenant has had on the development of Judaism either indicates how ineffectual the deuteronomistic advocacy of it was in the post-exilic period or suggests that it was intended to be a restatement of the old covenant in terms of future celebrations of the original exodus rituals (cf. 23.7f. for an equally mistaken notion of how the future will see the past). The tendency of some Protestant writers to see in the passage the first enunciation of the central principle of Protestantism, i.e., every man is his own priest and every man is his own prophet, is a misreading of the text.[32] The text rules out *teachers*, not intermediaries, priestly or prophetic. What it says is that every man will be his own teacher. Now given the rise of hermeneutic as a reformation phenomenon (Dilthey)[33] and the splendid systems of theological thought developed and *taught* by Martin Luther, John Calvin, Jonathan Edwards, Karl Barth and their followers (to name but a few), it would be completely untrue to say that Protestantism has been a religion in which every man knew God without the benefit of teachers. Of course if knowing Yahweh in the text means the practice of justice and righteousness, then there is no good reason to think that Christians (Protestant, Catholic or whatever) know (or have known in the past) God any better than Jews, Muslims or devotees of any other religion (or none for that matter).

There is an argument which would see in the passage about the new covenant a counsel of despair rather than the high point of biblical religion. This argument takes two forms: the first stresses the poverty of imagination which cannot conceive of anything better (or more radical) than yet another version of a failed system; the second defines the prophetic task in moral terms and sees in the new covenant a surrendering of the moral element in prophecy. I have noted already the failure of the covenant as described by the deuteronomists, and how the new covenant is more of the same but with the cracks papered over. Perhaps this is more folly than despair. Against this approach it could be countered that, as covenant belongs to the deuteronomistic circles which were active during the exile, the failure of the covenant was more theoretical than actual. As a regulative principle for writing the history of the nation, it retrojected into Israelite history a pattern of covenant-making as a way of theologizing that history. This was the deuteronomists' response to the failure of the state to survive the Babylonian attacks, and so for the future they posited a covenant also, but with some modifications to take into account the defects of the past.[34] The second form of the argument defines prophecy as a moral force in the community, seeking to persuade the people to turn (*šūb*) from present policies and ways of life to different and more effective forms of living.[35] There can be no deliverance for the community unless it changes its way of life. If Zion is to be redeemed, it is by the practice of justice and righteousness (cf. Isa. 1.27). This is part of the prophetic notion that knowledge of Yahweh means *doing* justice and righteousness, pleading the cause of widow and orphan, defending the oppressed and seeking good (these features are so basic to the prophets that references are hardly needed, but cf. Amos 5; Hos. 6.6; Isa. 1.16f.; 5.1–7; Micah 1–3; 6.6–8; Jer. 22.15–17). Without a change in the community's practices there could be no future for the people. That is how the onslaughts of the Assyrians and the Babylonians were interpreted by the prophets – as punishments for corruption, injustice, exploitation and oppression of the poor (cf. Isa. 3.13–15). Without repentance there was no future. So to encounter a passage in a prophetic book which promises a golden future and a new covenant without repentance, and which envisages a period when there will be no need for such moral change *by* the people because Yahweh will change them automatically, is to enter a world where the prophets have conceded defeat and have withdrawn from the moral struggle to persuade people to change their ways. If people will not change, then to hope for God to change them is to move from the moral sphere to piety and transcendentalism. It is in this sense that the motif of the new covenant is a counsel of despair *if* it is to be attributed to Jeremiah (contrast the role of repentance in restoration in Jer. 31.18–20).

This brief digression on the new covenant as counsel of despair has been necessary in order to demonstrate one very good argument for not attributing the new covenant passage to Jeremiah. There are other, even better, arguments for such non-attribution (e.g., the deuteronomistic style of the text or the coontrast between the passage and those poetic oracles generally agreed to be by Jeremiah), but this is an important one which is very seldom made in the commentaries and books on Jeremiah. The new covenant motif is not necessarily a counsel of despair, if it comes from sources which did not emphasize the importance of human action in the way the prophets had. It is the stress on the absolute necessity of human activity (e.g., repentance or the practice of justice) in the prophets which makes the terms of the new covenant a retreat from moral responsibility in the community. Those circles (in particular the deuteronomists) which preferred to think of the community in terms of Yahweh's initiating activity created the covenant motif to describe Israel's history in paradigmatic terms. For them the possibility of a new covenant could not be seen as a counsel of despair, but as one more opportunity for succeeding where so often the community had failed. The new covenant remains a triumph of hope over experience but at least attributing it to the deuteronomists saves it from also being a counsel of despair.

Christian commentators have tended to stress the individualism of the new covenant and to see in this singling out of the individual a major advance in religion initiated by Jeremiah. Individualism combined with inwardness of religion are the essential features of the new covenant in this interpretation of the matter. It needs to be emphasized, however, that the covenant is made 'with the house of Israel and the house of Judah' (v. 31) and not with individuals. It may internalize the content of the covenant within the minds of the individuals constituting the two communities, but this is not individualism, nor is it that essence of religion which the philosopher A. N. Whitehead defined as 'what a man does with his own solitariness'.[36] What is envisaged by the text remains essentially the core of the deuteronomistic view of community religion, except that it will be realized more effectively in the future.

Rudolf Bultmann has drawn attention to the difficulty caused by talk of a new covenant (Jer. 31.31–34; Ezek. 37.26–28) which asserts that *individuals* keeping the moral demands of God constitute the covenant between Yahweh and the *people* of Israel.[37] Bultmann rightly points out that such individual activity removes the covenant from the sphere of historical and empirical reality, because it is not made with a real nation which can keep its stipulations qua nation (an essential ingredient of the biblical notion of covenant) but is kept by individuals. This arrangement Bultmann calls 'an eschatological concept'. Whatever it may be termed, his analysis is an important exposure of defects in the concept of covenant, as well as a percipient treatment of the new covenant pericope. Reflection upon the idea of covenant will demonstrate the problem: 'How is the covenant to be kept by the community?' If understood in a moral way, then the question is about percentages: 'Must everybody in the community keep the rules in order to preserve the covenant unbroken?' Would one person stealing, killing, coveting or whatever break the covenant, or would fifty-one per cent have to indulge in such activities in order to produce a broken covenant? But covenant as a community mode of living cannot be structured in terms of what individuals do; the important thing is what the community as a whole does. Such communal actions are very limited and usually confined to ritual practices, which is why the primary narrative in the Bible presents the covenant-making account in Exodus 19–24 in conjunction with lengthy cultic regulations (indeed the story of Sinai is presented in liturgical terms and is essentially a cultic story). The way to keep the covenant is by communal observances capable of being practised by all responsible members of the community (e.g., circumcision, fasts and feasts, sacrifices, dietary rules etc.). Bultmann has made an important point, but ruined it with his use of the term 'eschatological'. In reality covenant is an abstract term, a metaphor for organizing the community. It must be kept (or broken) in equally metaphoric terms, and the vision of a new covenant in Jer. 31.31–34 should not be removed from the sphere of communal activity, but seen as a variation on the standard deuteronomistic presentation of life in the community constructed by the metaphor of covenant.

The various aspects of Christian interpretations of the new covenant analysed in the above paragraphs have been considered in order to clarify what the traditionists, who produced the new covenant pericope, may have had in mind when they incorporated their ideas about the future into the Jeremiah tradition. During the exilic period some circles saw hope for the future in a new, permanent covenant involving the whole community and including the Davidic king (cf. Jer. 31.31–34; 32.36–41; 33.19–26; Ezek. 37.24–28). The internalization of the divine torah in Jer. 31.33f. is probably the equivalent of the new mind and new spirit of Ezek. 36.24–28. Hopes for the future have been modelled on the past, with a few modifications to deal with unresolved problems. Although the motif of the new covenant is not developed in either of the two traditions, it may represent a restoration programme (or an element in such a programme) put forward by deuteronomists and others for the shaping of the future community in Jerusalem. The two centuries after the fall of Jerusalem saw the development of various restoration programmes designed to determine the reconstruction of city and community (cf. Ezek. 40–48; the Ezra—Nehemiah material; the priestly editing of the primary narrative (Genesis–Deuteronomy); Isa. 56–66). Not all of these programmes were ever implemented, though they may all have contributed something towards the shape of fourth-century Jerusalem. Whether the deuteronomists ever succeeded in establishing the new covenant they envisaged is beyond finding out now, but the involvement of Ezra in various covenants may point to some success on their part (cf. Ezra 10.3; Neh. 9.38 [Heb. 10.1]). The new covenant was one strategy among many for reorganizing the post-exilic community, and fragmentary evidence for that strategy is carried by the Jeremiah tradition.

A note on internalization in the Jeremiah tradition. Arising out of this analysis of the internalization element in the new covenant motif, it is worth considering briefly the use in Jeremiah of the motif of internalization. Those commentators who have seen in the book of Jeremiah the beginnings of individualistic spiritual religion (Skinner among others), and who have tended also to praise this element as an advance in religious consciousness, would do much better to focus their attention on the book of Psalms than on Jeremiah, because more of the kind of religion they approve of is to be found there than in the very complex edition of Jeremiah. However, there are sufficient elements of internalization in Jeremiah to warrant a few comments. The account of Jeremiah's call (1.4–10) presents the prophet as having interiorized his commission. No occasion is provided for the event; in fact it is not even described as an event but as Jeremiah's awareness that he is called to be a prophet. In one of the soliloquies he is represented as saying: 'Thy words were found, and I ate them, and thy words became to to me a joy and the delight of my heart' (15.16). As Samuel Terrien observes: 'The process of prophetic revelation was fully interiorized. The word had been "inwardly digested".'[38] The presentation of a prophet who persistently failed to persuade the community to take him seriously, in a time when prophecy itself had become problematic, makes it hardly surprising that there should be some elements of internalization in the tradition. Internalization is one major form of escape from, or resolution of, failure. The retreat into a deep inner life (what today would be called 'a rich inner life of fantasy') is a way of dealing with such public problems as failure. Because the life of Jeremiah cannot be reconstructed from the tradition, this retreat or internalization may reflect community reactions to the exile (particularly the response of the deuteronomists) more than elements in the mental life of the prophet. But the presence of such internalization elements in the tradition points to some of the real social, political and religious problems of the exilic period which the redactors attempted to deal with in their presentation of a prophet who had to internalize so much of his experience.

The material known as the confessions (or soliloquies) is the best example of the internalization process at work in the tradition. Constructed out of the *Weltanschauungen* and language of the Psalms, these poems present the prophet (and represent the community) struggling with his experiences of the world and interiorizing them as a struggle with Yahweh. These confessions breathe the same atmosphere as the Psalms and the book of Job, and reflect an exilic community deeply troubled by the way its world has disintegrated and seeking divine vindication. The internalization of the prophet's struggle becomes an image of the community's self-awareness in the dark days of the exile.

The internalization element in the new covenant motif has been discussed sufficiently already not to demand further consideration here, but it is worth mentioning the fact that the internalization of torah removes the struggles and failures the community underwent during the exile, so that in the future all will know without any one having to tell them – a case of internalization as retreat from reality, from failure and from the kinds of conflict which characterized the life of the community in Jeremiah's time. Although the internalization mode of handling experience is not used in the material on prophetic conflict (apart from possibly in the divine council motif), commentators have used it in the attempt to justify or validate the 'true' prophet over against the 'false' prophet. Thus Walther Eichrodt, while admitting 'that there is no such thing as an external test by which to tell true prophecy from false, such as all reasonable persons may safely apply', argues that faith can judge the truth or falsehood of prophecy.[39] This faith which relates to having the spirit within is a withdrawal from the public world (where empirical evidence is important for argument) to an interiorized world where faith validates opinions rather than logic and argument. In the face of the problems posed by the plethora of prophets preaching different things it is small wonder that any group should retreat into faith or, as in the case of the traditionists working on Jeremiah, into models of internalization.

Just as the new covenant motif seems to have had little impact on the post-exilic community, so did its element of internalization. There is no evidence to suggest that the shaping of the post-exilic Jerusalem community internalized its religious focus (at least no more evidence than the book of Psalms and the book of Job). On the contrary, it became a greatly ritualized community and developed the cultic regulations laid down in torah. Centuries later, Jewish religion began to develop a highly interiorized form of spiritual religion which may have owed much to the exilic development of internalization, but which certainly had to wait for the emergence of that formidable group of religious thinkers and leaders, the Pharisees. If fulfilment of the new covenant expectation must be sought, let it be found in the achievements of the Pharisees, who helped to create the spiritual way of life of a very practical but deeply internalized rabbinical religion. Of their outlook, convictions, beliefs and achievements Ellis Rivkin has this to say:

> And when we ask ourselves the source of this generative power, we find it in the relationship the Pharisees established between the one God and the singular individual. The Father God cared about *you*; he was concerned about *you*; he watched over *you*; he loved *you*; and loved *you* so much that he wished *your* unique self to live forever. One's earthly father was here today and gone tomorrow; but the one Father God was here forever. One's earthly father was now just, now unjust, now kind, now harsh, now dependable, now whimsical; one's Father in Heaven was always just, kind, merciful and dependable. And the heavenly Father was ever present. One could talk to him, plead with him, cry out to him, pray to him – person to Person, individual to Individual, heart to Heart, soul to Soul. It was the establishment of this personal relationship, an inner experience, that accounts for the manifest power of Pharisaism to live on. It accounts for the power of Christ to live on. It accounts for the teachings of Muhammed to live on. For it would seem that there is no viable human alternative to the reality *within*, a reality that reassures each one of us that he or she is a precious person, a unique individual worthy of eternal life if each of us remains steadfast to a *politeuma* pressed deep within our souls where no external force can ravage it. *Internalization* is the only road to salvation.[40]

9

After the Fall:
Exiles and 'Exiles'

The final section of the Jeremiah text for analysis is chs. 37–44, where the material deals with the final days of the Jerusalem community and the aftermath of the Babylonian destruction of the city. Recent treatments of this section have raised a number of interesting points about the development of this stage of the Jeremiah tradition from an original concern with the survivors of the Jerusalem community to a later, and more developed, polemic against that group on behalf of the Babylonian exiles.[1] Such research is in line with the general argument of this book that the book of Jeremiah in its present form is primarily concerned with the presentation of Jeremiah the prophet as a means to advance certain ideological positions over against the claims of other groups in the exilic and reconstructionist periods. In the complex editing of the narratives in chs. 37–44, the redactors have built up further their case against the Jerusalem community and concomitantly strengthened their argument for the case of the Babylonian exiles.[2] The ways in which such factors have influenced the construction of the stories will be brought out in the following analysis of the text. It is, however, also important to note the way that material originally devoted to a specific viewpoint has been reshaped by redaction to produce virtually the opposite effect. This is a strong feature of biblical writing and indicates the significant contribution to meaning which the redaction of a text makes. It also, of course, means that redaction criticism must play an important part in the task of interpreting the biblical text.

The various interviews Jeremiah had with Zedekiah (chs. 37–38) have been analysed already (in ch. 6 above), so it is unnecessary to say much about them in this chapter.[3] The effect of the narratives about Jeremiah and Zedekiah is to show how, in spite of opportunities to change official policy, that king and his court persisted in ignoring (or disobeying) the prophetic word. Such persistent refusal to listen to the prophetic word brought with it the inevitable divine judgment against king, officials, city and community recounted in ch. 39. According to the various accounts in 37–39, the prophet spent most of the period locked up, and so plays no part in the siege or fall of Jerusalem. The community, under its king and courtiers, having rejected the prophetic word, there remains nothing for the prophet to do but languish in detention as the inert witness of the city's destruction.

The account of the fall of Jerusalem is given very briefly in Jer. 39.1–10. A further, and much more detailed, account is provided in Jer. 52 as a conclusion to the book of Jeremiah (cf. II Kings 24.18–25.30). However, the main interest of the redactors working on the Jeremiah tradition is with the role of Jeremiah in the periods before and after the Babylonian destruction of Jerusalem (though his absence from the account of Gedaliah's governorship of the community in Jer. 40.7–41.18 is noteworthy). The shortened form of the account of the defeat of Jerusalem in 39.1–10 provides only a very brief précis of the main events which terminated the siege. Verses 1–2 interrupt the flow of narrative from 38.28b (MT) to 39.3, and come from the deuteronomistic redactors using the material in the deuteronomistic history. The narrative flow (note transposition in RSV margin) would have read: 'now it came to pass when Jerusalem was captured that all the princes of the king of Babylon came and sat in the middle gate . . .' (LXX omits vv. 4–13 and reads v. 14 after v. 3, either representing a shorter, more compact text or skipping from the list of Babylonian names in v. 3 to the similar list in v. 13). For about eighteen months Jerusalem was besieged and the community suffered all the rigours of such campaigns until, by the time the siege was successfully concluded by the Babylonians, severe famine and deprivation had helped to devastate the city's population (cf. 52.6; Lam. 5.4–10). Finally the city wall was breached and the Babylonian army had access to the city. As with all governments in times of impending defeat for their nations, the king and his officials fled the city by night in an attempt to escape in the direction of the Arabah.[4] Their flight was in vain because they were pursued by some of the Chaldean army and captured in the plains of Jericho. There is a graphic allusion to this flight, its failure and the consequent death of Zedekiah in Ezek. 12.12f. As a Babylonian vassal, King Zedekiah had failed his suzerain, so he was taken as a captive to Riblah in Syria where Nebuchadrezzar had his headquarters. There sentence was

passed on him after, presumably, some form of trial (the phrase in
v. 5, 'and he passed sentence upon him' (*way^edabbēr 'ittō mišpā-
ṭîm*) implies a trial of some kind). His sons were killed and he had
his eyes put out before he was taken to Babylon as a prisoner of
war. Various palaces were burned, though neither account in the
book of Jeremiah refers to the destruction of the temple
(cf. II Kings 25.9; but the phrase 'the house of the people' in
Jer. 39.8 just might refer to the temple).[5] The walls of the city were
broken down, rendering the city incapable of being defended, and
many citizens were deported to Babylon. Some of the poorer elements left in the land were put in charge of the vineyards and fields
(v. 10), but the impression that most of the people were taken into
exile should be avoided, because a substantial number of important
people remained behind to organize life in exilic Judah.

In the account of the fall of Jerusalem and the organization of
community life under Gedaliah (39.1–10; 40.7–41.18), the prophet
Jeremiah is notably absent. He is also absent from the account in
II Kings. Such absence may not be surprising in view of the prophet
being locked up (or under house arrest) at the time, though it is
arguable that his absence from the accounts gave rise to the stories
about his imprisonment at the hands of king and princes. Wherever
the deuteronomistic history does provide an account of a prophet
involved in a city's struggle against the enemy, it is a story of
deliverance for Israel or Judah, ably assisted by prophetic intervention (cf. Elisha's involvement in the saving of Samaria, II Kings
6.8–7.20, and Isaiah's reassurance of Hezekiah during the Assyrian
siege of Jerusalem, which resulted in the deliverance of the city and
the massacre of 185,000 Assyrians, II Kings 19; Isa. 37). Such
stories are fine where the cities involved survived the threats, but
Jerusalem in 587 did not survive the Babylonian siege, so there
was no intervention for Jeremiah to effect. Hence his absence from
the account of the fall of Jerusalem. However, it was not a blame-
worthy absence (like David's from the battle on Mount Gilboa), for
the prophet is presented by the narrators as having struggled with
the king and his counsellors over a long period to persuade them to
give up their foolhardy scheme of resistance against the Babylonians.
There had been prophets about at the time trying to intervene
against the Babylonians with oracles of *šālōm*, but these were
self-deluded mantics deluding the community. They succeeded,
Jeremiah failed. So when the end of the siege came, and the king,
his courtiers and the community went into exile, there was nothing
further that Jeremiah could do:

> But if you will not listen,
>   my soul will weep in secret for your pride;
> my eyes will weep bitterly and run down with tears,
>   because Yahweh's flock has been taken captive. (13.17)

The material in 39.1–40.6 contains a number of accounts of Jeremiah's fate when Jerusalem fell.[6] In keeping with the deuteronomistic view of history as the sphere of the operation of the divine word and prophecy as the medium of that word, Nebuchadrezzar is represented as being aware of Jeremiah's existence, plight and outlook (39.11–12) and Nebuzaradan is presented as being familiar enough with Jeremiah's message to be able to paraphrase it back at the prophet (40.1–3). In 39.13f. Jeremiah is released from the court of the guard and committed to Gedaliah's care. So after the fall Jeremiah is freed and takes up residence among the people at Mizpah (39.14; cf. 40.6). For reasons not apparent to the modern analyst, the editors have included at this point (39.15–18) a piece about Ebed-melech (cf. 38.7–13). It would have made better sense if it had been placed after 38.7–13, but perhaps it was intended to relate to the release of Ebed-melech from service to Zedekiah, or meant to refer to his surviving the siege and its aftermath. Unfortunately the text does not expand the matter sufficiently to provide any information on this point. As a similar prophetic oracle is given relating to Baruch (45.1–5), also equally inconclusive and curiously located in the tradition, the motif of such an escape may be seen as a redactional element used in the construction of the Jeremiah tradition.

Jer. 40.1–6. A rather different account of Jeremiah's escape is given in this passage. It tells how Jeremiah was taken, bound in chains, along with all the other captives due for deportation to Babylon, and then released at Ramah (some miles north of Jerusalem) by Nebuzaradan. Nebuzaradan makes a little deuteronomistic speech (vv. 2f.), releases the prophet and offers him the choice of accompanying them to Babylon or remaining in Judaean territory as a free man (free to do what he likes or free to join Gedaliah, the governor of Judah). He is given a food allowance and a present and released. So he goes to Mizpah and joins Gedaliah. It is an idyllic picture of a prophet highly valued and respected by the Babylonians, who extend the freedom of the land to the prophet. This is how prophets of Yahweh should be treated! Strange things may well happen during military occupations (*pace* Bright), but this idyll

contradicts 39.11–14 and should be seen as a redactional legend.
There is some textual confusion in 40.1 which, as it stands, has no
object of the phrase 'the word that came to Jeremiah from Yahweh . . .', but attributes the deuteronomistic words in vv. 2f. to
Nebuzaradan, the captain of the Babylonian guard. No wonder later
Jewish thought made Nebuzaradan become a righteous proselyte in
his latter years.[7] If v. 1a introduces a prophetic oracle, then vv. 2b–
3 may be the summary of that oracle, but as v. 2a restates (from a
different source?) part of the activity in 39.13–14a, v. 1b may be a
parenthetical explanation deriving from a different story of how
Jeremiah was released. In transmission the text has become disrupted, so it is difficult now to suggest what the original might have
read.[8]

The two different accounts of how Jeremiah was released from
detention and came to take up residence among the associates of
Gedaliah at Mizpah indicate yet again one of the major features of
the construction of the Jeremiah tradition: the double accounts or
versions of so much of the material in the book. These variations
on themes and motifs reveal the complex nature of the Jeremiah
tradition and rule out easy solutions which posit a biographer taking
notes as events unfolded. A number of stories were told about the
prophet in relation to the city, the kings, the prophets and other
persons in the community (Judaean and Babylonian). Such stories
have been built up by the traditionists, reflected upon and developed
into theological statements about the exilic period. By telling the
stories in different versions, the traditionists are permitted greater
scope for theological reflection, and the book becomes a much more
multi-layered account of prophecy in relation to the changing fortunes of the community. Whatever the explanation offered for the
many double versions of stories may be, it should strongly emphasize the features of variation and complexity in the tradition.

Jer. 40.7–41.18. An account is now given of life among the Judaean survivors of the Babylonian invasion and the destruction of
the land. It portrays a few features of life in the community governed
by Gedaliah until his assassination. However, it is not from a source
concerned with Jeremiah, because he does not appear in it at all. A
much briefer account of Gedaliah's governorship and assassination
is given in II Kings 25.22–26 (nothing of either account appears in
Jer. 52). Presumably the deuteronomistic editors have used a common source for both accounts, but the material in the Jeremiah
tradition gives many more details.[9] The absence of Jeremiah from

the account is strange, and suggests a rather different view of the early exilic community in Judah from that put forward by the editors of the tradition. In this view the community existed without the activity of the prophet (a view rather typical of the deuteronomistic history). The inclusion of such an extract in the Jeremiah tradition allows the redactors to present a community falling apart without the presence and involvement of Jeremiah. The insertion of the material also allows the redactors to set the stage for the next narrative about Jeremiah (chs. 42–43).

A striking feature of the Gedaliah material is the picture it draws of Judaean life after the fall of Jerusalem. The forces which had opposed the Babylonians in the open countryside are still at liberty (40.7–10), many Jews who had fled from Judah during the invasion now return to Mizpah and harvest the vines, the olive groves and the summer fruit (40.11f.), and, apart from Gedaliah himself, there are important figures, including members of the royal house, in the territory (cf. 41.1). All these features suggest a less than catastrophic invasion of Judah by the Babylonians. The invasion had been aimed at reducing Jerusalem and its king to a state of servitude to Babylon, and this was achieved eventually after a protracted siege. It was the king, as a Babylonian vassal sworn to loyalty to Babylon, who was the main target of the invasion, rather than the territory (the medieval rabbinic commentators, Rashi and Qimhi, clearly view Zedekiah's resistance as a breach of his oath of loyalty to the Babylonians, hence the legal matter in 39.5). The ruination of the city and the deportation of leading officials and citizens restored Babylonian domination. The appointment of Gedaliah as governor effectively made Judah a province of the Babylonian empire. Thus peace was restored to the Judaean territory. The tendency of some of the biblical sources to present the events of this period as removing *all* the royal family, officials and important figures (leaving only the 'poorest of the land'; cf. 39.10; 40.7) should not mislead the modern reader into accepting such a presentation as necessarily true. The account in 40.7–41.18 shows a rather different situation prevailing, one in which there was a great deal of mobility in the territory, agricultural production was flourishing, and members of important families had not been deported. As no information is provided in any of the accounts about the duration of Gedaliah's governorship, it is difficult to be certain when the events of 40.7–41.18 took place. There is reference to a third deportation of Jewish captives by the Babylonians in Jer. 52.30, which dates such an event to c. 583/2. This might well have been the Babylonian response to

the assassination of Gedaliah.[10] If it is related to Ishmael ben Neth-
aniah's revolt against Gedaliah's governorship, and therefore against
Babylonian dominance (an early Judaean liberation front?), it suggests that Gedaliah was governor for about five years before his
assassination. Over such a period the harvests referred to in 40.10,
12 would have had time to develop after the invasive forces of
Babylon had devastated the land. But the well-being of the community suggested in 40.7–12 should be allowed to balance the pictures drawn elsewhere in the biblical traditions of a terribly
devastating invasion of the land by the Babylonian army. The siege
and its aftermath were indeed terrible, but the whole land may not
have suffered so extreme a fate. However, it must be remembered
that the traditions in this section contain quite often distinctive
information which may not fit in precisely with the data available
in other traditions about the fall of Jerusalem and its aftermath.

In 40.13–16 Gedaliah is warned that one of the resistance leaders
is plotting against his life at the instigation of the Ammonite king
(v. 13). Gedaliah had no reason to believe this information, or preferred not to believe it so as to avoid taking action which might have
upset the peace of the community and have brought the Babylonians
against it in a punitive action. He took no precautions against a
possible plot and even refused an offer to have Ishmael murdered.

The account of Gedaliah's assassination is given very briefly in
41.1–3. Ishmael, with ten men, attends a meal in Mizpah and during
its course he kills Gedaliah and also puts to the sword all the Jews
with Gedaliah and the Babylonian soldiers stationed at Mizpah. It
is therefore an armed revolt against Babylonian authority and the
execution of a collaborationist, namely Gedaliah. At least, that is a
possible interpretation of the act. The biblical text reports the matter
very briefly and does not elaborate on it. As a member of the royal
family Ishmael cannot have liked the Babylonians very much after
their cruel treatment of the king's sons (cf. 39.6), nor as an anti-
Babylonian will he have been disposed kindly towards Gedaliah.
Behind the story there are tensions which had contributed to the
destruction of Jerusalem in the first place, i.e., the struggle between
different parties within Judaean politics (e.g., pro-Egyptian and
pro-Babylonian). The Ammonite involvement in the assassination
(cf. 40.14), assuming it to be a realistic account and not a pejorative
element in the story, may have been directed against a unified
Judaean community, but that is unlikely to have been Ishmael's
reason for the act. It must be remembered that the whole period in
which the Jeremiah tradition is set was one of fierce political and

ideological battles between rival factions for power in the community, and that any act of collaboration with the enemy (and Babylon was always *the* enemy in this period) could be denounced as treason. The assassination of Gedaliah may have been the result of such an attitude. The period in which the killing took place, the seventh month (the time of the autumn pilgrimage and feast), was to be commemorated in later years (cf. Zech. 7.5; 8.19), though whether in honour of Gedaliah's memory or for other reasons is not known.

The story presents Ishmael as a killer given to massacring innocent people. In 40.4–9 he is involved in further killings just after the murder of Gedaliah. Again it is difficult to determine just why he should murder seventy pilgrims from the northern territory, but he may have been committed to a policy of effective action taken on as wide a scale as possible and designed to cripple the Babylonian control of Mizpah. On the other hand, it is equally possible that he just wanted to take revenge on as many people as opportunity afforded. The seventy pilgrims are presented as part of an eighty-strong pilgrim party on its way to the temple site in Jerusalem, stopping off at Mizpah to pay its respects to Gedaliah, there to perform mourning rites for the destruction of the house of Yahweh. If the dating of Gedaliah's assassination to 583/2 is correct, then this pilgrimage can hardly have been an act of lamentation for the destruction of the temple, but must have been part of some other ritual occasion. Perhaps during the exile, or during the early period immediately after the fall of the city, the temple site still functioned as a sacred place for worship and offerings.[11] Whatever was behind the pilgrimage, few of the pilgrims ever got to Jerusalem, but their corpses were thrown into a large cistern in the town (v. 7). The reference to Mizpah's fortifications in v. 9 (referring to King Asa's activities in the past; cf. I Kings 15.22) may indicate that Ishmael had plans to use the town as part of his strategy against the Babylonians. The capture of the town's people, including the king's daughters left there in Gedaliah's care by the Babylonians (so not all the important people went into exile to Babylon), and the intended transportation of them to the Ammonite territory (all achieved by only Ishmael and ten men against soldiers as well as officials [cf. v. 16]!) suggest a development of the story well beyond the framework of an original account of the assassination of Gedaliah.[12] Different strands of tradition-building (cf. the somewhat different Greek account of the events of ch. 41) have contributed to the story, and in doing so have produced a curiously incredible account bordering on the absurd at times.

Ishmael's attempt to kidnap and transport the whole Mizpah community to Ammonite territory is foiled by Johanan ben Kareah and the other leaders of the Judaean forces (41.11–16). As to their source of information ('when . . . [they] heard of all the evil which Ishmael . . . had done', v. 11) the text is silent. Presumably not all the people of Mizpah had been taken captive (contra v. 10, unless it is treated as hyperbole), so some escaped and informed Johanan and his companions. They pursued after Ishmael and caught up with him at the great waters in Gibeon. This location is not on the route to Ammon, so it may be necessary to identify Mizpah with a town other than the one usually identified as the Mizpah of this story.[13] There the captives deserted Ishmael and returned to Johanan. Ishmael escaped with eight of his men (so only two were killed or captured in the encounter) and went to the Ammonites. Johanan, his companions and the captives – soldiers,[14] women, children, and officials – returned from Gibeon but not to Mizpah. They went and stayed near Bethlehem instead and prepared to flee to Egypt (41.17f.). This planned flight is accounted for by the redactors in terms of the group's fear of Babylonian reprisals against the Judaeans for the assassination of Gedaliah. The real effect of the verses is to provide a lead-in for the next tradition block, dealing with the prophet Jeremiah.

How is the absence of Jeremiah from the narratives in 40.7–41.18 to be accounted for? It is a notable absence made all the more emphatic by the sudden recourse of the community to Jeremiah in 42.1ff. Presumably there were various stories in circulation about the activities of the community associated with Gedaliah, and the redactors of the Jeremiah tradition used some of these to build up a picture of that community in such a way that it contributed to their overall presentation of Jeremiah. The independent origins of the tradition about Gedaliah and the Judaean community between 587 and 583/2 are indicated by the absence of Jeremiah from it. The story simply does not know Jeremiah as a member of that community, hence it has no place for his activities. The redactors have stitched together two independent sets of tradition, one associating Jeremiah with Gedaliah's community, in which he is very active, and the other giving an account of the disastrous experiences of the community at the hands of Ishmael. The answer to the question about what Jeremiah was doing while Ishmael and his ten men were terrorizing the community is probably a very simple one: he was doing nothing because the tradition of that story did not have him as a member of the community. Once again the redactors have used material originally foreign to their concerns, have incorporated it into their tradition-building, and then have used their own traditions to continue their presentation of the life of the prophet. Perhaps for them Jeremiah was a silent sufferer of all the horrors of Ishmael's campaign against the community, but, as the traditions stand, it is more probable that they were unaware of the anomalies caused by associating together the two independent sets of tradition.

Jer. 42–43. An alternative account of life in the land of Judah after the fall of Jerusalem is now presented in which Jeremiah, not Gedaliah, is the central figure (contrast 42.9–12 with 40.9f.). This account knows nothing of the assassination of Gedaliah or the subsequent misadventures of the community, but is tied into that cluster of stories by the motif of going to Egypt. In the completed tradition of Jeremiah, the story may appear to presuppose the events of 40.13–41.18, but a careful examination of ch. 42 will not reveal any direct connections. The association is purely one created by the juxtaposition of the chapters. It remains curious, however, that in the presentation of the prophet Jeremiah, a prophet regularly presented as speaking to the community leadership on every occasion of note, there should be absolutely no comment from the prophet on the revolt against Babylon constituted by the assassination of Gedaliah, or on the perilous situation of the community after such events. This remarkable absence of comment suggests that the material in 40.7–41.18 may have been so independent of the Jeremiah tradition circles originally that its appearance now in that tradition must be due to the latest stages of the construction of the book of Jeremiah. The story of Gedaliah, which the deuteronomistic historians used in II Kings 25 and Jer. 52, circulated and was developed along legendary lines as an account of the chaotic conditions of the territory after the fall of Jerusalem. The Jeremiah tradition has been used to carry some of those legends, but has not been adjusted to make any links between the different streams of tradition. Analysis of the text reveals that the sections are mutually independent of one another, whereas a very cursory reading of the text may reinforce the presupposition that there is an *implicit* connection between the stories.

In 42.1–5 the commanders of the forces, in particular Johanan and Azariah[15] ben Hoshaiah, and all the people approach Jeremiah the prophet and request him to pray to Yahweh for guidance for

them. Jeremiah agrees to the request. The people then respond that
they will act according to whatever Yahweh says through Jeremiah.
What follows is a lengthy series of deuteronomistic-style sermonic
replies (vv. 6–22) which indicates the influence of the deuteronomists in the construction of this pericope. It is rather difficult to be
sure which bits belong to the original story and which pieces are
part of the deuteronomistic construction. The kernel of the story
appears to be contained in vv. 1–5, 7–9a, 17*, but commentators
and authors of monographs differ in the precise delineation of the
core, so there is room for disagreement here.[16] The gist of the
prophet's reply seems to be that the community should remain in
Judah and not attempt to go down to Egypt. However, such a
discernment of the kernel is an oversimplification, because the material has been expanded so considerably that the whole account is
deuteronomistic through and through. So much of vv. 13–22 anticipates the community's response in 43.1–7 that it is out of place
in the prophet's statement, but this point presupposes that there is
an original story with a later development by the deuteronomistic
redactors. It may be more realistic to see in the account a deuteronomistic creation which presents the prophet as an intercessor for
the community (cf. 37.3; for intercession in relation to the exilic
community cf. 29.7, though there it is not prophetic but communal
intercession). At the same time it is important to note that the
narrative contrasts remaining in the land with going to Egypt and
associates that remaining in Judah with divine blessing and makes
the Egyptian journey an object of divine displeasure. So the story
has its origins in a positive view of the Judaean community, and
therefore should be contrasted with other views in the Jeremiah
tradition which make the exiles in Babylon the object of Yahweh's
blessing.

This is the most important feature of the narratives contained in
the block of traditions formed by chs. 40–44 (37–39 form an extended preface to the block). The future is not in Babylon, it is
certainly not in Egypt, but *it is in Judah.* The lengthy deuteronomistic diatribe in 42.13–22 against the projected visit to Egypt
indicates the strength of that conviction about Judah being the
proper sphere of divine blessing in the exilic period. The conventional deuteronomistic phrases, used elsewhere in the tradition
against the inhabitants of Jerusalem who were not prepared to
surrender to the Babylonians, are used here to denounce the proposed journey to Egypt. Those who go down to Egypt are threatened
with 'sword, famine and pestilence' (vv. 17; 22; cf. vv. 14, 16; see

also 43.11), a motif used a number of times in the construction of
the Jeremiah tradition (e.g. 14.12; 21.7, 9; 24.10; 29.17f.; cf. 28.9;
and in modified form ['sword . . . famine'] in 5.12; 11.22; 14.15,
18). The community in Egypt will not only lead a blighted existence
there, but will become 'an execration, a horror, a curse, and a taunt'
(v. 18; cf. 44.12, which combines both sets of phrases). What is
especially interesting about these two motifs applied to the Egyptian
exiles with such vigour is that they are both employed with equal
vigour against the people in Jerusalem who survived the first Babylonian invasion and deportation:

> Thus say Yahweh of hosts, Behold, I am sending on them sword,
> famine, and pestilence, and I will make them like vile figs which
> are so bad they cannot be eaten. I will pursue them with sword,
> famine, and pestilence, and will make them a horror to all the
> kingdoms of the earth, to be a curse, a terror, a hissing, and a
> reproach among all the nations where I have driven them.
> (29.17f.; cf. 24.9f.)

The different settings of the application of the two motifs produce
an insight into the polemics of the exilic period. The exiles in
Babylon despised the remnant in Jerusalem and the Jerusalem community despised the exiles in Egypt. The same language is used to
disparage both despised groups but the social context is rather
different in each case. The material in chs. 24 and 29 (for the
relation between these two chapters cf. 24.2f., 8–10; 29.17) represents the pro-Babylonian exilic community stage of the editing of
the tradition. The substance of the attack in chs. 42–43 is indicative
of a pro-Judaean community strand in the Jeremiah tradition. Taken
together, they cancel each other out, but they ought to be viewed
as different stages and strands in the construction of the tradition.
Quite clearly the motif of Yahweh's building up of the Judaean
community demonstrates that during the exile those survivors of
the Jerusalem catastrophe who stayed in Judah believed that Yahweh was with them and that the future lay with them rather than
elsewhere. The sermons against going down to Egypt (cf. the ban
on returning to Egypt in Deut. 17.16) reflect this viewpoint. The
use of one of the leitmotifs of the tradition in 42.10 (cf. 1.10 and
my comments on the use of the leitmotif in ch. 2 above) and also
in 24.6 confirms the view that both communities (the Judaean and
the Babylonian exiles) saw themselves as the special recipients of
divine care and therefore as having the status of being God's people
during the exile. The distance between the two groups allowed each

to develop this viewpoint in isolation, though the construction of
the tradition has included (ironically) both viewpoints. That the
presentation of each ideological position is cast in the same deuteronomistic language suggests that either discrete groups of deuteronomists edited the different blocks of material, or the same editing
processes were used to present the diverse material in a relatively
uniform way. The significance of the two sets of traditions about
how the Judaean community and the exiles in Babylon saw themselves in relation to Yahweh's purposes is that no uniform theological or ideological stance can be posited for the book of Jeremiah in
terms of its constituent parts. The final edition may have had some
such purpose in mind, but the traditions constituting the Jeremiah
tradition must be differentiated into their distinctive elements and
allow to play a dialectical role in determining the variety of meanings
in the book of Jeremiah.

In Jer. 43.1–7 the response of the community to the prophet's
intercession is given as a hostile rejection of Jeremiah's advocacy of
settling down in Judah (advice which is very similar to that offered
to the Babylonian exiles in the letter of 29.3–9). The reply contains
elements of the attack on the prophets motif: the men who criticize
Jeremiah are described as 'insolent men' (v. 2, *hāʾᵃnāšīm haz-
zēdīm*; LXX omits the adjective); such a description reflects
Deut. 18.22, where the prophet whose word does not come to pass
is dismissed as speaking 'presumptuously' (*bᵉzādōn*, cf. Deut.
18.20). The response to the prophet is an accusation of being
a false prophet, and uses two of the most common motifs in the
prophetic conflict narratives: 'You are telling a lie (*šeqer*). Yahweh
our God[17] did not send you (*lōʾ šᵉlāḥᵃkā*) to say, "Do not go to
Egypt to live there" ' (43.2). Jeremiah is accused of telling a lie and
of not being sent by Yahweh. Ironically these are two of the most
common accusations made in the tradition against the opponents of
Jeremiah (cf. 14.14; 23.21, 25, 32; 28.15; 29.9), and their use
against Jeremiah here demonstrates the ease with which they may
be used by any group against another group. It also illustrates and
confirms the argument advanced above in ch. 7 that the accusation
carries no integral element of evidence or proof of the truth of its
content. It is a technical response to a statement with which the
individual or audience disagrees and, given varying stances and
viewpoints, it would falsify every prophet who ever prophesied.
That is precisely why such accusations do not constitute evidence
of falseness against a speaker but represent conventional replies
from the opposition. The accusations 'You are telling lies', 'You

have not been sent by Yahweh' are formal elements in the social conflict between prophets or between prophets and the community. Their occurrence in the text indicates a context of prophetic conflict but does not constitute evidence for the truth of one party rather than the other.

What is particularly curious about this exchange between the community and Jeremiah is the role Baruch is accused of playing in the matter: 'but Baruch the son of Neriah has set you against us, to deliver us into the hand of the Chaldeans, that they may kill us or take us into exile in Babylon' (v. 3). Throughout the tradition there is a consistent presentation of Jeremiah as a prophet ranged against the community and speaking for a policy of change in political outlook. During the Babylonian crisis he is presented as advocating surrender to the enemy (what today would be called high treason and punishable by the death sentence), an attitude described as 'weakening the hands of the soldiers who are left in this city, and the hands of all the people' (38.4). But nowhere in the tradition is there any suggestion that Jeremiah was put up to do this by other people; he is always presented as being his own man (or Yahweh's, if there is a difference) and speaking his own mind (or Yahweh's). So it is most unusual to find here the suggestion that he is only the front man for Baruch's scheming. It is so out of character that it requires some form of investigation or explanation. Without pursuing the matter too far, and in view of the paucity of information available, the following comments may be warranted. The material in 40–44 is different from the other blocks in the tradition, so a different perspective on Jeremiah might be expected in the narratives. We have noted already the prophet's absence in 40.7–41.18 and I have explained that absence in terms of the origins of the material. Such origins may contribute to the view of Jeremiah in 43.2f., especially the opposition to him expressed in language reflecting the polemic against the prophets. Furthermore, the role of Baruch in 43.3 (cf. ch. 45) suggests a source beginning to develop the figure of Baruch in his own right. Much later tradition developed Baruch as an important literary and visionary figure (see the apocryphal Book of Baruch and the pseudepigraphical Apocalypse of Baruch) and he figures largely in Aggadic writings.[18] The first stages in this development may well have been the material in chs. 43, 45 and this would account for the strange accusation that he was the influence behind Jeremiah on this occasion. This independent element within the tradition presents him as beginning to emerge as a figure in his own right, whereas elsewhere in the tradition he has social status, is a witness to Jeremiah's land transaction, acts as his amanuensis but has no character of his own. He is a passive figure in those traditions, but in 43.3; 45.3 elements of characterization are provided for him, and as such these constitute the beginnings of his development into an independent figure with a life of his own.

The outcome of the rejection of Jeremiah's warnings against going to Egypt is a mass exodus (enforced in places) to Egypt (43.4–7). The irony of such a flight is that Jeremiah and Baruch are taken also, so they presumably ended their lives in exile in Egypt (later traditions have different accounts of what happened to both men in Egypt). The reason for going to Egypt given in v. 3 is a persuasive one. Ishmael's revolt against Babylonian authority would have brought swift and severe retribution against the community. In spite of the benevolent views of the Baylonians taken in the tradition (cf. similar views taken of the Romans in the gospels; the anti-Babylonian oracles in Jer. 50–51 are an exception to the *Realpolitik* of the tradition, just as the attitude towards Rome taken by the NT Apocalypse is an exception to the *Realpolitik* of the gospels and the writings of Paul), the Babylonians were not nature's gentlemen, extending kindness and charity to the human race. Like all empires dominating smaller states, they could be remarkably vicious and domineering (not perhaps as cruel as the Assyrians, but Ps. 137.8f. probably expresses the genuine view of the community on the matter), so the reason for leaving Judah put forward by Azariah and Johanan must be seen as a good one. The optimism of the redactors may reflect the pro-Babylonian stance behind most of the tradition's construction. A structuralist approach to the narratives in the Jeremiah tradition would emphasize the symmetry of the different blocks of material whereby the rejection of the prophet's warnings by the Judaean community resulted in the Babylonian deportations in the first place and the flight to Egypt in the second place. Both rejections emptied the land of its people and produced two communities in exile. The asymmetry of the accounts lies in the fact that only one of these exilic communities, the Babylon group, constitutes a positive entity for the future. The other, the Egyptian group, has little or no future at all. The narratives relating to both groups give the impression that the land vacated was virtually left empty (apart from elements which did not count) and the focus of these accounts is on the exilic groups. Thus 43.5f. specifically states that everybody was taken to Egypt. With the flight to Egypt there is an ironic inversion of the exodus from Egypt and the tradition, probably intentionally, writes off that exilic group for such an action. Elements in the narratives about the group in Egypt stress the negativity of such a course of action (cf. v. 7, 'they did not obey the voice of Yahweh'), and it becomes apparent that the community has fled from the destructive anger of Babylon, only to encounter the destructive anger of Yahweh in and against Egypt (cf. 43.10–13; 44.26–30). As there are no positive oracles on behalf of the Egyptian group in the collection of material in chs. 42–44, the tradition block must have come from sources hostile to the refugees in Egypt, either from Palestinian or Babylonian milieux.

The symbolical action of Jeremiah directed against Egypt in 43.8–13 has been analysed in the chapter on dramatic and symbolical actions of the prophet. It is part of a highly developed and much extended tradition of hostility towards Egypt and therefore towards the Judaean refugees down in Egypt. There are problems of interpretation in the section, particularly in relation to the fact that the Babylonians did not extend their empire into Egypt successfully. Egypt remained independent until it was conquered by Cambyses and brought under Persian rule. However the failure of such predictions should not obscure their real purpose, which is to denounce the Egyptian forces and the community in exile there. Such denunciations are a feature of the prophetic traditions, though the Babylonian campaign against Egypt appears in the Ezekiel tradition as the resolution of other problems in prediction (cf. Ezek. 26; 29.1–20). The action of Jeremiah is problematic also in its details, but the pericope is a rare example in the tradition of the incorporation of material against the nations into the presentation of the prophet's activities. The use in v. 11 of elements also found in 15.2 is indicative of redactional activity.[19]

Jer. 44. The material on the fall of Jerusalem and its aftermath is brought to a conclusion by a prolix attack on the communities in exile in Egypt. It is not in fact a continuation of the attack in 43.8–13, which related to Tahpanhes, but is directed against 'all the Jews that dwelt in the land of Egypt, at Migdol, at Tahpanhes, at Memphis, and in the land of Pathros' (v. 1). It therefore presupposes a well developed system of Jewish communities resident in Egypt rather than a hastily assembled group of refugees implied by 43.4–7. Such communities had been in the process of developing since the fall of Samaria in 721 and were to become a very important part of Diaspora Judaism. The deeply antagonistic material against such communities in ch. 44 is a measure of the hostility felt by certain groups rather than a sign of percipience in understanding the important role in the development and preservation of Jewish religion such settlements were to play. The terminology and ideas of ch. 44 are strongly deuteronomistic, and the chapter contributes much more to our understanding of deuteronomistic attitudes than it does to the reconstruction of Jeremiah's views on such matters. There is a deuteronomistic résumé of history in vv. 2–10 which sets out in exaggerated form the destruction of Jerusalem and Judah to such an extent that 'Behold, this day they are a desolation, and *no one dwells in them*' (v. 2). This unrealistic representation of the facts of the exile allows the redactors to demonstrate the truth of their theology: the vast devastation of the land took place because the communities failed to listen to the prophets (v. 4), were thoroughly wicked and idolatrous (v. 3), and preferred idolatry to paying heed to the prophets (v. 5). The main elements of this analysis have been noted at various points in the tradition (cf. 7.22–26; 11.7–11; 25.1–14), but here they are applied to the Egyptian communities. Their responsibility is greater than the Jerusalem and Judaean communities because they have seen what was done to such communities and therefore ought to have changed their ways (for this type of argument in the tradition cf. 3.6–11; 23.13f.). 'Have you forgotten the wickedness of your fathers, the wickedness of the kings of Judah, the wickedness of their (Heb. his) wives, your own wickedness, and the wickedness of your wives, which they committed in the land of Judah and in the streets of Jerusalem?' (v. 9).

The ideological nature of this sermon must be quite evident to every modern reader, not only because it applies the same critique to every community no matter what its circumstances, but also because its strongly rhetorical content is far closer to rhetoric than analysis. It is a mixture of threats against the Judaeans and the Egyptian communities which is not easy to separate out into discrete strands. Were the communities in Egypt as a punishment for their sins in Judah, or had they gone there to escape other threats (e.g. 43.3)? Who precisely is being addressed in the first sermon? According to v. 7 it is the remnant in the midst of Judah, but according to v. 8 it is the people living in Egypt. Such vague generalizations, using stereotypes instead of precise analysis, are characteristic of ideological denunciations. They are highly unrealistic, but many ideological positions are at variance with fact (that is partly what makes them ideological), so instead of treating them as statements of fact we should inquire about their function in this particular section of the tradition. The application to the Egyptian communities of the denunciations already used to condemn the Jerusalem community indicates the redactors' determination to dismiss from significance the Judaean exiles in Egypt. Just as the communities in Jerusalem and Judah had been condemned throughout the tradition, so now the survivors of the fall of Jerusalem are to be rejected from having any part in future developments brought about by Yahweh. This is not just polemic masquerading as piety. It goes much deeper than that. It is denunciation on behalf of something else, something not openly stated in the text. The redactors are writing off as without significance communities they regard as rivals of the community for which they speak. To gain the perspective needed to discern this ideological bias, it is necessary to view the matter from a vantage point afforded by the whole tradition. The only communities of which the tradition speaks with hope are Israel in the early oracles (cf. 31.2–6, 15–20), and the Babylonian exiles in one of the latest strands in the tradition. The positive oracles about Israel are most probably reapplied to the exiles in general (if not to the whole Diaspora of a later period – thereby contradicting the denunciations in ch. 44?), so the only specific target of restoration in the tradition as it now stands may well be the Babylonian exiles (cf. 24; 29.1– 14). Is the complete denunciation of the Egyptian communities incorporated into the tradition in order to underline the redactors' firm conviction that the future lies only in exile? This conviction needs to be made more precise by qualifying it to read: *only in exile, and then only among the Babylonian exiles, is there any hope for the future*. The way the traditions in chs. 37–44 are arranged, whatever their original setting or intention may have been, so as to depict a disintegrating community giving way to a remnant at the mercy of killers, and finally fleeing to Egypt, where it begins to replicate the past history of the Jerusalem community by developing idolatrous ways, suggests that the final organization of the material is designed to advance the claims of the Babylonian exiles and to reject all other claims as coming from wicked communities doomed to further annihilation. How well this reading of the text fits the facts available in ch. 44 may be confirmed by a further analysis of the contents of the chapter.

The complete annihilation of the Judaean remnant in Egypt is very clearly stated in vv. 11–14, 26–30. Using stereotyped language, the deuteronomists threaten the community with divine destruction: 'Behold, I will set my face against you for evil, to cut off all Judah' (v. 11; cf. vv. 7f.). In Egypt they will be consumed by sword and famine 'from the least to the greatest', and will become 'an execration, a horror, a curse, and a taunt' (v. 12). The same punishment meted out to Jerusalem will befall the community in Egypt: 'I will punish . . . with sword, with famine, and with pestilence' (v. 13). *None* shall 'escape or survive or return to the land of Judah' (v. 14), though a later glossator has modified the comprehensiveness of the annihilation by adding the phrase 'except some fugitives'.[20] To make their conviction clear, the redactors repeat some of the elements of this attack in vv. 26f.: 'Behold, I am watching (*šōqēd*) over them for evil and not for good; all the men of Judah who are in the land of Egypt shall be consumed by the sword and by famine, until there is an end of them' (v. 27). The gloss at the end of v. 14 is here developed more fully into a statement about the few survivors who do manage to return to Judah; they will be 'few in number' (*mᵉtē mispār* v. 28). It is more likely that this verse has influenced the gloss in v. 14 and that vv. 26–28 belong to the latest stages of the development of the chapter. The way the text accommodates statements to the effect that everybody will be annihilated, and then modifies such statements by admitting to some survivors, indicates its rhetorical nature. It is arguable, however, that the modification represents a later stage of textual development, produced by sources which were aware of the return to Judah of refugees from Egypt. The problem with hyperbole is that, although ideal for sermons, it is a poor vehicle for dealing with reality. The stress on the annihilation of the community in vv. 26–28 is part of the central denunciation of idolatry in the sermon (vv. 15–25), and it is completed by the introduction of a sign confirming the sermon's predictions (vv. 29f.). Such a sign is very unusual in the Jeremiah tradition (cf. Isa. 7.10–17) and is most probably the work of the deuteronomists. The sign is usually taken as a prophecy after the event by someone aware of the palace intrigues of Amasis and Pharaoh Hophra, in which eventually Hophra was killed and Amasis reigned as Pharaoh till c. 526. As these events took place c. 570, the sign was probably constructed not long after that. The survival of Egypt and its friendly relations with Babylon during the closing decades of the Babylonian empire helped to vitiate the force of the predictions in this chapter. In such peaceful relations the Judaean communities in Egypt probably also enjoyed a stable existence.

The sermon has been expanded greatly by a lengthy diatribe against idolatry in vv. 15–25. The substance of this polemic is a reworking of the material on the same cult in 7.17f., where it is directed against practices in Jerusalem and the cities of Judah. The reapplication of the polemic to the communities in Egypt is further evidence of the deuteronomistic reuse of material first used against Jerusalem, to make an equation between the Judaean communities which underwent divine judgment and the Egyptian communities. Such an equation effectively removes those communities from any considerations of future hope and, at the same time, reinforces the hopes put forward for the Babylonian exiles. In effect, it strengthens their claims to be the sole community for which Yahweh cares and has plans of restoration. The polemic is essentially reflection upon reflection, i.e., in its original setting in 7.16–20 it is part of a highly convoluted attack on the cultic practices of the Judaean community, constructed by the deuteronomists as part of their denunciation of the people, but in 44.15–25 it is extended to apply to an entirely different group. It is a secondary use of material already functioning as secondary (i.e., redactional comment) in its primary setting. Again it is evidence of the ideological nature of the deuteronomistic attack on the community. It could be argued that the original setting for the polemic is ch. 44, and that it has been summarized in 7.17f., but this is much less likely to be the case because of the many expansions in 44.15–25. The detailed discussion of idolatry is a mark of the deuteronomistic outlook which, throughout the history of the kings of Israel and Judah, in the framework of Deuteronomy and at times in the Jeremiah tradition, obsessively analysed the disasters that befell the nations of Israel and Judah as the result of national idolatry. The charge of idolatry is part of the theodicy put forward by the deuteronomists, and to find such a lengthy denunciation of a particular cult in Jer. 44.15–25 is clear evidence of strong deuteronomistic activity in the tradition. Apart from passing references to Baalistic practices, there are no analyses of idolatry in Jeremiah's work. The one other lengthy consideration of idolatry in the Jeremiah tradition is 10.1–16, which is a complicated mixture of polemic against idols and a hymn celebrating the incomparability of Yahweh. It is not part of Jeremiah's work, but probably should be seen as an exilic addition to the tradition from cultic sources, either priestly or cult prophets.[21]

The discussion between Jeremiah and all the people in vv. 15–25 on the subject of the idolatrous cult is a very interesting one, whatever its origins or redaction. The specific cult is described as burning incense and pouring out libations to 'the queen of heaven' (vv. 17–19, 25); in 7.18 baking cakes for the queen of heaven is the central feature of the cult.[22] Although there are difficulties in identifying the precise cult alluded to here (either a specific Ishtar-Isis cult or a more general worship of astral deities) and problems about which period saw the flourishing of the cult (Manasseh's, Josiah's or later kings?), the argument used by the people to justify the practice should be studied by every religious group devoted to the empirical ('experience shows that . . .') approach to religion. The essence of the defence of popular religion is simply: 'It works'. When the community were loyal in their devotion to the cult they prospered, but ever since they had given up the cult they had experienced nothing but invasion and famine (vv. 17f.). If the argument represents a historical one, rather than a deuteronomistic construction, it may be a description, in very general terms, of the relative peace and prosperity enjoyed under Manasseh's long reign and the violent disruptions of life under Josiah, followed by various invasions during the reigns of the subsequent kings. The irony of the argument is that it is a mirror image of the deuteronomistic argument that well-being comes from pursuing a particular form of religion and deviation from that form leads to disaster. Given this style of argumentation (i.e., the argument from experience to theology), it is a moot point which approach is a proper assessment of the situation. Certainly there is as much force in the popular argument as there is in the deuteronomistic argument, because the argument from experience is a technique indifferent to ideology. It will support a wide range of diverse ideologies because experience requires a framework to give it meaning (as T. S. Eliot says in his *Four Quartets*, 'We had the experience but missed the meaning'). Different frameworks will read the 'same' experiences differently. For the community, working within its religious outlook, it was self-evident that devotion to the cult of the queen of heaven was an effective way of prosperous living. To the deuteronomists, such a cultic devotion was the very cause of the disasters which the community saw as the result of the lapse of the cult. The general argument is very similar to the popular myth about the fall of the Roman empire being due to the increase in licentious behaviour among the Romans, which politicians and religious leaders (who should know better) like to maintain as confirming their own particular ideological resolutions of society's problems. The Roman historians themselves did not advance this view in their analysis of the downfall of the empire, but argued that it was the influx of foreign cults, especially Christianity, which had led to the corruption of the community and deprived the empire of the protection of its ancient gods.[23] It would be foolish to attempt to explain complex social conditions by simple accounts of causation, and the fact that such folly has been practised

since at least the time of the deuteronomists is no defence for
continuing to indulge in such fantasy.

A further remarkable feature of the polemic against idolatry in
the sermon is the rather different reason given for the destruction
of the Judaean community. It is a very typical deuteronomistic
argument which attributes the destruction to Yahweh's judgment
against the community for burning incense to such cults: 'Yahweh
could no longer bear your evil doings and the abominations which
you committed; therefore your land has become a desolation and a
waste and a curse, without inhabitant, as it is this day. It is because
you burned incense . . .' (44.22f.). This is the argument of the
deuteronomistic edition of Jeremiah, which glossed the tradition in
terms of an anti-idolatry polemic. However, we have seen already
that a large block of the Jeremiah tradition is devoted to presenting
the collapse of Judah as the result of either prophets who misled
the community or the refusal of the kings, Zedekiah in particular,
to listen to Jeremiah (cf. chs. 26–38). The different accounts may
be taken as the end result of a very substantial tradition-building
process which produced a multi-layered account of the causes of the
exile.

Exiles and 'exiles'. The sermon against idolatry concludes the
section of traditions about the fall of Jerusalem and its aftermath.
There is a brief coda in ch. 45, which addresses a word of hope to
Baruch, but it has no connection with the narratives in chs. 37–44
(cf. 45.1, which dates the piece to the fourth year of Jehoiakim,
i.e., c. 605). Whatever the original source of some of these narratives
may have been (e.g., 40.7 – 43.7 may have come from a Jerusalem
source), they now stand in a context constructed by the deuteronomists designed to denigrate the Jerusalem and Judaean communities. Such denigration is intensely functional, and serves the purpose
of eliminating all communities other than the exiles in Babylon from
the future purposes of Yahweh. To this end a mythic view of the
exile is produced whereby the land of Judah remains uninhabited
during the exilic period (cf. 'no one dwells in them', 44.2; 'without
inhabitant', 44.22; 'leaving no remnant', 44.7; 'to cut off *all* Judah',
44.11). A similar view appears in the later writings of the Chronicler
when he describes the period of exile as a time when the land was
empty for seventy years: 'all the days that it lay desolate it kept
sabbath, to fulfil seventy years' (II Chron. 36.21). It is a mythic (or
ideological) view of the exile, and indicates a non-historical attitude
which required the land to be empty so that the exilic community

could return to it and repopulate it. That return would constitute a new beginning in a land purified by the absence of people for seventy years and repopulated by a people purified by the experience of exile. It is all highly theological and, as in all ideological accounts of reality, not to be confused with the historical experience of exile. It was a good deal more untidy than the deuteronomists or the Chronicler imagined, and the reality was quite different. Judah was not uninhabited during the exile; various communities survived and lived through the period. The Egyptian Jewish refugee communities also thrived throughout the period and after. Furthermore, when the exile was over (it must be remembered that the description of the period as 'exilic' is derived entirely from the perspective of the communities which were in exile and not from the communities which remained in Palestine – the term indicates the success of the deuteronomistic myth!), the communities in Egypt and Babylon continued to thrive *there* and only a few exiles returned to the homeland. The future of Judaism lay with different communities in different countries and not simply with exiles returning from Babylon. It is, therefore, very necessary to distinguish sharply between historical reality and ideological factors in the representation of that reality. To do otherwise is to be misled completely by the deuteronomistic construction of reality to reflect its own ideology.

The ideology of the redactors of the Jeremiah tradition is used in the tradition to carry their viewpoint by the presentation of Jeremiah the prophet, and by the sustained representation of the Jerusalem and Judaean communities as incorrigibly corrupt, to the point of having no part to play in the future. It is correct to say that the deuteronomists' view is: 'Only in exile and only among the exiles is there hope for the future', but that principle needs to be made more precise so as to reflect the proper nuances of the redactors. 'Only in the Babylonian exile and only among the Babylonian exiles is that hope to be found.' It is a fine example of partisan politics.

10

From Chaos to Covenant:
Uses of Prophecy in Jeremiah

No single image of the prophet exists in the tradition. Rather is it made up of many streams of tradition flowing into a central reservoir constructed by the traditionists over a lengthy period of time. Beginning with the enigmatic poet figure whose poems attacked the conduct and complacency of the community, the tradition has been built up, to change the metaphor, into a multi-storey edifice with many levels contributed by many sources. The poetic figure remains as the basis of it all, but the overall picture is one of a magisterial authority figure mediating the divine word through sermon, prayer and action. From an aloof poet haranguing the community to the central character in the nation standing between it and disaster the many layers of the tradition reveal how the sixth century responded, in one way, to the loss of statehood. Too much theology and ideology was shaken by the events of the period between 597–587 for the old ways to be maintained without some rethinking. Loss of royal house and temple, monarchy and priesthood, courtiers and intelligentsia, accompanied by severe depopulation caused by invasions, starvation, famine, slaughter and deportations, registered deeply in the nation's consciousness and gave rise to many movements of response and readjustment. Among the most thoroughgoing and significant responses was the creation of the Jeremiah tradition.

The stages by which the poet became a deuteronomistic prophet are very difficult to determine, and it is also far from clear when the tradition was completed. Judging by various later additions to the tradition (e.g., the Topheth material in ch. 19; the levitical elements in 33.17–22; the oracles against Babylon in chs. 50–51) the latest strands may belong to the post-exilic, i.e., the Persian, period. However, the main concerns of this analysis have not been with the origins, composition and development of the Jeremiah tradition, but with the various uses made of prophecy throughout the book.

These are more manageable concerns than a theory of how the book of Jeremiah came to be in its present form. All the main blocks of material in the tradition have been considered, except for the oracles against the nations. These oracles (chs. 46–51) are usually the element omitted from general treatments of Jeremiah and, as in Skinner's treatment, I have avoided giving them a separate chapter. One reason for this omission – though the oracles contain many interesting features – is the rather conventional nature of the material (they are what the book of Jeremiah has in common with many of the prophetic traditions), which renders them less a distinctive use of prophecy in Jeremiah than the other blocks of tradition; another reason is the wish to have more time to think about them before providing an analysis of them.[1] They are touched upon at various points throughout my book, so they are not entirely neglected, but economies of space have militated against giving them a separate treatment. Among commentators there is no agreement about whether they are genuine oracles of Jeremiah or secondary additions to the tradition. I am inclined to agree with those who regard them as secondary, especially the oracles against Babylon.[2] I find it difficult to accept the tradition that Jeremiah was a great friend of the Babylonians and also preached such invective against them. Of course that is probably also a secondary tradition, but it develops out of the basic tradition more coherently than the oracles against the nations. The material against Babylon is too late for the prophet (50.2, with its explanation in v. 3, presupposes the Persian conquest of Babylon c. 539), who is unlikely to have been a lively and still active centenarian. It is quite possible that some genuine Jeremiah material may be preserved among the oracles, and on that point I have an open mind. The conventional nature of the oracles, also found especially in the Isaiah and Ezekiel traditions, suggests a common source in ancient Israel which encouraged its professional prophets to attack the nations. In the traditions of prophets who attacked Judah and Israel (cf. Amos 1–2; 3–9), rather than indulged in such chauvinistic behaviour, such oracles are disjunctive. This does not rule out the possibility that these prophets were conventional also, but it does raise serious questions about how radical they really were.

Any discussion of the oracles against the nations inevitably raises this perennial issue of the consistency of the canonical prophets, or of any person in ancient cultures for that matter. Space does not permit a discussion on cultural relativism and the nature of truth in the ancient world, but a brief comment may be justified. It is always a very difficult matter to determine to what extent ancient writers were aware of contradictions and inconsistencies in the works they produced. In religion and politics, contradictions and inconsistencies are even more difficult to detect (this is probably as true today as it was in the ancient world). To the believer, no matter what system the belief is invested in, everything is coherent and consistent, whereas to the outsider contradictions and inconsistencies abound. It is the story of the emperor's new clothes: those who share the paradigm see them, the outsider cannot see them.[3] Yet it is not as simple as that because the Greek historians (especially Herodotus and Thucydides) could distinguish between fact and fantasy, history and fable, and some of the biblical writers could recognize a contradiction when they saw one. The various answers to the question 'Who killed Goliath?', David (I Sam. 17), Elhanan (II Sam. 21.19), were sorted out into a consistent account by the Chronicler (I Chron. 20.5). So the Chronicler must have been able to spot a contradiction and feel strongly enough about it to correct it. Others may not have noticed the contradictions, which therefore did not bother them. Had such contradictions been pointed out, it might have been a different matter. So perhaps we should distinguish between a toleration of unnoticed contradictions and a positive eye for spotting them. Other contradictions only arise out of contingent juxtapositions, such as the combination of books in a collection. This is the main source of contradictions in the Bible, e.g., both Paul and James use Gen. 15.6, but they use it to prove precisely opposite propositions (cf. Gal. 3.6–9 with James 2.20–24). Taken separately, such opinions may cause little difficulty, but, fortuitously combined together in the same sacred book centuries later, they constitute a formidable contradiction. These things considered, it is a difficult task to decide to what extent the chauvinism of the oracles is compatible with the trenchant critique of the prophet's own nation in the prophetic traditions. As with so many issues in the interpretation of prophecy, it is a matter of probabilities which can only be determined by a sophisticated *blend* of subjectivity (judgment) and objectivity (textual analysis) on the part of the sensitive scholar.

The real effect of the inclusion of the oracles against the nations in the Jeremiah tradition is the evidence it provides of how the traditionists saw the prophet. He was not a radical innovator who spoke only against his own people, but a conventional prophet who also proclaimed disaster for the neighbouring nations. The presentation combines chauvinism with radicalism; indeed it stresses the conventional role of Jeremiah by fitting him into a long line of prophets who 'prophesied war, famine, and pestilence against many countries and great kingdoms' (28.8). That is why the tradition contains perhaps the greatest amount of material against the nations in the prophetic traditions.[4] In the introduction to the tradition the redactors stress this fact by making Jeremiah 'a prophet to the nations' (1.4; cf. v. 10). As the communities in Palestine, Babylon and Egypt settled down to life in foreign lands or under foreign dominance, it became very important to construct a working relationship with these powers. The Jeremiah tradition may be regarded as one such development, though the oracles against the nations may not support that view unless it can be shown that they belong to a different strand of development. However, if the oracles are scrutinized, it will be seen that they attack the neighbouring states (e.g., the Philistines [!], Moab, the Ammonites, Edom, Syria, Kedar and the kingdoms of Hazor, and inevitably Egypt) and the doomed Babylon, but nowhere is the Persian empire attacked. Now this is a feature of all the collections of oracles against the nations in the prophetic traditions. Not one of them offers a devastating critique of or threat of doom against the Persian authorities. This negative feature of such collections indicates two things (at least). The chauvinistic habit of ranting against the other nations came to an end with the fall of Babylon. The radical changes introduced by Persian governmental organization made many of these nations provinces within the empire; as such they, including the Judah-Jerusalem community, were in no position to revolt or preach against the imperial authorities. The hopes for a sudden reversal of fortunes expressed in Hag. 2.21–23 are too general to identify the Persian empire explicitly, and are the final expression of an attitude completely out of place in the new regime. The presence of the oracles in Jer. 46–51 in the Jeremiah tradition indicates one further stream of tradition which flowed into the collection and helped to construct the book of Jeremiah. They come from a period before the effective establishment of the Persian government and represent a view of life rapidly disappearing. The concern with placating or co-operating with foreign governments expressed in the letter of 29.7 (in contrast to the sentiments expressed in chs. 50–51; cf. Ps. 137.8f.) was to become the normal way of life. If such a concern accounts for 29.7 and the other narratives which express a favourable attitude to the Babylonians, then the stream which contributed chs. 46–51 to the tradition must have come from discrete sources. One group of traditionists contributed them to the Jeremiah tradition, thereby spoiling the effect of the pro-Babylonian material in the tradition. Such diversity of traditions within the one book shows the different contexts and periods involved in the production of the tradition, and makes it that much harder to schematize its development and composition. The streams have not produced a unified book but a collection of variegated traditions which are held together loosely by the creation of the figure of the prophet.

The presentation of the prophet is the linking element between so many discrete elements in the tradition, and this factor may help to explain the shape and size of the book of Jeremiah. It is the largest of the prophetic collections, but has no centre without the figure of Jeremiah. Just as the Isaiah tradition is made up of many reworkings and reinterpretations of salvation motifs, and the Ezekiel tradition focuses on cultic perspectives on the exile, the Jeremiah tradition builds up the figure of a prophet. This distinctive feature of the tradition may be due to the strong influence of the deuteronomists at various stages of the tradition's growth. Apart from their interest in history as the encounter between king and community and the divine word mediated by the prophets, some of their circle incorporated into the deuteronomistic edition of the laws (Deuteronomy) the notion of a prophet to whom the community should pay attention (Deut. 18.15–18). The figure of Jeremiah may well have been a spelling out of this ruling.[5] Throughout the Jeremiah tradition, the prophet is portrayed as a preacher the community ought to have listened to but regularly rejected. As a consequence of this obdurate attitude the community was destroyed. King, individuals, and community are all presented as rejecting the prophet, and as a result of such failure to hear the prophet the Babylonians invade and destroy the land. The obscure poet Jeremiah is made into a paradigmatic figure through the deuteronomistic handling of the tradition. The retelling of various stories allows many different elements of the redactors' view of prophecy to be demonstrated in a concrete way. Hence the creation of the *prophet* Jeremiah. Such must be considered one of the major uses of prophecy in the book of Jeremiah, and it is probably not an exaggeration to say that such a presentation has contributed a great deal to the popular view of a prophet.

If we seek to confirm such a presentation of a prophet from other biblical writings, it will invariably be from the prophets featured in the deuteronomistic history. Little or nothing is said about most of the figures behind the traditions in the book of the twelve: Jonah is too midrashic to count for much in this matter, the Amos incident

(Amos 7.10–17) is the most problematic in that tradition, and Hosea's marriage is too symbolical to establish a pattern of prophetic
behaviour. To find paradigms of prophets, we must look either in
the deuteronomistic history or in the other two large traditions,
Isaiah and Ezekiel. The Isaiah material yields very little information
on how prophets behave, because it consists mostly of poetic oracles
which lack biographical details. The small element of biographical
material in Isa. 6.1–8.18; 20.1–6 (chs. 36–39 do not count as they
belong to the deuteronomistic history; cf. II Kings 18.13–20.19) is
therefore a feature of the tradition which immediately calls for
scrutiny because of its distinctiveness in a lengthy collection of
virtually anonymous oracles.[6] Apart from a few exchanges between
the prophet and the elders of the exiles, Ezekiel is mainly represented by very long speeches and visions. There is a protracted call
narrative for him and a number of actions are ascribed to him.
However, as he is clearly an exilic figure, we may expect biographical
material to appear in his tradition. It is not on the same scale as the
Jeremiah tradition, but then there is no individual prophet's tradition which contains so much biographical material as the book of
Jeremiah does. That fact should alert the intelligent reader to ask
the question: 'Is there something special about the book of Jeremiah?' It will not do to say, 'Jeremiah did more than any other
prophet', or 'All the other prophets *said* a great deal but Jeremiah
did many things.' We have no grounds for thinking that Jeremiah
stood out among a group of peculiarly inert prophets. It is much
more likely that the particular nature of the material in Jeremiah
signals an important fact about the tradition. It was created by
people who were very interested in portraying a prophet in terms
of his life, his activities and his relations with important members
of society. Other traditionists were not, so the traditions they produced focused on the poems and sayings attributed to their figures.
But the Jeremiah tradition was produced by redactors who developed the poems into an account of the life and times of the prophet.
To what extent any of the material they used reflected or was based
upon the real life of Jeremiah cannot be determined from the tradition. Everything has been subsumed under their concern to create
a tradition which would carry their ideology during a time of crisis
and which would give them power in the reconstructionist period.
The tradition probably began with the poems but provided prose
insertions which occasionally interpret the poems. Other poems and
laments were created and incorporated into the tradition, which was
then developed by a series of narratives which reconstructed the

poet as a prophet engaged in dialogue with or preaching to the community, the royal court or important officials in the community. None of these elements is in the tradition merely to tell the story of a prophet, but each account may be related to the problem of creating a theodicy which would justify the disasters which destroyed the community between 609 and 587.

Adherents of the Skinnerian approach will protest that to assume such a development of the tradition is to ignore the explicit statements in the text. On the contrary, it is to take note of what the text says but in relation to what *all* the texts say. The double or different accounts of the same occasion or event provide distinctive perspectives for viewing the relation between the prophet and the community, but hardly give factual reports of anything. All the time the prophet Jeremiah strides through the tradition as the true prophet, the central focus of the community's life. This is not only hindsight; it is ideology. This kind of ideology is to be found in deuteronomistic writers and so, when it is found in Jeremiah, it must be traced to them. To argue that Jeremiah really was the great prophet the tradition says he was is to beg the question. If the community disregarded him, he cannot have been the great prophet later generations imagined him to have been.[7] The whole story is told from a later perspective, and Jeremiah fills the role set for him by the tradition. This is where the analogy with the quest of the historical Jesus works for the Jeremiah tradition. Just as we can never be sure *now* whether statements attributed to Jesus in the gospels were said by him or of him by the early church, so we can never be sure that sayings or actions attributed to Jeremiah belonged to him originally or were created by the redactors. Whatever confidence there might be in accepting some elements of the gospels as representing something close to the historical Jesus, there is much less for Jeremiah. The Jesus story was eventually committed to writing in the light of what had happened to him and afterwards in the development of the church. The life of Jeremiah came to be written because of the events which destroyed the community and the way they vindicated the prophet. This may suggest a connection between Jeremiah and the way the tradition developed. I am not suggesting that there were no such connections, but that from the basis of the poems the tradition developed in a number of ways which had very little to do with the original figure, and very much to do with the redactors and the needs of the communities in the sixth century. Such developments exist for the Isaiah and Ezekiel traditions; it would be foolish to imagine that the Jeremiah tradition did not so develop.

The collapse of the state during the period of 597–587 led to the emergence of a number of communities created by Judaeans surviving the catastrophic years. These grew up in Egypt, Babylon and especially in Judah. Even in Jerusalem life continued and, although conditions after the siege were not ideal, people eked out a subsistence which became the basis for a future reconstruction of the city and its hinterland. Such communities were to play a very important part in the life of the nation over the next few centuries, and helped to create Judaism. Without the communities in Egypt and Babylon it would be difficult to imagine what Judaism might have been like or how different it would have been. Between the two destructions of Jerusalem (587 and 70 CE) conflict within these communities was the great creative force which did much to shape the Judaism which emerged after the fall of Jerusalem in Roman times. Stress on this factor of the communities is intended to explain why the redaction history of the book of Jeremiah is so important, and also why the functions of the various tradition blocks should be examined.

One of the major features which differentiates the historical critical approach to the Bible from precritical and traditional approaches is the view that the various books in the Bible do not have single authors but are the products of many writers, often writing over a lengthy period. This approach to the biblical literature allows for a much more realistic understanding of what is going on in any particular book or tradition. It also permits an investigation of the text in relation to some of the forces which may have given rise to it. The text is no longer seen as just the product of its writers and redactors but as having much greater significance than that. It is the response of various elements in the community to issues arising in and for the community. It is an attempt to deal with such issues by means of the production of a tradition which is partly constructed to meet such needs and partly produced by such needs. There is therefore a very strong connection between a tradition and the community out of which it grows. This production is also related to crises within the community. The impetus to edit or produce a particular tradition may come from such crises, so that a biblical work may be a series of responses to the problems thrown up by a critical period in the community's life. In this sense some of the biblical writings should be seen as attempted answers to the questions posed by the community's experiences of crisis.[8] This approach helps to account for why the sixth century was such a productive period for creating traditions in the Judaean communities (e.g., Jeremiah, Ezekiel, the deuteronomistic history, possibly Job and the priestly writing). The collapse of the nation's institutions and the exilic experience of various groups made the past very important, yet demanded responses for the future. Among these responses the production over a lengthy period of the Jeremiah tradition must be considered one of the most important achievements of the community.

I stress the role of the community in the production of the Jeremiah tradition for a number of reasons. It draws attention away from the popular myth of the heroic individual performing in and writing his own book (whether actually writing it or directing Baruch in its production makes little difference). It recognizes the time element in the creation of the tradition, and the way community issues shape the end product of the process. In fact it is a way of emphasizing that the composition of the tradition is more a process than an event. Over a period of time, different elements are brought together and the tradition emerges out of the combination of these elements, which are then supplemented by further elements. Slowly the tradition is built up, as different elements shape a response to the crisis facing the community and expansions come about by the addition of discrete features to the central body of work. Starting off from a collection of poems critical of the community and warning of impending invasive destruction, the tradition is created by prose commentaries on the poems which construct a life of the prophet in conflict with the community. This is developed to such a length that it is clear from reading Jeremiah that the disaster of the fall of Jerusalem is *the* crisis to which the tradition is *the* response. Sense is made of that disaster by identifying its causes and the guilty parties. However, making sense of the past is not a sufficient response to the crisis, because the communities living after the collapse of city and state need hope for the future. So the tradition develops the future aspects of the matter to encourage various groups to live through the difficulties of the period and to look forward to a better future. Community needs, then, are a very important feature of the tradition building impetus and can be divided into two categories: a need to come to terms with the past, to have it explained and sense made of it (the theodicy elements in the tradition achieve the meeting of such a need); then a need for future hope, a resolution of the current state of affairs so that the community has something to work towards. Because different communities are involved (Judaean, Egyptian, Babylonian), different responses to the future are to be found in the tradition. A post-exilic edition of the tradition may have focused on just the Jerusalem community, but, as it now stands, the book has elements addressed to the exiles in Babylon and the groups left in Judah. The absence of any reference to a future hope for the exiles in Egypt may indicate a strongly polemical attitude to such groups, or it may point to the development of the tradition in an anti-Judaean community direction. Because the communities in Egypt represent Judaean forces which left Judah to escape further Babylonian interference (Jer. 41–44), the very pointed threats against *all* the Judaeans in Egypt probably represent a concealed advocacy of another group's claim to Judah and Jerusalem. Given the positive attitude expressed elsewhere in the book of Jeremiah towards the exiles in Babylon, the final stage of the tradition may have been undertaken with their interests in mind.

The disagreement among scholars about the location for the composition of the tradition, be it in Palestine, Egypt or Babylonia, is understandable because of the lack of direct information on the subject. A case can be made out for each location, though each case may only be able to use some of the information available. If the interests of the community are taken as the central factor behind the redaction and due allowance is made for conflict between the communities of an ideological nature, then it may be possible to see in the final forms of the tradition the claim of a particular group to the control of the Jerusalem community. This possibility depends upon viewing the later stages of the redaction as arising in Palestine in response to the struggle for power in the reconstructed community. We know from Haggai, Zechariah, the material appended to Isa. 40–55 (Isa. 56–66), and the Ezra-Nehemiah traditions that from 520 to the late fifth century the Jerusalem community was engaged in fierce struggles over the shape and direction of the community. What should be done? who should do it? what about the neighbouring communities? how was the future organization of the city to be constructed? As part of the answers to these questions, the material on the Babylonian exiles in the Jeremiah tradition may have been designed to credit the claims of returning exiles with the imprimatur of the prophet Jeremiah. Their claim to the city was based on Jeremiah's identification of them as the people favoured by Yahweh and restored to their own land. This claim is a counter-claim to a similar one made by those who remained in Judah (cf. Jer. 42.1–12), a claim also backed by Jeremiah's authority. So we have two groups claiming Jeremiah's backing for their control of Jerusalem and Judah. As the Judaean group's claim is developed in the tradition into an account of how the group fled to Egypt, thereby deserting Judah and facing the wrath of Yahweh, we must assume that the redactors have edited and produced a narrative which undercuts the Judaean claims. It makes a good deal of sense to see such a dismissal as part of the counter-claim of the Babylonian exiles who returned to Palestine at various periods in the Persian era. The great ideological presentations of Palestine during the exile come from an exilic perspective which does not admit of an occupied territory during the period, so the writing off of the claims of other groups is greatly facilitated by such a presentation. The presence in the Jeremiah tradition of pericopes siding with the Babylonian exiles suggests an element in that community struggle after the ending of the Babylonian period. It may also contribute to the view that one of the strongest reasons for the production of the Jeremiah tradition along the lines it now takes is as a contribution to one of the parties in the struggle within the community.

The underwriting of a group's claims by a prophet is a stage in the development of the image of Jeremiah in the tradition. It also points to an argument for why the tradition, unlike the other prophetic traditions, has such a concentration of narratives about the life of a prophet. The narratives of Jeremiah the prophet have not only been developed in line with the deuteronomistic view of prophecy but have also been constructed to carry the claims of a specific group within the larger community struggles of the reconstructionist period. It is not simply the teaching of the prophet, however important that may be for the theodicy, which is contained in the tradition; the development of the prophet interacting with the Judaean community contributes to the force of his affirmation of the Babylonian exiles. The other traditions stress the content of the prophetic oracles, but the Jeremiah tradition goes much further in its development of prophecy by constructing a life for the prophet. In this life the prophet is ranged against various official strata in the community, denying their hopes and aspirations for the future. Each encounter with an official body ends in the rejection of the prophetic word and the concomitant rejection of the community. In the midst of these encounters the prophet writes to the deportees, who have gone into exile to Babylon, assuring them that their future is secure and that they will eventually return home (29.1–14; cf. 32.37–44). The *figure* of the prophet became as important as the oracles associated with him in the late sixth century (hence the material in Isa. 6–8), and if we are to understand how Jeremiah came to be regarded as a 'great' prophet, in spite of the singular lack of success in his lifetime, then we must seek such an understanding in the complex issues involved in rebuilding the community in the Persian era. The needs of the community contributed to the deuteronomistic development of the prophet as a historical figure working within the earlier community.

There is a tendency in much writing about the Bible to assume, or to argue from the position, that a major figure, be it Moses, David, Isaiah or Jeremiah, emerged in the community fully developed as a great person.[9] This is an unrealistic, as well as a false, interpretation of the matter. Nor is it simply a matter of later generations coming to recognize the greatness of a person in his own time. It is much more a case of the development of that person through a number of traditions until his later status is retrojected into the past and he appears always to have been what he has become now. His greatness is the creation of the developed tradition rather than the cause of that tradition. This is not to deny Jeremiah significance, but to recognize the creativity of the tradition building. The vindication of his critique by the events following 597 and 587 helped to develop the tradition which then moulded him in the form of a deuteronomistic prophet and presented him in a substantially different light from that of his original status. Just as Winston Churchill's many failings as a politician have been eclipsed by his performance during the 1939-45 war, so that many people think of him in such heroic terms for his whole life, so the collapse of Jerusalem enhanced Jeremiah's reputation and gave rise to the development of him as the great prophet. It would be a mistake to read back into history the later views and presentation of the prophet.

Part of the development of Jeremiah into the figure of the great prophet is achieved by the use of traditional language to construct his soliloquies. The strong influences of the formal language of the Psalms, especially the laments, and the book of Job have been emphasized in this book, and the presentation of the prophet in such terms anchors him in the general experience of the community. As part of the formal response to the tragic events of the fall of Jerusalem, the redaction represents the prophet bemoaning his lot in terms reflecting the communal reactions to the catastrophe. It is very difficult to determine whether only one level of representation is present in the text or many levels portray prophet, community and exilic elements. This polyvalent material therefore allows a wide latitude of interpretation: it is the outpouring of Jeremiah's own confessions, it is the redactors' shaping of those confessions, it is the community's response to the tragedy, it is the laments of various sixth-century groups, it is a later presentation of the community's responses to grief under the image of the prophet, or it is even a theologization of the divine suffering brought about by the destruction of the people. It would be foolish to insist that only one meaning should be drawn from the material; the language is too formal and, as with so much poetry, too ambiguous to be on solid ground if only one interpretation is taken. Yet it is also unsatisfactory that such ambiguity should undermine the attempt to understand the poems. However, the strong links between the language of the soliloquies and that of the Psalms and Job within the context of the exilic period provide some evidence for the contention that the redactors have fused images of the prophet with images of the community responding to the disaster which befell city, community and country.

The contrast between the image of the prophet delineated in these soliloquies and the poet behind the oracles is striking. In the oracles the community is denounced and consigned to destruction, whereas in the soliloquies the prophet is presented as dissociating himself from his message (cf. 17.16). In the oracles the community is evil and deserving of destruction, but in the soliloquies the speaker is innocent, conspired against and suffering wrongfully. Such a contrast can be found in some of the lament psalms: on some occasions the community confesses itself to be guilty, on other occasions the community pleads its innocence. Both responses were made to the events which destroyed the state. The ambivalence of such responses can only be noted here, because it would take too long to investigate the tendency in the biblical writings, especially poetic and cultic sections, for polarities of opinion to be expressed. Events may be caused by Yahweh or created by men (cf. the conquest of Canaan by Joshua's armed campaigns and the cultic reading of that conquest in Ps. 44.2f. [Heb. vv. 3f.]), or a man may be innocent, and yet despise himself and repent (e.g. Job 1.1; 42.6). The catastrophe of Jerusalem's destruction could be interpreted as Yahweh's punishment of the community for its sinfulness, but it could also be seen as the suffering of the innocent for the sake of God (cf. Ps. 44.17–22 [Heb. vv. 18–23]; Isa. 53; the book of Job). It may be argued that these examples of the suffering of the innocent should not be related to the exile, but there are as good grounds for such an interpretation of them as there are for other views. For an individual or a community to claim to be both innocent and guilty may appear to be contradictory, but in theology contradictions are usually called paradoxes. Some Protestant positions should have no difficulty here, given Luther's great principle of *simul iustus simul peccator*, 'both justified and a sinner'. However, the two positions need not be contradictory, because they may not be put forward together. The accusation of guilt may be met with an affirmation of innocence, though in the Jeremiah tradition there are liturgical elements indicating the confession of guilt (cf. 3.21–23; 14.7–9, 19–22). Might it not be the case that the soliloquies represent the communities in exile, or even in Judaean territory, lamenting their state and pleading their innocence, whereas the accusations of wickedness and confessions of guilt represent other strands in the tradition? In the light of this possible explanation, the soliloquies may be a strand of exilic response which saw the community as the victim of wicked oppressors (a strand which resonates quite well with the oracles against the nations). This would be another use of prophecy in the tradition, whereby it carried those elements of protest or complaint at outraged virtue during the long period when Jerusalem lay in ruins and the Babylonians dominated the whole territory. As spokesman for the community the laments are put in the prophet's mouth and he speaks the laments of the oppressed community. Thus his greatness as a man standing for the community's well-being is further established. It is an interesting way of handling the text and suggests yet another reversal of images within the tradition. The figure who preached against the nation's well-being has become the speaker on its behalf in the development of the tradition.

Many uses of prophecy in the book of Jeremiah have been discussed in this analysis and, if space permitted, many more could be investigated. However the salient features of the general argument have been given in sufficient detail to convince the reader of the case being made or to dissuade against such a view being taken. The two main features isolated in the book's title 'From *chaos* to *covenant*' are intended to describe the outer limits of the material investigated. From the chaotic conditions of Judah in decline to the very late strands in the tradition which hoped for a return to old standards but with new emphases, the processes which produced the Jeremiah tradition continually arose out of the needs of the community. If some of the elements in the tradition focus more directly on the creation and presentation of the prophet Jeremiah, that should not deflect our attention from the very important communal aspects of tradition building. Contrary to conventional belief, the canonic processes which gave rise to scripture were not just the work of gifted individuals but arose out of the community and, like so much other work produced in antiquity and the medieval ages (e.g., the great megalithic monuments and the magnificent cathedrals of European civilization), were the products of many anonymous groups.[10] Confronting the chaos produced by the invading hordes of Babylonians (external chaos) and the disintegration of the community produced by false cults and ideologies (internal chaos), the growth of the tradition was prompted by many reactions to the needs of the community. Explanatory responses (theodicy), complex redactional developments, hopes for the future, projected programmes, and more traditional reactions against the other nations have all contributed to the rich network of traditions forming the book of Jeremiah. In spite of the very lengthy narratives and deuteronomistic sermons, there is no coherent pattern in the book. The images of chaos and the new covenant are used, but not developed very fully (cf. 4.23–26; 31.31–34). They are there, but whatever they represent is not unfolded. Yet the two images cover the whole range of the period, from the disintegration of the kingdom to the almost utopian vision of the future where harmony has been restored within the community. It is not a case of a group of redactors putting together all the strands in a coherent, cogent order so as to produce a blueprint for the future attached to a map of the past. Rather is it a complex gathering together, though not with too much order or connection, of many strands, elements and features covering a lengthy period and developed from many sources. These have been fused together into a nexus of many layers which, to change the metaphor, is almost geological in its complexity. The material has been gone over time and again in order to extract from it a wide variety of perspectives for viewing the community and the prophet. It has been added to and reshaped perhaps too often for us to be able to discern a single strand running throughout the tradition, for it is not that kind of book.

The great differences between the Hebrew and Greek developments of the tradition indicate further hermeneutical complexities in the understanding of the prophet by many different communities, and also suggest that a rather different view was taken of Jeremiah in the communities from that taken of Isaiah. If the Isaiah tradition has about it a fixity which graduates towards the canonic, the Jeremiah tradition has a fluidity which expresses a more dynamic or protean aspect than a canonic one. Yet it is the Jeremiah tradition which carries most of the material about prophets and their activities in the prophetic traditions. The book of Isaiah focuses on the teaching (*tōrāh*), whereas the book of Jeremiah focuses on the prophet.

The distinction owes something to the activities of the deuteronomists, but may also point to developments in the period and needs
in the community which were met by such a presentation. Here the
explanations attempted become too speculative to be useful, but the
differences between the two great prophetic traditions are certainly
worth considering and, if possible, mapping. However, such a task
is unwarranted at this stage of my book.

The contexts out of which biblical books have come are something
we know very little about. What little we do know has been gained
from persistent and percipient questioning of the text, as well as the
use of information afforded by archaeological materials bearing on
the period depicted in the text. Lacking full information about the
communities and settings which produced the books makes it much
more difficult to interpret them, because so much information is
determined by knowing its context or origin. Without such knowledge some things are very difficult to understand.[11] If we knew
much more about the processes which produced the Jeremiah tradition it would be easier to construct an account of its composition
and to understand better the meaning of many of its elements.
Because we do not have that knowledge all theories about the book
must remain speculative; but that is not a denigration of such
speculation; rather is it a recognition of the need for a responsible
and judicious postulation of theories about the composition and
signification of the book of Jeremiah. I have suggested a number of
motifs in the tradition which point to the communal activities behind
the shaping of the text. The interaction of community and tradition
produced by the needs of the period appears to me to be a better
account of the book than the flat Skinnerian approach which makes
the biographical approach the basis of the tradition. It accounts for
more in the tradition, though it does have its weaknesses, as all
approaches have. Where it gains over the Skinnerian view is its
recognition of the various distancing moves in the tradition which
reveal the redaction contemplating and creating the prophetic figure
by means of narratives. The degree of development and reflection
in the tradition is also better brought out by such an approach,
though the functioning of piety is less well served (see Appendix
II). There are gains and losses in any approach, and many will feel
that in losing the person of the prophet in exchange for a deeper
insight into the way traditions are created and developed they have
lost more than they have gained. What is a loss to some will be a
gain to others. It is all a matter of perspective.

It has become fashionable in the field of biblical commentaries to include in the discussion a section on the history of exegesis. Such an inclusion has many virtues, though brevity is seldom one of them. The history of ideas and the history of the ways texts have been interpreted are fascinating aspects of scholarship, but to incorporate them into biblical commentaries is a daunting task because of the sheer amount of material available for treatment. The multitudinous traditions of Judaism, Christianity (especially Catholic and Protestant), humanism, rationalism, Marxian and secular philosophies as well as the wide range of literature (poetry, drama, novels, short stories) relating to the Bible are so enormous that to produce a history of exegesis and interpretation would compound Qoheleth's worst fears that 'of making many books there is no end'. Only by ignoring most of the material and selecting a few major figures in Jewish and Christian biblical exegesis is it possible to give a semblance of feasibility to the project.[12] Yet in spite of the difficulties involved in such an approach, there may be something to be said for attempting to outline some of the factors involved in the history of the exegesis of a *particular* biblical book. Space does not permit a proper treatment of the history of the exegesis and interpretation of the book of Jeremiah here, but a few comments may be appropriate.

The dichotomy between text and interpretation in biblical studies is a very artificial one which easily misleads the reader into thinking there are two distinctive activities involved. There are not. The text itself is already composed of many interpretative moves and decisions. Although the text is the object we interpret, it is itself the product of interpretation. To ignore that factor is to fail to understand the nature of hermeneutic. Throughout this book I have emphasized the large amount of interpretative activity which gave rise to the text in the first place, so interpretation has already begun when we approach the text. We may choose to extend that interpretative movement beyond the limits of the specific book under scrutiny, and such an extension takes us into the history of exegesis and interpretation. But in order to keep work within manageable proportions it is necessary to set strict limits to what will be investigated. Hence the tendency to separate text from subsequent interpretation. Such a separation may be justified, provided that why it is being done is recognized, and allowance made for it in the treatment of the subject.

The figure of Jeremiah emerges out of a number of interpretative activities which produced the tradition: the poet behind the poems becomes the conventional prophet acting in relation to the community and its leaders. Then he becomes a deuteronomistic preacher offering king or community the possibility of repentance at every turn. His early visions of hope are reinterpreted to apply to the Diaspora communities (just as his early oracles of doom are reapplied to the Babylonian threat). Other elements, e.g., the preaching against the nations, are incorporated into the collection, and the tradition of a multifaceted prophet is developed. There is such a large proportion of interpreted material within the tradition that any history of the exegesis and interpretation of the book of Jeremiah would have to have a very lengthy first chapter on the book itself! The distinctive Hebrew and Greek traditions of Jeremiah constitute two major sources for investigating the history of interpretation, which continue to generate research programmes. We have already noted a number of elements in the book of Jeremiah, e.g., the seventy years of 25.11f.; 29.10, and the figure of Baruch, which are developed significantly in later traditions. The influence of the Jeremiah tradition on the New Testament, apart from contributing to the title of that collection, is quite considerable.[13] To trace the varied uses of Jeremiah in early Judaism and Christianity would require a separate volume, especially for the patristic period.[14] With the Reformation there came a new impetus for writing commentaries on biblical books, partly inspired by the great medieval rabbinic commentators such as Rashi and Qimhi. Commentaries on Jeremiah by Rashi, Qimhi and John Calvin are only the iceberg tip of work done on Jeremiah in the period from the eleventh to the sixteenth century, but to give a proper account of the interpretation of Jeremiah in that period would demand yet another book.[15] In the post-Reformation period, the development of the historical-critical method, under the influence of rationalism, gave rise to the modern hermeneutical approach to scripture which brought with it another set of approaches and interpretations.

It would be folly to attempt to set out the different approaches to Jeremiah in literature, poetry and drama.[16] The image of the lonely prophet courageously attacking king and people is one that appeals to radical political theology today, and it is not surprising to find that Jeremiah was virtually a folk hero for radical theologians involved in American politics of the 1960s and 1970s. The Czechoslovak dissident philospher Vitezslav Gardavsky was working on a book on Jeremiah before his death in 1978.[17] Such an approach to Jeremiah is fine as an application of certain aspects of the tradition in the analysis of modern society, but it has to be controlled very carefully, otherwise too many illegitimate transfers of meaning will be made. Its attractiveness is part of the temptation to oversimplify the use of biblical material for interpreting the complexities of modern life. We do not live in the world of the Bible, so in order to use biblical motifs a whole series of transformations must be undertaken, which so empty the motifs of substance that the exercise is not worth pursuing (see Appendix II). If this kind of activity is to be engaged in, then it may be better to analyse the biblical material and compare such an analysis with analyses made of the world in which we live. Family resemblances between the analyses may permit some observations to be made about similarities and dissimilarities of situations and responses. However, such uses of biblical traditions indicate a further dimension of the history of interpretation and extend the complex range of material to be treated.

Conclusions. Sufficient summaries of my approach to and treatment of the Jeremiah tradition have been provided throughout this book to alleviate the need for a lengthy concluding section. The two main emphases in the book are: the life of Jeremiah presented in the tradition is neither a historical nor a biographical feature, but part of the interpretation and presentation of the redactors; throughout the tradition there is a good deal of evidence for a complex use of prophecy which provides many insights into community struggles of the sixth century. At the same time the book is intended to be an introduction to Jeremiah and so focuses on textual and interpretative issues. These have been treated sketchily because of the preliminary nature of the book, but they will be developed much more fully in subsequent work.[18] Unfortunately there is too much material in the book of Jeremiah, raising too many interpretative issues, for one book or commentary to deal satisfactorily with all its elements, aspects and features.

The approach to the life of Jeremiah aspect of the tradition has suggested that the way the life of Jesus was developed in the gospels may be analogous for a study of Jeremiah. To this suggestion should be added a further comparative example, the life of Socrates. There is a substantial amount of material in ancient classical literature on the life of Socrates (e.g., portraits of the philosopher have been provided by Aristophanes, Aristotle, Plato and Xenophon, to name but a few), and the different ways the man was seen by different people and periods is a very interesting study which may have something to contribute to Jeremiah studies.[19] Where the Jeremiah tradition differs from the material on Socrates and Jesus is that all the elements contributing to a life of Jeremiah have been incorporated into the tradition; so it is not possible to do a comparative study of different books. However, a comparative analysis can be carried out of the discrete traditions within the book of Jeremiah and this, along with a structuralistic approach to the narrative sections, would provide an absorbing study. The interpretation of the figure of Jeremiah and of different motifs in the book begins in the tradition and provides no grounds for separating the tradition and its development in later centuries into two discrete categories.[20] The wide range of uses of prophecy in Jeremiah reflects the complex struggles of the various communities scattered about Palestine, Egypt and Babylonia during the sixth century. Because we have little hard evidence about these communities, it is necessary to study the traditions produced in the period for inferential information about these communities. In stressing the element of conflict throughout the book of Jeremiah, I have kept in mind the saying of Heraclitus: 'Conflict is the father of everything.'[21]

APPENDIX I

Some Books on Jeremiah in English

Not only is the book of Jeremiah a difficult book to understand, but also there are very few recent commentaries in English on the text. This makes the task of understanding it even more difficult for the intelligent reader who knows no Hebrew, Greek or German. The dearth of English commentaries on Jeremiah in the past sixty years is hard to explain, though the sheer amount of hard work involved in producing a commentary is enough to protect the book from all but the hardiest of exegetes. If the past is another country, its literature is equally alien, and none more than Jeremiah. The vexed problems and many issues which have to be resolved before a satisfactory working approach to a commentary is achieved have contributed to the dearth of first-class commentaries on the book of Jeremiah. I can think of no other major book in the Hebrew Bible which is without a full-scale commentary in English. However, the 1980s will see the rectification of this anomaly. The absence of a Jeremiah commentary from the old International Critical Commentary series is being made good by William McKane for the new series of that Commentary. This will be a magisterial philological work which, no doubt, will be first class and indispensable when it appears. It will be in two volumes (the usual division of 1–25 and 26–52), as will Douglas Jones's New Century Bible on Jeremiah. As that commentary is virtually finished, it should be making its appearance within the next eighteen months. John Thompson's *The Book of Jeremiah* (New International Commentary on the OT, Grand Rapids 1980) was published too late for use in this book. It is the first of the Jeremiah commentaries promised for the 1980s to appear and is very welcome. Although conservative in approach (the Skinnerian line is taken), it is not dogmatically so. A lengthy commentary (819 pages), it treats the text as the record of Jeremiah's utterances and certain critical incidents in his life (for an evaluation of it see my forthcoming review in *SJT*). I am myself working on Jeremiah for the Old Testament Library commentary series, but this will not appear before 1985 at earliest. In Germany Siegfried Herrmann is producing the comprehensive BKAT, on Jeremiah and that with McKane's commentary should define the direction of Jeremiah research for some decades to come. Other series of commentaries are mooted and they will include volumes on Jeremiah. So in spite of the long dearth of competent commentaries in English on Jeremiah, the future for Jeremiah studies looks extremely bright.

Any student of Jeremiah will know that the current lack of full-scale commentaries on Jeremiah is quite a recent phenomenon. From the turn of the century up to the end of the Kaiser war, English commentaries tended to match the commentaries in German. Outstanding British scholars wrote commentaries or published translations of Jeremiah which included generous notes and introductions (I have in mind here the work of G. A. Smith, S. R. Driver, A. C. Welch, C. J. Ball, W. H. Bennett, A. S. Peake, A. Streane, J. Skinner, L. Elliott-Binns). In the 1920s and 1930s many studies were produced of Jeremiah, though most of them were lightweight in comparison. Since then the commentaries, with the notable exception of the smaller series, the *Interpreter's Bible* and the *Anchor Bible*, have dried up, though the occasional lightweight book on Jeremiah did appear. Unless I have misjudged recent scholarship, there has been an increase since the mid-1960s of serious books and monographs on the subject and this increase will, I believe, continue to grow. It is certainly time that the Jeremiah tradition came in for some of the scrutiny which the Isaiah and Ezekiel traditions have had in English. In this appendix I wish to consider in very brief terms some of the books on Jeremiah written in English over the past three decades. This information may help the reader to gain an impression of the work done on the tradition, and may also provide some idea, in conjunction with the rest of my book, of how the future treatment of Jeremiah will be different from this work.

Elmer A. Leslie's *Jeremiah: Chronologically arranged, translated, and interpreted* (New York and Nashville 1954) is a brave attempt to set out and discuss the chapters of Jeremiah in relation to their chronological order. Apart from the chapters belonging to the period 598–587, which are fairly clearly dated in the tradition, this approach involves devoting a rather large chapter (280–331) to what he calls 'Supplements and Adaptations from the Diaspora'. It could not be otherwise, because there is a great deal of undated material in Jeremiah and even in the dated material there is much secondary or additional writing. The approach is Skinnerian, with a very lucid commentary style which incorporates the work of German commentators, especially that of Volz and Rudolph, extremely well. His 'Abiding Values in Jeremiah' (332–40) chapter does not strike me as being particularly illuminating on the tradition, because many of the values he finds there could also be derived from other prophetic traditions.

J. Philip Hyatt's commentary in the *Interpreter's Bible* (1956) has been used in the course of this book, so little need be said about it here. It suffers from the severe limits of the series, namely too little space, which even at that must be shared with two versions of the text and an expository section. However, the exposition section by Stanley Romaine Hopper should be noted here, because it is a splendid piece of highly literate comment in which insights and observations on Jeremiah are interspersed with quotations from Auden, Bunyan, Coleridge, Dante, Eliot, Emerson, Hölderlin, Hopkins, Jung, Kierkegaard, Rilke, Tillich, Wilde and Yeats (to name but a few). It is a very satisfying read. Philip Hyatt, who contributed so much to Jeremiah studies, also wrote *Jeremiah: Prophet of Courage and Hope* (New York and Nashville 1958). This is a short book (128 pages) and too general to be very useful, but it is a good indication of how many writers on the subject of Jeremiah wish to stress the element of hope in the book. It is too Protestant to have the measure of Jeremiah.

The Torch Bible Commentaries volume on Jeremiah is by H. Cunliffe-Jones (London 1960). Its brevity lessens its value, but for a long time it and volume 5 of the *Interpreter's Bible* were the most accessible books on Jeremiah for most students, so it deserves credit and recognition. It is a useful and straightforward treatment of the text which is sober and sensible.

Sheldon H. Blank's *Jeremiah: Man and Prophet* (Cincinnati 1961) has been used at various points in this book, but a few further comments may be warranted here. It is a very sanguine and selective reading of Jeremiah, but a good example of the Jewish interpretation of Jeremiah as the prophet of *hope* (hope being something you *do*). It is good on the exposition of the confessions as prayer, and takes the Buber-Heschel line on the 'pain of God'. Although Skinnerian in its approach, Blank's reading of Jeremiah is an appealing one, and indicates what generations of Jews have found in the tradition: 'A promise is a promise, they insisted; a commitment is a commitment. God can no more repudiate a promise than he can be unjust. He cannot be capricious. Constancy is the very essence of God' (154).

Joseph Woods' *Jeremiah* (Epworth Preacher's Commentaries, London 1964) is written for the preacher, and therefore limited in its contribution to the understanding of the Jeremiah tradition. Copious use is made of the Methodist Hymn Book, therefore the tone of the book is rather evangelical. This is useful for the busy preacher, but the seeker after knowledge may find it less than helpful. Its approach is completely Skinnerian, but there are occasional insights which make the reading of these small books worth the effort spent in locating them.

John Bright's *Anchor Bible* (1965) is used throughout this book, so little need be added here. The series is a mixed one and the *Jeremiah* volume is disappointing in some ways. It has a good introduction and a useful translation of the text. However, Bright is too conservative to explore the complex depths of the text successfully. He is too prepared to accept its surface meaning and to intuit Jeremiah's mental states to develop the redactional factors along constructive lines. John Bright's contribution to Jeremiah studies is a formidable one and every scholar is much in his debt. That is precisely why this volume disappoints so much, because from him more was expected. The sections on Jeremiah in his *Covenant and Promise* (1977) also contribute to the discussion, but along equally conservative lines.

R. K. Harrison's *Jeremiah and Lamentations: An Introduction and Commentary* (Tyndale OT Commentaries, London 1973) is a short (192 pages) and very conservative commentary. Its appeal is likely to be limited to readers of a similar persuasion. I find its excessive use of the New Testament makes the work more of a book for private devotions than for understanding the prophet of the sixth century or the circles which produced the tradition.

Ernest Nicholson's two-volume commentary, *The Book of the Prophet Jeremiah*, in the Cambridge Bible Commentary series on the NEB (Cambridge 1973 and 1975), has the strengths of Nicholson's lucid exposition of the material and the weaknesses of the series, namely working with the NEB and the lack of space to develop the discussion. Taken with the Torch Bible commentary it will provide the uninitiated with an introduction to the book and some of the textual and exegetical issues involved in the interpretation of Jeremiah.

Like Philip Hyatt and John Bright, William Holladay is a formidable contributor to Jeremiah studies and the footnotes of this book are studded with references to his journal articles. His *Jeremiah: Spokesman out of Time* (Philadelphia 1974) is a popular introduction to Jeremiah (comparable to Hyatt's small volume). Apart from the usual presentation and discussion of the main features of the tradition, he also argues that Jeremiah was out of place in his own time. This view allows him to match up certain features of the tradition with aspects of our own time. I can see the point of this kind of exercise, but I do not find its results persuasive in any sense. A straining after contemporary relevance in biblical studies seems to me to be a misguided way of handling the Bible (see my Appendix II). At best I think the perceptive scholar can show what is involved in the biblical tradition and then, tracing various stages in the history of ideas up to modern times, show how there are (or are not as the case may be) some family resemblances between now and then. There is some value in this approach, but caution and insight demand that we be modest in making any claims about relevance. Holladay has also published *The Architecture of Jeremiah 1–20* (Lewisburg and London 1976) which, although extremely dense in its arguments about the order in which parts of the text developed, may help to introduce readers to the complexities of rhetorical criticism. The book uses many of the rhetorical criticism arguments developed by Jack Lundbom (a student of Holladay's), and argues the case for identifying specific elements in the tradition with the contents of the original roll produced by Baruch. An interesting book, but not easy to read.

Solomon Freehof's *Book of Jeremiah: A Commentary* (The Jewish Commentary for Bible Readers, New York 1977) is a very simple commentary designed for Jewish students of the Bible. Readers who have mastered some of the more difficult commentaries referred to in this book will not gain much from it, but Rabbi Freehof's book does have one outstanding virtue – it makes available in a well-assimilated way comments on Jeremiah from the great medieval rabbinic commentators, Rashi and Qimhi, and also from some more recent Jewish commentators, such as Samuel David Luzzato. After reading so many pious volumes of Christian writers on Jeremiah it is salutary to be reminded that Jeremiah was a Jew. In my opinion far too many writers on the subject forget this basic datum, and I would advocate that all students of the Jeremiah tradition should read Blank and Freehof in order to correct any tendency towards this misconception of the nature of the tradition.

There are a number of important works and monographs on Jeremiah which have been used in this book, e.g., Berridge (1970), Nicholson (1970), Overholt (1970), and Raitt (1977), and, as they are in English, they may be recommended to the serious reader.

However, they are not introductory works but highly technical, discursive books which require a good deal of hard work to master. They are but the beginning of what will become a stream of books and monographs on the important issues in the study of Jeremiah.

These, then, are most of the significant books written on Jeremiah over the past three decades. To the reader who wishes to pursue the subject further I recommend the learning of German – that will open up an even larger world of books on the Jeremiah tradition.

APPENDIX II

A Note on Using Jeremiah Today

The questions which will be asked by certain people reading this book are of two kinds: the ordinary question of relevance, 'What is the point of studying an ancient book like Jeremiah?' and the theological question, 'Is there no word from the Lord for today from the book of Jeremiah?' The first question is easier to answer than the second, because the study of ancient texts has an intrinsic value of its own without necessarily being relevant to today. Such a study might prove to be relevant, but only after the work had been done, certainly not in a priori terms. The theological question is extremely difficult to deal with, because it arises out of so many presuppositions which really need to be investigated before ancient texts are disinterred from their resting places. The preacher who needs more sermon fodder might be better advised to question the wisdom of reducing texts to sermons. Perhaps the Protestant overvaluation of the sermon should give way to a new perspective on the Bible. To suggest that much more hard work than may be warranted by the result is the way the second question should be answered may not be very acceptable to those who would ask it. But if there is no balm in Gilead, who will be happy with the anodyne products of the house of Roche? The answer to the first question is apparent to any intelligent person who is prepared to think about a task undertaken and well done. I cannot answer the second question because I believe that each person and community (both separately and together) must *work out* in dialogue with the text whether there is a positive answer to the question or not, as the case may be. Addressing today's issues and problems with today's techniques properly worked out may be as close as we can get to the world of Jeremiah. In achieving this the Jeremiah tradition may or may not contribute something to our work. It is in being open to the negative use of the tradition, i.e., the possibility that it may have nothing to offer us, that I am unable to use the traditional framework which asks the question in the first place. That framework presupposes that there *is* a word from the Lord for today in Jeremiah. I think we should be much more open than that closed system of reference.

A concrete example of the folly of such closed system questions may be seen in the work done on Jeremiah by Elliott-Binns, whose Westminster Commentary (1919) and *Jeremiah: A Prophet for a Time of War* (1941) explicitly relate the prophet's work to a Britain facing war or coming out of the trauma of a recently fought war. As treatments of the book of Jeremiah they are fine pieces of work, but in relating Jeremiah's time to Britain of the Kaiser war and the impending Hitler war, they make a connection which is at best a very superficial one. Jeremiah warned his people of impending doom because of their wickedness and, later, advised them to surrender to the Babylonian enemy, which he considered to be the servant of the living God. Now transpose these terms to Britain in 1936–39 and the following is Jeremiah's message to the British people: You are a vicious, corrupt and wicked nation, about to be punished for your sins by God's servant, Herr Hitler, and I counsel everyone of you to surrender to the German army, thereby saving yourselves alive. Yet at no point in his second book does Elliott-Binns take this reading of Jeremiah. He talks a good deal about the nastiness of the Germans, comparing them to the Assyrians, but he never plays the prophet against his own people. Of course, if there is one book in the Bible which is completely unsuitable for use in the time of such a war it is the book of Jeremiah! The nastiness of the enemy was not his concern, and treason in the face of the enemy did not bother him. What worried him was his own people; they were the real enemy, and against them he turned his wrath and his scorn. In order to make his work fit our modern age we have to empty all his statements of their significance and then apply them in a banal and pietistic way. It would do our intelligences more credit and preserve the integrity of the Bible in a better way if we did not use the Jeremiah tradition for such purposes.

It is not my intention to hold a good man such as Elliott-Binns up to ridicule, but his work provides the best example of the folly of working in this way. More recent writers such as Philip Hyatt and William Holladay have also insisted, in their minor writings on Jeremiah, that he is a prophet for today. It would appear to be an occupational hazard of writing commentaries on the Bible that relevance must be sought for these ancient texts. Clearly we are not living in sixth-century Judah and, equally clearly, the sayings of Jeremiah are not addressed directly to us. What things we might have in common with the ancient world in respect of being human and living in social groups we share with all ancient literature, so we have no greater argument for Jeremiah's relevance than for the fragments of Heraclitus. This does not rule out the possibility that the Jeremiah tradition might have something to say to us; it just admits the possibility that it may have nothing to contribute. In the following paragraphs I will attempt to give my reasons for being sceptical of the *success* of projects which try to relate ancient literature to the modern world.

If the message of the book of Jeremiah is, as I see it, something like this: 'There is not, and cannot be, any permanent security, whether in God, theology, ideology, nationalism, patriotism, ritual, ancestry, history or whatever' and 'We must always relate to the past and be open to the future in constantly changing ways' – then his message may be useful for and transferable to our own times. To get to this concession I have had to ignore what the prophet said or what the tradition has done with his sayings in order to translate the sense of the book into some rather simple principles which might provide guidance for modern communities. Other commentators would disagree with my synopsis of Jeremiah's message, and that is the first major obstacle to such an enterprise. It is unlikely that we will be able to agree upon a common statement of the book's message. I would prefer to avoid summarizing the tradition and simply let the words stand, whether they are relevant or irrelevant. If my summary is accepted for argument's sake, then it has to be pointed out that many prophets have something similar to say, and that many Greek philosophers have said things like these, sometimes in a better way. What Jeremiah contributes to the discussion is the particularity of his times and the way it is said in the tradition. However, if my summary can be matched with contemporary circumstances, perhaps the tradition can be used. What have to be matched are the horizons of the text with our own horizons (see the philosophical hermeneutic of Hans-Georg Gadamer) and in such a way that the integrity of both are maintained; then perhaps some progress can be made. But this is not a process which can be hastily achieved in order to preach sermons; it involves diligent analysis and reflective interpretation which treat more than the surface of the text. It also involves a high quality of individual interpreter. A Martin Luther or a Karl Barth may be able to project their own meaning on to Paul sufficiently to influence a generation of thought, but even their schemes disintegrate as more and more exegetes discover just how much Luther or Barth and how little Paul there is in their systems.

The methods of treating the Bible as commodity or fetish (especially at home in fundamentalism, but other groups have employed them) I have ruled out as an insult to intelligence and integrity, and as a way of reducing the Bible to the level of a blasphemous fable. If the book of Jeremiah is to be made to speak to today (outside of the most crude forms of 'word of God' theologies), then among the questions which must be asked are those which question the whole project itself. It is because I do not think we can just assume that it *must* speak to contemporary society that I am sceptical of the project. Even in terms of a 'word of God' framework of reference, it would not follow that every book of the Bible was relevant to any given situation. Some situations might be addressed by Job, Qoheleth, Esther or the Song of Songs, and others might be spoken to by Jonah, James, Ruth or Titus, and yet others have no book which fitted their situation. Only a fiercely dogmatic position could insist that the Bible must speak to every age and situation or that every book in the Bible was relevant to all ages. But such a dogmatic position (so often the historical position of theology in Protestant traditions) is virtually the same kind of dogmatic stance as is opposed by Jeremiah in the tradition. The dogma of Yahweh's protection of Jerusalem is attacked in the tradition as a lie, just as Hananiah's dogma of the saving grace of Yahweh is branded as a lie. Surely here is a word from Jeremiah if any will receive it – yesterday's dogma is today's lie! But who among the churches can receive this saying? All the emphases on Bibles, creeds, dogmas and what our fathers before us believed add up to the kind of situation against which Jeremiah fought in vain. To enshrine his tradition in the same way so that we revere it is to have learned nothing from his work. To insist that what the prophet Jeremiah said then is still relevant or valid for today is to indulge in freezing the spirit in the written word so that we have to await another prophet who will free us from the tyranny of yesterday's prophets. This, then, is the theological problem which I see at the base of all talk about the word of God in a written form. It approximates to the status of an idol. It tyrannizes the community and produces the enslavement of minds which the past five centuries have amply demonstrated. I am therefore unhappy with making Jeremiah a party to such tyranny and enslavement. In freeing the tradition from the constraint of having to be relevant perhaps it will be incarnated in other forms, perhaps not. That is the essence of freedom and openness.

Such, then, are some of the reasons which make me respond so negatively to the question: 'Has Jeremiah a word from the Lord for us today?' Too negatively, perhaps, but I have not ruled out the way of hard work which will grapple with today's problems, informed by how others met the problems of their own time. We may learn nothing from them but examples of courage, persistence and application. That may be enough. However, some intrepid souls may find that their situation is more conducive than other people's to mining the depths of the tradition in order to furnish stocks for illuminating their world. One such person might have been Vitezslav Gardavsky, who was working on a Jeremiah project until he died as a result of the hounding of the authorities, who had systematically degraded him since the invasion of Czechoslovakia in 1968. He deserves to be remembered with respect for his fierce courage and integrity. His project involving Jeremiah sounds as though it might have been an advance on the more usual application of the prophet's significance for our times, in that he wished to show how Jeremiah attempted to deprive the rich of their certainties and to rob the poor of their hopes. To speculate on what the finished project might have been like is to attempt to go down that passage towards a door into the rose-garden which we will never open, to rephrase Eliot's words. Nothing I have said in this appendix rules out the project Gardavsky was involved in before his death. For those who are prepared to do the hard work entailed, and who live in circumstances out of which such a project naturally arises, there is material in Jeremiah which may be transformed for our time. But I emphasize these two necessary conditions, without which the work done will not be worth doing. To do a shallow work of exegesis, and then match it up with a superficial analysis of contemporary life, is to earn a condemnation from the tradition itself: 'You have healed the people's wound too lightly by speaking a lie and making them believe what can do them no good.'

ABBREVIATIONS

AB	Anchor Bible, New York
AOAT	Alter Orient und Altes Testament, Kevelaer
ATD	Das Alte Testament Deutsch, Göttingen
BDB	F. Brown, S. R. Driver and C. A. Briggs, *A Hebrew and English Lexicon of the Old Testament*, Oxford 1907, reprint of 1966
BHS	Biblia Hebraica Stuttgartensia, Stuttgart 1970
BHT	Beiträge zur historischen Theologie, Tübingen
BJRL	*Bulletin of the John Rylands Library*, Manchester
BKAT	Biblischer Kommentar, Altes Testament, Neukirchen-Vluyn
BWANT	Beiträge zur Wissenschaft vom Alten und Neuen Testament, Leipzig, Stuttgart
BZAW	Beihefte zur *Zeitschrift für die alttestamentliche Wissenschaft*, Berlin
CBQ	*Catholic Biblical Quarterly*, Washington
EB	Études Bibliques, Paris
EJ	*Encyclopedia Judaica*, Jerusalem 1971–72
ET	English translation
EvTh	*Evangelische Theologie*, Munich
ExpT	*The Expository Times*, Edinburgh
FRLANT	Forschungen zur Religion und Literatur des Alten und Neuen Testaments, Göttingen
HAT	Handbuch zum Alten Testament, Tübingen
HTR	*Harvard Theological Review*, Cambridge, Mass.
HUCA	*Hebrew Union College Annual*, Cincinnati
IB	*The Interpreter's Bible*, 12 vols., Nashville 1951–57
ICC	The International Critical Commentary, Edinburgh and New York
IDB	*The Interpreter's Dictionary of the Bible*, Nashville 1962
IDB Suppl	*IDB, Supplementary Volume*, Nashville 1976
Interpr	*Interpretation*, Richmond, Va
JBL	*Journal of Biblical Literature*, New Haven, Conn., Missoula, Mont.
JNES	*Journal of Near Eastern Studies*, Chicago

JSOT(SS)	*Journal for the Study of the Old Testament* (Supplement Series), Sheffield
JSS	*Journal of Semitic Studies*, Manchester
JTS	*Journal of Theological Studies*, Oxford
KAT	Kommentar zum Alten Testament, Leipzig, Erlangen
LCL	Loeb Classical Library, London and New York
LXX	Septuagint
MT	Masoretic Text
NCB	New Century Bible, London
NEB	New English Bible, Oxford and Cambridge 1970
NICOT	New International Commentary on the Old Testament, Grand Rapids, Michigan
OTL	Old Testament Library, London and Philadelphia
RB	*Revue Biblique*, Jerusalem, Paris
RSV	Revised Standard Version of the Bible, London and New York 1952
SBLDS	Society of Biblical Literature Dissertation Series, Missoula, Mont.
SBLMS	Society of Biblical Literature Monograph Series, Missoula, Mont.
SBT	Studies in Biblical Theology, London and Naperville, Ill.
SEÅ	*Svensk Exegetisk Årsbok*, Lund
SJT	*Scottish Journal of Theology*, Edinburgh
SOTS	Society for Old Testament Study
StTh	*Studia Theologica*, Lund
TGUOS	*Transactions of the Glasgow University Oriental Society*, Glasgow
UF	*Ugarit-Forschungen*, Münster
VT	*Vetus Testamentum*, Leiden
VTS	Supplements to *Vetus Testamentum*
WMANT	Wissenschaftliche Monographien zum Alten und Neuen Testament, Neukirchen-Vluyn
ZAW	*Zeitschrift für die alttestamentliche Wissenschaft*, Giessen, Berlin
ZTK	*Zeitschrift für Theologie und Kirche*, Tübingen

SELECT BIBLIOGRAPHY

P. R. Ackroyd, *Exile and Restoration: A Study of Hebrew Thought of the Sixth Century BC*, OTL, 1968
—'Historians and Prophets', *SEÅ* 33, 1968, 18–54
J. M. Berridge, *Prophet, People, and the Word of Yahweh: An Examination of Form and Content in the Proclamation of the Prophet Jeremiah*, Basel Studies of Theology 4, Zürich 1970
J. Bright, *Jeremiah: Introduction, Translation, and Notes*, AB 21, 1965
S. H. Blank, *Jeremiah: Man and Prophet*, Cincinnati 1961
R. P. Carroll, *When Prophecy Failed: Reactions and responses to failure in the Old Testament prophetic traditions*, London and New York 1979
G. W. Coats and B. O. Long (eds.), *Canon and Authority: Essays in Old Testament Religion and Theology* (presented to Professor W. Zimmerli), Philadelphia 1977
J. L. Crenshaw, *Prophetic Conflict: Its Effect Upon Israelite Religion*, BZAW 124, Berlin 1971
G. Fohrer, *Introduction to the Old Testament*, ET Nashville 1968, London 1970
S. Herrmann, *Die prophetischen Heilserwartungen im Alten Testament: Ursprung und Gestaltwandel*, BWANT 85, 1965
W. L. Holladay, *The Architecture of Jeremiah 1–20*, Lewisburg and London 1976
J. P. Hyatt, 'The Book of Jeremiah: Introduction and Exegesis', *IB* 5, 1956, 775–1142
E. Janssen, *Juda in der Exilszeit: Ein Beitrag zur Frage der Entstehung des Judentums*, FRLANT 69, 1956
O. Kaiser, *Introduction to the Old Testament: A Presentation of its Results and Problems*, ET Oxford and Minneapolis 1975
G. Lisowsky, *Konkordanz zum Hebräischen Alten Testament*, Stuttgart 1958[2]
J. R. Lundbom, *Jeremiah: A Study in Ancient Hebrew Rhetoric*, SBLDS 18, 1975
A. D. H. Mayes, *Deuteronomy*, NCB, 1979
A. L. Merrill & T. W. Overholt (eds.), *Scripture in History and Theology: Essays in Honor of J. Coert Rylaarsdam*, Pittsburgh 1977
E. W. Nicholson, *Preaching to the Exiles: A Study of the Prose Tradition in the Book of Jeremiah*, Oxford and New York 1970

T. W. Overholt, *The Threat of Falsehood: A Study in the Theology of the Book of Jeremiah*, SBT 2.16, 1970

K.-F. Pohlmann, *Studien zum Jeremiabuch: Ein Beitrag zur Frage nach der Entstehung des Jeremiabuches*, FRLANT 118, 1978

T. M. Raitt, *A Theology of Exile: Judgment/Deliverance in Jeremiah and Ezekiel*, Philadelphia 1977

H. Reventlow, *Liturgie und prophetisches Ich bei Jeremia*, Gütersloh 1963

W. Rudolph, *Jeremia*, HAT, 1968[3]

W. Schottroff, 'Jeremia 2, 1–3: Erwägungen zur Methode der Prophetenexegese', *ZTK* 67, 1970, 263–94

J. Skinner, *Prophecy and Religion: Studies in the Life of Jeremiah*, Cambridge 1922

J. A. Soggin, *Introduction to the Old Testament: From its origins to the closing of the Alexandrian canon*, rev. ed., London and Philadelphia 1980

W. Thiel, *Die deuteronomistische Redaktion von Jeremia 1–25*, WMANT 41, 1973

P. Volz, *Der Prophet Jeremia*, KAT, 1922

G. Wanke, *Untersuchungen zur sogenannten Baruchschrift*, BZAW 122, 1971

A. Weiser, *Das Buch des Propheten Jeremia*, ATD 20/21, 1960[4]

R. R. Wilson, *Prophecy and Society in Ancient Israel*, Philadelphia 1980

NOTES

Introduction

1. So M. A. Screech, *Aspects of Rabelais's Christian Comedy*, Inaugural Lecture at University College, London on 2 February 1967, London 1968, 9. How differently these three Christian gentlemen understood the nature of Christianity and how tragic it is that, while there are still so many followers of Calvin and Loyola, so few Christians alive today are followers of Rabelais. The burning of Michael Servetus on 27 October 1553 is one of the least admirable aspects of Calvin's work.

2. *Duino Elegy* I, line 13 in Rainer Maria Rilke, *Duino Elegies: The German text with English translation, introduction and commentary* by J. B. Leishman and S. Spender, London 1963⁴, 24f.

3. Cf. 'For no worse evil can happen to a man than to hate argument', *Plato* I: *Phaedo*, trs. H. N. Fowler, LCL, 1938, 308f. I have translated *pathōn* as 'disease' rather than 'evil'. In the statement Socrates compares being a misologist (misology: 'hatred of argument') to being a misanthropist. Of course by misology he meant 'hatred of *reasoned* argument' rather than simple argumentativeness. Many people argue, fewer use reasoning.

4. *The Ethics of Aristotle: The Nicomachean Ethics*, trs. J. A. K. Thomson, Penguin Classics, London 1955, 27f. For the Greek text and a similar translation see Aristotle, *The Nicomachean Ethics* I, ch. iii, §§ 1, 4, trs. H. Rackham, LCL, 1934, pp.6–9. As I hope this book will make clear, I do not regard the Jeremiah tradition (text and substance) as affording *precise* information about Jeremiah. The approach to the tradition must be a tentative one, eschewing dogma and *Diktat*.

1. The Quest of the Historical Jeremiah

1. For the classic status of Skinner's book, see P. R. Ackroyd, 'John Skinner: Prophecy and Religion', *ExpT* 89, 1977–8, 356–8.

2. In spite of being preceded by Isaiah in modern Bibles (not always the case in the past) and having fewer chapters than Isaiah, Jeremiah is in fact the longest of the three major prophetic traditions: Isaiah, Jeremiah, Ezekiel. This is confirmed by a verse count (Jeremiah: 1364 verses; Isaiah: 1291 verses; Ezekiel: 1273 verses) and the length of the printed Hebrew text in BHS (Jeremiah: 116 pages; Isaiah: 105 pages; Ezekiel: 94+ pages).

3. Sheldon Blank, *Jeremiah: Man and Prophet*, 3; cf. A. C. Welch, *Jeremiah: His Time and His Work*, London 1928, 235.

4. An Ishmael in the sense of Gen. 16.12: 'He shall be a wild ass of a man, his hand against every man and every man's hand against him', rather than the Ishmael of Melville's *Moby Dick*, but the rage and obsession against evil shown in the tradition have a dimension comparable to Melville's view of the world.

5. E.g., J. R. Lundbom, *Jeremiah: A Study in Ancient Hebrew Rhetoric*; cf. W. L. Holladay, *The Architecture of Jeremiah 1–20*. Because Baruch acts at Jeremiah's dictation the arrangement of material is traceable to Jeremiah. Lundbom (120) can even write about what 'Jeremiah (and Baruch) say silently' with reference to a new temple in contrast to what Ezekiel says 'loud and clear'.

6. The most thoroughgoing exposition of this volte-face is given in T. M. Raitt, *A Theology of Exile*, esp. 106–27. While disagreeing with Raitt's general thesis I must acknowledge that I found his book stimulating and an advance on much of the treatment of this subject.

7. For the notion of bifid compositions in the Bible see R. K. Harrison, *Introduction to the Old Testament*, London 1970, 787–9 (applied to Isaiah); F. Cawley and A. R. Milliard in *The New Bible Commentary Revised*, London and Grand Rapids, Mich. 1970, 628 (applied to Jeremiah); cf. Harrison, *Jeremiah and Lamentations: An Introduction and Commentary*, Tyndale OT Commentaries, London 1973, 33, where he prefers a different approach.

8. It is the argument of John Bright ('The Date of the Prose Sermons of Jeremiah', *JBL* 70, 1951, 15–29) that the deuteronomistic prose is in fact the rhetorical prose of the late seventh and early sixth centuries in Judah and so was used by Jeremiah, the deuteronomists and others. In disagreeing with this view we can still recognize the formidable contribution to Jeremiah studies made by Bright; see his *Jeremiah*, AB 21, 1965. For a general treatment of Jeremiah see his *Covenant and Promise: The Future in the Preaching of the Pre-exilic Prophets*, London 1977, 140–98.

9. On the LXX tradition of Jeremiah see A. W. Streane, *The Double Text of Jeremiah (Massoretic and Alexandrian) Compared together with an Appendix on the Old Latin Evidence*, Cambridge 1896; J. G. Janzen, *Studies in the Text of Jeremiah*, Harvard Semitic Monographs 6, Cambridge, Mass. 1973; cf. S. Talmon, 'Aspects of the Textual Transmission of the Bible in the Light of Qumran Manuscripts', *Textus* 4, Jerusalem 1964, 95–132 (now reprinted in *Qumran and the History of the Biblical Text*, ed. F. M. Cross and S. Talmon, Cambridge, Mass. and London 1975, 226–63); E. Tov, 'The Nature of the Hebrew Text underlying the LXX: a Survey of the Problems', *JSOT* 7, 1978, 53–68.

10. On these complex factors see the standard OT introductions: e.g., O. Eissfeldt, *The Old Testament: An Introduction*, ET Oxford and New York 1965; also those of Fohrer, Kaiser and Soggin (see Select Bibliography). On prophecy in general see J. Lindblom, *Prophecy in Ancient Israel*, Oxford 1962, Philadelphia 1963; R. R. Wilson, *Prophecy and Society in Ancient Israel*; for the development of the prophetic books see S. Mowinckel,

Prophecy and Tradition: The Prophetic Books in the Light of the Study of the Growth and History of the Tradition, Oslo 1946.

11. On these titles see B. S. Childs, 'Psalm Titles and Midrashic Exegesis', *JSS* 16, 1971, 137–50; idem, *Introduction to the Old Testament as Scripture*, London and Philadelphia 1979, 520–22.

12. The idea that the original poetic material may have been accommodated at a later stage of the tradition to prophecy I owe to my Edinburgh colleague, Graeme Auld, and I acknowledge here the stimulus of correspondence and conversations with him. For a brief statement of the position see his review article 'Poetry, Prophecy, Hermeneutic: Recent Studies in Isaiah', *SJT* 33, 1980, 567–81.

13. On this see M. Noth, *Überlieferungsgeschichtliche Studien: Die sammelnden und bearbeitenden Geschichtswerke im Alten Testament*, Tübingen 1943; 3rd. ed. 1967. An English version is now available as *The Deuteronomic History*, *JSOT* SS 15, 1981. For a treatment of Noth's work see D. A. Knight, *Rediscovering the Traditions of Israel: The Development of the Traditio-Historical Research of the Old Testament, with Special Consideration of Scandinavian Contributions*, SBLDS 9, rev. ed. 1975, 143–76.

14. On the relation between Deuteronomy and the deuteronomistic history see E. W. Nicholson, *Deuteronomy and Tradition*, Oxford and Philadelphia 1967, 107–18; for the deuteronomistic editing of Deuteronomy see A. D. H. Mayes, *Deuteronomy*, NCB, 1979, 41–7. On Jeremiah see J. P. Hyatt, 'The Deuteronomic Edition of Jeremiah' in *Vanderbilt Studies in the Humanities* I, Nashville 1951, 71–95. See also H. W. Wolff, 'The Kerygma of the Deuteronomic Historical Work' in W. Brueggemann and H. W. Wolff, *The Vitality of the Old Testament Traditions*, ET Atlanta 1975, 83–100, 141–3, and for the influence of deuteronomistic thought on Lamentations see B. Albrektson, *Studies in the Text and Theology of the Book of Lamentations*, Studia Theologica Lundensia 21, Lund 1963, 214–39; on Amos cf. W. H. Schmidt, *ZAW* 72, 1965, 168–93.

15. On this scribal school see M. Weinfeld, *Deuteronomy and the Deuteronomic School*, Oxford 1972. Weinfeld (320–65) sets out the characteristic features of deuteronomistic phraseology and these elements allow for the identification in Jeremiah of such a strand; on these elements cf. W. Dietrich, *Prophetie und Geschichte: Eine redaktionsgeschichtliche Untersuchung zum deuteronomistischen Geschichtswerk*, FRLANT 108, 1972, 70–79. The formal scribal features of the school makes one doubt Bright's view (*JBL* 70) that everybody in the period spoke like a scribe!

16. On this see Mowinckel, *Prophecy and Tradition*, and the various accounts given in OT introductions.

17. Cf. T. H. Robinson, 'Baruch's Roll', *ZAW* 42, 1924, 209–21; J. Muilenburg, 'Baruch the Scribe' in *Proclamation and Presence: Old Testament Essays in honour of Gwynne Henton Davies*, ed. J. I. Durham and J. R. Porter, London 1970, 215–38; G. Wanke, *Untersuchungen zur sogenannten Baruchschrift*, BZAW 122, 1971; C. Rietzschel, *Das Problem der Urrolle: Ein Beitrag zur Redaktionsgeschichte des Jeremiabuches*, Gütersloh 1966.

18. Fohrer, *Introduction*, 393.

19. See the introductions on this point; also Holladay, op. cit., 169–74;

Rietzschel, op. cit., 130f.; and J. P. Hyatt, 'The Book of Jeremiah: Introduction and Exegesis', *IB* 5, 1956, 787f. The second collection may be
implied by Jer. 36.32.

20. Space does not permit a full exposition of this view of Baruch's role
in the tradition, but see Rietzschel, *Das Problem der Urrolle*, for a treatment
of the dramatic elements in Jer. 36 and Wanke, op. cit., for a rejection of
the traditional view of Baruch's memoirs. Cf. M. Kessler, 'Form-Critical
Suggestions on Jer. 36', *CBQ* 28, 1966, 389–401; C. D. Isbell,
'II Kings 22.3–23.24 and Jeremiah 36: A stylistic comparison', *JSOT* 8,
1978, 33–45.

21. For a lucid discussion of this viewpoint see E. W. Nicholson, *Preaching to the Exiles*.

22. On these additions see Mayes, *Deuteronomy*, 149, 368f.

23. For the notion of 'family resemblances', a very useful way of making
connections without positing direct influences, see L. Wittgenstein, *Philosophical Investigations*, ET Oxford and New York 1972, I, §67.

24. On the general meaning of the term see E. Shils, 'Ideology', *International Encyclopedia of the Social Sciences* 7, New York and London 1968,
66–75; for a very brief discussion of its political senses see D. Braybrooke
in *The Encyclopedia of Philosophy* 4, New York and London 1967, 124–7.
On ideology as false consciousness see K. Marx and F. Engels, *The German
Ideology*, ET New York 1964, London 1965. Probably the best and most
useful book on all aspects of ideology is Hans Barth, *Truth and Ideology*,
originally Zürich 1945, ET Berkeley and London 1976.

25. Mowinckel originally gave this in *Zur Komposition des Buches Jeremia*,
Kristiania 1914, but modified it in subsequent writings, cf. *Prophecy and
Tradition*. For summaries and accounts of his work see the introductions
and Bright, *Jeremiah*, lxiii–lxxiii.

26. It is a pity to find Bright (*Jeremiah*, lxxiii) dismissing as 'a wholly
subjective procedure' attempts to distinguish genuine from non-genuine
words of the prophet. This is a charge normally made by fundamentalists
who do not understand the nature of literary or artistic judgment because
of their positivistic presuppositions. All matters of judgment entail a large
degree of subjectivity and Bright should know better, especially as on the
same page he asserts '*one feels intuitively* that a summary of the words used
by him has been preserved rather exactly' (writing of Jer. 7.1–15; italics
are mine). Now who is being subjective!

27. E.g., H. Weippert, *Die Prosareden des Jeremiabuches*, BZAW 132,
1973; cf. W. L. Holladay, 'A fresh look at "source B" and "source C" in
Jeremiah', *VT* 25, 1975, 394–412.

28. E.g., Nicholson, *Preaching to the Exiles*; K.-F. Pohlmann, *Studien
zum Jeremiabuch*.

29. *Preaching to the Exiles*, 137.

30. For the different possibilities see Nicholson (Babylon), Pohlmann
(Palestine), and Hyatt (Egypt). The Egyptian location is derived from
Baruch's involvement in the process and, as he went into exile to Egypt
with Jeremiah, he must have produced the tradition there in Egypt. There

is a logical view here, but it has little substance if the view about Baruch being a deuteronomistic creation is correct.

31. For further details see M. Noth, *The History of Israel*, London 1960²; B. Oded, 'Judah and the Exile' in *Israelite and Judaean History*, ed. J. H. Hayes, J. M. Miller, OTL, 1977, 435–88.

32. An invaluable treatment of this period is P. R. Ackroyd, *Exile and Restoration*. See also his 'Faith and its reformulation in the post-exilic period: sources', and 'Faith and its reformulation in the post-exilic period: prophetic material', *Theology Digest* 27, 1979, 323–46; C. F. Whitley, *The Exilic Age*, London 1957, Philadelphia 1958.

33. Noth, *The History of Israel*, 292. For a useful summary of this view see S. Herrmann, *A History of Israel in Old Testament Times*, ET, rev. ed., London and Philadelphia 1981, 289–97. For a more detailed treatment of Palestine as the centre of activity see E. Janssen, *Juda in der Exilszeit*.

34. See D. W. Thomas, 'The Sixth Century BC: A Creative Epoch in the History of Israel', *JSS* 6, 1961, 33–46.

35. Cf. J. W. Miller, *Das Verhältnis Jeremias und Hesekiels sprachlich und theologisch untersucht mit besonderer Berücksichtung der Prosareden Jeremias*, Van Gorcum's theologische Bibliothek 28, Assen 1955; D. Baltzer, *Ezechiel und Deuterojesaja: Berührungen in der Heilserwartung der beiden grossen Exilspropheten*, BZAW 121, 1971; Raitt, *A Theology of Exile*. All three prophets (Jeremiah, Ezekiel, Second Isaiah) need to be treated together in order to produce a proper exilic theology, so it is a pity to see Raitt, who rightly argues for including Jeremiah as an exilic work, limiting his study to Jeremiah and Ezekiel. For a treatment of all the relevant material see Ackroyd, *Exile and Restoration*, 50–217.

36. On this element see J. W. Miller, 'Prophetic Conflict in Second Isaiah: The Servant Songs in the Light of Their Context' in *Wort – Gebot – Glaube: Beiträge zur Theologie des Alten Testaments. Walter Eichrodt zum 80. Geburtstag*, ed. H. J. Stoebe, Zürich 1970, 77–85. The problem of the servant as prophet or Israel is similar to the problem of interpreting the confessions of Jeremiah as referring to the prophet or the community. I do not think the Jeremiah material is any easier to interpret than the Second Isaiah motif.

37. What I have in mind here is a complex investigation of the three traditions as responses to the events of the sixth century so as to underline the differences and similarities and to delineate the emergence of theologization processes. The theology of the pathos of God has been a vein worked from the prophetic tradition by A. Heschel, *The Prophets*, ET New York 1962 and, under his influence, by U. Mauser, *Gottesbild und Menschwerdung: Eine Untersuchung zur Einheit des Alten und Neuen Testaments*, BHT 43, 1971, 78–114 (on Jeremiah). Heschel's influence on recent theology is another debt Christianity owes to Jewish thought.

38. *The Quest of the Historical Jesus: A Critical Study of its Progress From Reimarus to Wrede*, London 1911². The original German title was *Von Reimarus zu Wrede: eine Geschichte der Leben-Jesu-Forschung*, Tübingen 1906; later editions were published under the title *Geschichte der Leben-Jesu-Forschung*. Although Schweitzer may be somewhat out of date now,

and a new quest is eagerly pursued by hopeful theologians, his descriptive account is still valuable, and doubts will always remain about the degree of certitude with which the gospel sayings may be attributed to Jesus.

39. See his results stated briefly in *Quest*, 396–401.

40. The parallel between the two quests has been noted by some scholars, e.g., A. H. J. Gunneweg, 'Konfession oder Interpretation im Jeremiabuch', *ZTK* 67, 1970, 395–416 (noting the parallel uses of psalms for both figures); D. K. Jobling, 'The Quest of the Historical Jeremiah: Hermeneutical Implications of Recent Literature', *Union Seminary Quarterly Review* 34, 1978, 3–12 (as the title indicates, this article focuses directly on the resemblances between the research programmes; cf. esp. 6–8); W. Schottroff, 'Jeremia 2, 1–3: Erwägungen zur Methode der Prophetenexegese', *ZTK* 67, 1970, 263–94 (a strong call for using redaction-critical methods for determining authenticity and recognizing similarities between this approach and synoptic gospels research); see also E. Gerstenberger, 'Jeremiah's Complaints: Observations on Jer. 15.10–21', *JBL* 82, 1963, 393–408. Probably the strongest attack on the reconstructing the life of Jeremiah approach (or Skinnerian approach, as I call it) is that of H. G. Reventlow, *Liturgie und prophetisches Ich bei Jeremia*. For a recent attempt to defend the biographical approach see J. M. Berridge, *Prophet, People, and the Word of Yahweh*; cf. W. Johnstone, 'The Setting of Jeremiah's Prophetic Activity', *TGUOS* 21, 1967, 47–55.

41. For books in English on Jeremiah see Appendix I. As well as the many monographs, festschrifts and journal articles on Jeremiah, there are also conferences devoted to the topic, e.g., the Colloquium Biblicum Lovaniense XXXI was on 'The Book of Jeremiah' (Louvain, 18–20 August 1980). For literature on Jeremiah see S. Herrmann, 'Forschungen am Jeremiabuch', *Theologische Literaturzeitung* 102, Leipzig 1977, 481–90; G. Fohrer, 'Neue Literatur zur alttestamentlichen Prophetie (1961–1970): VII. Jeremia', *Theologische Rundschau* 45, Tübingen 1980, 109–21. Some journal articles are important as general treatments of Jeremiah, e.g., Schottroff, *ZTK* 67, 1970, 263–94; M. Weinfeld, 'Jeremiah and the Spiritual Metamorphosis of Israel', *ZAW* 88, 1976, 17–56; also P. R. Ackroyd, 'Aspects of the Jeremiah Tradition', *Indian Journal of Theology* 20, Serampore 1971, 1–12. The amount of material on Jeremiah is too vast to be listed in this book, and warrants a bibliographer's attention.

42. The commentaries most frequently used in this work, and therefore usually referred to in the notes by author (and page number) only, are Bright, AB 21, 1965; A. Condamin, *Le Livre de Jérémie: Traduction et Commentaire*, EB, 1936; B. Duhm, *Das Buch Jeremia*, Kurzer Hand-Commentar zum Alten Testament, Tübingen and Leipzig 1901; Hyatt in *IB* 5; W. Rudolph, *Jeremia*, HAT 12, 1968³; P. Volz, *Der Prophet Jeremia*, KAT 10, 1922; A. Weiser, *Das Buch des Propheten Jeremia*, ATD 20/21, 1960.

2. The Call of Jeremiah

1. These superscriptions are not a uniform series, but vary greatly

throughout the prophetic traditions (cf. Obad. 1; Jonah 1.1–3; Joel 1.1; Hab. 1.1). On these see G. M. Tucker, 'Prophetic Superscriptions and the Growth of a Canon' in *Canon and Authority*, ed. G. W. Coats and B. O. Long, 56–70; cf. H. M. I. Gevaryahu, 'Biblical Colophons: A Source for the "Biography" of Authors, Texts and Books', *Congress Volume Edinburgh 1974*, VTS 28, 1975, 42–59.

2. See the commentaries on individual prophetic books for exegetical treatments of the call narratives; also K. Baltzer, 'Considerations regarding the Office and Calling of the Prophet', *HTR* 61, 1968, 567–81. For the pre-prophetic material see W. Richter, *Die sogenannten vorprophetischen Berufungsberichte: Eine literaturwissenschaftliche Studie zu 1 Sam 9, 1–10, 16, Ex 3f. und Ri 6, 11b–17*, FRLANT 101, 1970.

3. N. Habel, 'The Form and Significance of the Call Narratives', *ZAW* 77, 1965, 297–323. On the formal aspects of prophetic language see C. Westermann, *Basic Forms of Prophetic Speech*, ET London and Philadelphia 1967.

4. On prophetic legends see A. Rofé, 'The Classification of the Prophetical Stories', *JBL* 89, 1970, 427–40; idem, 'Classes in the Prophetical Stories: Didactic Legenda and Parable' in *Studies on Prophecy: A Collection of Twelve Papers*, VTS 26, 1974, 143–64.

5. Cf. Kaiser, *Introduction*, 212–5, esp. 214 n. 12; Soggin, *Introduction*, 224–8. On cult prophets in general see A. R. Johnson, *The Cultic Prophet in Ancient Israel*, Cardiff 1962²; and his more recent restatement of the argument of that book in *The Cultic Prophet and Israel's Psalmody*, Cardiff 1979.

6. On tradition history see the works cited in ch. 1, n. 13 above. On form criticism see *Old Testament Form Criticism*, ed. J. H. Hayes, Trinity University Monograph Series in Religion 2, San Antonio 1974.

7. Cf. Richter, op. cit., 57–133; B. S. Childs, *Exodus*, OTL, 1974, 47–89.

8. The complexities of the section are ably discussed by Childs, ibid. Cf. Noth, *Exodus*, ET, OTL, 1962, 38–47; and Richter, op. cit., 131–3, 182f., for further comments; also Reventlow, *Liturgie und prophetisches Ich bei Jeremia*, 47–50.

9. Cf. Richter, op. cit., 134–5; R. G. Boling, *Judges*, AB 6A, 1975, 128–37. For prophets in the non-prophetic material see R. Rendtorff, 'Reflections on the Early History of Prophecy in Israel', *Journal for Theology and the Church* 4, New York 1967, 14–34; W. Zimmerli, 'Der "Prophet" im Pentateuch' in *Studien zum Pentateuch* (W. Kornfeld zum 60. Geburtstag), ed. G. Braulik, Vienna, Freiburg, Basel 1977, 197–211.

10. For angelic appearances cf. Gen. 16.7, 14; 21.17–19; 22.11–14; 31.11–13; Ex. 3.2; 23.33ff. For angel/messenger as an aspect of Yahweh see A. R. Johnson, *The One and the Many in the Israelite Conception of God*, Cardiff 1961², 28–33; on angels in the Genesis narratives see D. Irvin, *Mytharion: The Comparison of Tales from the Old Testament and the Ancient Near East*, AOAT 32, 1978, 91–104.

11. See the commentaries for the textual problems, esp. G. F. Moore, *Judges*, ICC, 1895, 173–99.

12. On the call of Samuel see the commentaries, esp. J. Mauchline, *1 and 2 Samuel*, NCB, 1971, 56–61; H. W. Hertzberg, *I and II Samuel*, OTL, 1964, 39–44; also M. Newman, 'The Prophetic Call of Samuel' in *Israel's Prophetic Heritage: Essays in honor of James Muilenburg*, ed. B. W. Anderson and W. Harrelson, New York and London 1962, 86–97.

13. The present redaction of I Samuel complicates the matter with its interpolation of 2.27–36, an account of the anonymous man of God's revelation to Eli of the coming downfall of his house, which renders Samuel's vision unnecessary; on the call of Samuel see Richter, op. cit., 13–56.

14. On *wayyityaṣṣab* (v. 10) meaning 'nocturnal revelation' cf. Job 4.16; S. R. Driver, *Notes on the Hebrew Text of the Books of Samuel*, Oxford 1890, 34. The term 'vision' (*mar'āh*) in v. 15 probably denotes what he had seen, cf. Gen. 46.2; Num. 12.6; Dan. 10.16; and esp. Ezek. 1.1; 8.3; 40.2. The reticence of detail in the story is typical of such biblical accounts, as Hertzberg (op. cit., 42) observes: 'The OT is generally very restrained in this connection (cf. Isa. 6 and Ex. 33); here, too, there is more in hints than in explicit statements.'

15. The division of Isa. 6.1–9.7 is a complicated matter involving translational and interpretative difficulties, especially in 8.16ff. For comments on aspects of this section see Carroll, 'Translation and Attribution in Isaiah 8.19f.', *The Bible Translator* 31, 1980, 126–34; on the larger issues see O. Kaiser, *Isaiah 1–12*, OTL, 1972, 71–130; H. Wildberger, *Jesaja 1–12*, BKAT X/1, 1972, 230–61 (on ch. 6), 230–389 on the whole section. See also I. Engnell, *The Call of Isaiah: An Exegetical and Comparative Study*, Uppsala Universitets Årsskrift 1949:4, Uppsala and Leipzig 1949.

16. Cf. Kaiser, *Introduction*, 221–6. In my book *When Prophecy Failed*, 132–44, I dealt with Isa. 6.1–9.6 from the canonical viewpoint of treating the story as it stands. Justified as this approach may be, an entirely new perspective on the text is gained by viewing it as an exilic redaction relating to questions about prophecy, community and the movement towards a canonic view of prophecy. For a treatment of some of these issues see P. R. Ackroyd, 'Isaiah I–XII: Presentation of a Prophet', *Congress Volume Göttingen 1977*, VTS 29, 1978, 16–48.

17. On this see O. Keel, *Jahwe-Visionen und Siegelkunst: Eine neue Deutung der Majestätsschilderungen in Jes 6, Ez 1 und 10 und Sach 4*, Stuttgarter Bibelstudien 84/85, Stuttgart 1977, 46–124; cf. F. Horst, 'Die Visionsschilderungen der alttestamentlichen Propheten', *EvTh* 20, 1960, 193–205.

18. Cf. Habel, op. cit., 312 n. 35.

19. The phrase may be demonstrative (e.g., Zech. 8.11) or contemptuous, and is used in traditions which normally refer to the nation as 'my people', i.e., Yahweh's people. It occurs in the Isaiah tradition at 6.9; 9.16 (Heb. v. 15); 28.11, 14; 29.14 and also in Micah 2.11. Its dominant occurrence is in the Jeremiah tradition; cf. 4.10f.; 5.23; 6.21; 7.16, 33; 11.14; 13.10; 14.10f.; 15.1, 20; 16.10; 21.8; 23.32; 27.16; 29.32; 36.7; 38.4. This clustering in the Jeremiah tradition does not prove Isa. 6.9f. to be an exilic usage, but the *probability* points in that direction. Note that 'this people' in Isa. 6.9f. does not specify Israel (as in 9.16) or Judah (cf. 1.1; 2.1), so is suitably indefinite, as befits a likely exilic redaction.

20. On I Kings 22 see S. J. de Vries, *Prophet Against Prophet: The Role of the Micaiah Narrative (I Kings 22) in the Development of Early Prophetic Tradition*, Grand Rapids 1978; on Ezekiel see the next three notes.

21. See W. Zimmerli, *Ezekiel* 1: *A Commentary on . . . Ezekiel, Chapters 1–24*, Hermeneia, Philadelphia 1979, 81–141; W. Eichrodt, *Ezekiel*, OTL, London 1970, 49–74; Keel, op. cit., 125–273.

22. There is a three-phase process of introduction in Ezek. 1–3 and its similarity of redaction to Hag. 1.1; Zech. 1 may indicate a canonic treatment of the exilic/post-exilic prophetic traditions (cf. Zimmerli, op. cit., 101).

23. For analytical details see Zimmerli, ibid., 142–78.

24. For exposition and analysis see J. L. Mays, *Hosea*, OTL, 1969, 20–45; H. W. Wolff, *Hosea*, Hermeneia, Philadelphia 1974, 3–45.

25. On this see Wolff, ibid., 14–17; whether Gomer had participated once in the local cult or was a regular worshipper (i.e., in biblical terms a 'sacred prostitute') is open to debate. Too much ink has flowed already on this topic for me to add to the flood.

26. For discussion of this chapter with bibliographical details see Wolff, 56–64.

27. See the commentaries for details, e.g., J. L. Mays, *Amos*, OTL, 1969, 133–40; H. W. Wolff, *Joel and Amos*, Hermeneia, Philadelphia 1977, 305–16. See also P. R. Ackroyd, 'A Judgment Narrative between Kings and Chronicles? An Approach to Amos 7.9–17' in *Canon and Authority*, 71–87; G. M. Tucker, 'Prophetic Authenticity: A Form-Critical Study of Amos 7.10–17', *Interpr* 27, 1973, 423–34; T. W. Overholt, 'Commanding the Prophets: Amos and the Problem of Prophetic Authority', *CBQ* 41, 1979, 517–32. The verbless sentence in Amos 7.14a makes the reply of Amos too ambiguous to resolve the vexed problem of what precisely he said to Amaziah. If the reader needs to be convinced that biblical language, especially that of prophecy, can be extremely ambiguous at times, then a perusal of the literature on this single issue will provide that convincement. On this much debated issue, among many discussions, see H. H. Rowley, 'Was Amos a Nabi?', *Festschrift O. Eissfeldt*, ed. J. Fück, Halle 1947, 191–8; S. Lehming, 'Erwägungen zu Amos', *ZTK* 55, 1958, 145–69; the discussion in N. H. Richardson, *JBL* 85, 1966, 89; Z. Zevit, *VT* 25, 1975, 783–90; idem, *VT* 29, 1979, 505–9; Y. Hoffmann, *VT* 27, 1977, 209–12; Soggin, *Introduction*, 241f., 245f.; and the commentaries.

28. Cf. Ackroyd, op. cit., 77–81; there is a growing literature on I Kings 13 which threatens to be as overwhelming as the material on Amos 7.14; see M. A. Klopfenstein, '1. Könige 13' in *PARRĒSIA: Karl Barth zum achtzigsten Geburtstag am 10.Mai 1966*, ed. E. Busch, Zürich 1966, 639–72; E. Würthwein, 'Die Erzählung von Gottesmann aus Juda in Bethel: Zur Komposition von 1 Kön. 13' in *Wort und Geschichte: Festschrift K. Elliger*, ed. H. Gese and H. P. Rüger, AOAT 18, 1973, 181–90; A. Jepsen, 'Gottesmann und Prophet: Anmerkungen zum Kapitel 1.Könige 13' in *Probleme biblischer Theologie: Gerhard von Rad zum 70. Geburtstag*, ed. H. W. Wolff, Munich 1971, 171–82. F. Crüsemann ('Kritik an Amos im deuteronomistischen Geschichtswerk: Erwägungen zu

2.Könige 14.27' in *Probleme biblischer Theologie*, 57–63) thinks that II Kings 14.27 was directed against the preaching of Amos. See also W. E. Lemke, 'The Way of Obedience: I Kings 13 and the Structure of the Deuteronomistic History' in *Magnalia Dei: The Mighty Acts of God*, Essays on the Bible and Archaeology in memory of G. Ernest Wright, ed. F. M. Cross, W. E. Lemke and P. D. Miller, New York 1976, 301–26.

29. On this cf. H. Schult, 'Amos 7.15a und die Legitimation des Aussenseiters' in *Probleme biblischer Theologie*, 462–78.

30. Cf. Wolff's comment (*Joel and Amos*, 314): 'The vision reports say nothing of such a command by Yahweh. Nevertheless, the balance of the evidence is in favor of the assumption that Amos perceived his commission in connection with the visions.' Cf. his comments, ibid., 295f.

31. For analysis and exegesis see the commentaries and also Berridge, *Prophet, People, and the Word of Yahweh*, 26–62; Habel, op. cit., 305–9; Lundbom, *Jeremiah*, 96–9; Reventlow, *Liturgie*, 24–77.

32. On its range and incidence see *BDB*, 654f.; cf. J. Macdonald and B. Cutler, 'Identification of the *Na'ar* in the Ugaritic texts', *UF* 8, 1977, 27–35. Apart from the Samuel material, the use of *na'ar* to describe King Solomon (I Kings 3.7) may point to the influence of the deuteronomists on the Jeremiah call narrative.

33. There is a very useful discussion of biblical metaphor and hyperbole in G. B. Caird, *The Language and Imagery of the Bible*, Duckworth Studies in Theology, London 1980, esp. 110–7, 144–59.

34. The simplest explanation for this influence is that the two sets of tradition were edited or produced by a common circle of traditionists using the same motifs to construct prophetic paradigms. On common elements between the two figures see W. L. Holladay, 'The Background of Jeremiah's Self-Understanding: Moses, Samuel, and Psalm 22', *JBL* 83, 1964, 153–64; idem, 'Jeremiah and Moses, Further Considerations', *JBL* 85, 1966, 17–27.

35. Lundbom, op. cit., 98f.

36. Jer. 15.16 has some textual difficulties, as LXX reads it differently from MT, reading 'those who despise your words'; see the commentaries at this point. The idiom *mṣ' dbr* is found elsewhere only in II Kings 22.13; 23.2.

37. Cf. Zimmerli, *Ezekiel 1*, 136f.

38. See the commentaries here. While I disagree with some of the views put forward by rhetorical criticism as practised by Lundbom and Holladay, there is a good deal of material in their work which advances the understanding of Jeremiah. Jer. 1 is a very sophisticated piece of editing which indicates more about the redactors' aims than it does about the prophet's experiences.

39. On this see G. von Rad, *Studies in Deuteronomy*, SBT 9, 1953, 74–91; cf. idem, *The Problem of the Hexateuch and other essays*, Edinburgh and New York 1966, 205–21. Less likely is Lundbom's view (op. cit., 98) that the word being watched over is what Yahweh has put into the prophet's mouth.

40. See the commentaries for discussion; Bright (*Jeremiah*, 5) writes:

'The picture in the prophet's mind is ambiguous and disputed; but it seems to be one of a cooking pot, or wash pot, boiling over a fire, and tipping so that its contents ("face," i.e., surface) are about to spill in a southerly direction.' Others relate the vision to a heated crucible and derive its terms from metallurgy; see H. W. Jüngling, 'Ich mache dich zu einer ehernen Mauer: Literarische Überlegungen zum Verhältnis von Jer 1, 18–19 zu Jer 15, 20–21', *Biblica* 54, Rome 1973, 1–24; here he is followed by S. Terrien, *The Elusive Presence: Toward a New Biblical Theology*, Religious Perspectives 26, New York 1978, 256f. Cf. Reventlow, *Liturgie*, 82–7.

41. On this kind of development in the prophetic traditions see Carroll, 'Inner Tradition Shifts in Meaning in Isaiah 1–11', *ExpT* 89, 1978, 301–4; D. R. Jones, 'The Traditio of the Oracles of Isaiah of Jerusalem', *ZAW* 67, 1955, 226–46.

42. For this motif see O. H. Steck, *Israel und das gewaltsame Geschick der Propheten: Untersuchungen zur Überlieferung des deuteronomistischen Geschichtsbildes im Alten Testament, Spätjudentum und Urchristentum*, WMANT 23, 1967. The ideological nature of the motif in the Bible should be clear from the fact that virtually none of the prophets was killed, but by NT times the motif appears to have reached the level of a dogma.

43. See B. S. Childs, 'The Enemy from the North and the Chaos Tradition', *JBL* 78, 1959, 187–98.

44. In 1.5 some Greek traditions read 'nation' for 'nations', which would make Jeremiah a prophet to his own nation; this makes better sense, but few commentators have accepted it (Skinner, *Prophecy and Religion*, 29 n., rejects as 'utterly unacceptable' the suggestion that it should be changed to 'my nation'). On the motif see H. Michaud, 'La vocation du "prophète des nations" ' in *Maqqél shôqédh: la branche d'amandier. Hommage à Wilhelm Vischer*, Montpellier 1960, 157–64.

45. See above ch. 1, notes 28–30, for discussion on possible sources of the redaction. The strong sense of return to Judah in the salvation oracles suggests a Palestinian location for the tradition (cf. Jer. 32).

46. Cf. Pohlmann, *Studien*; Janssen, *Juda in der Exilszeit*.

47. *Shorter Oxford English Dictionary*, 323. Cf. Greek *chiasmos*: diagonal arrangement, crisscross (Gk. *chiazein*, 'to mark with a *chi*'). For a discussion of chiastic structures in Jeremiah see Lundbom, 61–112.

48. On the analysis of the verse see the commentaries; also S. Herrmann, *Die prophetischen Heilserwartungen im Alten Testament*, 165–9. The way the chiasmus has been fractured by redaction or transmission makes one less impressed by the claims of Lundbom and Holladay for rhetorical criticism. It is an important approach to the text, but the redaction or transmission has been content to destroy the chiastic symmetry in order to incorporate into the statement a number of elements from the tradition. Rhetorical criticism should be pursued, but not to the point where semantics must give way to stylistics.

49. Although the terms of 1.10 are used here in the deuteronomistic principle of repentance, it is not at all clear to what extent the element of repentance should be understood as an implicit element in 1.10. Is the prophet commissioned to declare the divine judgment or promise to such

nations or to preach repentance to them? It rather looks as if elements have been extrapolated from the occurrences of these terms in the tradition and used to construct the call narrative.

50. The last phrase in 45.4, 'that is, the whole land', is omitted in the Greek, see BHS; it is an explanatory gloss which applies the terms to the land, rather than the nations.

51. This explanation holds good even if such exiles had returned to Jerusalem, because there still remained much work to be done there before the exilic party's ideology became the dominant one in the community. On the struggles of that period see Isa. 56–66 and the Ezra-Nehemiah material.

3. Early Rhetoric: Prophet against Community

1. Some scholars prefer to see 627 as the year of his birth (e.g., Hyatt, Holladay) so that he began work c. 609 when Josiah died (cf. Isa. 6.1), or even as late as 605, the year of the battle at Carchemish. On these possibilities see Hyatt, 'Jeremiah and Deuteronomy', *JNES* 1, 1942, 156–73; idem, *IB* 5, 779; C. F. Whitley, 'Carchemish and Jeremiah', *ZAW* 80, 1968, 38–49. Although these views resolve some of the problems of dating Jeremiah's work in the reign of Josiah, they do not satisfactorily account for all the problems. I have followed the traditional dating because that is what the redaction of the Jeremiah tradition presents as the period of the prophet's activity.

2. Apart from the works referred to in ch. 1, nn. 27, 28 above, cf. the following: T. R. Hobbs, 'Some Remarks on the Structure and Composition of the Book of Jeremiah', *CBQ* 34, 1972, 257–75; O. Loretz, 'Die Sprüche Jeremias in Jer. 1, 17–9, 25', *UF* 2, 1970, 109–30; H. H. Rowley, 'The Early Prophecies of Jeremiah in their Setting' in *Men of God: Studies in Old Testament History and Prophecy*, London and New York 1963, 133–68; W. McKane, 'Relations between Poetry and Prose in the Book of Jeremiah' in *Congress Volume Vienna 1980*, VTS forthcoming.

3. BHS sets it out as poetry. On its poetic structure see R. Althann, 'Jeremiah IV 11–12: stichometry, parallelism and translation', *VT* 28, 1978, 385–91.

4. For strophic analysis of the Jeremiah text see the commentaries of Condamin, Rudolph, Volz and Weiser; cf. W. L. Holladay, 'The Recovery of Poetic Passages of Jeremiah', *JBL* 85, 1966, 401–35.

5. A good example of the treatment of original prophecy plus *Nachleben* is Zimmerli's magisterial commentary on Ezekiel. The criticisms of this approach made by Childs (*The Old Testament as Scripture*, 369f.) should be noted, but equally serious objections may be made against Childs' alternative account of canonical interpretation; cf. *JSOT* 16, 1980, 2–60; and the reviews by Carroll, *SJT* 33, 1980, 285–91; B. W. Anderson, *Theology Today* 37, Princeton NJ 1980, 100–8. For an assessment of Childs' contribution to the contemporary discussion of canon see Carroll, 'Canonical Criticism: a Recent Trend in Biblical Studies?', *ExpT* 92, 1980, 73–8; idem, 'Childs and Canon', *Irish Biblical Studies* 2, 1980, 211–36.

6. This probability assumes two things: (1) there was such a thing as an

early collection of oracles; (2) the tradition about Baruch represents something real, though not necessarily a historical scribe called Baruch. On 2.1–3 as a redactional preface to the early oracles (thus making 1.1–2.3 all redactional rather than original Jeremiah material) see W. Schottroff, 'Jeremia 2, 1–3: Erwägungen zur Methode der Prophetenexegese', *ZTK* 67, 1970, 263–94.

7. This is a characteristic feature of biblical language and is not limited to the prophetic literature. It is a defect of Caird's book (*The Language and Imagery of the Bible*) that he does not consider it at any point. It is perhaps evidence of the hard times and effete culture into which the Bible has fallen that its most ardent supporters are blind to this dimension of biblical language. For brief treatments of bawdy language in the Bible see E. Ullendorff, 'The Bawdy Bible', *Bulletin of the School of Oriental and African Studies* 42, London 1979, 425–56; on the language and interpretation of the Song of Songs see M. H. Pope, *Song of Songs: A New Translation with Introduction and Commentary*, AB 7C, 1977.

8. Cf. the nice touch with which J. Chotzner (*Hebrew Humour and Other Essays*, London 1905, 10) refers to Ezekiel's strong language: 'Of Ezekiel's humour no specimens can be given here. It is, like Swift's, rather coarse, and not altogether palatable. The curious may be referred to the sixteenth and twenty-third chapters of the Book of Ezekiel.'

9. For *ṣ'h* as an obscene term see *BDB*, 858. Bright (*Jeremiah*, 11) translates it as 'sprawled, (a-whoring)'.

10. The precise meaning of these lines is not clear to me. They may be euphemisms for sexual activity ('feet' is a standard biblical euphemism for 'genitals'), but the strong language of the poems suggests that euphemistic terms would be out of place. See W. McKane, 'Jeremiah II 23–25: Observations on the Versions and History of Exegesis', *Oudtestamentische Studiën* 17, Leiden 1972, 73–88, esp. 79f., 86–8. I am grateful to Professors William McKane (St Andrews University) and Edward Ullendorff (London University) for correspondence on this matter. I still think there are bawdy undercurrents in 2.25.

11. *hāmôn* in 3.23 means 'noise made by a crowd' and is translated by Bright (20), following G. A. Smith, *Jeremiah*, London 1929⁴, 102, as 'hubbub' (Smith explains the line to mean 'the riotous festivals on the highplaces'). Whether these denunciations should be understood to refer to literal or metaphoric behaviour is very difficult to determine. Many commentators hedge their bets by taking both senses as the meaning of the texts, e.g. J. Calvin, *Commentary on Jeremiah and Lamentations* I, ET, Edinburgh 1850, 270, though he prefers the figurative interpretation because the community had no spiritual chastity; cf. J. A. Bewer, *The Prophets in the King James Version with Introduction and Critical Notes*, Harper's Annotated Bible series, New York and London 1949/50, 189.

12. An obscure line with no satisfactory resolution of the difficulties caused by the words *m'yuzzānîm* and *maškîm*: *yzn* 'to have heavy testicles' (?) is probably to be preferred to *zūn*, 'feed', hence *maškîm* (Volz, 59 n., describes this word as 'unintelligible') 'testicles' (*ma'ašîkîm* cf. BHS; unattested in biblical Hebrew but found in post-biblical Hebrew); Bright

(36) just translates 'sleek and lusty' and refuses to comment on the linguistic difficulties.

13. Cf. NEB margin; some prefer to emend the word to *yitgōrārū*, 'visited' the brothels (cf. Rudolph, 38; Bright, 36 n.; BHS; Volz, 59 n.; LXX *kateluon*).

14. Here I understand the plural imperatives of 5.1 (*šōṭṭū . . . rᵉʾū . . . dᵉʿū . . . baqšū . . . timṣᵉʾū*) to be addressed to the community by the prophet (cf. J. A. Thompson, *Jeremiah*, NICOT, 1980, 233 n. 1, 236 + n. 1); however, if the speaker of the oracle is Yahweh, as many commentators take it to be, then the plurals are difficult to interpret. Some would emend *wᵉʾeslaḥ* 'that I may forgive her', which certainly indicates Yahweh is the speaker (cf. LXX addition of 'says Yahweh' at end of verse), to *wᵉnislaḥ* 'that we may forgive' (e.g., Duhm). If the deity is the speaker, who then are those addressed? The divine council perhaps (cf. the similar plurals in Isa. 40.1f.) or Yahweh's response to advisers (heavenly?) who plead for mercy for the community (cf. Gen. 18.23–33)? As with so many other difficulties in the interpretation of Jeremiah, I am deeply grateful to Professor McKane for his generous correspondence with me on these issues.

15. 9.20 in Hebrew. The image of death coming up through the windows is found in Canaanite literature, but that may not have directly influenced the metaphor used here. On the Canaanite material see B. Margalit, *A matter of 'Life' and 'Death': a Study of the Baal-Mot Epic (CTA 4–5–6)*, AOAT 206, 1980, esp. 45–50.

16. Bright (67) translates 'for every brother's as crafty as Jacob', cf. Hos. 12.2–4 (Heb. vv. 3–5). A community of Jacobs would be as disastrous as a community of prophets (in spite of the wish expressed in Num. 11.29).

17. Rudolph (36; also in BHS) omits *wābōhū* in v. 23 and translates as 'das Chaos'. Caird (op. cit., 113f.) sees the piece as a good example of prophetic hyperbole. The similarity of Gen. 1.2 and v. 23a may point to the piece coming from the same circle of traditionists, rather than being influenced by Gen. 1. On its interpretation see the commentaries; for the view that it is an apocalyptic insertion into the tradition see V. Eppstein, 'The Day of Yahweh in Jeremiah 4, 23–28', *JBL* 87, 1968, 93–7.

18. On the Scythian hypothesis, which is largely abandoned these days, see Skinner, 35–52; cf. H. Cazelles, 'Sophonie, Jérémie et les Scythes en Palestine', *RB* 74, 1967, 24–44.

19. On the difficult interpretation of these confessions see ch. 5 below.

20. On the Micah traditions see J. L. Mays, *Micah*, OTL, 1976, 36–92; B. Renaud, *La formation du livre de Michée: Tradition et Actualisation*, EB, 1977, 1–148.

21. There are some references to oppression within the community, but these are strikingly few in number in comparison to the charges against the whole community – the book of Jeremiah is not a prophetic tradition which gives as much comfort to the Marxian analyst as do the Amos, Micah or Isaiah traditions (insofar as any prophetic book can be fitted into a Marxian scheme of analysis). Cf. Jer. 2.34; 5.26–29; and the deuteronomistic material in 7.5f., 9. I draw attention to this feature of Jeremiah in order to

outline the *Gestalt* of the tradition in contrast to other prophetic traditions. Too much should not be made out of it.

22. On the difficulties in the text see BHS and the commentaries. Most commentators are too intelligent to accept the picture of the community presented by this rhetorical attack. Commenting on ch. 26 Bright (172) observes 'There *were* good men in Judah', so we are warned 'against accepting Jeremiah's pessimistic evaluation of his people (e.g., v. 1–5; ix 1–8) without qualification'. Among others who make a similar point note Y. Kaufmann, *The Religion of Israel: From Its Beginnings to the Babylonian Exile* (abridged ET by M. Greenberg), New York 1972, 402, where he argues that there had been improvements in society since the eighth century. Such improvements would explain the point I make in n. 21 above. Space does not permit me to delineate Kaufmann's argument any further, but it is a fine piece of polemic against facile theological arguments all too often employed by Christian writers on the Bible, i.e., that Israel was destroyed because of its sinfulness – in Nebuchadrezzar's time *and* in the first century of the Christian church). The section in Kaufmann (401–46) on Jeremiah and Ezekiel is a judicious account of difficult material and is to be recommended for its realistic presentation of exilic prophecy.

23. For a good treatment of this motif in the tradition see T. W. Overholt, *The Threat of Falsehood: A Study in the Theology of the Book of Jeremiah*, SBT 2.16, 1970.

24. T. E. Lawrence, *The Seven Pillars of Wisdom*, ch. 3. I owe the quotation to Caird, op. cit., 110, whose treatment of hyperbole and absoluteness in the Bible (110–17) is a useful balance to the frenzied quest for meaning characteristic of some biblical interpretations.

25. On the book of consolation see Herrmann, *Die prophetischen Heilserwartungen*, 159–241; also ch. 8 below.

26. For a useful discussion of these prophetic traditions in relation to the theodicy motif, see Raitt, *A Theology of Exile*, 83–105. On the concept of theodicy see M. Weber, *The Sociology of Religion*, ET Boston 1963, London 1965, 138–50; in relation to Israelite prophecy see his *Ancient Judaism*, ET Chicago 1952, London 1953, ch. 12, 297–335.

27. There is some truth in the view that 'The Old Testament is the epos of the Fall of Jerusalem' (J. C. Todd, *Politics and Religion in Ancient Israel*, London 1904, quoted in N. K. Gottwald, *Studies in the Book of Lamentations*, SBT 14, 1954, 63 n. 1), though it should not be overexaggerated. Certainly the collapse of Jerusalem had a profound effect on the community and refracted many of its traditions, so that the subsequent contents and shape of the Bible were greatly determined by the epoch inaugurated by that fall.

28. Kaufmann, *The Religion of Israel*, 402; cf. Raitt, op. cit., 92–4.

29. On the positive aspects of the material in Jer. 37–44 see P. R. Ackroyd, 'Historians and Prophets', *SEÅ* 33, 1968, 37–54; also his *Exile and Restoration*, 56–8; cf. Pohlmann, *Studien*.

30. The works of Janssen, Nicholson and Pohlmann, already cited, bear on this issue, but too many imponderables are involved in the discussion

for a dogmatic position to be maintained on any resolution of the problem of where the tradition was produced.

31. The evidence for such conflict and controversy is to be found in Ezek. 40–48, Haggai-Zechariah, Isa. 56–66, the Ezra-Nehemiah material and most likely in the Jeremiah tradition. Apart from histories of the period see M. Smith, *Palestinian Parties and Politics that Shaped the Old Testament*, New York and London 1971.

32. With this poem we begin to encounter deuteronomistic editing in the poetry; for an invaluable treatment of this complex matter see W. Thiel, *Die deuteronomistische Redaktion von Jeremia 1–25*. This book represents pages 1–452 of his dissertation, *Die deuteronomistische Redaktion des Buches Jeremia*, Humboldt-Universität Berlin 1970. On 3.1–4.2 see the commentaries and Thiel, op. cit., 83–93; Holladay, *Architecture*, 46–54; D. K. Jobling, 'Jeremiah's poem in III 1–IV 2', *VT* 28, 1978, 45–55.

33. On *šūb* in the Jeremiah tradition see W. L. Holladay, *The Root ŠŪBH in the Old Testament with particular reference to its usages in covenantal contexts*, Leiden 1958, 128–39. For 4.3f. as transition see the commentaries and Thiel, 93–7.

34. On the disputation form see Westermann, *Basic Forms*, 201; on 3.1–5 see esp. B. O. Long, 'The Stylistic Components of Jeremiah 3.1–5', *ZAW* 88, 1976, 386–90; J. D. Martin, 'The forensic background to Jeremiah III 1', *VT* 19, 1969, 82–92; on the legal aspects of the piece see T. R. Hobbs, 'Jeremiah 3 1–5 and Deuteronomy 24 1–4', *ZAW* 86, 1974, 23–9; C. Carmichael, *The Laws of Deuteronomy*, Ithaca and London 1974, 203–7; cf. Mayes, *Deuteronomy*, 322f. See also W. Brueggemann, 'Jeremiah's Use of Rhetorical Questions', *JBL* 92, 1973, 358–74.

35. See the discussion in Skinner, 89–107; H. H. Rowley, 'The Prophet Jeremiah and the Book of Deuteronomy' in *From Moses to Qumran: Studies in the Old Testament*, London and New York 1963, 187–208; and in ch. 4 below.

36. Bright (26f.) thinks the failure of v. 10 might refer to Hezekiah's reform rather than Josiah's. This is most unlikely, because in Jer. 26.19 there is a tradition of a successful repentance in Hezekiah's time. Judah survived the Assyrian invasion but fell to the Babylonians, therefore reforms were successful in the earlier period but not in the later period.

37. Cf. Thiel, 119f. The strong emphasis on unwillingness or incapacity with reference to repentance in these oracles is in striking contrast to the picture of the prophet in chs. 26–37 regularly offering deliverance if the king or community will only change its policy. For these later accounts of the prophet's activities and the different traditions they represent see Wanke, *Untersuchungen zur sogenannten Baruchschrift*; also my discussion below in chs. 6 and 9.

38. This difficulty is similar to the one in Amos 7.14, where the negative is taken by some scholars to be an asseveration (see the works referred to in ch. 2, n. 27 above). In Jer. 30.11 the phrase is used to indicate the destruction of the nations (*kī 'eʿśeh kālāh bᵉkol-haggōyim*), so it is probable that in 4.27; 5.1 it represents a redactional note promising some survival of elements after the destruction. Hyatt (850) thinks 5.1 indicates

the deuteronomist's awareness that the land was not fully destroyed in 587; the phrase in 4.27 (cf. 5.10) is seen by him to be a mitigating gloss (841). Lundbom (op. cit., 40, 148) is inclined to take *lō'* in these verses as having an asseverative force. On such asseveratives see C. F. Whitley, 'Some Remarks on *lū* and *lō'* ', *ZAW* 87, 1975, 202–4; cf. F. Nötscher, *VT* 3, 1953, 372ff. Both possibilities have to be allowed for, so the interpretation of the phrases depends upon the interpreter's judgment with respect to the redaction of the tradition. Indeterminacy of meaning is a major problem in the interpretation of biblical statements, especially in the prophets.

39. On the text see BHS; Thiel, 214–7. For *nḥm* see D. W. Thomas, *ExpT* 44, 1933, 191f.; he understands it to mean 'draw breath (of relief), breathe again'. Although *nḥm* is used of the deity in the Jeremiah tradition, in the later liturgies it is combined with *šūb* to mean 'God turns and breathes again' (cf. Joel 2.14; Jonah 3.9). Provided this is not a concealed attempt to avoid the metaphor of Yahweh repenting, it is an interesting way of treating the terms; in response to Thomas see G. B. Mitchell, *ExpT* 44, 428.

40. Deut. 30.1–10 is built around the motif of *šūb*; cf. Mayes, 367–9.

41. Cf. Janssen, op. cit., 75f., where he argues from Judg. 10.6–16 that the deuteronomists maintained that the only hope for Israel during the exile was a return of the kind displayed in the time of Jephthah. Cf. H. W. Wolff, 'The Kerygma of the Deuteronomic Historical Work' in *The Vitality of Old Testament Traditions*, 83–100.

42. On covenant see D. J. McCarthy, *Treaty and Covenant: A Study in Form in the Ancient Oriental Documents and in the Old Testament*, Analecta Biblica 21A, Rome[3] 1978; if the treaty forms of the Ancient Near East are behind the development of the covenant motif, then repentance seems even less likely to have a covenantal basis. Too many biblical scholars accept repentance as having its roots in covenant to be listed here but cf. Holladay, *The Root ŠŪBH*; T. Raitt, 'The Prophetic Summons to Repentance', *ZAW* 83, 1971, 30–49; idem, *A Theology of Exile*, 37–49. Such a view is fine if the motif of repentance is a deuteronomistic creation, but if it has its origins in prophecy then I rather think it must be accounted for in a different way. As I tend to take a similar view of covenant to that of L. Perlitt, *Bundestheologie im Alten Testament*, WMANT 36, 1969, though modified to the extent of recognizing covenant elements of a pre-deuteronomistic nature (the regulative use of covenant for Israel's history is deuteronomistic in origin), I do not regard covenant as a significant feature of eighth-century prophecy; so *if* repentance is genuine in the prophets of that period, I do not see it as having a covenantal matrix.

43. Cf. Skinner, 165–84; and the discussion of these accounts in ch. 4 below. See also Nicholson, *Preaching to the Exiles*, 68–71.

44. Some of the steps in this movement are obscure, but for a treatment of the general concept see P. R. Ackroyd, 'The Vitality of the Word of God in the Old Testament: A Contribution to the Study of the Transmission and Exposition of Old Testament Material', *Annual of the Swedish Theological Institute* (Jerusalem) 1, Leiden 1962, 7–23.

45. Two invaluable works on the remnant motif are W. E. Müller, *Die Vorstellungen vom Rest im Alten Testament*, Leipzig 1939, and G. F. Hasel, *The Remnant: The History and Theology of the Remnant Idea from Genesis to Isaiah*, Andrews University Monographs V, Berrien Springs 1972.

46. S. Schechter, *Aspects of Rabbinic Theology*, New York 1961, quoting *Pesikta von Rab Kahana*, ed. Buber, Lyck 1868, 160a–163b.

47. In Jewish thought repentance replaced sacrifice when the temple cultus was destroyed in 70 CE; on its range and significance cf. G. F. Moore, *Judaism in the First Centuries of the Christian Era: The Age of the Tannaim* I, Cambridge, Mass. 1927, 497–534; J. J. Petuchowski, 'The Concept of "Teshuvah" in the Bible and the Talmud', *Judaism* 17, New York 1968, 175–85; Schechter, op. cit., 313–43; A. Cohen, *Everyman's Talmud*, London and New York 1949, 104–10.

48. The notion of false repentance is stated in Jer. 3.10; for a brief view of fraudulent repentance see *Midrash Rabbah on Genesis* 9.2, 5. It is not easy to determine what constitutes false repentance, and the references given here do not persuade one that it is a meaningful concept. It looks too much like rationalization in the avoidance of a real problem to be convincing. It seems to be based on the distinction between intention and action, but special pleading is quickly involved if it is asserted that people perform certain actions only to gain God's favour, when that precisely is what repentance entails. If the paradigm of repentance is Nineveh's response to Jonah, then it is very difficult to see what false repentance might entail. The subject really needs a much fuller discussion than space permits here.

49. See A. I. Kook, *Orot ha-Teshuvah*, translated as *Rabbi Kook's Philosophy of Repentance*, New York 1968; cf. *EJ* 14, cols. 73–8.

50. As a humanistic concept, the idea of repentance is a very important way of stating that the past is not completely determinative of the future. It is a corollary of human freedom and responsibility. It involves the possibility of change, hence appeals to the existentialist approach to life. Man determines himself and may go on determining himself without fear of being trapped by the past. As a theological concept it involves a deity who also changes in response to man's actions. Arising out of the metaphors used by the prophets to describe human and communal activities, it came to be posited of God himself. A reciprocal relationship is built up between God and man through the turning of both to each other. Its strongly humanistic elements have made it less than appealing to some theological traditions, which prefer a deterministic world-view based on predestination. However, the breadth of its scope and the sheer power of its imaginative construction of the future make it one of the finest concepts to have been developed by man. It is the human side of the dialectical relationship between God and man and, given such a dialectical structure, it deserves to be analysed more fully than I have space for in this book.

4. Temple Sermon and Covenant Preacher

1. On the treatment of 7.1–8.3 see the commentaries and Thiel, 103–34.

The popularity of the temple sermon (7.1–15) with preachers is such that the canonical presentation of Jeremiah preaching it is the way most readers treat it. For a judicious treatment of it see Skinner, 165–84; on formal aspects of the section see C. D. Isbell and M. Jackson, 'Rhetorical criticism and Jeremiah VII 1–VIII 3', *VT* 30, 1980, 20–6.

2. For the formal analysis of 7.1–15 see G. Fohrer, 'Jeremias Tempelwort (Jeremia 7 1–15)' in *Studien zur alttestamentlichen Prophetie (1949–1965)*, BZAW 99, 1967, 190–203; H. G. Reventlow, 'Gattung und Überlieferung in der "Tempelrede Jeremias", Jer. 7 und 26', *ZAW* 81, 1969, 315–52; see also J. A. Wilcoxen, 'The Political Background of Jeremiah's Temple Sermon' in *Scripture in History and Theology: Essays in Honor of J. Coert Rylaarsdam*, ed. A. L. Merrill and T. W. Overholt, Pittsburgh 1977, 151–66; and the works referred to in n. 17 below.

3. Cf. Thiel, 290–5, for a discussion, with a table setting out comparative features of 7.1–15; 22.1–5; 17.19–27 (291), of the deuteronomistic sermons which offer the community an alternative to its current way of life. This type of preaching is not the creation of D, but is at home in the deuteronomistic circles, cf. I Kings 9.4–7, operating during the exilic period (so Thiel, 118). For a rather different account of these prose sermons see the article by W. L. Holladay, 'Prototype and Copies: A New Approach to the Poetry-Prose Problem in the Book of Jeremiah', *JBL* 79, 1960, 351–67.

4. Cf. Skinner, 170ff.

5. See the various discussions in Bright and Nicholson. The difficulty with the argument that the sermons represent the gist of what Jeremiah said is that it is impossible to show how they would differ if he had not said anything at all comparable to the sermon. From the deuteronomists' viewpoint, the sermons represent what a prophet would have said on any given occasion, and this makes it rather difficult to determine the extent to which the prophet may have contributed his own distinctive element. Herrmann and Rudolph tend to see the deuteronomistic material as *revisions* of what Jeremiah originally said, rather then free deuteronomistic creations. I tend, with others, to see the contribution of the deuteronomists as a much more creative element in the construction of the Jeremiah tradition.

6. This is necessarily a very general statement and intended as a *Gestalt* of prophecy from Amos to Jeremiah. The attack on sacrifice in the prophetic traditions (e.g. Hos. 6.6; Amos 4.4f.; 5.25; Isa. 1.10–17; Micah 6.6–8; Jer. 6.20; 7.21–23) is a limited one and, as the references indicate, often appears in the framework (e.g., Isa. 1), the redaction (e.g., Jer. 7) , or a problematic section.

7. See esp. Reventlow, *ZAW* 81, 334–41.

8. See the commentaries on this point. Danish archaeological excavations have suggested that Shiloh was destroyed in the late eighth century (see M.-L. Buhl and S. Holm-Nielsen, *Shiloh, the Danish Excavations at Tall Sailun, Palestine, in 1929, 1932, and 1963*, Copenhagen 1969; also J. van Rossum, 'Wanneer is Silo verwoest?', *Nederlands Theologisch Tijdschrift* 24, Wangeningen 1970, 321–32; R. A. Pearce, 'Shiloh and Jer. VII 12, 14, and 15', *VT* 23, 1973, 105–8). For arguments, not always persuasive, against

this position see J. Day, 'The destruction of the Shiloh sanctuary and Jeremiah VII 12, 14' in *Studies in the Historical Books of the Old Testament*, ed. J. A. Emerton, VTS 30, 1979, 87–94. As the hearers of the Jeremiah tradition would not know what *had* happened centuries before their time, their familiarity with Shiloh as a cult centre will have been determined by the deuteronomistic history presentation in I Samuel; so Jer. 7 should be taken in conjunction with the history as a theological presentation of deuteronomistic ideology rather than a straightforward historical account.

9. In 7.3 the words *waʰšaknāh 'etkem*, 'I will cause you to dwell (in this place)' may be revocalized (cf. BHS: Aquila; Vulgate) as *wᵉʾeškᵉnāh 'itkem* 'I will dwell with you'. The MT vocalization relates to the community's survival in the land which is more in keeping with the whole passage (cf. v. 15, 'I will cast you out'); whereas the proposed revocalization relates to the divine presence in the temple.

10. For the triple repetition of a word or phrase cf. 22.29. What the RSV translates as 'this' in the Hebrew is *hēmmāh*, 'these', a possible reference to the complex of buildings constituting the temple. It could, however, be an abbreviation for the phrase *hammāqōm hazzeh*, 'this place', i.e., the temple. Cf. BHS; Thiel, 108–9; Rudolph, 50; LXX understands it as *estin* 'it is'.

11. Cf. II Kings 18–19; Isa. 36–37. On the complicated issue of the inviolability of Jerusalem see J. H. Hayes, 'The Tradition of Zion's Inviolability', *JBL* 82, 1963, 419–26; B. S. Childs, *Isaiah and the Assyrian Crisis*, SBT 2.3, 1967; R. E. Clements, *Isaiah and the Deliverance of Jerusalem: A Study of the Interpretation of Prophecy in the Old Testament*, *JSOT* SS 13; 1980. If Jer. 7.1–15 is an attack on a dogma of Zion's divine protection, then it is ironical that the Isaiah tradition should have contributed so much to the dogma. But one generation's prophecy is the next generation's superstition!

12. Omitted in Greek of v. 13 but translated in v. 25 as *hēmeras kai orthrou*, 'by day and early morning'. The metaphor here of God rising early in the morning to speak, through the prophets, to the people should be balanced with other metaphors of divine activity in the Bible: e.g., not sleeping (cf. Ps. 121.3f.) or sleeping (cf. Ps. 44.23 [Heb. v. 24]). Doctrine should not be built on *any* of these metaphors – context or function of metaphor is everything in the interpretation of biblical metaphor.

13. On the desert motif in Jer. 2.2f.; Hos. 9.10; Deut. 32.10–14, see R. Bach, *Die Erwählung Israels in der Wüste*, Dissertation: Bonn 1952. On some of the complexities of the desert traditions and their functions in the Bible see Carroll, 'Rebellion and Dissent in Ancient Israelite Society', *ZAW* 89, 1977, 176–204.

14. Cf. Thiel, 128–34; he provides a table setting out the comparative material on the Moloch sacrifice polemic in 7.30–34; 19.5–12; 32.34f. (*Tabelle* 3,131). For the principle of giving children to Yahweh (without specification of the means) cf. Ex. 13.1f., 11–16; 22.29b. The phrases in Jer. 7.31, 'which I did not command, nor did it come into my mind' may well be a polemic against the beliefs indicated by the Exodus texts (cf. Ezek. 20.25f.). The reference to burning (*liśrōf*) the children in

Jer. 7.31 (cf. II Kings 23.10) may be an exaggeration of a cult which dedicated children to the god by passing them through fire. There are numerous references to this cult in the Hebrew Bible which may be translated
to mean either sacrificing the children by fire or dedicating them by fire.
The verb used is *ha'ᵃbīr* (or various hiphil forms of *'br*), which means 'to
cause to pass, pass through' and should probably be translated in most
cases as 'dedicate'. This is its clear meaning in Ex. 13.12 (cf. v. 2 *qaddeš-
lī*, 'consecrate to me'). RSV gives 'you shall set apart to Yahweh';
cf. Lev. 18.21, where RSV has 'devote them by fire to Molech' ('by fire'
is unwarranted because it is not in MT, which simply has *lᵉha'ᵃbīr*, 'dedicate' or 'pass through'; though note that the Samaritan Pentateuch has
lᵉha'ᵃbīd, 'cause to serve', and LXX has 'to serve'). All the occurrences in
the deuteronomistic history (II Kings 16.3; 17.17; 21.6 [= II Chron. 33.6];
23.10) could be translated 'he passed his son/sons and daughters through
the fire', i.e., 'dedicated them to the service of a particular cult' (possibly
sacred prostitution, which would fit the context of Lev. 18, a series of
prohibited sexual practices, cf. vv. 19–23). RSV margin recognizes this
possibility for II Kings 16.3; 17.17. It also fits the prohibition against
magical practices in Deut. 18.10 (cf. RSV margin), where sacrificing children is out of keeping with the context. The references to the practice in
Jer. 7.31 (cf. the more normal phrasing in Jer. 32.35, which is a variation
on 7.31 – or vice versa); Ezek. 16.21; 23.37 are blatantly pejorative descriptions of a cult practice which, although illicit by some standards, was
decidedly not vicious. But propagandist abuse is seldom accurate. In
Ezek. 20.26, 31 the language used is similar to that in the deuteronomistic
history and it may be translated as 'pass through' or 'dedicate'. (For those
who prefer to take the pejorative references in Jer. 7 and Ezek. 16; 23 as
the way to understand all the other references [including Ex. 13.12!], the
following consideration might meet with their approval: if the kings of
Judah were in the habit of burning their children, what a great pity it was
that Josiah stopped the practice. Otherwise he might have burned Jehoiakim
as a child and thereby have made Jeremiah's life much easier in the future!)
For a view of *ha'ᵃbīr* as 'pass through' see the Talmud (*b.San*.64a), where
the practice is related to cultic prostitution. A brief statement of the correct
understanding of the practice can be found in N. H. Snaith, 'The cult of
Molech', *VT* 16, 1966, 123f.

15. RSV translates *bᵉha'ᵃbīr* as 'in making them offer by fire', where
'dedicate' or 'pass through' (fire understood) might be less eisegetical. The
phrase in Ezek. 20.26, *bᵉha'ᵃbīr kol-peṭer rāḥam*, is virtually the same as
ha'ᵃbartā kol-peṭer-reḥem in Ex. 13.12 (cf. Ex.34.19f.). On the interpretation of the Ezekiel references see Zimmerli, *Ezekiel* 1, 344, 411f. (he
certainly relates the practice to killing, and supports Elliger's view, 'Das
Gesetz Leviticus 18', *ZAW* 67 1955, 17, that Moloch worship involved the
sacrifice of newly born children who were the result of immoral cultic
intercourse); Eichrodt, *Ezekiel*, 270–3. As biblical legend informs us that
Abraham was once tempted to burn his son Isaac as a sacrifice (cf. Gen. 22),
the motif of dedicating children (especially sons) to god/God by fire is
clearly a complex one in the biblical traditions.

16. After a lengthy discussion of just *one* cultic practice it would be inadvisable to devote another lengthy footnote to this even more complex matter. For diverging viewpoints see Kaufmann, *Religion of Israel*, 430–2; M. Smith, 'The Veracity of Ezekiel, the Sins of Manasseh, and Jeremiah 44.18', *ZAW* 87, 1975, 11–16; cf. the brief discussion in Carroll, *When Prophecy Failed*, 49–52.

17. For analysis of the chapter see the commentaries; Reventlow, *ZAW* 81, 315–52; F. L. Hossfeld and I. Meyer, 'Der Prophet vor dem Tribunal: Neuer Auslegungsversuch von Jer 26', *ZAW* 86, 1974, 30–50. On aspects of the trial see Skinner, 171–4; R. Davidson, 'Orthodoxy and the Prophetic Word: A Study in the Relationship between Jeremiah and Deuteronomy', *VT* 14, 1964, 407–16.

18. Micah 3.12; cf. BHS, LXX on the text. Cf. Mays, *Micah*, 92. Two things may be said about the citation of this text: it is a unique occurrence in the prophetic tradition and it is a very strange, discrete account of Hezekiah's reign. In II Kings Hezekiah's reign is presented as a very good one, full of piety and success, but not one that required the king/community to repent. When the king fell sick the prophet Isaiah did not advise him to repent but prayed for him (cf. II Kings 20.1–11; Isa. 38). Indeed, if there is one motif ill-suited to the story of Hezekiah as it appears in II Kings and Isa. 36–39 it is repentance (cf. Isa. 38.3; II Kings 20.3). So a tradition such as Jer. 26.19 is a radically different account of the ideal king (or what is more likely, it is an ad hoc argument invented by the traditionists for the trial story of Jeremiah). Cf. Ackroyd, 'Historians and Prophets', *SEÅ*, 26.

19. On 26.24 cf. Bright, 170; Rudolph, 171. Volz, 92, deals with ch. 26 immediately after 7.1–15 and understands the confrontation to be the fulfilment of 1.18f.; king, priests and people are ranged against the prophet (98). Others (e.g., H. Cunliffe-Jones, *Jeremiah*, Torch Bible Commentaries, London 1960, 177–80) think that during the trial the people changed their view of the matter and switched sides. The inconsistencies in the story point to the complex development of various strands making up the story (see Reventlow here). We should perhaps take 26.1–19 to be the story and see vv. 20–24 as an addition from a later period (cf. Volz). Jer. 26, like so much else in the Bible, is tantalizing in the information it gives and that which it withholds, so we are not able to interpret every element in the story in a consistent way.

20. A failure in the sense that Micah fully expected Jerusalem to be blotted out (1.5; 3.12) and was wrong. How ironic it is that a later generation of traditionists (Jer. 26.18f.) should use his work to indicate a *successful* relationship between a prophet and the king/community.

21. Suggested by Rudolph, 171 (tentatively). My own view is that 26.18f. is a creation of the traditionists working on the Jeremiah tradition (not all deuteronomists held the same opinions on every topic, so there is no inconsistency in maintaining that one group worked on the history and another, perhaps in a different period, developed a version of Jeremiah).

22. For a slightly different view of the story see Carroll, 'Prophecy, Dissonance and Jeremiah XXVI', *TGUOS* 25, 1976, 12–23.

23. Cf. Thiel, 139–56 (with a table on 149 setting out the connections

between 11.3–5, 7f. and 7.22–26). Bright, 89, thinks the section 'reflects Jeremiah's actual sentiments and activity'.

24. Cf. Rudolph, 77–81, for a discussion of this question.

25. On this see Perlitt, *Bundestheologie im Alten Testament*; cf. my comments in ch. 3, n. 42 above.

26. Here I am in agreement with Mayes, *Deuteronomy*, 85–103. I think the same principles argued for there can be applied to the presentation of Jeremiah as a deuteronomistic preacher.

27. *Prophecy and Religion*, 89–107; for the example of engagement not leading to marriage see 106.

28. Ibid., 106.

29. Ibid., 106f.

30. R. G. Collingwood, *Speculum Mentis or The Map of Knowledge*, Oxford and New York 1924, 134f. For Collingwood 'the highest religion' means Christianity.

31. Cf. Skinner, 103–5.

32. There are too many examples in the history of Judaism to choose from, but what I have in mind has been expressed admirably by Sigmund Freud in an address to the Society of B'nai B'rith on 6 May 1926: 'Because I was a Jew I found myself free from many prejudices which restricted others in the use of their intellect; and *as a Jew I was prepared to join the Opposition and to do without agreement with the "compact majority"*.' See *The Complete Psychological Works of Sigmund Freud*, vol. 20, London and New York 1959, 272–4, quoting 274 (italics mine). The phrase 'compact majority' comes from Ibsen's *Enemy of the People*.

33. In spite of James Barr's valiant attempts to stem the flood of fundamentalism (see his *Fundamentalism*, London 1977, and 'The Problem of Fundamentalism Today' in *Explorations in Theology 7: The scope and authority of the Bible*, London 1980, 65–90, 146f.), it continues to overflow the banks of Western culture as hordes of more than once born fanatics revive ancient idolatries. Jer. 8.8 may be a useful way of relating the Jeremiah tradition to this contemporary blight.

34. Arend van Leeuwen, *Critique of Heaven: The first series of the Gifford Lectures entitled 'Critique of Heaven and Earth'*, London and New York 1972, 129 (italics in the original). I know no better statement of the problem than this. On the problem of routinization see M. Weber, 'The Routinization of Charisma' in *The Theory of Social and Economic Organization*, ET London and New York 1947, 334–54.

35. See the arguments of Kaufmann cited in n. 16 above.

36. Along such lines see M. Smith, *Palestinian Parties and Politics that Shaped the Old Testament*; cf. E. Rivkin, *The Shaping of Jewish History: A Radical New Interpretation*, New York 1971, 3–41.

5. The Confessions of Jeremiah: Towards an Image of the Prophet

1. Throughout this chapter I use the RSV translation of the poems (with its thou's and thy's) but it is so unsatisfactory a translation that I am tempted to provide my own. However, that would be to deny the reader

a common public text against which to check my comments, so I have persisted with the use of the RSV. The delineation and interpretation of the 'confessions' constitute some of the most difficult issues in understanding Jeremiah, a book already noted for the number of difficult interpretative problems in it.

2. See 'The Soliloquies' in *Augustine: Earlier Writings*, ed. J. H. S. Burleigh, The Library of Christian Classics VI, London and Philadelphia 1953, 23–63. They are a mixture of prayer, argument, meditation and dialogue between Augustine and someone he chooses to call Reason. Some commentators prefer to call the Jeremiah material 'prayers' (e.g., Blank) or 'intimate papers' (e.g., E. A. Leslie, *Jeremiah: Chronologically arranged, translated, and interpreted*, New York and Nashville 1954, 137–54). See n. 4 below for further views on the subject.

3. *Prophecy and Religion*, 202f. In spite of the similarity between the views of Skinner and Blank on Jeremiah's confessions as prayer, Blank (*Jeremiah*, x) claims that he has not been influenced by Skinner. See also Blank, 'The Confessions of Jeremiah and the Meaning of Prayer', *HUCA* 21, 1948, 331–54.

4. For analysis of these sections see Blank, *Jeremiah*, 105–28; Reventlow, *Liturgie*, 205–57; Skinner, 201–30; Thiel, 157–229 passim; also W. Baumgartner, *Die Klagegedichte des Jeremia*, BZAW 32, 1917; F. D. Hubmann, *Untersuchungen zu den Konfessionen Jer 11, 18–12, 6 und Jer 15, 10–21*, Forschung zur Bibel 30, Würzburg 1978. Note that Baumgartner treats the material as *Klage*, 'complaint', 'grievance' poems rather than confessions, though he quickly resolves the question of the influence of the cultic psalms on the poems in order to present an account of Jeremiah's inner life.

5. Note the lack of an address form in 11.18, where MT begins with *wayhwh*, 'and Yahweh . . .', cf. LXX, which omits *wa-*, see BHS. Some would transpose 12.6 to the end of 11.18 (BHS, Rudolph, Blank); others even interpolate 12.6 into 11.18 (e.g., Volz, 134); see the commentaries for the variety of ways in which 11.18–12.6 have been rearranged to provide a more logical account of the material.

6. For an analysis of the poems in relation to the Book of Psalms see Baumgartner, op. cit., and Reventlow. On 12.1–5 see W. McKane, 'The Interpretation of Jeremiah XII, 1–5', *TGUOS* 20, 1965, 38–48. On Ps. 44 cf. A. A. Anderson, *The Book of Psalms* I, NCB, 1972, 336f.

7. Most of this verse is an addition to its present context; it may have come in from the drought liturgy in 14.1–6, where it would fit quite well (cf. BHS; Blank, 111 n. 12).

8. For a different understanding of *bōteaḥ*, 'fall down', see G. R. Driver, 'Difficult Words in the Hebrew Prophets' in *Studies in Old Testament Prophecy* presented to Professor Theodore H. Robinson, ed. H. H. Rowley, Edinburgh and New York 1950, 59–61, where he argues for the meaning 'fall flat on the belly'.

9. I am inclined to agree with Reventlow's (cf. *Liturgie*, 257) cautious handling of it.

10. See the discussion of Cornill's view in Skinner, 112f. n. 2; cf. Bright, 89f.

11. *Liturgie*, 242–51.

12. On this point see C. Westermann, 'Struktur und Geschichte der Klage im Alten Testament', *ZAW* 66, 1954, 44–80, esp. 52–4; cf. idem, 'The Role of the Lament in the Theology of the Old Testament', *Interpr* 28, 1974, 20–38.

13. MT reads 'Yahweh said'; RSV follows LXX *genoito*, 'be it so'. The Jewish Publication Society's Bible *The Prophets: Nevi'im: A new translation of the Holy Scriptures according to the Masoretic text*, 2nd section, Philadelphia 1978, 556, 'The Lord said: Surely, a mere remnant of you will I spare for a better fate!', admits that the meaning of the Hebrew is uncertain (I take that to be the point of enclosing the two lines between the supralinear *b-b*).

14. Cf. BHS for the range of variations on this difficult word *šērītīkā* (Qere form); Blank translates as 'I have served you well'; see the comments of Bright, 109.

15. Verses 12–14 probably do not belong to the piece; I have included v. 12 here in order to demonstrate how the poems are broken up by intrusions and additions. Cf. 17.1–4 for a possible source (cf. Rudolph); Bright wisely omits vv. 12–14 from his translation.

16. The disruptions of the text of the poems are serious obstacles to their interpretation and indicate their troubled history of transmission. A more comprehensive approach to the book of Jeremiah would involve a tedious amount of redaction criticism and the formulation of a possible theory of redaction for the Jeremiah tradition.

17. LXX is quite different here: 'those who disregard your words' (taking *mṣ'* as *n'ṣ*) 'consume them' (*klm* for *'kl*); cf. BHS, the commentaries; Blank, 110; Bright, 110. Some would omit the opening words of the section 'you know (Yahweh)'.

18. There is no agreement among commentators on the relation of v. 21 to the rest of the poem; some would omit the verse, others part of the verse. It looks like an addition after the formal termination of 'says Yahweh', but the full redaction has many examples of such fracturing of the rhetorical flow of the text.

19. 15.11 *'et-hā'ōyēb* (Syriac adds 'from the north'; cf. v. 12, where in MT 'iron from the north' is less than meaningful). See BHS; cf. Reventlow, 214, and the commentaries; Jewish translation suggests the emendation in v. 12, 'He shall shatter iron – iron and bronze!' LXX understands v. 12 quite differently.

20. A close comparison of the Hebrew text of 15.13f. and 17.3f. will show that they are essentially the same text, with minor variations of a stylistic nature and one or two more substantive changes (note *'br* in 15.14 appears as *'bd* in 17.4). Gerstenberger ('Jeremiah's Complaints: Observations on Jer. 15.10–21', *JBL* 82, 1963, 394–6) thinks vv. 13f. may once have been an oracle of promise; LXX omits 17.1–4, so may have recognized the verses as a copy of 15.13f. (unless they were absent from its Hebrew text). Cf. Rudolph, 96, for the relation between 15.12 and 17.1.

21. RSV conceals the MT here by using 17.4 ('drive away' for 'cause to

serve' 15.14), without a note in the margin to indicate such a change of the consonantal text. This is a regular feature of English translations which makes the task of the exegete much harder and almost demands that commentators provide their own translation into English. Translation is the primary element in biblical interpretation, and the different ways the text may be translated indicate the varieties of interpretation available. On the thought of 15.13 cf. Isa. 43.3.

22. On prophets as intercessors cf. Amos 7.1–9; Gen. 20.7; Reventlow, *Liturgie*, 140–205; and in more general terms see A. B. Rhodes, 'Israel's Prophets as Intercessors' in *Scripture in History and Theology*, 107–28; H. W. Hertzberg, 'Sind die Propheten Fürbitter?' in *Tradition und Situation: Artur Weiser zum 70. Geburtstag*, ed. E. Würthwein and O. Kaiser, Göttingen 1963, 63–74; J. Scharbert, *Heilsmittler im Alten Testament und im Alten Orient*, Quaestiones Disputatae 23/24, Freiburg 1964, 153–224.

23. On the interpretation of the Psalms see the relevant commentaries and H. J. Kraus, *Theologie der Psalmen*, BKAT XV/3, 1979; on the range of interpretation available for one psalm cf. Carroll, *VT* 21, 1971, 133–50. On the general interpretation of the confessions see P. Welten, 'Leiden und Leidenserfahrung im Buch Jeremia', *ZTK* 74, 1977, 123–50; on 15.10–21 in particular cf. J. Bright, 'A Prophet's Lament and Its Answer: Jeremiah 15:10–21', *Interpr* 28, 1974, 59–74. The position of Reventlow, which I only partly follow here, is severely criticized by Bright in his article 'Jeremiah's Complaints: Liturgy, or Expressions of Personal Distress?' in *Proclamation and Presence*, 189–214. For a very balanced statement of an extremely complex issue see Soggin, *Introduction*, 285.

24. *qr' šm 'l* is used for naming individuals but not for naming them by the divine name. In 15.16 the phrase is *kī-niqrā' šimkā 'ālay* and denotes divine ownership, usually of the nation or its institutions (for a secular use of the phrase cf. II Sam. 12.28; Isa. 4.1).

25. Cf. Reventlow, 220f.; Gerstenberger, 401; Gunneweg, 'Konfession oder Interpretation im Jeremiabuch', *ZTK* 67, 1970, 405; Baumgartner, 36.

26. Diogenes Laertius, *Lives of the Eminent Philosophers* IX, ch. 11, § 62, trs. R. D. Hicks, LCL, 1925, II, 474f.

27. Cf. BHS, LXX on v. 18a. Reventlow (225 n. 155) observes that the final phrase 'that fail' (*lō' ne'*mānū*) is an epexegesis to 'deceitful' ('*akzāb*).

28. The pious commentator or reader should be warned against the temptation to take this text too literally or to establish a principle of human depravity from it. If taken in either of these ways it quickly becomes a Cretan liar paradox: the man who said that the human mind is incurably deceitful, being human, had an incurably deceitful mind. Perhaps this statement of his is an example of such a deceived or deceitful mind! As the context is a series of wisdom sayings (on Jer. 17.5–8; cf. Ps. 1), it would be better to interpret 17.9 in terms of a polemic against the wise (cf. 8.8–10; 9.23f. [Heb. vv. 22f.]), and to attribute the hyperbolic force of the statement to the rhetoric of argument.

29. Gerstenberger (op. cit., 401) prefers to interpret the matter in terms

of the prophet as Yahweh's representative: 'The prophet's suffering is representative of God's own suffering.' For the theological development of this motif of the pathos of God see A. J. Heschel, *The Prophets*, 221–78; U. Mauser, *Gottesbild und Menschwerdung*, 102–14. For the weeping prophet motif (e.g. Jer. 13.17) outside the Jeremiah tradition cf. Isa. 22.4 (a stray element from the Jeremiah tradition?).

30. The section 8.18–9.22 (Heb. v. 21) became the ritual reading in the synagogue for the 9th Ab commemoration of the destruction of the Jerusalem temple in 70 CE.

31. The metaphor of sickness can describe the wound or the reaction, destruction or disease. On the modern use of the metaphor for describing social conditions (e.g., fascism is a cancer in society) see S. Sontag, *Illness as Metaphor*, New York 1978, London 1979.

32. Cf. Skinner, 212–5; Bright, 112.

33. Cf. the escape stories of Jer. 26; 37; 38. Gerstenberger (op. cit., 407) attributes the poem in 15.10–21 to the deuteronomist and sees its point as one of hope: 'Historical events had demonstrated that the incomprehensible could happen: God had put Israel out of his sight (15.1). Prophetic intervention had been useless (14.11ff.). Was this the absolute end for Yahweh's people? The deuteronomist answers "no," because the prophet himself, as a member of this weak and unreliable Israel, becomes a paradigmatic figure of salvation. ". . . I am with you to save and deliver you . . ." (v. 20b) is the final pronouncement over the prophet. Thus Jer. 14f. ends on a more hopeful note. One man has found grace with Yahweh. This is a ray of light which shines out in the darkness of the unconditional doom expressed in 14.2–15.9.'

34. Cf. Skinner (17.9f., 14–18); Blank (17.14–18); Reventlow (17.12–18); Baumgartner (17.12–18); Volz (17.14–18); Rudolph (17.14–18); Weiser (17.12–18); Bright (17.14–18).

35. Cf. BHS (Qere-Ketib). RSV has incorporated into 17.13 a second object for the verb 'they have forsaken' from a gloss at the end of the line in the MT. It is better omitted and the line read as 'for they have forsaken the fountain of living water'. Cf. 2.13, which has influenced the gloss here (probably put in by a scribe who did not wish the text to be obscure in any way).

36. MT has for v. 16, 'as for me, I did not press from being a shepherd (*mērō'eh*) after you', which does not make a great deal of sense. The difficulty can be resolved by redistributing the letters of *mr'h* as *y* (haplography of (*'st)y*) *m r'h* = *yōm rā'āh* 'day of evil' cf. vv. 17–18. Cf. Skinner, 205 n. 3. In v. 16b the phrase 'you know' (*'attāh yādā'tā*) may be taken with the preceding line (so MT; RSV) or with the following words (e.g., Bright).

37. Reventlow entitles 17.12–18 'Prayer in the temple' (229). The view of the temple here (cf. 12.7) could hardly be further from the attitude taken towards it in the temple sermon, so if there is anything of Jeremiah behind the temple sermon this section (or verse) must come from a very different source. The redactional context of the poem indicates a temple orientation.

38. Cf. Isa. 5.19; Ezek. 12.21–27. In my book *When Prophecy Failed*,

82, I dealt with these references as evidence of popular scepticism directed against the prophets. This is a reasonable approach to the text but it does not take into account the complex redactional background to the text, nor does it treat Jer. 17.15 as a possible word of promise. Here I would take a different approach and see the text asking different questions from those I tackled in my previous book. Cf. Skinner, 211f., for my first approach.

39. The identity of the enemy or evildoer in the Psalms is very complex; for an admirable treatment of Mowinckel and Birkeland on the subject see G. W. Anderson, 'Enemies and Evildoers in the Book of Psalms', *BJRL* 48, 1965, 18–29.

40. The interpretation of individual and collective images in the Psalms is very difficult, so I would not expect the Jeremiah material to present an easier interpretative task. On individual elements in the Psalms cf. Gerstenberger in *Old Testament Form Criticism*, 198–205; also W. Brueggemann, 'Psalms and the Life of Faith: A Suggested Typology of Function', *JSOT* 17, 1980, 3–32.

41. LXX omits 'not' before 'hear'; cf. Rudolph, 122; Skinner, 206. *qšb*, 'heed', should be understood in the sense of 'carefully watch' (for an occasion of offence), cf. Jer. 20.10. Perhaps the MT 'let us not heed his words' is a development of the tradition in terms of the motif of the community's deliberate rejection of prophecy.

42. MT *y⁽ʳⁱbāy*, 'my adversaries'; translations and commentators tend to read *rȋbȋ*, 'my plea', see LXX.

43. Verse 20b, 'they have dug a pit for my life', is a variation on v. 22b; cf. the commentaries for a variety of ways of explaining the repeat. Skinner's discussion (223–30) of Jeremiah's vindictiveness in the poems in terms of 'Jeremiah had not learned the lesson of the Cross . . .' (230) is both anachronistic and beside the point. The liturgical nature of the poems makes the plea for vengeance comparable to similar vindictiveness in the Christian apocalyptic tradition (cf. Rev. 16.1–7; 19.1–3).

44. Cf. Lundbom, 45f. Baumgartner divides into 3 sections, Skinner into 2 (omitting v. 13), Blank only has 1 section (vv. 7–11), Rudolph has 3 (7–9, 10–13 (omitting 12), 14–18); cf. Gunneweg, 409–12. Reventlow does not treat 20.7–18 (it probably does not fit his cultic thesis as well as the other poems). In following the verse divisions of Baumgartner and Rudolph I am aware that a strong case can be made out for dividing the section into 7–10, 11–13, 14–18. On the whole section see also D. J. A. Clines and D. M. Gunn, 'Form, Occasion and Redaction in Jeremiah 20', *ZAW* 88, 1976, 390–409.

45. LXX reads this line as 'for I will mock with my bitter speech', which suggests *'śḥq* for MT's *'z⁽q*; cf. Skinner, 207.

46. For *ḥzq* 'seize' in the sense of rape a woman cf. Deut. 22.25; II Sam. 13.11; Judg. 19.25; cf. Rudolph, 130f.; Heschel, *The Prophets*, 113f. Heschel writes: 'These terms used in immediate juxtaposition forcefully convey the complexity of the divine-human relationship: sweetness of enticement as well as violence of rape' (114). Clines and Gunn (' "You tried to persuade me" and "Violence! Outrage!" in Jeremiah XX 7–8', *VT* 28, 1978, 20–27) argue that the terms should be understood to mean persuade

rather than rape. Whatever the merits of their argument, I do not think they are justified in accusing those who understand the reference to be sexual of committing the error of what James Barr (*The Semantics of Biblical Language*, London and Toronto 1961, 218) calls 'illegitimate totality transfer'. There are sufficient overtones in Jer. 20.7–8 to warrant a sexual interpretation, though other interpretations may be possible also.

47. Verse 10, *māgōr missābīb*, 'terror on every side', is understood differently by LXX ('gathering round' = '*gr*?, cf. BHS). Omitted by Skinner (207 n. 2).

48. 20.12 = 11.20 (with minor variations: the difference between the verses is that 20.12 reads *bōḥēn ṣaddiq rō'eh*, 'who tries the righteous, who sees . . .' and 11.20 reads *šōfet ṣedeq bōḥēn*, 'who judges righteously, who tries . . .').

49. Ps. 31.14 (MT) *ki šāma'tī dibbat rabbīm māgōr missābīb* = Jer. 20.10 (MT). Bright (132f.) suggests that it may have been a nickname for Jeremiah: 'Apparently Jeremiah had used the expression so often that it was becoming a nickname. One can imagine one man in the crowd nudging another as Jeremiah passed, and whispering, "there goes old Magor-missabib."' ' Cf. Holladay, 'The Covenant with the Patriarchs Overturned: Jeremiah's Intention in "Terror on Every Side" ' (Jer. 20:1–6)', JBL 91, 1972, 305–20.

50. On this difficult passage see D. L. Petersen, *Late Israelite Prophecy: Studies in Deutero-Prophetic Literature and in Chronicles*, SBLMS 23, 1977, 33–8, 50f.

51. On this see Lundbom, op. cit., 46–8; Holladay, *Architecture*, 151–8.

52. Cf. BHS, Rudolph, 132, on 'that man' (v. 16) as possibly 'that day' (cf. v. 14, which curses the *day* of his birth); cf. Skinner, 208 n.

53. Cf. 'One can neither exaggerate the agony of spirit revealed here, nor improve upon the words which Jeremiah found to express it. There is, indeed, little in all of literature that compares with this piece, and nothing in the Bible except perhaps the third chapter of Job, to which it is very similar. Whether Job develops the thought of this passage, or whether both derive from a common tradition is a question that cannot be answered with assurance; but kinship between the two is undeniable' (Bright, 134). As Dean Swift used to read Job 3, rather than Jer. 20.14–18, on his birthday it should be clear that the Job passage is the more forceful of the two.

54. Cf. 'The Book of Job is a mighty fugue based on the cry of the lamentation; it alone indicates the underlying significance that the lament has in Israel for talk of God, that is, for theology' (C. Westermann, *Interpr* 28, 23). For the lament as a primary element in Job see Westermann, *Der Aufbau der Buches Hiob*, BHT 23, 1956, 25–55 (for comment on Job 3 and Jer. 20.14–18 see 31–33).

55. On Job in relation to the exile cf. E. Dhorme, *A Commentary on the Book of Job*, London 1967, clxvif.; A. Hurvitz, 'The Date of the Prose-Tale of Job Linguistically Reconsidered', *HTR* 67, 1974, 17–34; Ackroyd, *Exile and Restoration*, 245f. (and the bibliographical information cited in his footnotes there).

56. Whether as extended metaphor, symbolic or dramatic action, or

whatever, see the discussion in Lindblom, *Prophecy in Ancient Israel*, 137–48, 165–73; also Fohrer, 'Die Gattung der Berichte über symbolische Handlungen der Propheten' in BZAW 99, 92–112. Hosea's marriage is a more complicated case of real action(?) with additional symbolic significance.

57. Cf. Thiel, 169–77. On the interpretation of the piece see Bright, 95f.; C. H. Southwood, 'The spoiling of Jeremiah's girdle (Jer. XIII 1–11)', *VT* 29, 1979, 231–7.

58. See Bright and the commentaries. Leslie (op. cit., 87f.) bravely rejects both this interpretation and Rudolph's vision approach, to insist upon the action involving a *real journey*. Presumably the prophet took witnesses with him on this hazardous journey so that they could confirm his actions, if not his meaning!

59. For the vision interpretation see Rudolph, 93.

60. I say 'simplest', but of course I mean 'in my opinion it is the simplest'; the scholarly debate on the meaning of the section hardly suggests that there is a simple, let alone a simplest, meaning to the story at all. Southwood (*VT* 29) thinks the spoiling of the girdle relates to the 'foe from the north' motif. I certainly prefer an interpretation which makes the Mesopotamian element the cause of the spoliation rather than a vague figure for idolatry.

61. Cf. Thiel, 195–201; Fohrer, op cit., 98; see the commentaries for analyses of the verses.

62. The reader who demands practical advice from reading the Bible should be warned against searching it for guidance on marriage. At God's command Hosea married a whore, Jeremiah did not marry, Ezekiel did not mourn the death of his wife (Ezek. 24.15–27), and Isaiah fathered a child on a prophetess (Isa. 8.1–4). As these examples illustrate, the range of marriage and celibacy is covered, and unless the reader happens to be a depressed prophet living in Jerusalem c. 627–597, celibacy may not be a wise move. The reason given for Jeremiah's refusal to marry (Jer. 16.4) reminds one of the early days of the CND Aldermaston marches, when idealistic young people refused to marry or have children because there was no future for either activity. The later marches were participated in by some of these people accompanied by the very children they once were not going to have! I daresay Jeremiah's resolution was a firmer one.

63. Cf. Thiel, 218–27; Rudolph, 125–7; also McKane in his forthcoming commentary.

64. Cf. Jer. 36.23; on some of the factors involved here see A. C. Thiselton, 'The Supposed Power of Words in the Biblical Writings', *JTS* 25, 1974, 283–99; also my discussion in *When Prophecy Failed*, 58–61. Thiselton's arguments need to be taken much further before they yield some illumination here. On Jehoiakim's action, which may be taken simply as a gesture of contempt, see ch. 6 below.

65. Note the elaboration of the section in v. 18 to include Jerusalem and the cities of Judah. 25.26 uses a cipher *Sheshak* to refer to Babylon. This cryptographic device is known as athbash (*ssk* is athbash for *bbl*), a technique whereby letters of the alphabet in reverse order are substituted (in English this would entail zyx = abc). Apart from 25.26, athbash occurs in

Jer. 51.41 (*Sheshak*) where it is unnecessary because the poems are clearly directed against Babylon (cf. 51.1, 2, 4, 5, 6–8, 11, 12, 24, 29–31, 34–37, 41–44, 47–50, 53, 54–56, 58). In 25.26 LXX omits the cipher *Sheshak*, but appears to have understood an athbash in 51.1 where for MT *lēb qāmāy* it reads (LXX 28.1) *Chaldaious* 'Chaldeans' (= *kśdym*).

66. Rudolph, 163, see the commentaries for further explanations.

67. Cf. M. de Roche, 'Is Jeremiah 25.15–29 a Piece of Reworked Jeremianic Poetry?', *JSOT* 10, 1978, 58–67.

68. The precise meaning of the text here is difficult because of linguistic obscurities; on these cf. BHS and the commentaries.

69. The piece is dated to the fourth year of Zedekiah's reign (51.59) and refers to a Babylonian visit by the king which is otherwise unknown. It may have been a development of the tradition in the light of ch. 27, which speaks of planned rebellion in that period. Seraiah ben Neriah is Baruch's brother, so the story probably came from circles working on the redaction of the tradition which attributed it to Baruch. See the commentaries for discussion; also Wanke, op. cit., 136–9.

70. MT adds at the end of v. 64 'and they shall weary themselves' (*w'yā'ēfū*), a gloss from the end of v. 58.

6. *Conflict I: Concerning the Kings of Judah*

1. The most likely meaning of the phrase 'those who handle the law' (*tōfśē hattōrāh*) is 'the priests', i.e., those who administer torah (Rudolph, 16); cf. the priestly role set out in Deut. 33.10. This interpretation is also borne out by the parallelism of the two lines. Hyatt ('Torah in the Book of Jeremiah', *JBL* 60, 1941, 385–7) has suggested that it refers to a subdivision of the priesthood which was skilled in interpreting the law (and which also was the predecessor of the later scribes); see also his commentary, 814. The tripartite leadership in 2.8 is made up of priest, rulers and prophets; cf. 18.18 for the variation priests, wise men and prophets. So some would associate these handlers of torah with the wise (i.e., scribes) of 8.8 (cf. Volz, 18f.).

2. On 21.1–23.8 see Thiel, 230–49; and the commentaries. For the role of Jeremiah as intercessor (21.1ff.; cf. 37.1–3; 42.1–6) see Reventlow, *Liturgie*, 143–9.

3. On these two motifs see Wanke, *Untersuchungen*, 144–56; cf. M. Kessler, 'Jeremiah Chapters 26–45 Reconsidered', *JNES* 27, 1968, 81–8.

4. On the inconsistency here see Rudolph, 133f.; cf. Hyatt, 977. For further inconsistencies on the death of kings see the comments on Jer. 22.18f.

5. So Rudolph, 136.

6. On this see L. Köhler, 'Justice in the Gate', in *Hebrew Man*, London 1956, 149–75.

7. Cf. BHS, the Versions and commentaries; Bright, 140–1. For 'inhabitant of the valley' (*yōšebet hā'ēmeq*) as 'enthroned over the valley' see Weiser, 182. For a fragment from the Isaiah tradition with similar

motifs cf. Isa. 10.16–19 (on its interpretation see Wildberger, *Jesaja*, 405–11).

8. Cf. BHS for Qere-Ketib readings; in v. 6 the Cairo geniza fragments omit 'king', thus making 'house' = 'temple'. It is not entirely clear from the text whether palace/temple, city or land is being threatened. Note that in v. 7 'I will *prepare* . . .' is the translation of *qiddaštī*; this meaning of *qdš* would fit 1.5, 'before you were born I prepared you'; cf. 6.4, where *qadšū* is translated 'prepare' (for 'war').

9. Cf. 'We are then left with a grand conspiracy of silence on the subject of the death of Josiah because, given the OT premises, no one could satisfactorily account for it theologically. The fact is that the death of Josiah proved to be the relatively small but sharp-edged rock on which the OT concept of divinely motivated history foundered', S. B. Frost, 'The Death of Josiah: A Conspiracy of Silence', *JBL* 87, 1968, 381. It may be more realistic to say that the death of Josiah was a limiting case in the deuteronomistic presentation of history; the Chronicler was able to resolve the problem by applying a different theological perspective.

10. Cf. 'Note the extreme "democracy" of the notion of society which Israel's faith fostered: the king and the carpenter are "neighbors" ', Bright, 141f. I think this is to overemphasize the semantic aspect of *rēʿēhū*, 'neighbour'. The recent tendency in the writings of Mendenhall and Gottwald to stress the democratic and egalitarian aspects of ancient Israel's social life warrants a sustained riposte which space does not permit here (for some evaluative remarks see my reviews of N. Gottwald, *The Tribes of Yahweh*, New York and London 1980, forthcoming in *SJT* and *Religious Studies*).

11. Cf. BHS; perhaps the phrase 'then it was well with him' ('*āz ṭōb lō*) would be better read after 'did not your father eat and drink', and understood in the sense of 'he enjoyed himself' (cf. Bright, 142, for this meaning). The repeated '*āz ṭōb* in v. 16 should be omitted. LXX understood vv. 15f. quite differently.

12. For eating and drinking in a context of covenant making see Ex. 24.9–11 (some would argue that the reference to eating in Ex. 18.12 implies the making of a covenant between Jethro and Israel; so Buber, *Moses*, Oxford 1946, 94ff.); on this aspect of the covenant motif cf. McCarthy, *Treaty and Covenant*, esp. 273–6. Harrison's (*Jeremiah*, 117f.) interpretation of Jer. 22.13–17 as making a contrast between Jehoiakim's ostentation and 'the *austere* and moral way of life followed by Josiah' (my italics) is a very curious understanding of 'eating and drinking'. Whatever the precise content of the phrase it is highly unlikely to have meant austerity (a case of eisegesis?).

13. See the commentaries; cf. II Kings 24.4. It is difficult to determine whether such accusations have a real or a formal significance. What adds to the difficulty, especially in view of Jer. 26.20–23, is the fact that the prophet Jeremiah survived a long career of denouncing kings yet was never killed by one, not even the 'vicious' Jehoiakim. It should be noted that the Jeremiah tradition never permits Jeremiah and Jehoiakim actually to en-

counter one another (hence Jehoiakim's absence in ch. 26 and Jeremiah's absence in ch. 36).

14. RSV provides 'saying' at two points in 22.18; it is not in MT. See BHS and LXX on the difficulties in the verse. M. J. Dahood ('Two textual notes on Jeremiah', *CBQ* 23, 1961, 462–4) argues that the words *'ādōn*, 'lord', and *hōdōh*, 'majesty', should be understood to mean 'father' and 'mother', referring to the king as the community's father and mother.

15. LXX[B] of II Chron. 36.8 adds to the note on Jehoiakim's burial (completely absent from MT) 'was buried in the garden of Uzza with his fathers' (for such a location cf. II Kings 21.18, 26); for a brief discussion of the various ways in which the data have been interpreted cf. Hyatt, 983f.

16. In spite of the arguments of my *When Prophecy Failed*, the evidence from the Bible suggests that there was an inconsistent attitude to contradictions. Cf. '. . . it is not impossible that the prediction of Jeremiah actually was unfulfilled. The lack of literal fulfilment would not have disturbed the prophet; and it is by no means certain that ancient scribes and editors were careful to include in the prophetic books only predictions that were known to have been fulfilled. To suppose this is to attribute to ancient scribes and editors modern editorial methods' (Hyatt, 983f.). There is some truth in this statement, but the matter is more complicated (otherwise the Chronicler's correction of the Goliath incident in I Chron. 20.5 would be unnecessary).

17. The theory that the deuteronomistic history was produced in two editions, one pre-exilic and the other exilic, may help to relieve the starkness of this failed prediction; see F. M. Cross, *Canaanite Myth and Hebrew Epic: Essays in the History of the Religion of Israel*, Cambridge, Mass. and London 1973, 285–9. Conventionalist twists (on these cf. *When Prophecy Failed*, 112–7, 216 + n.), such as interpreting peace (II Kings 22.20) to mean 'dying before the country is invaded', may help, but are probably more indicative of problems than solutions.

18. Cf. Rudolph, 141; Hyatt, 984; and the commentaries.

19. Cf. Thiel, 242–6; Hyatt, 985.

20. On citations from the people in the Jeremiah tradition see W. J. Horwitz, 'Audience Reaction to Jeremiah', *CBQ* 32, 1970, 555–64; T. W. Overholt, 'Jeremiah and the Nature of the Prophetic Process' in *Scripture in History and Theology*, 129–50 (cf. idem, *CBQ* 41, 1979, 262–73); in relation to prophecy in general see J. L. Crenshaw, *Prophetic Conflict: Its Effect Upon Israelite Religion*, BZAW 124, 1971, 23–38.

21. Cf. BHS for LXX omissions and variations. The statement in v. 30, 'for none of his offspring shall succeed', may be either an addition or indicative of the lateness (Zerubbabel's time or even later) of the oracle. It would then be an incorporation into the Jeremiah tradition, thereby lending it weight, of an anti-Zerubbabel oracle. Cf. Ezek. 17.11–21 on Coniah. The failure of that line, indeed of the whole royal house, is made into a prophetic prediction.

22. See discussion in *When Prophecy Failed*, 162–6. Such disagreements are not limited to prophets; great men or geniuses seldom like each other either: e.g., Leonardo da Vinci and Michelangelo both worked in Florence

on commissions during the same period (1500–1505) but, according to Vasari, they strongly disliked each other (see G. Vasari, *The Lives of the Artists* [Penguin Classics], London 1965, 270). The problem of relativism for this discussion is best stated in William Blake's lines: 'The Vision of Christ that thou dost see/Is my Vision's Greatest Enemy:/Thine has a great hook nose like thine,/Mine has a snub nose like to mine' (from *The Everlasting Gospel*, 1818; see *The Complete Writings of William Blake*, ed. G. Keynes, London and New York 1966, 748). J. B. Payne (*Encyclopedia of Biblical Prophecy: The Complete Guide to Scriptural Predictions and their Fulfilment*, London and New York 1973, 337) produces a curious argument that the divinity of Jesus Christ is somehow connected with this prediction. Otherwise as Messiah his birth from the line of Jechoniah and Zerubbabel (cf. Matt. 1.12) would have disconfirmed this prediction of Jeremiah's!

23. See commentaries for discussion of the issues involved. There are variations in the text on the way Zedekiah's name is spelled (*ṣidqiyyāh/ ṣidqiyāhū*). On messianism in the Hebrew Bible I take the view that it only developed in the Roman period as an apocalyptic-political movement, so only metaphors and images within such a movement are derived from biblical traditions. J. L. McKenzie, *A Theology of the Old Testament*, London and New York 1974, 23f., sensibly states the issue thus: 'I have been convinced for years that messianism is a Christian interest and a Christian theme; that it is a Christian response to the Old Testament and should be treated as such; that in a theology of the Old Testament . . . messianism would appear neither in the chapter headings nor in the index. It is not only not a dominant theme, but in the proper sense of the word it is doubtfully a theme of the Old Testament at all. This theme is imposed upon the theologian by theological factors foreign to his area of study.' To this statement I would add it is also very much a *Jewish* interest and theme, though one belonging to the post-biblical period and utilizing motifs from biblical traditions. See also J. Becker, *Messianic Expectations in the Old Testament*, ET Philadelphia 1980.

24. LXX places 23.7f. at the end of the chapter, i.e., after the polemic against the prophets, which is quite inappropriate.

25. For analysis see Wanke, *Untersuchungen*, 6–91, on chs. 26–29; 36; and 91–133 on chs. 37–43.

26. MT of 27.1 reads 'the reign of Jehoiakim'; a few manuscripts read 'Zedekiah'. As 27.3, 12 refer to Zedekiah, v. 1 should be amended accordingly (cf. RSV); the error may have been induced by 26.1. BHS suggests reading 'in the fourth year' (cf. 28.1) for MT 'in the beginning of the reign'. 27.1; 28.1 are in somewhat confused states as they now stand in MT.

27. Cf. Wanke, 156.

28. Cf. 26.9, where the use of *wayyiqqāhēl* for the *assembling* (*qāhāl* = the religious assembly of the people) of the whole people suggests a formal tribunal; see Wanke, 83–8; Hossfeld and Meyer, *ZAW* 86, 35–7.

29. See Wanke, 59–74; Kessler, 'Form-Critical Suggestions on Jer 36', *CBQ* 28, 1966, 389–401; also C. D. Isbell, *JSOT* 8, 1978, 33–45.

30. See my remarks on this aspect of the tradition in ch. 1 above (also

nn. 17–20 there); cf. Kessler, 'Jeremiah Chapters 26–45 Reconsidered', *JNES* 27, 1968, 81–8.

31. The variations on the prophet's role in all these stories has been analysed by Wanke, who sees different authors (none of whom is Baruch!) behind three blocks of material (19.1–20.6, 26–29; chs. 37–43; 45; 51.59–64). A different interpretation of the function of these chapters is offered by H. Kremers, 'Leidensgemeinschaft mit Gott im Alten Testament: Eine Untersuchung der "biographischen" Berichte im Jeremiabuch', *Ev Th* 13, 1953, 122–40. He wishes to see in the material a 'passion of Jeremiah' story (what he terms *Leidensgeschichte*); he also offers such an account of Baruch. However, in my handling of the material I follow the general approach of Wanke.

32. Three times it is said that 'Jeremiah remained in the court of the guard' (37.21; 38.13, 28). For the view that chs. 37, 38 are two accounts of the *same* story see Skinner, 258f.; Bright, 233. Hyatt, 1076, rejects such a view; cf. Rudolph, 239.

33. For a similar accusation that certain nobles 'weaken the hands' of the people see the Lachish Letters (No. VI): translated by W. F. Albright in *Ancient Near Eastern Texts Relating to the Old Testament*, ed. J. B. Pritchard, Princeton³ 1969, 322; for text see H. Torczyner, *Lachish* I: *Lachish Letters*, London and New York 1938, 101–19.

34. LXX omits the phrase *'îš sārîs* in 38.7 which RSV translates as 'eunuch'; the term may have that meaning, but not necessarily, and is better understood as a designation of a court official (cf. Rabsaris in 39.13, 'the chief' of such officials; cf. 29.2); see Hyatt, 1075. Although the picture of a eunuch assisting a celibate is a touching one and material for a sermon, it may be more accurate to see the rescue being carried out by an important court official. I have therefore omitted any reference to him being a eunuch in the text of my book.

35. Much has been made of this lie in recent writing on prophetic conflict (e.g., Crenshaw, *Prophetic Conflict*, 59). If an absolutist position is taken on the Bible, i.e., of the kind fundamentalists take, then rightly the lie should be exposed. However, taking the redactional context approach, it is more reasonable to see it as an element in the story-telling rather than as a focus for exegesis. It does, however, muddy the waters with regard to prophecy and morality in terms of a criterion of validity; cf. discussion in *When Prophecy Failed*, 192f.

36. See S. Bok, *Lying: Moral Choice in Public and Private Life*, Brighton and New York 1978, a book which raises many interesting questions for ethicists and moralists. For the problem of lying from a theological viewpoint see D. Bonhoeffer, 'What is Meant by "Telling the Truth"?', *Ethics*, ed. E. Bethge, London and New York 1971², 326–34.

37. Lundbom (op. cit., 25–7) does not treat it this way, but fixes the inclusio between 1.1 and 51.64. In early rabbinic tradition Jeremiah was the first volume in the prophetic canon (latter prophets) and so followed II Kings. When Isaiah was promoted to that position, the connections between II Kings 24 and Jer. 52 became less obvious.

38. Cf. Ackroyd, *Exile and Restoration*, 78–83; *SEÅ*, 42f.; E. Zenger,

'Die deuteronomistische Interpretation der Rehabilitierung Jojachins', *Biblische Zeitschrift* 12, Paderborn 1968, 16–30.

7. *Conflict II: Concerning the Prophets*

1. For a good treatment of the Ezekiel material see Eichrodt, *Ezekiel*, 159–84.

2. The literature on the subject is growing steadily; see Carroll, *When Prophecy Failed*, 184–98; Crenshaw, *Prophetic Conflict*; F. L. Hossfeld and I. Meyer, *Prophet gegen Prophet. Eine Analyse der alttestamentlichen Texte zum Thema: Wahre und falsche Propheten*, Biblische Beiträge 9, Fribourg 1973; H.-J. Kraus, *Prophetie in der Krisis: Studien zu Texten aus dem Buch Jeremia*, Biblische Studien 43, Neukirchen-Vluyn 1964; I. Meyer, *Jeremia und die falschen Propheten*, Orbis Biblicus et Orientalis 13, Freiburg and Göttingen 1977; E. Osswald, *Falsche Prophetie im Alten Testament*, Sammlung gemeinverständlicher Vorträge und Schriften aus dem Gebiet der Theologie und Religionsgeschichte 237, Tübingen 1962; T. W. Overholt, *The Threat of Falsehood*; G. von Rad, 'Die falschen Propheten', *ZAW* 51, 1933, 109–20; Reventlow, *Liturgie*, 121–40; J. A. Sanders, 'Hermeneutics in True and False Prophecy' in *Canon and Authority*, 21–41; T. Seidl, *Formen und Formeln in Jeremia 27–29: Eine literaturwissenschaftliche Untersuchung*, 2 vols., Arbeiten zu Text und Sprache im Alten Testament 5, St Ottilien 1978; S. J. de Vries, *Prophet Against Prophet*; A. S. van der Woude, 'Micah in dispute with the pseudo-prophets', *VT* 19, 1969, 244—60. The attack on the prophets in Jer. 23.9–32 is very popular with preachers, e.g., R. Niebuhr, 'The Test of True Prophecy' in *Beyond Tragedy: Essays on the Christian Interpretation of History*, New York and London 1938, 89–110; cf. P. Tillich's title sermon in *The Shaking of the Foundations*, London 1962, 11–21. The subject warrants the attention it has received and the length of this chapter (relative to the other chapters) is evidence of its complexity. I have in mind to produce a monograph on the substantive issues once I have completed the commentary on Jeremiah.

3. The precise meaning of 5.31, 'the prophets prophesy falsely and *the priests rule at their direction*', is not clear; it could either be that the priests rule at the instruction of the prophets or, what is more likely, the priests rule by their side (i.e., together they operate to give the people what they want). See the commentaries.

4. So RSV; as BHS sets out the Hebrew it is probably a poetic, rather than a prose, piece; for a variation on the content of 4.9f. cf. 14.13f.

5. On deuteronomic (i.e., derived from the book of Deuteronomy) and deuteronomistic (i.e., derived from the redaction circles which produced the history and editions of prophetic texts) elements in Deut. 13.1–5 see Mayes, *Deuteronomy*, 230–4.

6. Cf. BHS; a few manuscripts read 'peace *and* truth' (cf. 33.6 and the Versions).

7. I have italicized the phrase '*in my name*' to draw attention to the fact that these prophets were Yahwistic prophets speaking in Yahweh's name, rather than devotees of other cults speaking by Baal (contrast 2.8; 23.13).

Contrast the terms of the community's punishment in 14.16 with the threats in 6.12 = 8.10. One reflects the experience of exile, the other the threat of invasion and conquest.

8. For analysis and exegesis of the cycle see the works cited in n. 2 above; also Thiel, 249–53. Original Greek text reads *en tois prophētais*.

9. See the commentaries; even Thiel's analysis indicates only the slightest influence of deuteronomistic thought in the section. Perhaps the cycle had an independent origin and development before being incorporated into the Jeremiah tradition. It contrasts quite strikingly with the material on prophets in Jer. 27–29, so may demonstrate that a number of discrete traditions about prophets were, at some stage, taken into the tradition.

10. Cf. BHS for difficulties in the text; v. 10b may be an addition cf. 12.4a; 14.4.

11. Cf. Bright, 152; Meyer, *Jeremia*, 116f. In Jer. 29.23 the reference is probably to adultery as sexual involvement with other people, but that meaning cannot be transferred to 23.14 without making illegitimate hermeneutical moves.

12. To translate 'wormwood' into its modern equivalent as 'absinthe' or 'vermouth' would be to mislead modern readers. Such terms convey to some people a pleasant drink rather than a bitter experience.

13. Omitting 'who prophesy to you' (*hannib'īm lākem*) with original Greek; see the commentaries on this point.

14. Cf. Thiel, 250. Its occurrence outside deuteronomistic influence is in Ps. 81.13, a psalm with strong legal overtones (i.e., decalogue echoes); cf. Fohrer, *Introduction*, 290.

15. MT *mī 'āmad*, 'who has stood?', whereas RSV reads as *mī mēhem 'āmad*, 'who among them has stood?' (cf. v. 22); cf. BHS, Rudolph.

16. Bright, 152.

17. Cf. II Kings 9.17; 17.13, 23; 21.10; 24.2. On Amos 3.7, as a deuteronomistic element in the tradition, see Wolff, *Joel and Amos*, 181, 187f.; also W. H. Schmidt, 'Die deuteronomistische Redaktion des Amosbuches', *ZAW* 77, 1965, 168–93.

18. This divine wish to kill is in contrast to the assertion in Ezek. 18.32; 33.11 that the deity does not desire (*ḥfṣ*) the death of anybody. With I Sam. 2.25 contrast I Sam. 3.13. In the Israelite cult Yahweh was confessed to be the one who 'kills and brings to life' (I Sam. 2.6); he was also the one who causes miscarriages, unpremeditated murders (Ex. 21.13), and the general destruction of the community (II Sam. 24.10–14). As such the deception of prophets, and of the community through them, is a minor divine feat. Against such pictures of divine sovereignty all humanizing traditions of biblical religion struggle in vain.

19. On this see the writings of Crenshaw and Overholt listed in n. 2. On Jer. 23.22 see Carroll, 'A Non-Cogent Argument in Jeremiah's Oracles against the Prophets', *StTh* 30, 1976, 43–51.

20. For the divine council motif see B. W. Anderson, *IDB* 2, 654–6; D. Neiman, *IDB Suppl*, 187f. As the motif appears in Homer (cf. *Iliad* VIII. 1–40; XX.1–30), Ugaritic writings and other cultures apart from the Hebrew Bible, it should be viewed as either a literary fiction or a mythological

trace in the Bible. It figures in the prophetic traditions of Amos, Isaiah, Jeremiah and Second Isaiah in particular.

21. On the messenger motif cf. Westermann, *Basic Forms of Prophetic Speech*, 98–128; see also R. N. Whybray, *The Heavenly Counsellor in Isaiah xl. 13–14: A Study of the Sources of the Theology of Deutero-Isaiah*, SOTS Monographs 1, Cambridge 1971.

22. See the commentaries, especially Cornill's suggestion discussed in Hyatt, 994. J. Woods (*Jeremiah*, Epworth Preacher's Commentaries, London 1964, 102), in my opinion, gets it right when he comments: 'One might think that God was in the pocket of these hucksters, but in fact He is far away from them.'

23. Cf. Holladay, *JBL* 83, 1964, 153–64; *JBL* 85, 1966, 17–27.

24. E.g., 'Here we see Jeremiah take a significant step forward, away from the irrational and toward the rational' (Leslie, *Jeremiah*, 227). When I say 'reduces the prophet to being a philosopher and only half a person' I intend no slur on philosophy or philosophers. If prophecy becomes a rational activity, then it might as well be abandoned and philosophy taken up; that is a high view of philosophy as rational activity. How philosophers come to terms with the irrational or imaginative aspects of being human is a rather different problem.

25. Cf. 'There should be no need to emphasize, in this century of radio sets and electronic devices, that many dreams may be assemblages of thought-elements that convey no information whatsoever: that they may just be *noise*', P. B. Medawar, 'The Act of Creation' in *The Art of the Soluble: Creativity and Originality in Science*, London 1969, 98 (italics in the original).

26. On this see Crenshaw, op. cit., 56–61; cf. *When Prophecy Failed*, 190–2.

27. Cf. *When Prophecy Failed*, 188–98. I have discussed this aspect of the matter in my Balmore Group discussion paper (read to the Group in Glasgow on 10 June 1980), 'Is biblical pseudoprophecy a pseudoproblem?'. I would hope to incorporate points made in that discussion into any subsequent work done on the problems of prophetic authenticity.

28. In spite of the length of this chapter I have hardly discussed the substantive issues involved in prophet conflict at all. Hence the need for a book-length treatment of the subject.

29. It is one of the more interesting and useful features of Wilson's *Prophecy and Society in Ancient Israel* that he treats prophetic conflict in terms of accusations of witchcraft (see 210f., 248–51). This insight could be developed to make more sense of the material under discussion. Prophecy in Israel functioned the way witchcraft or divination functioned in neighbouring states (hence association of material in Deut. 18.9–22), so quarrels and fierce opposition are to be expected among prophets. I do not share Mary Douglas's sanguine view ('Purity and danger revisited', *Times Literary Supplement* 4042, 19 September 1980, 1045) that Israel did not need witches because it had prophets, because the conflict between prophets was as fierce as the social conflict created by societies with witchcraft accusations available for discriminating against elements in the community.

30. Cf. BHS for difficulties in the text. For discussion of the section see W. McKane, '*Maśśā*' in Jeremiah 23 33–40' in *Prophecy: Essays presented to Georg Fohrer*, ed. J. A. Emerton, BZAW 150, 1980, 35–54.

31. It may be somewhat harsh to accuse the commentator of a 'turgid piece of work'; after all, it may represent an important discussion in the period when it was produced. Apart from the six occurrences of *maśśā* in vv. 34–38, the stem (*nś*') is also used twice in v. 39; cf. BHS and the Versions.

32. On late prophecy see Petersen, *Late Israelite Prophecy*; McKane (*BZAW* 150, 53–4) relates the section to decisions which have to be made by individuals (also households) and sees it as having greater cohesiveness with vv. 9–32 than commentators generally allow.

33. MT of Jer. 27.1 should probably read 'in the fourth year of the reign of Zedekiah', cf. 29.1; see BHS and the commentaries.

34. For deuteronomistic elements see vv. 5, 8, 13; LXX omits vv. 1, 7, 13–14a and parts of 21–2. The chapter is one where MT and LXX differ the most in the tradition. 27.16–22 are probably part of the later development of MT. On analysis and exegesis of ch. 27 see Wanke, op. cit., 19–36.

35. See the commentaries on this issue; cf. Jer. 52.17–23. The presence of sections on the temple furnishings in the tradition suggests the period of rebuilding the temple to the time of Ezra's mission to Jerusalem (cf. Ezra 5.13–15) as the matrix of these elements being added to the tradition. See P. R. Ackroyd, 'The Temple Vessels: a continuity theme' in *Studies in the Religion of Ancient Israel*, VTS 23, 1972, 166–81.

36. As well as the works listed in n. 2 and the commentaries on ch. 28, see also D. Lys, 'Jérémie 28 et le problème des faux prophètes ou la circulation du sens dans le diagnostique prophétique' (Hommages à Edmond Jacob), *Revue d'histoire et de philosophie religieuses* 59, Strasbourg 1979, 453–82; H. Mottu, 'Jeremiah vs. Hananiah: Ideology and Truth in Old Testament Prophecy', *Radical Religion* 2.2/3, Berkeley, California 1975, 58–67.

37. Except for v. 1, which reads 'Hananiah . . . said to me' (i.e., Jeremiah); as the rest of the chapter has Jeremiah in the third person, perhaps *'ēlay*, 'to me', should be understood as an abbreviation for *'el-yrmyh*, 'to Jeremiah'; cf. BHS.

38. LXX is much shorter and probably a more original text; see Bright, 200, 202.

39. RSV v. 8, 'war, *famine*, and pestilence' is a translation derived from the conventional listing in deuteronomistic texts; MT actually reads 'war, disaster (*ûl*ʰ*rā'āh*), and pestilence'; many manuscripts read *rā'āh* as *rā'āb*, 'famine'.

40. Cf. Osswald, op. cit., 21; 'The image of God which emerges from Jeremiah's oracles is that of a deity who is radically innovative, never bound by the decisions of the past'; so W. L. Holladay, 'Jeremiah' in *IDB Suppl*, 471. Whatever truth there may be in this assertion, it is most certainly not the way the redactors constructed or understood the tradition.

41. On this see *When Prophecy Failed*, 45–55, and the essays in *Tradition and Theology in the Old Testament*, ed. D. A. Knight, London 1977.

42. For a discussion of this limiting factor in tradition see M. L. Henry, *Prophet und Tradition: Versuch einer Problemstellung*, BZAW 116, 1970.

43. On this cf. Carroll, *The Bible Translator* 31, London 1980, 126–34; Ackroyd, VTS 29, 16–48.

44. See the commentaries for various divisions of the chapter; most are agreed that vv. 16–20 belong to another context but disagree over whether vv. 10–14 should be seen as part of the original letter.

45. In my opinion vv. 10–14 are secondary (against Bright; Hyatt is less certain about their authenticity). For discussion of the meaning of the 'seventy years' motif see ch. 8 below.

46. Given the contacts between Jer. 29 and Dan. 9 (the seventy years motif) and the Babylonian setting of the exiles in Jer. 29 and of Daniel and his friends, the following proposition suggests itself: 'false prophets burn and true prophets/servants of God do not' (i.e., Zedekiah and Ahab were roasted in the fire, whereas Daniel's three friends survived their visit to the furnace, Dan. 3). It is, however, too risky a test for determining authentic prophets that all claimants to the office of prophet should be asked to submit themselves to the burning fiery furnace ordeal! It might, of course, reduce considerably the number of false prophets.

47. For one of the better treatments of the tension between Torah and prophecy see J. Blenkinsopp, *Prophecy and Canon: A Contribution to the Study of Jewish Origins*, Notre Dame and London 1977; on Torah as centre see *When Prophecy Failed*, 121–3.

48. From scholars as traditional as Eichrodt (*Ezekiel*, 157, 176) to scholars as modern as Crenshaw (*Prophetic Conflict*, 49–61) there is agreement on this point. They do differ on what follows from this lack of a valid criterion for authenticating prophecy (e.g., Eichrodt reverts to the argument from faith), but space does not permit a pursuit of the various suggestions here.

49. This favourite aphorism is used in Matt. 7.15–20 in relation to discerning false prophets, but in Luke 6.43–45 it is related to discriminating between good and evil people.

50. For a brief treatment of a very difficult issue see D. M. MacKinnon, 'Tillich, Frege, Kittel: Some Reflections on a Dark Theme', *Explorations in Theology* 5, London 1979, 129–37, 201f. As usual MacKinnon has his finger on an important issue but does not develop it very far. The complexities of this issue are further justification for a book-length treatment of prophetic conflict.

51. See Crenshaw's muddying of the waters (op. cit., 49–61); for reservations about some of his arguments see *When Prophecy Failed*, 192f.

52. For the literature on this narrative see ch. 2 n. 28 above; there is a very fine exegetical treatment of I Kings 13 in K. Barth, *Church Dogmatics* II/2, Edinburgh and New York 1957, 393–409. See also Hossfeld and Meyer, op. cit., 21–7.

53. L. S. Coser, *The Functions of Social Conflict*, London and New York 1956, 118. Coser's analysis is a distillation of Georg Simmel's theories of

social conflict, developed in the light of theoretical and empirical findings. For a critical analysis of Coser's position see J. Rex, *Key Problems of Sociological Theory*, London 1961, New York 1962, 115–35.

54. Coser, op. cit., 156f.

55. On this cf. Wilson, *Prophecy and Society in Ancient Israel*, 73–6, 210f., 248f., This insight needs to be developed as an analytical tool for prophetic conflict.

56. 'Jeremiah vs. Hananiah: Ideology and Truth in Old Testament Prophecy', *Radical Religion* 2.2/3, 1975, 58–67. Mottu is not blind to the possibility of ideology in Jeremiah's position; his analysis is a stimulating one which needs to be incorporated more widely into the discussion about prophetic conflict.

57. 'Life without Principle', in *The Writings of H. C. Thoreau: Reform Papers*, ed. W. Glick, Princeton 1973, 167.

58. See *The Samaritan Chronicle No. II (or: Sepher Ha-Yamim): From Joshua to Nebuchadnezzar*, ed. J. Macdonald, BZAW 107, 1969, 163f., 184, 187f.

59. Ibid., 187–8. Note the charge: 'to claim for himself that he was a prophet of the Lord' (*yō'mar 'al nafšō kī hū' nābī' me'et yhwh*). How reminiscent it is of the charge in the Jeremiah tradition that they sent themselves and spoke out of their own minds!

60. A prime example of this principle is the Jewish view of Jesus; cf. B. Pick, *Jesus in the Talmud: His Personality, his Disciples, and his Sayings*, Chicago and London 1913.

8. The Book of Consolation and the New Covenant

1. See in particular Herrmann, *Die prophetischen Heilserwartungen im Alten Testament*, 159–241; S.' Böhmer, *Heimkehr und neuer Bund: Studien zu Jeremia 30–31*, Göttinger theologische Arbeiten 5, Göttingen 1976; Raitt, *A Theology of Exile*, 128–222; also the commentaries on Jer. 30–33. The oracles of salvation in Jer. 30–31 which may be attributed to Jeremiah divide the commentators into those who locate them in the Josiah period, i.e., Jeremiah's early preaching of salvation for the north, and those who put them into the period after the fall of Jerusalem. I think the first possibility is the more likely, as during that period there was a wave of enthusiastic belief in the imminent destruction of Assyria. Such a belief contributed to an 'Assyrian' edition of the Isaiah tradition (on this see H. Barth, *Die Jesaja-Worte in der Josiazeit: Israel und Assur als Thema einer produktiven Neuinterpretation der Jesajaüberlieferung*, WMANT 48, 1978), so it is reasonable to suppose that the young Jeremiah may have been caught up in the mood of time.

2. This is very much the approach taken in the OT Introductions of Fohrer and Kaiser.

3. Cf. the arguments of R. E. Clements, 'Patterns in the Prophetic Canon' in *Canon and Authority*, 42–55. The dialectical account of prophecy (on which see *When Prophecy Failed*, 16–21) need not depend upon finding elements of judgment *and* salvation in each prophet, but is based on such

elements collected together in the tradition associated with a particular prophet. This approach allows prophet, followers, redactors and editions to contribute to the dialectic of prophecy.

4. For a sophisticated argument which accepts the attribution of the salvation oracles to Jeremiah, see Raitt, op. cit.; cf. idem, 'Jeremiah's Deliverance Message to Judah' in *Rhetorical Criticism: Essays in Honor of James Muilenburg*, ed. J. J. Jackson and M. Kessler, Pittsburgh 1974, 166–85. To argue, as Raitt does, that only Jeremiah and Ezekiel would have had the authority to sanction such beliefs is question-begging, and assumes that they had the status in society of their own time which later generations and the construction of their traditions gave them. If this had been the case, their preaching would not have been rejected so thoroughly; it is, after all, part of the definition of having such social status that the community accepts as authoritative statements made by such persons.

5. Cf. Böhmer's analysis, op. cit. Throughout this chapter my comments are deeply indebted to Böhmer's careful analysis of Jer. 30–31.

6. On Jer. 24 cf. Reventlow, *Liturgie*, 87–94; Thiel, 253–61. The complex problem of the matrix of such elements in the Jeremiah tradition is discussed in the works (already cited throughout this book) of Ackroyd, Pohlmann and Wanke. Whether the sections supporting the Babylonian exiles are to be derived from a Babylonian or a Palestinian source and whether during or after the exile are issues underdetermined by the data available in the tradition.

7. On this cf. J. Mauchline, 'Implicit signs of a persistent belief in the Davidic Empire', *VT* 20, 1970, 287–303.

8. Note the shorter LXX text in v. 14.

9. Quoting Weinfeld, *Deuteronomy and the Deuteronomic School*, 145; the italics represent Weinfeld's comparison with the text of Jer. 25.11–13; 29.10, which he presents side by side with the Esarhaddon inscription. There is a considerable literature on the 'seventy years' motif, see Weinfeld, ibid., 143–6; C. F. Whitley, *VT* 4, 1954, 60–72; P. R. Ackroyd, *JNES* 17, 1958, 23–27; R. Borger, *JNES* 18, 1959, 74; also A. Orr, *VT* 6, 1956, 304–6; and the discussion in Ackroyd, *Exile and Restoration*, 240–4 + notes. See also the commentaries of Rudolph and Weiser for the sense of the seventy years as three generations (cf. Jer. 2.9 for the three generations of you, your children, and your children's children). The range of possible interpretations of the simple phrase 'seventy years' should be proof positive of the hermeneutical complexities of understanding the Bible.

10. In 31.38 MT lacks *bā'îm* (only the vowels are in the text), possibly due to haplography caused by *nᵉ'um* (cf. BHS). On 'days are coming' cf. Jer. 18.17; 33.14; 46.10, 21; 47.4; as well as its occurrences in Jer. 30–31. For an exhaustive treatment of the term see S. J. de Vries, *Yesterday, Today, and Tomorrow: Time and History in the Old Testament*, Grand Rapids, Mich., 1975, London 1976.

11. Cf. 23.19f., where the same piece occurs. It may be a phrase linking 30.23f. with 31.1 (so Hyatt, 1027); Bright (272 n.) adds *bînāh* (cf. 23.20), and translates 'When that day has passed/You will see this clearly and well.'

12. For detailed analyses see the commentaries, Böhmer, op. cit., and

Herrmann, op. cit. Brief summaries appear in Hyatt, 1022f.; Bright, 284–7.

13. In 30.5 the phrase 'we have heard' (*šāmā'nū*) is odd in view of 'for thus says Yahweh'; cf. BHS, which omits the introductory phrase and reads 'I have heard' (cf. 'I see' [*rā'ītī*] in v. 6); BHS also omits 'like a woman in labour' in v. 6.

14. On the motif of a priestly salvation oracle (*Heilsorakel*) see J. Begrich, 'Das priesterliche Heilsorakel', *ZAW* 52, 1934, 81–92 (= *Gesammelte Studien zum Alten Testament*, Munich 1964, 217–31); also C. Westermann, 'Das Heilswort bei Deuterojesaja', *EvTh* 24, 1964, 355–73.

15. Cf. Böhmer, op. cit., 58. On the day of Yahweh see L. Cerny, *The Day of Yahweh and Some Relevant Problems*, Prace z vedeckych ustavu 53, Prague 1948.

16. On *'ēdāh* in 6.18 cf. BHS, where transposition of 'ayin and daleth yields *dē'āh*, 'know'; as MT stands there is no proper parallelism between 'nations' and 'congregation'. Cf. the commentaries on Jer. 30.20.

17. On the exilic origin of Micah 5.2–4 cf. Mays, *Micah*, 111–7; cf. J. T. Willis, *VT* 18, 1968, 529ff.

18. Cf. the listing of opinions in Hyatt, 1028; Hyatt necessarily dates it to the time of Gedaliah because he does not believe Jeremiah was active in Josiah's time.

19. On the finding of grace in the desert motif cf. Hos. 9.10; Deut. 32.10; Bach, *Die Erwählung Israels in der Wüste*.

20. For analysis and exegesis see B. Lindars, 'Rachel Weeping for her Children – Jeremiah 31.15–22', *JSOT* 12, 1979, 47–62; see also B. W. Anderson, ' "The Lord Has Created Something New" – A Stylistic Study of Jer 31:15–22', *CBQ* 40, 1978, 463–78; P. Trible, 'The Gift of a Poem: A Rhetorical Study of Jeremiah 31:15–22', *Andover Newton Quarterly* 17, 1976, 271–80 (cf. her *God and the Rhetoric of Sexuality*, Overtures to Biblical Theology, Philadelphia 1978, 31–59).

21. See the commentaries. Lundbom (op. cit., 32–4) understands the line as 'the *female* protects the *soldier*' and sees this as making an inclusio with 30.5f.; the statement then becomes an ironic observation, 'My, a new thing on earth! the woman must protect the soldier.' Sexual ribaldry has some part to play in 31.22b; 30.5f., so Lundbom's interpretation is worth noting. Other interesting views may be found in the articles cited above in n. 20.

22. Cf. 'This couplet has been the despair of commentators. Its exilic terms, *created* and *female*, relieve us of it' (G. A. Smith, *Jeremiah*, London 1941⁴, 305 n. 1). Also 'The last clause is probably a grammatical note which has crept into the text from the margin' (so A. C. Welch, *The Book of Jeremiah: Translated into Colloquial English*, London 1928², 74 n. 3).

23. For the 'courting' interpretation see the Jewish Bible and S. Freehof, *Jeremiah*, The Jewish Commentary for Bible Readers, New York 1977, 188f.; both translate it as 'a woman shall court a man' (Freehof) or 'a woman courts a man' (*The Prophets: Nevi'im*, 595). Cf. Isa. 4.1 for a different use of role reversal in the future life of the community.

24. Cf. '. . . either *shall protect* . . . or . . . the woman (fig. of Isr.),

instead of holding aloof (*habbat haššōbēbāh*, v. 22), will, in the new future which Y(ahweh) creates, with affection *press round* her divine husband' (*BDB*, 686). Cf. Rashi's 'Do not be ashamed to seek after Me' (Freehof, 189). As with so much biblical metaphor, meaning is not always as clear as we would like it to be.

25. Horace's observation 'the doctors are divided' (*doctores scinduntur*) is a good summary of the history of biblical interpretation and indicates that indeterminacy of meaning is very much a feature of biblical literature. If the difficult phrase in Jer. 31.22b is a proverbial saying of the period, indicative of unusual change in social norms, its precise meaning may elude us. Without further background information it may not be possible to determine its meaning. Such background knowledge is important for determining the meaning of slogans which seldom have a cognitive context: e.g., how many people beyond 1980 will understand the meaning of the recent political legend, 'Nobody drowned at Harrisburg'?

26. Cf. Holladay, *Architecture*, 167; idem, 'Jer. xxxi 22B Reconsidered: "The Woman Encompasses the Man" ', *VT* 16, 1966, 236–9.

27. See the commentaries on 31.26; cf. Hyatt, 1035f. Bright (238) says 'I confess that I am baffled'; Rudolph and Weiser treat it as a citation; cf. 'The ecstatic state is here called "sleep," and as the prophecy had been of so unusually cheering a character, that sleep might well be called sweet' (so A. W. Streane, *The Book of the Prophet Jeremiah together with The Lamentations*, Cambridge Bible for Schools and Colleges, Cambridge 1913, reprinted 1952, 193).

28. Bright, AB, 287. I have italicized his phrase 'it ought never to have been questioned' in order to underline the strength of Bright's feelings on the subject. I cannot imagine why it ought *never* to have been questioned, because it looks so much like a secondary addition to the chapter that a strong argument would be needed to show why one should even think of attributing it to Jeremiah. Bright is not alone in his assessment of the passage, cf. 'This passage presents the most important single teaching of Jeremiah, where his religious thought reaches its climax. It is one of the mountain peaks of the O.T. and came to have great importance in the N. T.' (Hyatt, 1037). Further superlatives are showered on the section by Bright (*Covenant and Promise*, 194) and Hyatt (*Jeremiah: Prophet of Courage and Hope*, New York and Nashville 1958, 105–7) in their more popular writings on Jeremiah. Cf. 'It *must* have been written by Jeremiah, and is rightly regarded as his most noteworthy contribution to the ideal religion of the future' (Skinner, 332f.; my italics); cf. Thompson, *Jeremiah*, NICOT, 59–67, 115f., 579–81.

29. A sample listing of attitudes may be given as: a genuine Jeremianic piece (Smith, Elliott-Binns, Streane, Leslie, Hyatt, Rudolph, Bright), from another or later hand (Duhm, Blank, Nicholson, Böhmer). Although it would be true to say that most exegetes attribute it to Jeremiah, I suspect there is a growing body of opinion which sees it as redactional and secondary. It remains a popular piece for analysis and exegesis, e.g., J. Bright, 'An Exercise in Hermeneutics: Jeremiah 31.31–34', *Interpr* 20, 1966, 188–210; P. Buis, 'La Nouvelle Alliance', *VT* 18, 1968, 1–15; H. Weippert,

'Das Wort vom neuen Bund in Jeremia XXXI 31–34', *VT* 29, 1979, 336–51. For an argument which makes the 'new' element in the covenant relate to the making available of copies of the law in local synagogues, so that everybody now has access to the divine torah, see J. Swetnam, 'Why was Jeremiah's New Covenant New?' in *Studies on Prophecy*, VTS 26, 1974, 111–5 (cf. Volz's commentary for emphasis on the importance of the exilic origin of the synagogues for the development of the tradition).

30. On this cf. Perlitt, *Bundestheologie im Alten Testament*. There may have been pre-deuteronomistic uses of covenant, but it is the use of covenant as a regulative principle which is the deuteronomistic creation. In deuteronomistic thought everything revolves around the covenant motif. In my opinion Jer. 31.31–34 comes from deuteronomistic sources and not from Jeremiah (cf. Nicholson, *Preaching to the Exiles*, 82–4).

31. For the notion of *b'rīt* 'covenant' as 'obligation' (*Verpflichtung*) see E. Kutsch, *Verheissung und Gesetz: Untersuchungen zum sogenannten 'Bund' im Alten Testament* BZAW 131, 1973, esp. 6–16 (for his remarks on the new covenant see 143–9). There are many problems involved in sorting out the linguistic evidence of the Bible from the theological presuppositions of commentators, but, in my opinion, the arguments of Perlitt and Kutsch are such that the conventional view of the covenant needs to be rethought radically.

32. Cf. 'We do no injustice to Jeremiah if we say that he first enunciated, without realizing it, what has come to be a central principle of Protestantism. Every man is his own priest, and every man is his own prophet. When the new covenant is realized, every man knows God without the need of intermediary' (Hyatt, *Jeremiah: Prophet of Courage and Hope*, 106f.). Too many commentators express similar sentiments for me to list them all.

33. According to Dilthey ('Die Entstehung der Hermeneutik', in *Gesammelte Schriften* 5, Göttingen 1964, 317–37; translation in *W. Dilthey: Selected Writings*, ed. H. P. Rickman, Cambridge 1976, 247–63), hermeneutic arose as a Reformation response in opposition to the magisterium of the church.

34. Here then the 'new' element in Jer. 31.31–4 is in fact a deuteronomistic way of confirming the regulative use of covenant for the history of the nation's past. What the passage looks forward to is the *first* successful maintenance of covenant, but in view of its redactors' beliefs about past failures the future is thought of in terms of something new. To the modern analyst the matter may look like a counsel of despair, but for the deuteronomists, hopes for the future lay in making the covenant paradigm work. It therefore functions in their work in an aspirational way.

35. I would associate this view of prophecy with the writings of Martin Buber (cf. his *The Prophetic Faith*, New York 1960) and also with any account of prophecy which stressed the element of repentance as a moral demand in the preaching of the prophets. As such, the automatic divine action of internalizing torah bypasses the need for human response and returns prophecy to the cultic sphere from which it attempted to escape in the period from Amos to Jeremiah. Space does not permit the development

of the argument here to show the extent to which the new covenant passage is a defeat for prophecy as a moral force and enterprise.

36. A. N. Whitehead, *Religion in the Making* (Lowell Lectures, 1926), Cambridge 1927, 6.

37. Bultmann's much reproduced article 'Weissagung und Erfüllung' first appeared in *StTh* 2, 1949, 21–44, then in *ZTK* 47, 1950, 360–83; it was collected in his *Glauben und Verstehen* II, Tübingen 1952, 162–86. It was translated as 'Prophecy and Fulfilment' in Bultmann's *Essays Philosophical and Theological*, London and Philadelphia 1955, 182–208, and has also appeared elsewhere, e.g., in *Essays on Old Testament Interpretation*, ed. C. Westermann, ET Richmond, Va and London 1963, 50–75. For a discussion of some of his arguments, see W. Zimmerli, *The Old Testament and the World*, London and Richmond, Va 1976, 137–50. I think biblical theologians should have another look at Bultmann's arguments in order to work out a much more coherent account of covenant as a community factor rather than as something individuals might involve themselves in without conditions.

38. S. Terrien, *The Elusive Presence*, 256. Terrien notes the popularity of this image for Protestant divines after the reformation.

39. Eichrodt, *Ezekiel*, 176f. Faith, like experience (cf. Jer. 44.15–19), is not a criterion of anything because it may be used by any number of people to justify the most diverse views. The flat earthers and modern physicists both use faith, but how does such faith justify one view more than another? How is truth to be determined if faith validates arguments? There is no reason to believe that Hananiah's faith in Yahweh was any whit less than Jeremiah's.

40. E. Rivkin, *A Hidden Revolution*, Nashville 1978, London 1979, 310 (italics in the original). If 'internalization is the only road to salvation' (so Rivkin) we may see the Jeremiah tradition as helping to lay some of the early foundations of that road. However all I would argue for here is that the internalization elements in the tradition are insights rather than developed strategies for dealing with the future. Sufficient conditions were not produced until the Pharisees relocated Judaism after the fall of Jerusalem.

9. After the Fall: Exiles and 'Exiles'

1. See Pohlmann, *Studien zum Jeremiabuch*; Wanke, *Untersuchungen*, 91–133; cf. Ackroyd, 'Historians and Prophets', op. cit., 37–54. For general historical background see Janssen, *Juda in der Exilszeit*.

2. There is a very useful tabulation of the Hebrew text of Jer. 37–44, representing its development by setting out in two columns, the original kernel of the stories and the redactional development of these stories, in Pohlmann, 208–23 (with notes on 224f.).

3. For a lengthy analysis of Jer. 37–38 see Pohlmann, 49–93.

4. The phrase in 39.4, 'by way of the Arabah' (*derek hāʿⁱrābāh*) may indicate a flight to the steppe-land, i.e., the arid semi-desert region east of

Jerusalem, or it may refer to the Jordan depression south of Jericho; on this cf. J. Gray, *I and II Kings*, OTL, 1977³, 765.

5. Cf. F. Landsberger, 'The House of the People', *HUCA* 22, 1949, 149–55; cf. II Kings 25.9. Talmud *Megillah* 27a understands Jer. 39.8 to refer to the synagogue.

6. For detailed analysis see Pohlmann, 93–107; see BHS, LXX, commentaries for the text.

7. See briefly *EJ* 12, cols. 918f.; tractate *Sanhedrin* 95a–96b.

8. Cf. Bright, 244; LXX and commentaries. MT here is a good example of the rather precarious position advocates of the canonical approach to interpretation get themselves into, by insisting on using MT as the text for interpretation (Childs is particularly vulnerable here). The MT of Jeremiah raises all kinds of questions about such an approach.

9. For analysis of these sections see Pohlmann, 108–22; Hyatt, 1083–90.

10. See the commentaries on this point; cf. Gray, op. cit., 770–2; on the numbers involved in deportations see Ackroyd, *Exile and Restoration*, 20–31.

11. Jer. 41.5 does not constitute sufficient information to construct an account of the fortunes of the temple ruins during the period 587–516. See Ackroyd, ibid., 25–8; also·D. R. Jones, 'The Cessation of Sacrifice after the Destruction of the Temple in 586 BC', *JTS* 14, 1963, 12–31.

12. On this see Rudolph and Pohlmann, 119f.

13. Cf. Gray, op. cit., 770–2. The two possibilities are (1) Tell en-Nasbeh, about 8 miles north of Jerusalem; (2) Nebi-Samwil, south-west of Gibeon. Commentators differ on which Mizpah they think the story has in mind and the text is of no help in making the identification any clearer. Cf. J. Blenkinsopp, *Gibeon and Israel: The role of Gibeon and the Gibeonites in the political and religious history of early Israel*, SOTS monograph series, 2, Cambridge 1972, 98–100.

14. MT of 41.16 reads *gᵉbārīm 'anšē hammilḥāmāh*, 'men, i.e., men of war'; a few MSS read *gibborim*, 'warriors', cf. the Versions. As Ishmael had killed all the men and the Chaldean soldiers at Mizpah (41.3), it is difficult to imagine what soldiers Johanan can have brought back from Gibeon. Cf. Pohlmann, 119f. Treating 'soldiers' as a later gloss indicates the development of the story in the course of redaction and transmission.

15. On Azariah see LXX, also 43.2, which RSV follows. MT reads Jezaniah, cf. 40.8.

16. For detailed analysis see Pohlmann, 123–45. For differences of opinion in the division of ch. 42, cf. Thiel: vv. 1–5, 7–9a, 17* (*Dissertation*, 579f.); Warne: vv. 2–5, 7, 8a, 9aa, 19*, 22* (*Untersuchungen*, 130); Pohlmann: vv. 1*–5, 7–9*, 10, (11), 13, 14, 16; vv. (12), 15, 17, 18; vv. 19, 20, 21; v. 22.

17. In 43.2 LXX reads *pros hēmas*, 'to us', for MT *'ᵉlōhēnū*, 'our God', suggesting a possible original Hebrew *'ēlēnū*, 'to us'.

18. Cf. briefly *EJ* 4, 266f. Late legend had him move from Egypt to Babylon and even identified him with Ebed-melech. On the literature later attributed to him see C. A. Moore, *Daniel, Esther, and Jeremiah: The Additions. A New Translation with Introduction and Commentary*, AB 44,

1977, 255–358. Cf. Eissfeldt, *Introduction*, 592–4; Soggin, *Introduction*, 458–61.

19. See the commentaries for problems in the text of 43.8–13. Perhaps 43.11 should be in poetic form, as in 15.2 (which lacks the third line 'to the sword those who are doomed to the sword'). The rhetorical nature of the piece should be clear from the sentiment that Nebuchadrezzar would give 'pestilence' to Egypt. Such stereotyped statements have emotive rather than semantic force in the text.

20. 44.14 *kī 'im-pᵉlēṭīm*, 'except some fugitives', clearly contradicts the opening phrase of the verse *wᵉlō' yihyeh pālīṭ wᵉśārīd*, 'none shall escape or survive'. Cf. vv. 27f. for the same kind of absolute statement modified by development. It is easier to regard v. 14 as being glossed than v. 28, where the modification may occur to take cognizance of later reality; see commentaries on this point.

21. For discussion of Jer. 10.1–16, cf. Ackroyd, 'Jeremiah x.1–16', *JTS* 14, 1963, 385–90; Overholt, 'The Falsehood of Idolatry: An Interpretation of Jeremiah x.1–16', *JTS* 16, 1965, 1–16; Davidson, 'Jeremiah X 1–16', *TGUOS* 25, 1976, 41–58. Davidson has argued, conclusively in my opinion, for the lack of influence of Second Isaiah on this piece. Recently M. Margaliat ('Jeremiah X 1–16: a re-examination', *VT* 30, 1980, 295–308) has argued that the piece, including the Aramaic v. 11, comes from Jeremiah.

22. Cf. MT, BHS, LXX for *mlkt* as 'queen' (Versions) or 'hosts' (MT); vocalization makes a difference but only with reference to a specific cult; cf. W. E. Rast, 'Cakes for the Queen of Heaven' in *Scripture in History and Theology*, 167–80.

23. On this, apart from Edward Gibbon's incomparable *Decline and Fall of the Roman Empire*, see M. Grant, *The Fall of the Roman Empire – A Reappraisal*, Annanberg School of Communications, Radnor, Pa. 1976; Augustine's *City of God* also bears on the argument here.

10. From Chaos to Covenant: Uses of Prophecy in Jeremiah

1. For such an analysis see my commentary (whenever it appears). However, what follows in this chapter is an attempt to say something about these oracles.

2. See the commentaries for varying positions: Duhm, Volz, Skinner all reject them as non-Jeremianic. It is possible, on the analogy of Jer. 30–31, that they contain a nucleus of authentic material which has been expanded greatly by secondary additions (cf. Rudolph).

3. Next to the *Alice* stories of Lewis Carroll, I regard Hans Christian Andersen's story of 'The Emperor's New Clothes' as the finest parable or paradigm for analysing theological or political positions. In the story the child, i.e., the outsider, (how wisely the gospels have made a child the model of greatness in the kingdom) sees what nobody else can (or is prepared to say they can). It is a good case of what Edwin Muir ('The Good Man in Hell' in *Collected Poems: 1921–1951*, London 1952, 74) meant by the line 'speak the truth only a stranger sees'. So the visitor to a culture, religion, theology or political ideology may see anomalies and contradictions

to which its adherents are oblivious. Perhaps that is why contradictions in the Bible are more bothersome to modern readers than to the original creators of the books in the Bible.

4. It is debatable whether the oracles against the nations in the Jeremiah tradition are longer than in the Isaiah tradition; measuring the length of such collections is quite difficult. Nothing, however, is at stake whether the Jeremiah material is the longer or not.

5. Deut. 18.15–18 form a late addition to the law on the prophet, cf. Mayes, *Deuteronomy*, 279f., 282. On Moses and Jeremiah see the writings of Holladay already indicated.

6. Cf. Ackroyd, VTS 29, 16–48; Auld, *SJT* 33, 567–81.

7. This is a subtle variation of Rabbi Nachmanides' powerful argument against the truth of Christianity addressed to the Spanish king when he visited the synagogue in 1263: 'If our fathers who saw him (Jesus) and were acquainted with him did not listen to him, how then shall we believe and listen to the king who has no knowledge of him in actual experience but only through a remote report . . .' For a translation of the debate, with background information, see O. S. Rankin, *Jewish Religious Polemic of early and later centuries, a study of documents here rendered in English*, Edinburgh 1956, 157–235; text of debate on 178–210, quoting from 208. It is a good argument but not an invincible one. I use it to draw attention to the gap between the presentation of Jeremiah and the community's response to him.

8. The question and answer approach to interpretation is well developed by H.-G. Gadamer, *Truth and Method*, London and New York 1975, 325–41, from the work of Collingwood; on the logic of the question and answer approach to prophecy see *When Prophecy Failed*, 77–84.

9. For Jeremiah this seems to be the Skinnerian position. However great we think he is now, as a major prophet who was right all along, that is how great he was in his own time. Only the stubbornness of the community failed to recognize his genius. This seems to be the position of Raitt in his *A Theology of Exile*.

10. These have been demonstrated ably by form criticism and redaction criticism (or tradition history, as it is called with reference to the Hebrew Bible). Cf. 'The Bible is in its origin a *product* of the believing community. Modern biblical study has made this much more plain to us than it could ever have been in the past . . . Scripture arose *out of* the traditions of the community' (so Barr, 'The Bible as a Document of Believing Communities', in *Explorations in Theology* 7, 113f. (italics in original); see also his masterly 'Historical Reading and the Theological Interpretation of Scripture', ibid., 30–51). See also J. L. McKenzie, 'The Social Character of Inspiration', *CBQ* 24, 1962, 115–24. I have a discussion paper entitled 'Canonic Process: Community and the Creation of Scripture', which is in the process of being prepared for publication.

11. I have indicated already the importance of background information for determining the meaning of texts with the example of the contemporary slogan 'Nobody drowned at Harrisburg'; lacking such information makes the meaning of biblical texts much more indeterminate.

12. B. S. Childs is the great advocate and practitioner of this approach (cf. his *Exodus* and *Introduction to the Old Testament as Scripture*).

13. L. E. Binns, *The Book of the Prophet Jeremiah: With Introduction and Notes*, Westminster Commentaries: London 1919, lxxxviii–ix, lists NT passages influenced by Jeremiah (taken from the appendix to Westcott and Hort's Greek NT).

14. For this see C. Wolff, *Jeremia im Frühjudentum und Urchristentum*, Texte und Untersuchungen zur Geschichte der altchristliche Literatur 118, Berlin 1976. For patristic material see Origen's homilies on Jeremiah.

15. John Calvin has 5 volumes of commentary on Jeremiah (vol. 5, 298 is the end of Jeremiah; thereafter commentary on Lamentations begins). Fortunately Luther did not produce a commentary on Jeremiah. For Rashi and Qimhi see Rabbinic Bibles.

16. I shall not even try to give a brief listing of all the works which have used Jeremiah in one form or another, except to note Franz Werfel's novel *Hearken unto the Voice* and Stefan Zweig's drama *Jeremiah*. Gerard Manley Hopkins has a poetic version of Jer. 12.1ff., which prompts me to surmise that buried in the poetry of many languages and cultures may be a host of uses of Jeremiah motifs.

17. I owe this information to J. Bentley, 'Vitezslav Gardavsky, Atheist and Martyr', *ExpT* 91, 1980, 276f.; the central part of a trilogy, 'The Angel on the Point of the Sword', was to be about Jeremiah and was designed 'to deprive the powerful of their certainties and the poor of their hopes'. I am familiar with Gardavsky's work in its English form (*God Is Not Yet Dead*, Pelican 1973). Ever since 1968 the authorities have hounded him, and now that he is dead I would wish in this footnote to hold his memory in honour. Such men are too few in our time yet without their brave integrity maintained against terrible oppression we are all for a dark future. They deserve our gratitude, they warrant our remembrance.

18. See my OTL commentary in preparation; for other commentaries in preparation see Appendix I.

19. For a convenient grouping of this material see *Socrates: A Source Book* compiled and in part translated by J. Ferguson, London 1970.

20. Here I agree with Childs (*JSS* 16, 1971, 149) that midrashic interpretation is not a post-biblical distortion, but part of the biblical tradition itself. As such it is to be taken seriously. There is (as Jacob Weingreen argues in *From Bible to Mishna: The continuity of tradition*, Manchester and New York 1976, 143–54) a strong continuity (artificially broken up by canonization) between the forces which gave rise to biblical traditions and those which produced post-biblical literature.

21. Heraclitus, fragment LXXXIII: *polemos pantōn men patēr esti*; for text and commentary see C. H. Kahn, *The Art and Thought of Heraclitus: An edition of the fragments with translation and commentary*, Cambridge 1979, 66f., 207–10. I have understood *polemos*, 'war', in its more general sense, in Heraclitus, of 'conflict', i.e., a universal principle of opposition.

INDEX OF NAMES

INDEX OF SUBJECTS

INDEX OF BIBLICAL REFERENCES

(a) The Book of Jeremiah

(b) The Books of Deuteronomy, Psalms, Isaiah, Ezekiel, Hosea and Amos